TEACHING HISTORY IN HIGHER EDUCATION

What are the distinctive characteristics of the discipline of history? How do we teach those characteristics effectively, and what benefits do they offer students? How can history instructors engage an increasingly diverse student body? *Teaching History in Higher Education* gives instructors an innovative and coherent approach to their discipline, addressing the specific advantages that studying history can bring. Edward Ross Dickinson examines the evolution of methods and concepts in the discipline over the past 200 years, showing how instructors can harness its complexity to aid the intellectual engagement of their students. This book explores the potential of history to teach us how to ask questions in unique and powerful ways, and how to pursue answers that are open and generative. Building on a coherent ethical foundation for the discipline, *Teaching History in Higher Education* presents a range of concrete techniques for making history instruction fruitful for students and teachers alike.

EDWARD ROSS DICKINSON is Professor of History at the University of California, Davis, and an historian of modern Europe and the world. He is the author of *The World in the Long Twentieth Century* (Oakland, CA, 2018), *Dancing in the Blood: Modern Dance and European Culture on the Eve of the First World War* (Cambridge, 2017), and *Sex, Freedom and Power in Imperial Germany* (Cambridge, 2014).

TEACHING HISTORY IN HIGHER EDUCATION

Ethics, Aims, Methods

EDWARD ROSS DICKINSON
University of California, Davis

Shaftesbury Road, Cambridge CB2 8EA, United Kingdom

One Liberty Plaza, 20th Floor, New York, NY 10006, USA

477 Williamstown Road, Port Melbourne, VIC 3207, Australia

314–321, 3rd Floor, Plot 3, Splendor Forum, Jasola District Centre, New Delhi – 110025, India

103 Penang Road, #05–06/07, Visioncrest Commercial, Singapore 238467

Cambridge University Press is part of Cambridge University Press & Assessment, a department of the University of Cambridge.

We share the University's mission to contribute to society through the pursuit of education, learning and research at the highest international levels of excellence.

www.cambridge.org
Information on this title: www.cambridge.org/9781009519922

DOI: 10.1017/9781009519939

© Edward Ross Dickinson 2025

This publication is in copyright. Subject to statutory exception and to the provisions of relevant collective licensing agreements, no reproduction of any part may take place without the written permission of Cambridge University Press & Assessment.

When citing this work, please include a reference to the DOI 10.1017/9781009519939

First published 2025

A catalogue record for this publication is available from the British Library.

A Cataloging-in-Publication data record for this book is available from the Library of Congress

ISBN 978-1-009-51992-2 Hardback
ISBN 978-1-009-51991-5 Paperback

Cambridge University Press & Assessment has no responsibility for the persistence or accuracy of URLs for external or third-party internet websites referred to in this publication and does not guarantee that any content on such websites is, or will remain, accurate or appropriate.

Contents

		page
	Introduction	1
	I.1 The Purpose of This Book	1
	I.2 What Makes History Different?	11
	I.3 The Structure of This Book	20
1	**What Is History Like?**	24
	1.1 The Size and Shape of History	24
	1.2 How History Thinks I: Holism and Historicism	29
	1.3 How History Thinks II: Inductive and Idiographic Principles and Practices	54
2	**What Do Historians Do?**	61
	2.1 Interpretation and Inquiry	61
	2.2 Spooky Questions	71
	2.3 Between the Social Sciences and the Humanities: History and Theory I	78
3	**What Kinds of Stories Do Historians Tell?**	101
	3.1 The Literary Qualities of Historical Scholarship	101
	3.2 Debates about Causation: History and Theory II	109
	3.3 What Kinds of Causation Do Historians Consider?	117
	3.4 Productive Uncertainties	124
4	**What Kinds of Problems Do Historians Solve?**	130
	4.1 Some Common Problems of Historical Research and Interpretation	130
	4.2 The Objectivity Question: Postmodern Doubts about History	155
	4.3 Epistemological Doubt and Historical Practice	171
5	**What Does History Teach Us?**	183
	5.1 History as a Way of Thinking	183
	5.2 History and the Present	193
	5.3 An Aside: History Pedagogy and Civic Education	198
	5.4 Lessons of History	204

6 Principles and Guidelines for Teaching History — 215
   6.1 Respect for Our Students and for Our Discipline — 215
   6.2 Pedagogical Reciprocity: Teach Things Students Want to Know — 216
   6.3 Teach the Sources — 223
   6.4 Teach the Breadth of the Discipline — 230
   6.5 Pattern and Specificity: Case Studies — 233
   6.6 Teach Interpretation and Analysis — 237
   6.7 Teach through Inquiry — 243
   6.8 Concluding Thought — 248

Bibliography — 251
Index — 270

Introduction

I.1 The Purpose of This Book

What does History teach us? By History, with a capital "H," I mean not our knowledge of what happened in the past, the record of past events, but rather History as a field of inquiry, a "discipline" in the academic sense. History with a capital H is a way of learning and thinking about the past. It employs a particular mode of inquiry, defined by specific assumptions about the nature of knowledge about the past. It is the collective project of "historians" – the many people (some academics, some not) who study history, with a lowercase h, which is what happened in the past.[1] What do we gain when we learn to ask the kinds of questions that historians ask, to adopt the procedures that historians use to investigate those questions, and to develop the kind of answers historians build? In short, what benefits do people get from taking courses or completing degrees in the academic discipline of History? Education researcher Gaea Leinhardt gave a pithy formulation of the questions this book seeks to address: "What are the essential

---

[1] Many others have made this distinction. Michel-Rolph Trouillot distinguished in *Silencing the Past: Power and the Production of History* (Boston, MA: Beacon Press, 1995) between "historicity 1" (my lowercase history) and "historicity 2," "historical narratives" or "what is said to have happened" (my uppercase History) rather than what happened (pp. 29, 5). Keith Jenkins differentiates between "the past" (history) and "history" (History) in "Teaching History Theory: A Radical Introduction," in *History in Higher Education: New Directions in Teaching and Learning*, ed. Alan Booth and Paul Hyland (Oxford: Blackwell, 1996), pp. 75–95, here p. 76. Ross E. Dunn has distinguished between "history as account (Hac)" and "history as event (Hev)" in "Constructing World History in the Classroom," in *Knowing, Teaching, and Learning History: National and International Perspectives*, ed. Peter N. Stearns, Peter Seixas, and Sam Wineburg (New York: New York University Press, 2000), pp. 121–140, here p. 128, and Robert B. Bain, "'They Thought the World Was Flat?' Applying the Principles of *How People Learn* in Teaching High School History," in *How Students Learn: History in the Classroom*, ed. M. Suzanne Donovan and John D. Bransford (Washington, DC: National Academies Press, 2005), pp. 179–213, here p. 186. Steve Harris uses the same nomenclature as I have here in "Reading and Understanding History: An Introduction to Critical Thinking," (unpublished ms, 2022).

opportunities that teaching and learning in history provide? ... What powerful and unique opportunity does the content and disposition of history provide the teacher and the learner?"[2]

The final chapter of this book will return to the question "what does history teach us?" – that is, what can we learn from what happened in the past, or what lessons can we draw from history (with a small h)? But that is a much less useful question than the one Leinhardt posed. The idea that we can learn specific practical lessons from history is an example of what I call operational thinking. Operational thinking asks, "how do I solve this problem?"[3] Chapter 1 of this book will argue that the most fundamental postulate of History as a discipline, as a way of thinking, makes it difficult for historians to answer that kind of question. By its nature History asks instead two quite different questions, which are at the heart of what I call strategic thinking. Strategic thinking asks first: "What is the nature of this problem?" and second: "How did I come to have this problem?" – which can also be phrased as: "Why do I have this problem?" Operational questions lead to answers – to actionable knowledge that can guide decision-making. Strategic questions lead to more questions – to inquiry, which yields greater understanding. The relevant issue for operational thinking is: What is the practical usefulness of History as a form of intellectual endeavor? Strategic thinking focuses on a different issue: What is the logic of inquiry that is fundamental and unique to this form of intellectual endeavor? This book will argue that the answer to the second question is the most meaningful answer to the first question. History with a capital H is a unique and uniquely powerful mode of inquiry. The primary practical usefulness of studying History is that by doing so we learn that mode of inquiry. This is not to say that lessons and decisions are not important. It is just that they are not what History is best at. History is good at teaching us how to *inquire* in a unique and powerful way.

Leinhardt posed the questions this book addresses a quarter of a century ago, on the basis of a literature on history education that was at least

---

[2] Gaea Leinhardt, "Lessons on Teaching and Learning in History from Paul's Pen," in *Knowing, Teaching, and Learning History: National and International Perspectives*, ed. Peter N. Stearns, Peter Seixas, and Sam Wineburg (New York: New York University Press, 2000), pp. 223–245, here p. 224.

[3] For a recent example of a long list of lessons people believe they can draw from history, see "More about General Principles of Historical Knowledge," http://futurefocusedhistory.blog/more-about-general-principles-of-historical-knowledge.

a quarter century old at that time. The contemporary discussion of history education is certainly immensely more sophisticated than it was in the 1970s, but it is still carried on in fundamentally the same terms. There is, therefore, by now a vast literature on the topic, and this book relies heavily on the ideas that can be found in that literature and the research findings that underpin it. It is useful to distinguish between two broad genres. On the one hand, a rich and sophisticated body of work draws on the results of rigorous study of methods and practices, generated by scholarship on teaching and learning as it applies specifically to History. On the other, an equally rich and thoughtful literature draws on reflections on the nature and purposes of the discipline itself, and on the experience of university History professors in translating that reflection into pedagogical practice. These literatures overlap substantially. A central agenda of the scholarship on teaching and learning has been to develop effective discipline-specific pedagogies, including for History. And History professors have been deeply influenced by the scholarship on teaching and learning as they have gone about translating evolving understandings of the fundamentals of the discipline into teaching practice. It will be most fruitful, therefore, to think of these as two distinctive approaches to the same project.

In fact, there is essentially consensus in the literature about the aims of History teaching, and there has been throughout the past half century.[4] Of course any college or university course in History must impart information – what some call factual knowledge, others content, others still a coherent narrative. This is the first and indispensable aim of History education, because without that basic knowledge or narrative of what happened in the past, students have no foundation or framework for any sort of analytical approach to it. But the more important ultimate goal is to teach students a specific way of thinking, specific cognitive skills, that are uniquely important to the discipline – to train them, as Nikki Mandell and Bobbie Malone put it in 2008, in "thinking like an historian."[5] The research literature on teaching practice has found that the teaching methods individual History professors employ in the classroom constitute (as Alan Booth put it in 2003) "a long continuum extending from teacher-centered to student-centered approaches, and from content-delivery to the

---

[4] For the historical background to the emergence of this consensus, see Linda Symcox and Arie Wilschut, "Introduction," in *National History Standards: The Problem of the Canon and the Future of Teaching History*, ed. Linda Symcox and Arie Wilschut (Charlotte, NC: Information Age, 2009), pp. 1–11.
[5] Nikki Mandell and Bobbie Malone, *Thinking Like a Historian: Rethinking History Instruction* (n.p.: Wisconsin Historical Society Press, 2008).

facilitation of understanding." Some seek to engage students more through the excitement of learning to think independently and critically, to develop their ability to generate their own analyses and interpretations. Others emphasize the excitement of the "story" of history, the encounter with the diverse and unique people of the past and with the dramatic and powerful stories that History can tell about them. Others still focus on what the past can tell us about the present, on the broad patterns that we can distinguish in the past and about its relationship to our own lives. Whatever the specific emphasis and method, however, the "prevailing disciplinary orthodoxy" (as Booth puts it) is that History should teach not just a narrative of events, but also and more importantly a way to think.[6] History instruction should impart habits of inquiry, methods of analysis, and an historically sound conception of the nature of knowledge about the past. The aim, as John Tosh put it in 2008, is "equipping young people with a distinctive mode of thinking"; or in Robert Bain's formulation in 2009, not transmitting a body of knowledge but creating a "cognitive apprenticeship"; or again, as a study of History teaching internationally put it in the same year, History should teach above all "a way of thinking and reasoning, a method of inquiry."[7] To put it another way: the aim of History education is to teach students *how* to think, not *what* to think.

This broad consensus has held and expanded, at least in the English-language literature, for the past half century. British historians Alaric K. Dickinson and Peter J. Lee argued already in 1978, for example, that students should learn about History as "a way of finding out about the past rather than a body of received information."[8] Twenty-three years later, Sam Wineburg's *Historical Thinking and Other Unnatural Acts* offered

---

[6] Alan Booth, *Teaching History at University: Enhancing Learning and Understanding* (New York: Routledge, 2003), pp. 63, 52–57, 55.
[7] John Tosh, *Why History Matters* (Basingstoke: Palgrave MacMillan, 2008), p. ix; Robert B. Bain, "Into the Breach: Using Research and Theory to Shape History Instruction," *Journal of Education* 1898 (2008/2009): 159–167, here p. 160; Symcox and Wilschut, "Introduction," p. 3. This is a program that one can trace at least back to the 1920s and 1930s; see, for example, the discussions in Michael J. Douma, *Creative Historical Thinking* (New York: Routledge, 2018), pp. 38–39; David Sylvester, "Change and Continuity in History Teaching 1900–1993," in *Teaching History*, ed. Hillary Bourdillon (London: Routledge, 1994), pp. 9–26 (on the UK, but equally valid for the USA). For a more developed statement and program, see M. Anne Britt, Charles A. Perfetti, Julie A. van Dyke, and Gareth Gabrys, "The Sourcer's Apprentice: A Tool for Document-Supported History Instruction," in *Knowing, Teaching, and Learning History: National and International Perspectives*, ed. Peter Stearns, Peter Seixas, and Sam Wineburg (New York: New York University Press, 2000), pp. 437–470.
[8] Alaric K. Dickinson and Peter J. Lee, "'Educational Objectives for the Study of History' Reconsidered," in *History Teaching and Historical Understanding*, ed. Alaric K. Dickinson and Peter J. Lee (London: Heinemann, 1978), pp. 21–38, here p. 22.

1.1 *The Purpose of This Book*

what is probably the most influential statement of this goal: History teaching should impart the specific "forms of inquiry" characteristic of the discipline.[9] Joel M. Sipress and David J. Voelker offered a very similar formulation in 2009, suggesting that History teachers should focus on imparting the "central assumptions, forms of inquiry, and cognitive habits" that shape the discipline of History. It is *"historical thinking* itself, rather than a particular body of historical knowledge, that should be the emphasis of history education."[10]

Two issues, however, remain very much unresolved. One is that there is no agreement about how historians think, or at least should think. Instead, there is a very long history of bitter theoretical disagreement about that. This disagreement has persisted since the inception of the discipline some 200 years ago. Later chapters will address it in some detail; for now, it will suffice to say that some historians regard their discipline as a social science with aspirations to help achieve present aims, while others regard it as a discipline in the humanities, which aims to give its students a deeper understanding of what it means to be human. Iconic nineteenth-century figure Leopold von Ranke, who is often regarded as the founder of the modern discipline of History, explicitly addressed this issue already in the 1820s, when he dismissed theories about the meaning of history as "metaphysics" and rejected the idea that the job of history is "instructing the present for the benefit of future ages," in favor of simply showing "what actually happened."[11] As an undergraduate student in the 1980s I witnessed

---

[9] Sam Wineburg, *Historical Thinking and Other Unnatural Acts: Charting the Future of Teaching the Past* (Philadelphia, PA: Temple University Press, 2001), p. 41. A somewhat more opaque statement is in Lendol Calder, "Uncoverage: Toward a Signature Pedagogy for the History Survey," *Journal of American History* 92:4 (2006): 1358–1370: History education should focus on the "cognitive contours of history as an epistemological domain" (p. 1363).

[10] Joel M. Sipress and David J. Voelker, "From Learning History to Doing History: Beyond the Coverage Model," in *Exploring Signature Pedagogies: Approaches to Teaching Disciplinary Habits of Mind*, ed. Regan A. Gurung, Nancy L. Chick, and Aeron Haynie (Sterling, VA: Stylus, 2009), pp. 19–35, here pp. 23, 24, 25. There is a good book-length discussion of the first decades of this discussion in Peter N. Stearns, *Meaning over Memory: Recasting the Teaching of Culture and History* (Chapel Hill: University of North Carolina Press, 1993), which argues for an approach that centers on "the habits of mind the humanities should be establishing rather than merely the subject matter" (p. ix). See also Andreas Körber, "German History Didactics: From Historical Consciousness to Historical Competencies – and Beyond?" in *Historicizing the Uses of the Past: Scandinavian Perspectives on History Culture, Historical Consciousness and Didactics of History Related to World War II*, ed. Hille Bjerg, Claudia Lenz, and Erik Thorstensen (Bielefeld: Transcript, 2011), pp. 145–164, here p. 160; Inari Sakki, "Aims in Teaching History and Their Epistemic Correlates: A Study of History Teachers in Ten Countries," *Pedagogy, Culture, & Society* 27 (2019): 65–85.

[11] Leopold von Ranke, *The Secret of World History: Selected Writings on the Art and Science of History*, ed. Roger Wines (New York: Fordham University Press, 1981), p. 21; Leopold von Ranke, "The Pitfalls of a Philosophy of History (Introduction to a Lecture on Universal History: A Manuscript of the 1840s)," in *The Theory and Practice of History*, ed. Georg G. Iggers and Konrad von Moltke, trans

the late stages of an intense debate over the place of social science theory and of political commitments in History. As a graduate student in the 1990s I lived through a bitter controversy over the relationship between history and postmodern theory – what some now call "the theory wars."[12] In recent years the discipline has seen intense debates over the place within it of critical social theory – in particular postcolonial and decolonial theory, queer theory, and anti-racism. The latest episode in this ongoing debate occurred in the summer of 2022, when the president of the American Historical Association sparked a minor media firestorm by arguing that historians should steer clear of "presentism," meaning the desire to bring scholarship to bear on current issues of social or political importance. Some more activist historians saw this admonition both as politically regressive and as an attack on their own professional integrity.[13]

This fundamental disagreement will never go away. As this book will show, it is rooted in the nature and history of the discipline. This is not a crisis of the discipline; it is what the discipline is like. As Mary Fulbrook wrote in 1995, "Historians have never agreed about the nature of their craft"; from its very beginnings History was a discipline "with a remarkable diversity of objects of inquiry, and notions of methods and goals"; ever since it has been characterized by a "rather startling state of indecision (or, to put it more strongly, fundamental disagreement in principle) about the nature of historical investigation."[14] In the same year Allan Megill stated what I believe to be the prevailing assumption among historians today: "That there is a single History cannot be maintained, either subjectively as an enterprise" with a single unitary method "or objectively as an actual grand narrative" of the past. Instead we should adopt what he calls "The Multiplicity Postulate: Never assume that there is a single authorized

---

Wilma A. Iggers and Konrad von Moltke (Indianapolis, IN: Bobbs-Merrill, 1973), pp. 47–50, here p. 47.

[12] There is a useful discussion in Lisa Duggan, "The Theory Wars, or, Who's Afraid of Judith Butler?" *Journal of Women's History* 10 (1998): 9–19.

[13] James H. Sweet, "Is History History? Identity Politics and Teleologies of the Present," *Perspectives on History*, August 17, 2022, www.historians.org/publications-and-directories/perspectives-on-history/september-2022/is-history-history-identity-politics-and-teleologies-of-the-present. For the debate, see, for example, Kevin Gannon, "On Presentism and History; Or, We're Doing This Again, Are We?" https://thetattooedprof.com/2022/08/19/on-presentism-and-history-or-were-doing-this-again-are-we; Priya Satia, "The Presentist Trap," www.historians.org/publications-and-directories/perspectives-on-history/october-2022/responses-to-is-history-history; David Labaree, "Commentary on James Sweet's Essay about Historical Presentism," https://davidlabaree.com/2022/08/29/james-sweet-is-history-history-identity-politics-and-teleologies-of-the-present.

[14] Mary Fulbrook, *Historical Theory* (New York: Routledge, 1995), pp. 12, 14, 16.

historical method or subject matter."[15] A dozen years later Joanna Bourke observed that "there is no single discourse of history" (and, by implication, there never will be).[16] Laura Doan, in 2013, reached the same conclusion: "History is not (and never has been) a unified and coherent discipline."[17] German historian Otto Gerhard Oexle adopted a more ironic tone: "History has been since its origins at the beginning of the modern age, and still is, a discipline in crisis."[18] An essay of 2004 on teaching History in higher education was more blunt: historians "are notorious for disagreeing with each other about nearly everything."[19]

Second, in purely practical terms scholars of History education do not agree on the specific skills, habits of mind, and methods of inquiry that students of History should learn. Instead, the literature presents a wide variety of lists of such skills, habits, and methods. Lendol Calder, for example, suggested in 2006 that History survey courses should teach six specific "cognitive habits." History students learn to pose fruitful questions; to make connections between disparate evens and facts; to derive their reasoning from specific sources, the validity and reliability of which they examine carefully; to make inferences from fragmentary and limited evidence; to consider the multiple alternative perspectives that people in history display; and to recognize the limits of their own knowledge.[20] In 2007 Thomas Andres and Flannery Burke proposed "five Cs" of historical thought: Students in History learn to think about change; to think in complex ways about the context of events, texts, and people; about causality; about the role of contingency and chance in human history; and they learn to analyze complexity – because human societies, the subject of

---

[15] Allan Megill, "'Grand Narrative' and the Discipline of History," in *A New Philosophy of History*, ed. Frank Ankersmit and Hans Kellner (Chicago, IL: University of Chicago Press, 1995), pp. 151–173, here pp. 163, 168.
[16] Joanna Bourke, "Foreword," *Manifestos for History*, ed. Keith Jenkins, Sue Morgan, and Alun Munslow (New York: Routledge, 2007), pp. xi–xii, here p. xii. For a clear, brief discussion, see Zoltán Bolizsár Simon, "Historicism and Constructionism: Rival Ideas of Historical Change," *History of European Ideas* 45 (2019): 1171–1190.
[17] Laura Doan, *Disturbing Practices: History, Sexuality, and Women's Experience in Modern War* (Chicago, IL: University of Chicago Press, 2013), p. 41.
[18] Otto Gerhard Oexle, "Im Archiv der Fiktionen," in *Auf der Suche nach der verlorenen Wahrheit: Zum Grundlagenstreit in der Geschichtswissenschaft*, ed. Rainer Marie Kiesow and Dieter Simon (Frankfurt: Campus, 2000), pp. 87–103, here p. 87.
[19] Valerie Grim, David Pace, and Leah Shopkow, "Learning to Use Evidence in the Study of History," in *Decoding the Disciplines: Helping Students Learn Disciplinary Ways of Thinking* (San Francisco, CA: Jossey-Bass, 2004), pp. 57–68, here p. 57.
[20] Calder, "Uncoverage." For a list of these lists, see Sipress and Volker, "From Learning History to Doing History"; or Stéphane Lévesque, *Thinking Historically: Educating Students for the Twenty-First Century* (Toronto: University of Toronto Press, 2008), pp. 33–37.

historical study, are so complex.²¹ Alan Booth argued in 2004 that students in History learn to "read and use texts ... critically and empathetically"; to interpret "complex, ambiguous, and conflicting and often incomplete material"; to marshal arguments; to integrate information from many different sources, of different types, and often of fragmentary nature; and to examine alternative explanations.²²

Over the past two decades there have been influential efforts to generate authoritative statements of this agenda. Perhaps the most fruitful is the American Historical Association's "Tuning Project," launched in 2012. That project developed a broad roster of intellectual habits and academic skills History education should teach, and of the benefits learning those skills would bestow. In the United Kingdom another such list was generated as a Subject Benchmark Statement for History by the History Benchmarking Group, published by the Quality Assurance Agency for Higher Education in 2000.²³ While these efforts focus more on university and college-level History teaching, moreover, numerous other projects less explicitly focused on higher education have generated still further definitions of the skill set History teaches.²⁴

---

²¹ Thomas Andrews and Flannery Burke, "What Does It Mean to Think Historically? *Perspectives* 45:1 (2007), www.historians.org/publications-and-directories/perspectives-on-history/january-2007/what-does-it-mean-to-think-historically.

²² Booth, *Teaching History at University*, pp. 24–25. See further Alan Booth and Paul Hyland, "Introduction: Developing Scholarship in History Teaching," in *The Practice of University History Teaching*, ed. Alan Booth and Paul Hyland (Manchester: Manchester University Press, 2000), pp. 1–17; "Introduction," in *Knowing, Teaching, and Learning History: National and International Perspectives*, ed. Peter Stearns, Peter Seixas, and Sam Wineburg (New York: New York University Press, 2000); David Pace, "Beyond 'Sorting': Teaching Cognitive Skills in the History Survey," *History Teacher* 26:2 (1993): 211–220, and "The Amateur in the Operating Room: History and the Scholarship of Teaching and Learning," *American Historical Review* 109:4 (2004): 1171–1192; the websites of university-based projects, for example, at Virginia Technical University (www.historicalinquiry.com), George Mason University/Stanford University (http://historicalthinkingmatters.org), and the University of British Columbia (www.cshc.ubc.ca).

²³ The Tuning Project can be explored at www.historians.org/teaching-and-learning/tuning-the-history-discipline; *Subject Benchmark Statement: History* (Gloucester: Quality Assurance Agency for Higher Education, 2022), www.qaa.ac.uk/docs/qaa/sbs/sbs-history-22.pdf?sfvrsn=beaedc81_2. Another important milestone was the National Standards for History developed in 1996 by the National Center for History in the Schools in the United States; see National Center for History in the Schools, "History Standards," available at the University of California at Los Angeles Public History Initiative, https://phi.history.ucla.edu/nchs/history-standards.

²⁴ See, for example, Michael J. Salevouris and Conal Furay, *The Methods and Skills of History: A Practical Guide* (Chichester: Wiley-Blackwell, 2015); Mandell and Malone, *Thinking Like a Historian*, who identify (esp. p. 8) five "categories of inquiry" in History (cause and effect, change and continuity, turning points, the perspective of people in the past, and what the past tells us about the present); the Stanford History Education Group website, https://sheg.stanford.edu; the Common Core standards developed by a broad consortium of state school systems, www.corestandards.org/ELA-Literacy/RH/11-12; the Historical Thinking Project in Canada, http://historicalthinking.ca; Chauncey Monte-Santo, "Beyond Reading Comprehension and Summary: Learning

1.1 *The Purpose of This Book*

The picture of History that all these lists of skills, habits of mind, and attitudes give us is not completely chaotic; there is some overlap between them. But they certainly give us no coherent sense of what the aim of teaching History is. They are essentially descriptive. Collectively they offer us a grab bag of tasks – of particular things to try to teach our students. They do not offer us a clear definition of what we are teaching when we teach not a collection of loosely related skills, but a *discipline*, History. They do not offer us a mission.

Teachers of History, then, face two very serious intellectual problems: unresolvable epistemological disagreements about the nature of historical knowledge and how to gain it, and an essentially descriptive definition of what historians do. It appears from the available research that these problems quite seriously hamper instruction in History in higher education. A good deal of college- and university-level History instruction still does a poor job of teaching students how to think like historians. One study of 2018, for example, found that a tiny proportion of students even in advanced college History classes examine historical sources critically – by checking the date of publication, by thinking about the context in which they were produced at that time, and by considering who the author was and what his or her motives might have been. This is the most basic starting point for inquiry in the discipline of History; but most students, it appears, are not getting that message.[25] There may be a curricular explanation for that. A study of 2009 found that some History departments have in recent decades introduced special courses on historical methods for History majors in which students are asked to think explicitly about how historians think. It also found, however, that most departments still use a "pyramidal" curricular structure in which introductory courses "survey" topics; more advanced courses focus on narrower geographies and may introduce students to more historiographical debate and complexity; and students only engage in actually thinking

---

to Read and Write in History by Focusing on Evidence, Perspective, and Interpretation," *Curriculum Inquiry* 41 (2011): 212–249; American Historical Association, "Statement on Excellent Classroom Teaching of History" (updated 2017), www.historians.org/jobs-and-professional-development/statements-standards-and-guidelines-of-the-discipline/statement-on-excellent-classroom-teaching-of-history; Bradley Commission on History in the Schools, "Building a History Curriculum: Guidelines for Teaching History in Schools," *History Teacher* 23:1 (1989): 14; National Council for History Education, "Building a World History Curriculum: A Guide to Using Themes and Selecting Content" (1997), https://eric.ed.gov/?id=ED422238; United Kingdom Schools Council History Project, *A New Look at History* (Edinburgh: Holmes McDougal, 1976), www.schoolshistoryproject.co.uk/wp-content/uploads/2015/12/NewLookAtHistory.pdf.

[25] Sam Wineburg, Mark Smith, and Joel Breakstone, "What Is Learned in College History Classes?" *Journal of American History* 104 (2018): 983–993.

like historians themselves, by undertaking open-ended research projects on topics of their own choosing, in advanced seminars.[26] Since most students who take History courses are not History majors, this means that a very high proportion never get much formal exposure to what has, for the past half century, been regarded as the most important aspect of study in the discipline. Finally, recent studies have shown that a relatively high proportion of students fail, withdraw from, or get poor (D) grades in History courses, and that this is particularly true of students from less socioeconomically privileged backgrounds, above all those who are members of underrepresented minorities.[27] It appears, in short, that History instructors have not yet developed methods for effectively teaching their increasingly diverse student body to think like historians. There are clearly some structural reasons for these failings, related to the challenges of mass higher education under severe resource constraints.[28] But I believe they are the product as well of the absence of a clear conception of what we are doing when we are teaching History.[29]

In this book I want to offer a more coherent conception of what we are doing when we teach History, on the basis of fundamental intellectual postulates and characteristics that define the discipline. About midway through his 2018 book on teaching history in the digital age, *Why Learn History (When It's Already on Your Phone)*, Sam Wineburg observed that a "teacher who hopes to teach historical thinking must be able to articulate what makes history a unique form of knowledge, with its own ways of knowing and its own habits of mind."[30] That is the agenda of this book.

---

[26] Stephen D. Andrews, "Structuring the Past: Thinking about the History Curriculum," *Journal of American History* 95 (2009): 1094–1101.

[27] See particularly Andrew K. Koch, "Many Thousands Failed: A Wakeup Call to History Educators," *Perspectives on History* 55 (2017), www.historians.org/publications-and-directories/perspectives-on-history/may-2017/many-thousands-failed-a-wakeup-call-to-history-educators.

[28] For a good discussion of some of the structural reasons for these failings, specific to Canada but relevant for many other national contexts, see Ruth Sandwell, "On Historians and Their Audiences: An Argument for Teaching (and Not Just Writing) History," in *Becoming A History Teacher: Sustaining Practices in Historical Thinking and Knowing*, ed. Ruth Sandwell and Amy von Heyking (Toronto: University of Toronto Press, 2014), pp. 61–90, esp. pp. 83–86.

[29] That lack of clarity also contributes to a general failure systematically to prepare graduate students in History for teaching roles. See, for example, the incisive comment in Jonathan Zimmerman, "In Search of 'College-Level Teaching,'" *Journal of the Gilded Age and Progressive Era* 14 (2015): 429–432; Arlene Diaz, Joan Middendorf, David Pace, and Leah Shopkow, "The History Learning Project: A Department 'Decodes' Its Students," *Journal of American History* 94 (2008): 1211–1224, here p. 1211.

[30] Sam Wineburg, *Why Learn History (When Its Already on Your Phone)* (Chicago, IL: University of Chicago Press, 2018), p. 121.

I.2 What Makes History Different?

Identifying what defines the discipline of History cannot, however, entail denying or resolving the divisions, disagreements, and conflicts within the discipline. As Chapters 1 and 2 will show, those divisions derive not only from the complex history of the discipline but also directly from intellectual postulates that play a defining role in it. We cannot resolve them. But more important, we should not resolve them. They are one of the most important characteristics that make History a unique, and a uniquely valuable, field of study. Precisely the lack of consensus about how historians do, can, or should think is itself perhaps the most beneficial characteristic of History as a field of study. One of the greatest cognitive and intellectual benefits of the study of History in higher education derives from the fact that there is not *one* valid way to think like an historian. Historians think in quite *different* ways. This offers students the opportunity to cultivate a form of intellectual rigor that is not common in academic disciplines. The deepest aim of any academic training is to teach methodological rigor – that is, skill in employing a particular mode of inquiry. This is how academic study enables people to arrive at their own conclusions, to generate new knowledge and new insight. History, however, teaches two quite different modes of inquiry. Approached frankly, this epistemic division – this disagreement on the nature of historical knowledge and how to generate it – can cultivate perhaps the highest form of methodological rigor: the understanding that methodological rigor comes at a price. The lesson is not that sloppy thinking is better; it is that rigorous application of two methods can help us to avoid the blind spots created by rigorous application of only one.[31] Beyond that, approaching the acquisition of knowledge and of understanding in two different ways can allow us to see not only the limitations but also the specific benefits and potentials of each approach, and it can enable us to ask new questions to which neither alone would have led us. This is the rigor of intellectual flexibility. Developing it is one of the greatest potential benefits of the study of History.

---

[31] Allan Megill offers a concise statement of this position in "'Grand Narrative' and the Discipline of History," esp. pp. 166–167. Lutz Raphael has suggested that in practice most historians have now adopted a shared "epistemic culture" in which essentially empiricist assumptions are paired with an appreciation for the productivity of social science method in "The Implications of Empiricism for History," *The Sage Handbook of Historical Theory* (Thousand Oaks, CA: Sage, 2013), pp. 23–40, here p. 26. Other essays in the same collection, however, clearly do not conform to this model; see, for example, Michael Bentley, "The Turn toward 'Science': Historians Delivering Untheorized Truth," pp. 10–22.

The divided and divisive character of History is, furthermore, a great pedagogical resource because it gives History a unique intellectual attraction. The epistemological landscape – that is, the range of ways of thinking – into which History instructors invite students is open; there is more than one way forward. We can tell our students that they have options, that they can make choices, that they will need to see for themselves where those options and choices take them. Indeed, practicing historians and students in History have very powerful intellectual incentives to think simultaneously in different and even contradictory ways about their work. Laura Doan summed up this point with admirable economy in 2013: The study of History asks us not to decide on one particular way of thinking about the past, but to discern what different ways of thinking about it have to offer, and to develop "attentiveness to use value."[32] This is intellectually exciting. In History, we do not apply a formula; we think about what the particular value of applying different formulas might be. We can try them out and see what they yield; we can play them off against each other; we can use one to compensate for the weaknesses of another.

Acknowledging and exploring the profound disagreements within the discipline is, then, one of the most valuable *specific* benefits and *specific* attractions of studying *History*. Methodologically, History as a discipline is a mess – much more so than many other academic disciplines. That is not a problem either for scholars or for teachers of History. It is perhaps the greatest virtue of History as a subject of study and instruction in higher education. Seeking to achieve epistemological coherence is therefore not only pointless (given how vehemently historians disagree on the nature of historical knowledge and inquiry); it would also be intellectually and pedagogically counterproductive.[33]

I will offer here instead, therefore, an *ethical* definition of what it means to think like an historian, of what we are teaching when we teach History. The discipline of History asks us to adopt a particular ethical posture – a particular understanding of our relationship to other people. To think like an historian is to encounter people in the past as fully human and therefore as fully historical beings. And it is to do so as ourselves also fully human and fully historical beings. History asks us to engage with the people of the past in their full complexity, and with awareness of the full

---

[32] Doan, *Disturbing Practices*, p. 9.
[33] This is not at all a new program: it was advanced in very abbreviated form more than half a century ago by the Social Science Research Council. See David S. Landes and Charles Tilly, eds., *History as Social Science* (New York: Prentice-Hall, 1971), p. 1; excerpts at https://items.ssrc.org/from-our-archives/history-as-social-science.

complexity of the historical context that shaped them as people – their ideas, their values, their actions. And it asks us to acknowledge our own fully human complexity, and to be aware of the full complexity of the historical context that has shaped us as people too.

This ethical stance does not derive from any philosophical origin; adopting it is not an ethical choice. It is determined instead by two intellectual postulates that are foundational to the discipline of History – that is to say, without them the discipline of History would not exist.

The first of these is that everything human is historically conditioned. This is called "historicism." Historicism holds that we understand things (events, people, ideas, beliefs, institutions, practices, and so on) only when and to the extent that we understand the full historical context in which they came to be, the many different aspects of the historical situation in which we find them – including not only what was going on in the entirety of the society in which we find them, but also what had gone on before, what led that society to be what it was.

The second postulate derives logically from the first. It is that History is about everything. It does not try to isolate a particular aspect of the past and understand it through close analysis of factors we have predetermined to be defining of it, eliminating other variables, and according to principles that govern that particular aspect of human life – for example, the economy, religion, art, gender relations, warfare, class relations, environmental constraints, geographical influences, and so forth. Any historical situation consists of *all* these things; they are all interconnected, and there are no independent variables.

This is why History encounters people in the past as fully human and historical beings. It aims to understand their lives and behaviors, ideas and actions, their situation and choices, not in discrete fields (the economy, politics, culture, etc.) but as part of a social and historical whole. It engages with them in all their complexity, conscious both of their limitations and of their autonomy. Historians seek to understand people, as Joanna Bourke put it in the foreword to a volume titled *Manifestos for History* in 2007, as "unique, singular person[s] within specific times and geographical places." And we do that conscious, as Hayden White put it in the afterword to the same volume, of the ways in which they were "both enabled and hamstrung" by that specific historical context.[34]

---

[34] Hayden White, "Afterword," in *Manifestos for History*, ed. Keith Jenkins, Sue Morgan, and Alun Munslow (New York: Routledge, 2007), pp. 220–231, here p. 224. See also Bourke, "Foreword," p. xii.

There is an important further ethical consequence to these two postulates. History does not engage with human beings in the past in order to master them. Obviously, people in the past are dead, so we cannot master, motivate, or manipulate them. Further: the people of the past were real people, not fictional characters; they have already done everything that they are going to do. Unlike novelists, therefore, historians cannot invent people in the past and then make them do the things we want them to do in order to get our own message across. Historical people exist outside of our time, irreducibly independent of us. For the discipline of History people in the past are not things that historians aim to control. Malcolm Foley made this point eloquently in an essay of 2022: "As historians, we are primarily concerned with people in all their complexity ... we regard them not merely as subjects to be studied and experimented on with our hypotheses, but as people"; the historian enters into a relationship with people in the past "not to dominate and to exploit but to learn."[35]

Again, this is not the way History *should* be. This is the only way it *can* be. As Indrani Chatterjee put it in 2020, the "conceptual tools" of History "disrupt the ability of researchers to stand above and outside the very processes and things they seek to understand. They make mastery impossible."[36] Historians do not study people as cogs in a generic mechanism – economic, psychological, cultural, political. They do not study human behavior under specifically defined and delimited conditions. They study human actions, choices, and lives in full social contexts. The distinctive breadth of the discipline, then, fundamentally conditions its ethical foundation.

A further consequence of the foundational postulates of History, however, is that in studying History we encounter ourselves as fully human beings as well. Historians are not exempt from the assumption that everything human is historically conditioned. Historians are not outside observers of History. As English Marxist historian Eric Hobsbawm observed in 1994, "Historians do not and cannot stand outside their subject as objective observers ... All of us are plunged into the assumptions of our times and places."[37] Historians look at people in the past, but, in a sense, people in the past are also looking back. As we come to understand how

---

[35] Malcolm Foley, "History as Love," *Perspectives on History*, September 7, 2022, www.historians.org/publications-and-directories/perspectives-on-history/october-2022/responses-to-is-history-history.

[36] Indrani Chatterjee, "Whose History? What Theory? A Postcolonial Response," *History of the Present* 10 (2020): 166–168, p. 168.

[37] "Identity History Is Not Enough," in Eric Hobsbawm, *On History* (New York: New Press, 1997), pp. 266–277, here p. 276.

I.2 What Makes History Different? 15

they thought and why, under what constraints, how they acted, what their world was like, and how it influenced them, we begin to be able to some extent to see ourselves through their eyes – to identify also how *we* think, and why, what constraints *we* operate under, what *our* world is like, and how it influences us. We begin to understand how our historical context has conditioned us. This is what it means to say that we *encounter* the people of the past. In a sense, we do not "study" them, because while they are dead and therefore independent of us, we are *not* independent of them. We are not untouched by them. We do not just learn *about* them; we also learn *from* them.

This makes History a frightening and exciting discipline. Studying History can change us; it can change our understanding of ourselves and of our place in our own historical context in ways that we cannot predict or control. History is not just a process of asking questions and getting answers. We do not interrogate the people of the past to get from them the information we want. Encountering them as fully human beings means opening ourselves to what *their* questions were; it poses questions of *us*.

These are very abstract ideas. I would like to offer an example from my own life, not as an exercise in self-indulgence but to make the point a little more tangible. I grew up with no relationship to organized religion, but as part of a distinctive regional subculture. In the course of research for my dissertation I found that I needed a better understanding of late nineteenth- and early twentieth-century Protestant theology, in order to understand the motives, thinking, and actions of some of the people I was studying. Reading more deeply into key texts from the period, I came to understand that the subculture I identified with was a product of that theological tradition. I had been quite proud of what I thought was the uniqueness of the regional subculture I identified with, but I discovered that its fundamental assumptions, attitudes, and values were very largely a secular version of sectarian liberal Protestantism. Many years later, while writing another book about world history, I became interested in a particular early twentieth-century Indian immigrant to Great Britain. In order to understand his life better I read some of his published works; it became clear to me that many of my values are derived from the Islamic mystical tradition of Sufism (which he had helped bring to Europe). This is, in historical terms, not surprising; the intellectual life of the place and time in which I grew up, Northern California in the 1960s, was stirred and energized by its encounter with Sufism. As time has passed, I have come to understand more deeply how profoundly both these traditions have shaped my own commitments – social, intellectual, and even political. I continue to find this unsettling. I am not the autonomous person that, in my youth, I thought I was. But it has also been invigorating and liberating to understand this. It has given me the opportunity to explore the traditions and ideas that made me what I am, to examine them critically, to make some choices as to what I want to retain from them and what I want to modify. Among other things, it has helped make me somewhat more intellectually flexible. As a young professional historian, I was very much persuaded by the ideas of Leopold von Ranke. Later, I came to understand that this was partly because he too was a sectarian Protestant. I think recognizing that has helped to broaden my intellectual horizons, to consider with a more open mind the ideas of people who are not so persuaded by the approach he advocated.

There is one further important ethical consequence of the central postulates of History. As teachers of History, we understand our students to be fully human beings too. We encounter our students in the same way that we encounter people in the past, and ourselves. This means that here too we cannot aim for mastery.

Three considerations are important here. First, in purely practical terms, university students do not take history courses to be told what to think. They take them to figure out what they think, for themselves. They come to our classes with their own questions, interests, and agendas, shaped by their own historical contexts. Indeed, because the discipline of History is extremely broad – because it is about everything – it attracts a diverse student population who are interested in a vast variety of historical topics and approach them from a very wide range of perspectives, shaped by historical contexts that are very often radically different from our own. In this situation, History instructors do not get to tell their students how to understand the history they teach. In purely practical terms that is not the pedagogical situation in university History classrooms. If History instructors try to determine the outcome of students' encounter with History, many students will conclude that their instructors are arrogant and "clueless" and avoid taking their classes. But trying to dictate to our students the outcome of their encounter with the past would also limit our own intellectual opportunities. We can learn from our encounter with our students, just as we can learn from our encounter with the people of the past. The questions they ask, the things they find important, the lessons they draw from history – all these can enrich our own intellectual life enormously, but only if we listen to them. Further, a directive approach would be pedagogically self-defeating. In any History classroom students can learn from each other in the same way that their instructors can learn

1.2 What Makes History Different?

from them. That is an enormous pedagogical resource, and History instructors should not squander it by trying to dictate what everyone learns. What is more, attempting to tell our students what to think would be quite obviously self-contradictory. The fundamental assumption or postulate of the discipline of History is that everything human, including History instructors, is historically conditioned. The History instructor therefore, by simple logic, cannot step outside of history and tell other people what it means. That would not be modeling historical consciousness at all.

As History teachers, then, we do not get to determine outcomes. This is a very good thing, because students' aim of figuring out what they themselves think precisely aligns with the epistemology of History – the way that History understands what knowledge of the past is. Chapter 2 will address this issue. For now, suffice it to say that university-level instruction is very good at teaching students how to draw their own conclusions. We do not tell them what to think. Instead, we can show them *how* to think in a particular and distinctive way; we can create opportunities for them to explore the past and to encounter the people in it as fully human beings; we can offer them the techniques and methods of inquiry that historians have developed to do that; and we can offer them the understanding that they can only encounter the past as themselves fully human beings, from their own historically conditioned perspective. To quote from the introduction to a 1996 volume on teaching History in higher education: "Effective teaching is about facilitating student learning" by "guiding, advising and encouraging students" in the process of "constructing meaning for oneself on the basis of critical reflective practice rather than merely receiving and reproducing knowledge." The final essay in that volume concluded that "teaching might best be considered as the provision of a wide range of opportunities for learning" in this way.[38] I would add, however, that in doing this we are also creating opportunities to learn for ourselves – to expand our horizons, deepen our understanding, change our own minds. This should be self-evident. Educational theorists often speak of the need to create rich learning environments. Why would we, as instructors, learn less in a rich learning environment than our students do?

We can, then, understand teaching and learning History as a complex set of relationships founded on and characterized by reciprocity. I learn

---

[38] Booth and Hyland, "Introduction," pp. 8, 9; George Brown, "Assessing the Quality of Education in History Departments," in *History and Higher Education: New Directions in Teaching and Learning* (Oxford: Blackwell, 1996), pp. 298–319, here p. 304.

from my students; they learn from me; they learn from each other; we all learn from the people of the past.

Again, this can be unsettling, it can be anxiety-inducing. Both the people of the past and our students can challenge us in ways that we are not prepared to be challenged, and do not want to be or enjoy being challenged. I want to offer a word of reassurance, however. We can have faith in the power of History as a way of thinking, because we can have faith in the productivity of encountering other people as fully human beings (both them and us). Again without meaning to be self-indulgent, I can say that I write this from long experience. Looking back on thirty years as an historian, I treasure those moments in which I was most challenged by my job. In one such moment an undergraduate in a course on world history steered my class into a deeper discussion of the history of race and violence in twentieth-century America, creating an opportunity that other students very much appreciated. In another a graduate student obliged me to take seriously a social science theory that I had thought irrelevant. In a third an insightful critical comment by a colleague forced me to revise a paper completely (thanks to her, Hilda Smith, I ultimately won an article prize for that paper). In a fourth a wise colleague (Geoff Hume-Cook) from the Communication Department at my university told me that it would be more intellectually fruitful for me to stop arguing and start conversing. And on many occasions engaging with the interests, preferences, and ideas of students in my undergraduate classes has led me to investigate topics – and sometimes to come to conclusions – that I would never have approached otherwise.

In short, to study and to teach History is to go on an adventure. We do not control the outcome of an encounter with another fully human being; we do not know where it will take us. What happens on that adventure happens whether we plan it or not, whether we intend it or not, whether we like it or not. As German philosopher of history Hans-Georg Gadamer wrote in 1960, on this adventure "the question is not what we do, not what we should do, but what happens to us beyond our own willing and doing."[39] The aim of this book is not ultimately to provide a definite map, a fixed recipe for how to teach History or a list of skills it should teach students. Its aim instead is to reflect on how to make the adventure of studying and teaching History as exciting, as productive, and as unpredictable as we can.

---

[39] Hans-Georg Gadamer, *Methode und Wahrheit: Grundzüge einer philosophischen Hermeneutik* (Tubingen: Morh, 1965), p. XIV.

I do want to acknowledge an important limitation of this approach at the outset, which is that this book is written primarily for teachers in higher education – at the college and university level. I do not have experience of teaching in the schools, and teachers there face quite different challenges and opportunities. Particularly with regard to the closing chapters of this book, which address teaching methods in concrete and practical terms, many of the techniques I have developed for inviting students to embark on the intellectual adventure of historical study will be most relevant for History instructors in higher education. There are multiple reasons for that. One is that the curriculum in the schools is defined and constrained by content standards established by the states. The standards for California, with which I am familiar, are from the standpoint of the discipline of History outstanding, and this approach is entirely appropriate for History education at the primary and secondary school levels. Among other things, it lays the knowledge foundation for young people to go on to study History at the college and university level. But it does limit teachers' freedom to shape their own classes by requiring attention to particular topics. Second, the demands on teachers' time and energy in the schools are extreme and make more difficult a more open-ended and improvisational approach responsive to learners' particular interests and agendas. Third, teachers in the schools are for the most part teaching young people who are required to take their classes and may not be as motivated by curiosity and enthusiasm for the subject as students in higher education History courses. Perhaps most challenging at present, finally, History instruction in schools all over the Western world faces mounting pressure either to develop curricula that acknowledge the history, experience, and interests of an increasingly diverse student population or to return to a curricular model focused on the cultivation of a sense of shared national history, values, and civic culture.[40] History teaching has become

---

[40] There are excellent discussions of the history of these struggles in *Beyond the Canon: History for the Twenty-First Century*, ed. Maria Grever and Siep Stuurman (New York: Palgrave MacMillan, 2007) and Symcox and Wilschut, *National History Standards*. For the longer-term historical context, see Arie H. J. Wilschut, "History at the Mercy of Politicians and Ideologies: Germany, England and the Netherlands in the 19th and 20th Centuries," *Journal of Curriculum Studies* 42 (2010): 693–723. Useful assessments of recent developments in the USA are Megan Threlkeld, "Teaching the History Wars," *Perspectives on History*, April 18, 2023, www.historians.org/research-and-publications/perspectives-on-history/may-2023/teaching-the-history-wars, and James Grossman and Jeremy Young, "The Integrity of History Education: Bills Censoring K–12 Classrooms Censor Higher Education as Well," *Perspectives on History* February 8, 2023, www.historians.org/research-and-publications/perspectives-on-history/march-2023/the-integrity-of-history-education-bills-censoring-k%E2%80%9312-classrooms-censor-higher-education-as-well.

increasingly a political minefield, and teachers in some places must be careful if they do not want to be constantly at risk of losing their jobs.

Teachers in higher education are in a very different position. There is no set curriculum for History in higher education, and at that level professors have virtually complete autonomy in deciding what to address in their classrooms. As long as tenured professors run academic departments, no party in the various "culture wars" or "History Wars" (as the struggle to control History education has been called in Australia) that are playing out around the world will have significant leverage on what is taught in History courses in higher education.[41] And in higher education today most students in history classes are there because they want to be, not because they are required to be. A good deal of what I have to suggest in concrete terms regarding how to approach teaching history assumes that context.

Nevertheless, I do hope that the fundamental ethical orientation I advocate in this book will ring true for teachers of History at all levels, and that at least some of the practical techniques for "operationalizing" it – for building it into pedagogical practice – will be helpful for teachers in the schools. The intellectual benefits that can come from engaging with a divided and diverse discipline, from learning to ask strategic rather than operational questions, from abandoning the goal of mastery or control in favor of widening and deepening inquiry, from adopting an historicist approach to understanding the human condition – all these are as relevant for learners in primary and secondary schools as they are for students in higher education. I believe that in many or even most cases teachers in the schools have other concerns that, for concrete practical reasons (including sometimes job security), must take priority on a day-to-day basis over the kind of reflection about the nature and benefits of historical study this book offers. I hope that this book can be of use to them, though, when they do have time to think about the broader intellectual purposes of teaching in our discipline.

I.3 The Structure of This Book

In the chapters that follow, I will expand on what I have laid out in this Introduction in six successive steps. The first four of those steps are loosely

---

[41] Tenure is of course under vehement assault in some states in the USA; it has been severely eroded in the United Kingdom and parts of the Commonwealth since the 1980s; and tenure systems in the European Union generally secure the jobs of far fewer staff than in the Anglophone world. So far, however, there is little sign that History teachers in higher education will be subjected to explicitly political pressures, as schoolteachers in some places have been and continue to be.

related to the chronology of the development of History as a discipline – for of course History too is historically conditioned; it has become what it is through a complex historical process.[42]

Chapters 1 and 2 will address very basic characteristics of the discipline – its subject matter, how it understands the essential qualities of that subject matter, and the kinds of questions it asks. What does History ask *about*? How does it seek to *understand* what it asks about? And what is a good historical question – that is, a fruitful historical question, one that can lead us to meaningful answers, and is therefore worth asking, by the specific standards of History? Chapter 1 will focus on fundamental postulates that were central to the formation of the modern discipline of History at its inception, and that historians broadly agree on still. Chapter 2 will explore the profound division or divergence between the *different* ways historians think, which has always been evident but has become increasingly clear and explicit in the course of the development of the discipline in the twentieth century.

Chapters 3 and 4 will examine in greater depth some of the conceptual nuts and bolts of what historians do. How do practitioners of History build answers from the evidence their inquiry explores? What standards do they apply when trying to decide whether our conclusions are warranted by the evidence? What kinds of problems of evidence do historians face? How do they solve those problems? What do we mean when we say that we want to explore *why* something happened? What *forms* of explanation, what models of causation, do practitioners of History rely on? What kinds of conceptual tools do practitioners of History use? And how exactly can they be used productively, to create specifically *historical* understanding? Chapter 3 will focus on some questions and debates about historical knowledge and methods of historical inquiry that arose quite early in the history of the discipline, but became increasingly focused as a consequence of History's intensified engagement with the social sciences. Chapter 4 will discuss epistemological controversies that became particularly urgent in the course of History's encounter with postmodern theory.

---

[42] The literature on the history of History is gigantic. I have found useful, in recent years, Daniel Woolf, *A Concise History of History: Global Historiography from Antiquity to the Present* (Cambridge: Cambridge University Press, 2019); Shashi Bhushan Upadhyay, *Historiography in the Modern World: Western and Indian Perspectives* (Oxford: Oxford University Press, 2016); Norman J. Wilson, *History in Crisis? Recent Directions in Historiography* (Upper Saddle River, NJ: Prentice Hall, 2005); and – drastically outdated but still interesting partly for that reason – Norman F. Cantor and Richard I. Schneider, *How to Study History* (Arlington Heights, IL: Harlan Davidson, 1967).

The questions, debates, and controversies addressed in these two chapters can be organized into three broad categories. First, there were debates over whether History should adopt the methods of the social sciences or of the humanities. This is a debate that has focused on the relative importance of theory (hypotheses and the testing of hypotheses through research) and empiricism (open-ended research) in History. Second, again, there has been controversy about epistemological questions, questions about the nature of historical knowledge, about how we know what we think we know – or more accurately *why* we think we know what we think we know. This controversy has often focused on the issue of whether the facts that historians use to build the stories and arguments they present are found or constructed by historians – in other words, whether History is more a scientific or more a literary discipline. This is a very old question in History, but it has been of particular interest more recently to postmodernist theoreticians. Finally, there have been closely related arguments over the question of objectivity – whether or to what extent historical inquiry and historical knowledge can be value-free. Again, the argument of each of these chapters will be that debates and controversies of this sort constitute an enormous intellectual and pedagogical resource and benefit for historians and for the students they teach.

On the basis of the understanding of the discipline of History laid out in the first four chapters, Chapter 5 considers the question of what study in this discipline, uniquely among subjects of study in higher education, can teach our students. In this chapter I will also suggest that what History can teach our students is uniquely and urgently important today, as never before, for very good historical reasons. This chapter will discuss as well – again on the basis of the understanding of the nature of the discipline developed in the foregoing four chapters – the relationship between History education and civic education, specifically in democratic societies. Finally, it will argue that while History as a discipline is not good at answering operational questions and delivering actionable lessons, it does – uniquely among all academic disciplines – teach us the single most valuable lesson anyone can learn about the human condition.

Finally, Chapter 6 will define an approach to teaching History built around the findings of the foregoing four chapters. It will offer concrete methods for teaching in ways that address the specific and distinctive nature and strengths of History – including the strengths derived from its essentially divided character. And it will define approaches to those methods that are conformant with the ethical stance inherent in its fundamental postulates. The aim of this final chapter will not be to define a narrow program for how to teach History. Again, History is a big, diverse, and intensely divided discipline that gives the History instructor many pedagogical options. The aim is to offer a definition of fundamental pedagogical principles derived from the shared ethical foundation of the discipline and then to consider some specific approaches, methods, and techniques for teaching that seek to draw on its breadth, diversity, divisions, and internal contradictions.

CHAPTER I

What Is History Like?

1.1 The Size and Shape of History

The characteristic that most obviously makes History as a discipline different from other fields of knowledge is the enormous range of its subject matter. The field of inquiry of History is the entire human experience in every aspect, in every part of the world, since the invention of writing about 5,000 years ago (and historians draw on the neighboring field of archaeology to push that starting date back several thousand years). The one word that best describes the discipline in this respect is "capacious" – meaning roomy, ample, large, capable of containing a great deal. This is a quality that historians have treasured throughout the modern history of History. As the great German historian Leopold von Ranke remarked some 160 years ago, the creed of History is that "everything human is worth knowing." The American Historical Association put it even more plainly in 1990: "History is an encompassing discipline."[1]

This breadth is one of the greatest strengths of History instruction in higher education. At the university or college level learning is motivated by interest. In a well-designed History course, and in a well-designed curriculum for the History major, there is room for topics that will engage the particular interests, concerns, and experiences of almost any student. Beyond that, though, History as an extremely broad discipline gives students the opportunity to make complex connections across multiple fields of inquiry. In doing that, they can widen their interests and concerns, and come to understand better how their own particular interests and concerns are connected to a wider field of knowledge and understanding – and also to a wider world. By the very nature of the discipline, the study of History encourages students to expand their

---

[1] Leopold von Ranke, "A Fragment from the 1860s," in *The Varieties of History: From Voltaire to the Present*, ed. Fritz Stern (Cleveland, OH: Meridian, 1956), pp. 60–62, here p. 61; AHA Staff, "Liberal Learning and the History Major," *Perspectives* 28:5, p. 14.

horizons. That is intrinsically exciting. In my experience, it is in fact part of what makes higher education an extraordinary experience and a turning point in many students' lives.

In seminars with graduate and undergraduate students, I often use a simple exercise to encourage students to think about what the scope of the discipline entails for the practitioner: I ask students to identify the various subfields or areas of specialization in History, the kinds of sources that historians in each area of specialization use, the methods that are useful in the analysis of those sources, and the interpretive or theoretical traditions (historians sometimes call them "frameworks" or "lenses") that can be useful in making sense of what they find. Each year the list my seminar students construct includes at least the following:

- Military history
- Political history
- Intellectual history
- Religious history
- Cultural history
- Social history
- Microhistory
- Urban history
- Psychohistory
- The history of sexuality and gender
- Biography
- Economic history
- Population history
- Environmental history
- The history of science and technology
- The history of medicine
- Women's history
- Diplomatic history
- Imperial, colonial, and postcolonial history
- The history of childhood
- The history of the family
- Intersectional history
- Counterfactual history
- Historiography, the philosophy of history, and methodology

Given how enormous the field of history is, this is a partial list. In particular it does not include related fields that are historical in content but have developed their own very distinct specialist methods, questions, techniques, and traditions and their own journals, conferences, academic departments, and professional societies. They include archaeology, art history, historical sociology, dance history, music history, historical anthropology, historical geography, and more technical fields like historical preservation, numismatics (the history of coinage), paleography (the study of historical handwriting styles), epigraphy (the study of historical inscriptions), ethnomusicology, and heraldry. Finally, it does not include the historical work that scholars in other disciplines (and academic departments) produce, which is very often quite influential in the discipline of History – for example, the work of political scientists, anthropologists, sociologists, philosophers, and scholars in science and technology studies, cultural studies, religious studies, linguistics, literature and comparative literature departments, and the many disciplines of ethnic studies (Asian studies, African American studies, Chicano and Latinx studies, American studies).

What is more, these fields of specialization very often overlap considerably in practice. No historical problem can be fruitfully considered *only* from the perspective and using the methods of just one of these subfields. In fact, it is in the nature of History as a discipline that studies everything that no specialist is ever fully specialized; every historian has to look beyond the boundaries of her own particular interest to consider broader contexts. The outcome of political struggles for power in a particular city might reflect processes of social change driven by economic development. Religious conflicts might influence them. The capacities and functions of particular institutions (churches, military establishments, professional groups like guilds or lawyers' associations) might shape them. Individual people can help drive them. The tides of war can radically change the context in which they play out. They can be impacted by epidemic disease, by environmental change, or by natural disasters. To take one example, my own book on the history of child welfare policy in modern Germany required me to draw together research on the history of religion, social history, the history of medicine, political history, military history, the history of popular culture, urban history, and the history of academic disciplines like social statistics (a branch of sociology).

It is a consequence of the vast reach of History as a discipline that in colleges and universities History is sometimes housed organizationally in a grouping ("college," "division," or "school") of social science disciplines, while in other institutions it is grouped with the humanities. This is not a result of confusion about the nature of the discipline. History as a field of knowledge is distinctive in that it draws on the methods, traditions, and resources of both kinds of disciplines. Historians draw on the techniques of literary and textual analysis developed by scholars of literature and language, on the major theories developed by sociologists, on anthropologists' understandings of the dynamics of kinship networks or of ritual processes or of categories like "sacred" and "profane," on the findings and insights of historical geographers and cartographers, on the terminology and categories developed by political scientists, on the understandings of symbolic codes developed by art historians, on theoretical frameworks developed by feminist theory, queer theory, postcolonial theory, and so on. The techniques of postmodern discourse analysis (which help us, for example, to understand how particular professions or institutions interact with their target populations, or how understandings of social categories evolve through negotiation, debate, struggle, or conflict) have been enormously influential in History. Quantitative and statistical analysis can turn out to be an essential skill for almost any historian, studying almost any subject. One could go on for pages; the point is that breadth, interdisciplinarity, and eclecticism are fundamental qualities of the discipline.

Of course historians draw on the natural sciences as well. Environmental historians draw extensively on the findings of the hard sciences and of the social sciences (e.g., geology, geography, biology, or hydrology). Economic and population historians use medical knowledge to determine the health and nutritional statuses of historical populations by examining skeletal remains. Other historians draw on the findings of archaeologists, who use radiocarbon dating techniques to discover how old structures or other physical remains are. Historians of agriculture make use of the findings of biologists who use pollen counts in lake-bed deposits to reconstruct how local plant communities looked centuries or millennia earlier. Historians in multiple subfields (such as urban history, agricultural history, environmental history, even military history) now make use of geographic information systems (GIS) to analyze spatial relationships within human societies. There is even a field of "Big History" (as advocated, for example, by the International Big History Association) that draws on the findings of astrophysicists, evolutionary biologists, and planetologists to place human history in the context of the history of the universe, the planet, or the biosphere.[2]

---

[2] See, for example, Leonid Grinin, David Baker, Esther Quadackers, and Andrey Korotayev, eds., *Teaching and Researching Big History: Exploring a New Scholarly Field* (Volgagrad: Uchitel, 2014); Fred Spier, "Big History: The Emergence of an Interdisciplinary Science?" *World History Connected* 6 (2009), https://worldhistoryconnected.press.uillinois.edu/6.3/spier.html.

Historians have long treasured this expansive character of their discipline. As John Tosh reflected in the sixth edition of his widely influential study, *The Pursuit of History*, in 2015, "History is a hybrid discipline which owes its endless fascination and its complexity to the fact that it straddles" the division between the humanities and the social sciences, and "cannot be defined as either ... without denying a large part of its nature." The philosopher Wilhelm Windelband used more enthusiastic language 121 years earlier: "History produces images of ... human life in the total wealth and profusion of their uniquely peculiar forms and with their full and vital individuality."[3] To do that, it draws on almost every field of human knowledge.

The range of different kinds of sources on which practitioners of History draw to study these many aspects of the past is enormous. Obvious examples include the texts of laws (whether they were chiseled into stone in ancient Mesopotamia 4,000 years ago or published on the internet 10 years ago); business receipts (on clay tablets from the ancient city-state of Ur 3,000 years ago, or in electronic files generated in the 1990s); newspaper and magazine stories and advertisements in such publications, posters, pamphlets, and handbills; video clips of modern dance; the enormous volume of photographs generated by news organizations; the minutes of confidential meetings of charity organizations, women's groups, government committees, veterans' organizations; records of births, deaths, and marriages kept by local governments or by religious institutions; paintings, mosaics, inscriptions on headstones, sculptures, houses, and buildings; floor plans, blueprints, fire safety regulations and citations, local ordinances of every kind; novels, stories, myths, sagas, plays, chronicles, the lyrics of songs, poetry, parables and sayings, and language itself (the way grammar changed, the way people borrowed words from other languages, the frequency with which specific words were used, the ways that the meaning of words evolved); interviews with eyewitnesses, private letters, photographs, appointment calendars, or account books; memoirs, autobiographies, and diaries; tax records, court records in criminal or civil cases, census records, periodic surveys of landholdings and property (historically called catasters), deeds and conveyances in business transactions, wills and testaments, hospital records, school records, administrative documents of every imaginable kind (of fire services, police services, tax agencies, government ministries, provincial authorities, school authorities,

---

[3] John Tosh, *The Pursuit of History*, 6th edition (New York: Routledge, 2015), p. 43; Wilhelm Windelband, "Rectorial Address, Strasbourg, 1894," *History and Theory* 19:2 (1980): 169–185, here p. 179.

medical authorities, and so on); government statistical publications; the stenographic records of parliamentary sessions, constitutional conventions, school board meetings, or trade union conferences; almanacs and yearbooks; city guides and directories; city planning documents; scientific, medical, and professional journals; or the inexhaustible range of publications of scientific, philanthropic, professional, academic, religious, economic, charitable, recreational, public health, patriotic, cultural, educational, welfare, or advocacy organizations.

Historians value the careful analysis of all of these sources, but they also value the analysis, in a single investigation, of a multiplicity of sources. As Richard English put it in 2021, the "complex particularity" of any historical situation can be best grasped through "engagement with a vast range of mutually interrogatory sources," through "the attempt to hear as many competing voices as possible and to evaluate their implications."[4]

Working with even a small slice of these sources is one of the greatest benefits of studying History at university, and History instructors should ensure that their students get that experience. Few historical studies rely on just one form of evidence, and neither should History courses. As Leon J. Goldstein wrote in 1962 in a reflection on the nature of historical evidence, ideally in historical study "[t]here emerges in the course of research a constellation of kinds of historical evidence."[5] It will be of great benefit to students if that is true of History syllabi as well.

Such research sharpens our ability to see the limitations of evidence, it develops our capacity to widen our inquiry, and it fosters intellectual flexibility. It also poses exciting puzzles, demanding that we figure out what the juxtaposition of different kinds of information can tell us. The challenge of solving puzzles is intellectually exciting, and – again – intellectual excitement motivates learning.

1.2 How History Thinks I: Holism and Historicism

The extraordinary scope of History derives in part from its long-term evolution. History emerged and defined itself in the course of the nineteenth century, but has been expanding in methods, subfields, forms of evidence, and its relations with other disciplines ever since. This chapter and the next will review some of the specific consequences of that history.

---

[4] Richard English, "History and the Study of Terrorism," in *The Cambridge History of Terrorism*, ed. Richard English (Cambridge: Cambridge University Press, 2021), pp. 3–27, here p. 11.
[5] Leon J. Goldstein, "Evidence and Events in History," *Philosophy of Science* 29:2 (1962): 175–194, here p. 182.

Most historians are very familiar with it, but it is worth reviewing here briefly as a way of establishing some of its implications specifically for the *teaching* of History.

In the first place, then, many of the central postulates of History as practiced today derive from the nineteenth-century tradition of historicism. That term has a long and complex history and has meant different and sometimes diametrically opposed things in different contexts and times – so much so that one historian concluded by 2000 that it "has so many different or even contradictory meanings that it is all but useless."[6] In many cases it has been – as one recent study has remarked – "a term of abuse, a word of warning, and a derogatory concept" and a "convenient polemical device" used to denounce intellectual opponents. It has sometimes been associated with corrosive relativism, at other times with the intellectual and social arrogance of English liberal imperialism or, earlier, with Prussian authoritarianism and militarism or even the cultural and intellectual matrix in which Nazism thrived.[7] I will use it here instead in the sense that has come to be common among intellectual historians, to refer to a specific epistemological position that still commands widespread loyalty among historians.

As I have written in the Introduction, the central assumption of historicism in this specific sense is that every human phenomenon – social, cultural, intellectual, economic, psychological – is conditioned (that is, influenced though not absolutely determined) by its particular, specific, and unique historical context. As the historian of historicism Frederick Beiser explained it, to be an historicist is to

> recognize that everything in the human world – culture, values, practices, rationality – is made by history, so that nothing has an eternal form, permanent essence or constant identity which transcends historical change ... The particular causes that have brought human things into being make them what they are ... they depend on a specific context, a definite time and place ... particular circumstances at a particular time.[8]

---

[6] Willie Thompson, *What Happened to History?* (London: Pluto, 2000), p. 5.
[7] Herman Paul and Adriaan van Veldhuizen, "Introduction: Historicism as a Travelling Concept," in *Historicism: A Travelling Concept*, ed. Herman Paul and Adriaan van Veldhuizen (London: Bloomsbury Academic, 2021), pp. 1–12, here pp. 1, 3. On English historicism, see Priya Satia, *Time's Monster: How History Makes History* (Cambridge, MA: Harvard University Press, 2020), p. 3. Karl Popper famously used the term to mean exactly the opposite of what it meant in its original (German) intellectual context; see Karl Popper, *The Poverty of Historicism* (London: Ark, 1957).
[8] Frederick C. Beiser, *The German Historicist Tradition* (Oxford: Oxford University Press, 2011), pp. 2–3. For good historical overviews, see Georg G. Iggers, "Historicism: The History and Meaning of the Term," *Journal of the History of Ideas* 56 (1995): 129–152; Otto Gerhard Oexle, *Geschichtswissenschaft im Zeichen des Historismus: Studien zu Problemgeschichten der Moderne* (Gottingen: Vandenhoeck & Ruprecht, 1996).

1.2 *How History Thinks I*

This is what makes History capacious not just collectively as a discipline, but also in individual practice as a mode of inquiry. History assumes that we understand any object of study to the extent that we know its unique historical context in depth and detail, from multiple angles (e.g. social, economic, political, intellectual, environmental, epidemiological, etc.) and in multiple chronological registers (e.g., short-term, medium-term, long-term, or proximate). The more we know about that historical context, the more we understand our object of study.

The dynamic of historical inquiry, in this persisting historicist tradition, is therefore expansive. Most academic disciplines seek to define and delimit their subject matter with some precision; to develop a "tool kit" of recognized, defined, and approved methods, techniques, and practices appropriate to that delimited subject; and to establish a clear roster of accepted and legitimate forms of evidence and ways of applying methods and techniques to them. They also in most cases aim to refine their findings, to make them more precise and certain, often specifically to define *causation* as narrowly and definitively as possible. By doing that, they mean to codify the critical postulates that hold true in all related situations – for example, physical constants, the laws of thermodynamics, or the principles of atomic bonding and molecular structure.

This is the logic of the sciences – to focus inquiry narrowly in order to achieve unique and powerful insights. For the most part the sciences seek to limit the number of variables they must consider in any given inquiry in order to achieve analytical clarity and precision. Natural scientists in particular, but many social scientists as well, often aim for what is called parsimony, by which is meant reducing the number of variables involved in an explanation in order to come up with something reliable and actionable – a policy recommendation, for example, or a physical law governing the behavior of electronic circuits or chemicals or spacecraft. The sciences seek to extract predictable simplicity from confusing complexity. Often they aim as well for insights that will ultimately be useful for some particular practical purpose, such as curing disease, building more powerful machines, pursuing more effective economic or social policies, or dealing with the threats posed by radical sects or terrorist organizations. The centrality of the idea of statistical correlation in fields such as political science, psychology, economics, and much sociology is a reflection of that tendency. Its aim is to tell us which were the important or significant determining (causal) factors, and which we can leave aside as unimportant or incidental.

The discipline of History has usually done the opposite. For historicists the idea that a statistical measure can help us eliminate some factors as not particularly worthy of consideration is intuitively mistaken. Chapter 4 will examine more closely the characteristic ways in which historians tend to approach causation. For now, suffice it to say that historians are generally not much interested in establishing "a" cause or "the most important" cause because they assume that societies are extraordinarily complex, that many things are always going on in them in dynamically connected and related ways, and with multiple and complex consequences.

Historians therefore usually seek to expand their subject matter to encompass more of the complexity of historical contexts. They are interested in how *multiple* causes contributed in dynamic interaction with each other, not to one singular outcome, but to a range of outcomes, to the development of an entire society or of an important process (social, cultural, economic, demographic, political, etc.) within a society. As Keith Barton and Linda Levstik wrote in 2004, History relies on analysis of "the connections, relationships, and structures that tie together individual events" – again, of complex and dynamic contexts, not of disaggregated and isolated causal factors or variables.

A study published by the National Academy of Sciences put it this way already in 1970: whereas the social scientist aims to "simplify his problems by the exclusion of all but a few paramount variables," in "History ... the matter to be studied is inherently complex (some would say, infinitely complex) and resistant to simplification." (An historian would likely observe that the matter social scientists study is also infinitely complex; social science method merely oversimplifies it.)[9]

Historians are therefore not much persuaded of the likelihood that one can ever find out what one thing caused a singular result and will cause it again under similar circumstances. History aims to analyze and to understand the integrated totality of the human experience – not a narrow slice of it cut out and isolated for study. And there are no similar circumstances. Given how complex societies are, and given the universality of change over time, every historical situation is irreducibly different, unique. Sam Wineburg has put the point with – ironically – beautiful parsimony: in History, "Determining cause is less about isolating a mechanism than knitting together a textured understanding ... Parsimony in historical explanation often flirts with superficial reductionism."[10]

---

[9] Keith C. Barton and Linda S. Levstik, *Teaching History for the Common Good* (Mahwah, NJ: Lawrence Erlbaum, 2004), p. 69; Landes and Tilly, *History as Social Science*, p. 7.
[10] Wineburg, *Why Learn History*, p. 109.

The analytical approach the historicist tradition favors, then, seeks insight not by picking the human world apart into distinct and discrete fields and examining each in isolation, but rather by putting it together, by considering many aspects of a particular historical situation in dynamic relationship. History is holistic. It is true that there are many subfields and fields of specialization in History, each with its own traditions, interests, and conventions. Those subfields have multiplied and ramified for some two centuries now as the discipline has expanded far beyond its historicist roots, often in dialog with scholars and ideas from other disciplines. Nevertheless, historians in every subfield still tend to draw extensively on the methods, findings, questions, and research of those in multiple other subfields. As Martha Howell and Walter Prevenier put it in a 2001 handbook of historical method, historians for the most part still aim to "see social systems as integrated wholes" in which "economic, political, and ideological" – and we can add religious, cultural, environmental, intellectual, and so on – factors all interact and interconnect.[11]

Alan Booth put it this way: in History, "the more numerous, varied and structured the connections" a study makes between different facets of social life, "between different types of evidence; between rival interpretations of a topic; between the event or situation in question and the wider context ... the deeper the understanding." History is "fundamentally integrative."[12]

This holistic orientation is a thread that runs through discussions of History from its inception to the present. Leopold von Ranke defined the basic orientation already in the 1830s: "Since these [varied and multiple] aspects of society are never present separately, but always together – indeed, determining each other ... equal interest must be devoted to all of these factors."[13] One hundred and seventy years later American historian John Lewis Gaddis offered a particularly careful characterization of History as "ecological" in perspective, in that it aims to understand events in the totality of their social context. That word is particularly apt because ecology is not just the study of the entire environment, but rather the study of the ways in which the elements of the environment interact. At its most exciting, this is how History approaches studying "everything."

---

[11] Martha Howell and Walter Prevenier, *From Reliable Sources: An Introduction to Historical Methods* (Ithaca, NY: Cornell University Press, 2001), p. 91.
[12] Booth, *Teaching History at University*, p. 20.
[13] Leopold von Ranke, "On the Character of Historical Science (A Manuscript of the 1830s)," in Leopold von Ranke, *The Theory and Practice of History*, ed. Georg C. Iggers and Konrad von Moltke, trans. Wilma A. Iggers and Konrad von Moltke (Indianapolis, IN: Bobbs-Merrill, 1973), p. 40.

Historians seek to understand how multiple different factors interacted dynamically in any given historical situation, "because 'so much depends on so much else.'" To the social scientific goal of "parsimonious" explanation Gaddis contrasted the historian's "web-like sense of reality" that sees "everything as connected in some way to everything else." The historian would "think it irresponsible to seek to isolate – or 'tease out' – single causes for complex events. We see history instead as proceeding from multiple causes and their intersections. Interconnections matter more to us than does the enshrinement of particular variables." In most social science fields a "successful project is one that explains a lot with a little" – by identifying the really important and determining factors, the ones that really matter. In contrast, historians generally explain a lot with a lot, because the complexity and reach of History leads them to assume that "multiple causation is the only feasible basis" for real understanding.[14] John Tosh, in a 2008 essay, "Why History Matters," made the same argument using the term "holistic" rather than "ecological." Historians, he wrote, are "committed to a holistic approach, in which the object of inquiry is placed in its full social and cultural context ... This respect for context distinguishes them from economists and sociologists, who often draw on historical material, but in a highly structured way, designed to match a specific set of research questions" rather than in an open-ended and expansive inquiry.[15] I am particularly drawn to the concise formulation offered by Stefan Tanaka, an historian of modern Japan, in a reflection published in 2013 about the nature and potentials of the discipline of History in the digital age. His goal, as he described it, is to enable a "more expansive and heterogeneous" understanding of the past, one that appreciates the full "diversity of human experiences."[16] I have sometimes tried to encapsulate the point in an image: If the discipline of History ever dies, what will be written on its gravestone is "It was more complicated than that."

Again, historians often use the concepts of *context* and *contextualization* to define this fundamental characteristic of the discipline, of how historians think and work. History investigates things in complex, holistic, dynamic, messy context – as far as realistically possible in *full* context, encompassing *many* aspects of society at a particular time in dynamic

[14] John Lewis Gaddis, *The Landscape of History: How Historians Map the Past* (New York: Oxford University Press, 2002), pp. 54–55, 57, 64–65, 105.
[15] Tosh, *Why History Matters*, p. 22.
[16] Stefan Tanaka, "Pasts in a Digital Age," in *Writing History in a Digital Age*, ed. Jack Doughtery and Kristen Navrotzki (Ann Arbor: University of Michigan Press, 2013), pp. 37, 44.

relationship with each other *and* as they changed over time.¹⁷ Sam Wineburg has brilliantly analyzed how historians assess context in practice. Historians place documents and statements (for example) in context by comparing different texts with each other. They assess the author's background, experience, assumptions, and motives or aims. They evaluate the conditions under which a text was produced. They analyze the institutional, intellectual, and political incentives, constraints, and possibilities the author faced. They assess both explicit and implicit concepts, patterns, and biases evident in the vocabulary used in the text, or the references it contains, or the metaphors it uses. They often explore the contemporary usage and conceptual associations or connotations of key terms in a text. They establish its relationship to other texts. They investigate the social connections and commitments of the author in order to establish their place in the collective biography of the full range of people with whom they engaged and who might have influenced them.¹⁸ The aim is often specifically to understand the minds of people in that past moment – how they thought, how they saw the world, what they experienced, what meaning they derived from their experience, what their conscious motivations and understanding of their lives were, how they understood their position in the conditions and events around them, what they sought to achieve, what resources they had to achieve it, or to define it, how they thought they could use those resources, and how they understood their own actions.

Many historians use two particular metaphors to describe this characteristic of their work: that of *immersion* in the past, or that of *listening* to the people who lived it. Stefan Tanaka formulated this agenda in 2015: "The pleasure of research for many historians, myself included, is in the immersion in the sensibilities of another era" – something one does by "returning [texts] to the social context in which they originated and from which they drew form and meaning."¹⁹ Miles Fairburn, in one of the most useful available discussions of how historians work, offered another particularly clear formulation sixteen years earlier: Historians "'immerse' themselves in the documents so as to learn the meanings behind the idioms [patterns of speech] of another era." As practitioners of History, "we learn to understand how the people we are studying understood their own actions,

---

¹⁷ There is a fine discussion of this point in Michael J. Salevouris and Conal Furay, *The Methods and Skills of History: A Practical Guide* (Malden, MA: Wiley Blackwell, 2015), pp. 28–30; see also William H. Walsh, *Philosophy of History: An Introduction* (New York: Harper, 1958).
¹⁸ Wineburg, *Historical Thinking*, pp. 63–88.
¹⁹ Stefan Tanaka, "Reconceiving Pasts in a Digital Age," in *Historein* 15:2 (2015): 21–29, here p. 27; Tanaka, *History without Chronology* (n.p.; Lever, 2019), p. 157.

desires, beliefs, and rules."[20] One former chairman of the American Historical Association gave a concise summary in 2022: History "requires learning about other people, understanding them, and letting their voices and sensibilities be heard." One can say that a scholar is a fine historian if she has "learned from his [sic] sources and engaged them in respectful conversation . . . This is what historians do. We listen."[21] Greg Dening, writing in 2007, defined History as "dialogic," as an act of "listening" to people we recognize in their humanity as our equals.[22]

Again, the aim of this "immersion," or of "listening," is to develop a holistic, integrative understanding, to place people and events in the context of a complex web of social relationships, connections, influences, and histories. It is important that students understand that this is a foundational assumption of the discipline of History, and one that distinguishes it from other disciplines. I have found that unless we give students a sense that History is a coherent way of understanding the world, based on clear and explicit postulates, it can be difficult for them to understand clearly *why* they are being asked to master the investigative and analytical approaches and methods that historians employ. I think this makes intuitive sense. Students need to know what we are trying to teach them. Merely hoping that if we can just expose them to enough complicated case studies or narratives they will come to understand that everything in human life is conditioned by its history is not effective. Being confronted with such broad and diverse subject matter without the aid of "laws" or of fundamental and universally valid principles can seem overwhelming. This is particularly true because students are often accustomed from their studies in other disciplines to seek clearly delimited explanations or "results."

Making clear that we are offering them a specific mode of understanding the world, one that seeks to integrate many other modes of understanding, can in contrast be exciting for them. I sometimes suggest to my students that the aim of History is to "put the world back together" so that we can gain not just *knowledge about* some particular part of it, but *understanding of* how the parts work together.

---

[20] Miles Fairburn, *Social History: Problems, Strategies, and Methods* (New York: St. Martin's, 1999), p. 217.
[21] James Grossman and Waldo E. Martin, "A Tribute to Leon Litwack," *Perspectives in History* 60 (2022): 7–9, here pp. 7, 8.
[22] Greg Dening, "Performing Cross-Culturally," in *Manifestos for History*, ed. Keith Jenkins, Sue Morgan, and Alun Munslow (New York: Routledge, 2007), pp. 98–107, here p. 98.

An influential essay by Edgar Morin offers a formulation that I have found helpful for students: Holism "seeks explanation at the level of totality, in opposition to the reductionist paradigm that seeks explanation at the level of elementary components ... [T]he whole is more than a global entity – it has a dynamic organization ... Complexity is not merely the phenomenal froth of reality; it is in the principles themselves."[23] That last sentence is a difficult one; I think the heart of it is that we understand human affairs not when we understand how discrete parts of it, each governed by principles that we can discover by studying those discrete parts, interact, but rather when we understand that the interactions among those parts shape the parts themselves. In other words, we are not simply adding up discrete vectors, but understanding complexity as a dynamic system.

Some historians take this fundamental historicist position two radical steps further, adopting what we might call an "unconditional" historicist stance. That stance was probably more common fifty years ago than it is now; few historians today would adopt it, I think. But it is useful to think about the reasoning behind it, because it can be quite productive in History teaching.

The first of these steps is to argue that historians should suspend judgment altogether in favor of observing in as unbiased a manner as possible what people in the past thought, or said, or did. The goal is to set aside our own ideas and values temporarily and focus on the thoughts and actions of people in the past. As Miles Fairburn described it, the aim is to "achieve empathy with the minds – the conceptual world, the consciousness – of the people belonging to another culture" of the past.[24] If we enter into historical investigation with the aim of *judgment*, of imposing our own values on the past, we are easily distracted from the goal of *understanding* the past. If we come to our investigation with the habit of determining whether what people thought or did was right or wrong, we can be diverted from the task of discovering *why* they thought or did it.

This is a very old idea, but it is still very much alive. Again, Leopold von Ranke remarked already in 1824 that while some sought to assign to history the task of "judging the past," his own ambition was merely to "show what actually happened" and to understand it deeply and comprehensively.[25] Michael Salevouris and Conal Furay put the same point succinctly in their 2015 book on *The Methods and Skills of History*: "to interpret the past using the values and beliefs of the present will distort and misrepresent that past.

---

[23] Edgar Morin, "From the Concept of System to the Paradigm of Complexity," *Journal of Social and Evolutionary Systems* 15 (1992): 371–385, here pp. 372, 374, 381.
[24] Fairburn, *Social History*, p. 216. [25] Ranke, *Secret*, p. 21.

A distinguishing mark of the good historian is the ability to avoid judging past ages by the standards of the present, and to see those societies ... as those societies saw themselves."[26] And Joseph C. Miller – a former president of the American Historical Association and scholar of the particularly repellent history of slavery – offered a vehement restatement in 2012: "retrospective judgement," he argued, "contradicts the essence of thinking *historically*," the aim of which is to understand the past and the people who lived it, not to affirm our own values.[27] In brief: History should foster, and thrive on, not judgment but curiosity.

This is an idea that is very much alive, as well, in History pedagogy. As Kaya Yilmaz wrote in 2007 of History teaching in the schools, instructors very frequently aim to develop historical "empathy," an ability to understand "the past in its own terms," to understand how people in the past thought, in order to understand their motives in acting in the ways that they did. This is sometimes also called historical "perspective-taking" – the exercise of trying to understand how people in the past saw their own world and their place in it.[28]

This more extreme version of the historicist stance has been subject to vehement critique. In the late nineteenth and early twentieth centuries historicism thrived within universities and History departments that were dominated by upper-class and upper-middle-class white men. An influential British example is George Macaulay Trevelyan, Regius Professor of History at Oxford and scion of a prominent family, who spent his youth shuttling between Wallington Hall, a mansion in the north of England, and Welcombe House, a mansion in Stratford-upon-Avon in the south of England. Another was Geoffrey R. Elton, a vehement advocate of historicist detachment who held the same position at Oxford 40 years after Trevelyan did.[29] In recent decades the insistence of such figures that the historian should understand the past rather than judge it has come to seem to many critics to be a product of their very privileged position within a particular structure of social and cultural power – not of objectivity, but

---

[26] Salevouris and Furay, *The Methods*, p. 66.
[27] Joseph C. Miller, *The Problem of Slavery as History* (New Haven, CT: Yale University Press, 2012), p. 9 (emphasis in the original).
[28] Kaya Yilmaz, "Historical Empathy and Its Implications for Classroom Practices in Schools," *History Teacher* 40 (2007): 331–338, here p. 332.
[29] David Cannadine, *G. M. Trevelyan: A Life in History* (New York: HarperCollins, 1992). See, for example, George Macaulay Trevelyan, *An Autobiography & Other Essays* (London: Longmans, Green & Company, 1949), pp. 76–77; Trevelyan, *Clio, A Muse and Other Essays* (Freeport, NY: Books for Libraries, 1913), p. 151; G. R. Elton, *The Practice of History* (New York: Thomas Crowell, 1967).

of self-interest. They did not want patterns of power in past times to be judged because they were beneficiaries of the same patterns of power in their own times. They sought to depoliticize knowledge about the past – to deny its relevance to present social issues.

Priya Satia offered a summary of this critique in 2020: Early twentieth-century British champions of historicism were "abettors of those in power ... Britain's imperial career," for example, "depended on a particular historical sensibility that deferred ethical judgment to an unspecified future time" or rejected it entirely, blanking out critique of the origins, methods, and consequences of the exercise of imperial expansion and colonial domination. At the same time, their "conviction that history is necessarily a story of progress" implicitly validated that domination as a natural stage in the evolution of humanity. Dipesh Chakrabarty agreed, concluding that "Historicism enabled European domination of the world."[30] Haitian anthropologist Michel-Rolph Trouillot put the point in more general terms in 1995: the "traditions of the guild" of professional historians "forbid academic historians to position themselves regarding the present," seeing any such stance as "ideological" rather than scholarly. From "that viewpoint, power is unproblematic" – both power as it has been exercised in the past, and the forms of present social, institutional, cultural, and political power (often derived from historical forms of power and privilege) that shape historians' current assumptions and interpretations.[31]

Even aside from this principled and historically informed critique, students simply have a very hard time suspending judgment in the way unconditional historicism would favor. More important, they generally do not really believe that they should. They do not see any purpose in suspending judgment of, for example, slavery, mass murder, or ruthless and brutal economic or sexual exploitation. In fact, they often experience doing so as a kind of intellectual complicity. Further, my sense is that ever greater emphasis has been laid in the schools over the past decades on

---

[30] Satia, *Time's Monster*, pp. 1–2, 3; Dipesh Chakrabarty, *Provincializing Europe* (Princeton, NJ: Princeton University Press, 2009), p. 7. For a detailed study of the role of History in the formation of British imperial identity, see Reba N. Sofer, *Discipline and Power: The University, History and the Making of an English Elite, 1870–1930* (Stanford, CA: Stanford University Press, 1994).

[31] Trouillot, *Silencing the Past*, pp. 5, 151. In defense of historicism, it should be acknowledged that numerous historians have pointed out that in its original formulation in Germany it meant exactly the opposite of what its critics now claim. As one study of 2021 pointed out, historicism explicitly "rejected stadial accounts of history" – that is, the belief that history unfolds in stages – "and universal theories of social evolution," and countered the "rationalist-teleological notion of ... progress" that imperialists used to assert their own societies' superiority. Paul and Veldhuizen, "Introduction," p. 64.

developing young people's capacity for independent judgment – their ability to form and expound or defend their own opinions. This is surely appropriate; it has been a response to and a part of a broader, long-term democratization of public culture that has put emphasis on citizen's own capacity for judgment and independent thought rather than on respect for authoritative traditions and figures. It is also probably a response in part to the increasing diversity of most democratic societies, which has led to a declining emphasis on consensus and a rising appreciation for the capacity for critical judgment as an important skill for people who will inevitably encounter, in their interactions with fellow citizens, a wide range of views and perspectives.

Many students will likely be more convinced, then, by recent arguments within the historical profession in favor of "engaged history" – History that seeks to address present concerns, specifically issues of social justice. Claire Norton and Mark Donnelly wrote in 2019, for example, of a new "'ethical turn' in history" away from epistemological debates and toward historians' "ethico-political responsibilities" to "help campaigns for socio-political justice." Echoing Satia's (and other's) critiques, they advocate for paying attention to the fact that "the ways in which historians 'do history' have ideological and political consequences which too often go unrecognized" – for example, the tendency of the historicist approach to depoliticize our understanding of the past.[32] A year later Donald Bloxham argued that judgment is in any case unavoidable. On the one hand, our choice of language usually requires us to make implicit judgments – for example, we can write "appropriated" or "stolen," "settlement" or "invasion." On the other hand, "'Neutralizing' non-neutral phenomena by one's descriptions is not neutral either" – that is to say, again, that suspending judgment can be a form of moral complicity.[33]

Arguments like these cannot be dismissed as simply fashionable political correctness. There is a history reaching well back into the previous century of debate within the discipline of History between scholars committed to

---

[32] Claire Norton and Mark Donnelly, *Liberating Histories* (New York: Routledge, 2019), pp. 1, 2. See also, for example, *The Engaged Historian: Perspectives on the Intersection of Politics, Activism and the Historical Profession*, ed. Stefan Berger (New York: Berghahn, 2019); Marcia Sa Cavalcante Schuback, "Engaged History," in *The Ethos of History: Time and Responsibility*, ed. Stefan Helgesson and Jayne Svenungsson (New York: Berghahn, 2018), pp. 160–174; Jorma Kalela, *Making History: The Historian and Uses of the Past* (New York: Palgrave MacMillan, 2011); Christopher C. Martell and Kaylene M. Stevens, *Teaching History for Justice: Centering Activism in Students' Study of the Past* (New York: Teacher's College Press, 2021); Linda Symcox, "Internationalizing the U. S. History Curriculum: From Nationalism to Cosmopolitanism," in *National History Standards: The Problem of the Canon and the Future of Teaching History*, ed. Linda Symcox and Arie Wilschut (Charlotte, NC: Information Age, 2009), pp. 33–54.

[33] Donald Bloxham, *History and Morality* (Oxford: Oxford University Press, 2020), p. 9.

social justice and those committed to scholarly disinterest. An example would be the work in the 1970s of Jean Chesneaux, a French communist and environmentalist professor of History who became disillusioned with the academic discipline and argued that the "basic characteristics of the historian's rhetoric ... are those of capitalism as a whole" and "serve and reinforce the Establishment, the basic values of the capitalist system and the entire prevailing ideology." Those characteristics include the emphasis on the expertise of professionals, the focus on the technical requirements of work in the discipline, the interest in the past purely for its own sake, the goal of objectivity, the "publish or perish" imperative to produce scholarly work approved by colleagues and publishers, and the system of rewards that kept professors loyal to that conception of their work, such as prestigious jobs, fellowships, prizes, offices in professional and scholarly associations, media attention, publishing deals, and so on. Historians should instead, he suggested, embark on a "quest for the type of history the revolutionary struggle requires" and seek to "work not *on* but *with* the workers, the peasants, the people," assisting in creating "a history produced by the masses of people in terms of their own needs."[34] Oscar Handlin offered a blistering response to such views in 1979. Of those calling for relevant History, Handlin wrote "it is not knowledge they wish. Having already reached their conclusions, they seek only reassuring confirmation as they prepare to act ... At best, the usable past demanded of history consists of the data to flesh out a formula ... At worst, the demand made of the past is for a credible myth that will identify the forces of good and evil and inspire those who fight ... on one side of the barricades or the other."[35]

The balance between these positions has shifted in recent decades in favor of a more activist or engaged approach. But both positions remain very much alive – as, for example, the debate within the American Historical Association over "presentism" in the summer of 2022 (referenced in the Introduction) suggests. The discussion has been particularly active since about 2010, but in essence this is yet another long-lived and fundamentally unresolvable division within the discipline of History.[36]

---

[34] Jean Chesneaux, *Pasts and Futures, or What Is History For?* (London: Thames and Hudson, 1978 [1976]), pp. 3, 53, 107. For Chesneaux's environmental concerns, see esp. pp. 91–96 (emphasis in the original).

[35] Oscar Handlin, *Truth in History* (Cambridge, MA: Harvard University Press, 1979), pp. 403–404. For a good recent review of the discussion, see David Motadel, "The Political Role of the Historian," *Contemporary European History* 32 (2021): 38–45.

[36] We might date the more recent discussion conveniently from 2011, when Duke University Press began publishing the journal *History of the Present: A Journal of Critical History*. The following provide some orientation in the literature: Daniel Steinmetz-Jenkins, "Introduction: Whose

The terms of the current discussion are far less stark than those of the debate in the 1960s or 1970s; nevertheless, the epistemological questions – questions regarding the nature, purposes, and social functions of knowledge of the past – are fundamentally unchanged. But regardless of where individual professors of History stand on those questions, in my admittedly limited experience the great majority of students, whatever their political convictions, see the fundamental idea that History should serve our present needs, interests, and causes as self-evident. They are deeply interested in what a recent article on teaching history in higher education called "the history of now."[37] A very large proportion of students have, in other words, an operational conception of the value of the formal study of the past.

And yet, it has also been my experience that an emphasis on moral and political judgment *can* contribute to a real superficiality of historical understanding. I have found that students do sometimes stop investigating once they have formed an opinion of the rights and wrongs of an idea or action, and do not pursue a deeper, more complex or sophisticated comprehension of it – an *historical* understanding. The intellectual exercise of setting aside our own scale of values while we investigate someone else's can encourage students to examine in depth ideas that they find either particularly objectionable or particularly sympathetic.

I will give two brief examples. In my courses on twentieth-century Europe I have for some years now assigned excerpts from a particularly heinous misogynistic British anti-suffrage tract of 1913, Almroth Wright's *Unexpurgated Case against Woman Suffrage*.[38] Many students simply dismiss his ideas as reactionary and toxic – which they certainly were. But reading the essay closely, in the context of Wright's biography (which included many high honors for his medical work), is an excellent way to explore the relationships in early twentieth-century Britain between and among imperialism, political reform, biomedical science, racism, and gender relations. Making those connections can give students a much clearer understanding of the depth and intensity of opposition to women's suffrage, and of the profound implications, at that time, of the expansion of

---

Present? Which History?" in *Modern Intellectual History* 20 (2023): 559–570; David Armitage, "In Defense of Presentism," in *History and Human Flourishing*, ed. Darrin M. McMahon (Oxford: Oxford University Press, 2020), pp. 59–84.

[37] Patrick Iber and Jennifer Ratner-Rosenhagen, "The Present Is a Foreign Country: Teaching the History of Now," *Modern Intellectual History* 20 (2023): 651–662.

[38] Almroth Wright, *The Unexpurgated Case against Woman Suffrage* (1913), in *Controversies in the History of British Feminism. The Opponents: The Antisuffragists*, ed. Marie M. Roberts and Tamae Mizuta (London: Routledge/Thoemmes, 1995), pp. 1–86.

women's political and social rights. To undertake that analysis – to understand what was at stake for people at the time – students must set aside their visceral and, from any sane early twenty-first century perspective, entirely justified contempt for Wright's views.

As a second example, in the same course I often assign excerpts from Karl Marx and Friedrich Engel's *Communist Manifesto* as a way of giving students a greater understanding of the appeal of socialism in the early twentieth century. A very large proportion of my students have been told that Marxism was "wrong," and that history has proven that it was. They tend therefore to read the *Manifesto* cursorily on the assumption that something that was wrong cannot be very interesting. But obviously what is interesting to the historian about the *Manifesto* is not whether Marx was right that capitalism would lead to the progressive impoverishment of the working class, the enrichment of an ever-shrinking elite, the seizing up of the capitalist mechanism of accumulation, and revolution. What is interesting is not the answer ("Marx was wrong") but a question: What about the context of that period made Marx's reasoning persuasive to so many? The reasons for that were quite complex and would include at least three broad elements. One is that in the economic crisis and transformation of the period from the 1840s into the 1890s the experience of industrial societies appeared to be rather precisely predicted in Marx's pamphlet. Another is that the form of Marx's argument (social evolution through distinct stages, often called the "stadial" model) had a very long history in European societies, was very familiar to most Europeans, and had considerable intuitive intellectual appeal at that time. A third is that Marx's prediction of a future of harmony and peace echoed the Christian expectation of the Kingdom of God on Earth. Particularly when paired with autobiographies in which socialist workers recall their encounter with socialism as something like a conversion experience, in which they felt that scales had fallen from their eyes and they both understood their world for the first time, and for the first time had hope, this can give students a much deeper understanding of the appeal of socialism in that period.[39]

I think it is also important to recognize, however, that the dichotomy between "engaged" and "objective" History is not always very clear. Consider, for example, the observation by historian of Africa Emma

---

[39] There are useful worker's autobiographies in Alfred Kelly, ed., *The German Worker* (Berkeley: University of California Press, 1987). For a third example, explored in greater detail, see Wineburg, *Why Learn History*, pp. 84–91, and general reflection on p. 76. I believe many historians would regard Wineburg's argument as an example of the politically conservative bias of historicism, but it is interesting partly for that reason.

Hunter in 2022 that "the recovery of radical ideas" from the past by intellectual historians "can be a direct resource for political action in the present ... Exploring past ideas can pose specific challenges when sources speak in unexpected ways, with ideas which do not fit easily into dominant contemporary global frameworks." This sometimes "enables a critical questioning of the unspoken frameworks of the present."[40] In other words: Sometimes the best way to address our present concerns is to set them aside and listen to what people in the past have to say. Maria Elena Martinez made a similar point eight years earlier, in an essay addressing historical sexual identities. Martinez recognized the importance of "avoiding the collusion with power" that can result from relying on the concepts or perspectives we find in historical sources. But she also pointed out that imposing a familiar category (and the assumptions and expectations we associate with it) on historical people "who may not have recognized the practices, lifestyles, notions of body and self, and so forth that it references" can sabotage an "opportunity to discover in the past human possibilities and imaginings that were suppressed or left unfulfilled but that can provide guidance in the present for creating better worlds in the future."[41] This is, as Beverley Southgate put it in 2007, part of the unavoidable "schizoid nature of historical studies" – that very often the best way "to 'learn from the past'" things that are relevant to the present is to pursue "pure 'knowledge for its own sake.'"[42]

I think there is a fruitful way to approach this conundrum of historical "judgment" with students. That approach is to step back from politics or morality and consider the ethical stance that is at the foundation of the historicist tradition.

First, historicism asks that the historian respect the full humanity of the people she studies. People in the past are not simply "objects" of our study; they were (and are) "subjects" in the sense of being autonomous agents – with their own ideas, experiences, views, values, and lives. Again, the

---

[40] Emma Hunter, "Dialogues between Past and Present in Intellectual Histories of Mid-Twentieth-Century Africa," *Modern Intellectual History* 19 (2022): 630–638.

[41] Maria Elena Martinez, "Archives, Bodies, and Imagination: The Case of Juana Aguilar and Queer Approaches to History, Sexuality, and Politics," *Radical History Review* 120 (2014): 159–182, here pp. 173, 174. For a more abstract formulation, see Michel Foucault, "What Is Enlightenment?" in Michel Foucault, *Ethics: Subjectivity and Truth*, ed. Paul Rabinow, trans. Robert Hurley and others (New York: New Press, 1998), pp. 315–316.

[42] Beverley Southgate, "'Humani nil alienum': The Quest for 'Human Nature,'" in *Manifestos for History*, ed. Keith Jenkins, Sue Morgan, and Alun Munslow (New York: Routledge, 2007), pp. 67–76, here p. 69. See also Gabrielle M. Spiegel, "The Future of the Past: History, Memory and the Ethical Imperatives of Writing History," *Journal of the Philosophy of history* 8 (2014): 149–179.

historicist does not reduce them to the status of *things* to be studied; she recognizes them as *people* to be understood. This is the *ethical* message of Leopold von Ranke's observation that "everything human is worth knowing."[43]

Second, historicism also asks the historian to respect history and its role in shaping people. The people of the past were shaped by their own contemporary context and their own histories, which made them who they were, just as our own history has made us who we are. They had "historicity" – they were shaped by their own historical context, which we need to understand in its full complexity and scope if we are to understand *them*, their thoughts, and their actions. The people of the past, in short, are not simply markers that we shove around on a piece of paper until we have an arrangement that confirms our own beliefs, whether moral, political, religious, or whatever. *We* enter into *their* world, we "immerse" ourselves in it; we strive to understand where they stood in it, and how it looked to them.

This is an ethical stance, not a moral one. It defines how we approach or treat people, not what we think of them. Understanding what people thought, and how their history led them to think it, does not mean that we do not regard their beliefs or actions as moral or immoral. It does not mean that they "have an alibi" for deplorable actions, or that their admirable actions had no merit. Moral standards apply to beliefs and behaviors regardless of their origins or motives. An action (or an idea) is moral or immoral in the eyes of the person judging it; it is not moral or immoral only if the person who commits (or believes) it thinks it so. Understanding how people thought and where they stood in their world can mean seeing clearly how corrupt, cruel, self-serving, dishonest, or cowardly they were. It can mean appreciating how devoted, loving, principled, and courageous they were. To take only the most obvious examples of enslavement and genocide, the central aim of the historian is to understand how these practices came about and what consequences they had, but only a sociopath would not regard them as morally repugnant or see efforts to defend people against them as a matter of moral indifference. This response is in no way incompatible with the desire to understand them as historical realities. In fact, the historical literature on both is enormous precisely because our sense of their repugnance is so urgent. There is no reason students should try to suppress the feelings of disgust, grief, admiration, or enthusiasm that encountering the people of the past and the

---

[43] Ranke, "A Fragment from the 1860s," p. 61.

things that they said and did can elicit. On the contrary, these responses – judgments – can fuel the desire to understand.

This approach also does not imply a rejection of political judgment – it does not mean that we regard injustice or heroism in the past as not relevant to the present. History can often give us a sense for how precious some of our institutions and traditions are by revealing the terrible, vicious, and destructive things that were done in their absence, before they were created. It can also reveal how profoundly some of our institutions and traditions were shaped by and derive from terrible, vicious, destructive actions and conditions in the past, and how they perpetuate similar and related actions and conditions in the present. In neither case does it make any sense to the great majority of students to deny the political implications of those linkages between past and present – and neither does it make intellectual sense to ask them to do so. On the contrary, the moral or political urgency with which students regard such linkages can be the most powerful of all motivators for learning. How did the obviously vicious practices of the past evolve into the less obvious but pervasive injustices of the present? Who accomplished that, and for what purposes? Did that even happen because someone wanted it to, or rather as a result of social dynamics that drove choices in policy or in individual social behavior? What enabled the emergence of institutions or the predominance of ideas that underpin substantive practices of justice, equity, freedom, or creativity today? Did historical actors deliberately accomplish that, and if so how did they do it? Many students care deeply about questions like these, and that can lead them to pursue historical inquiry and learning with exceptional energy and determination. Present concerns can open the doors of historical inquiry, not shut them.

In short, the discipline of History does not ask us to suspend our own present concerns, commitments, and purposes. It *does* ask us not to study *only* those aspects of people's lives and worlds in the past that seem relevant to our own concerns. It asks us to enter into an open-ended inquiry into their lives and worlds. It asks us to treat them not as mere things, which can be dismissed without further inquiry once we have decided whether they were good or bad, or once we have made them answer *our* questions. Encountering people in the past is not an on/off, yes/no proposition; it is an encounter with humanity in its complexity and historicity.

In discussing this approach with students, I think it can be helpful to draw on a term developed by John Tosh, who wrote in 2008 of the possibility of a "practical historicism" – responsive to our concerns in the present, but loyal to the "scholarly conventions of the discipline." Thomas

J. Sugrue offered another useful formulation in 1998: that historians should maintain both "responsibility to the past" and "engagement with the present."[44] It is usually pointless to ask our students entirely to substitute curiosity for judgment, or to regard the past as morally or politically irrelevant to the present. Most will find neither approach plausible. What we can suggest to them instead is that right and wrong are not analytical categories, that judgment is not the endpoint of inquiry, and that we advance our understanding of the past not by deciding what category to put people in the past into (right/wrong, good/bad), but by deepening and expanding our inquiry into their world and their understanding of it.

The second tenet of "unconditional" historicism is the notion that historians should be guided in formulating research questions by their *sources*, rather than by some agenda established in advance – for example, on the basis of current issues of concern to them, or by a particular theoretical framework, or by sympathy with or hostility to a particular cause or set of values. We often describe these historians as working primarily in the tradition of textual analysis called hermeneutics, by which is meant the process of understanding what a text meant to people at the time of its production. Their argument is that what should be important to the historian, what she should investigate, is what appears important in the sources that she explores. What needs to be explained is not something that she picks out of the historical record because it is of interest to her here and today, but rather what she finds to have been of interest to the people of the place and period she is studying. Further, the categories that she should use in analyzing the thoughts and actions of people in the past are logically the categories that she finds in her sources, not in her own society, or in a currently influential theory. People in the past were not motivated by our ideas; their view of their world was not shaped by our categories; we can only understand their thoughts, words, intentions, and actions if we understand not how *we* think, but how *they* thought. If they thought something was important, that is a strong argument for looking into it.

German historian of Russia Jörg Baberowski puts it this way: History "does not encounter things armed with abstract concepts, but rather seeks to derive its concepts from close and verifiable observation of particular things."[45] In other words, ideally the encounter with what is in the sources

---

[44] Tosh, *Why History Matters*, p. 22; Thomas J. Sugrue, "Responsibility to the Past, Engagement with the Present," *Labor History* 39 (1998): 60–69.

[45] Jörg Baberowski, *Der Sinn der Geschichte: Geschichtstheorien von Hegel bis Foucault* (Munich: Beck, 2005), p. 67.

will define the historian's research agenda and the categories and concepts she uses in her analysis. Ludmila Jordanova explicitly used the familiar metaphor of immersion in suggesting something similar: "Much of the best history has proceeded by a kind of immersion in the sources, taking its explanatory devices out of those sources."[46]

A relatively small proportion of historians today believe that this can be a realistic description of how historians develop research agendas. At a minimum, most would probably agree that working with sources does not "define," but rather "refines" or "revises" an historian's research agenda. Any historian will begin the research process with her own interests and ideas, derived from many sources – her personal history and experiences, prior research, specific theoretical frameworks she finds interesting, or her own political commitments. This is a subject that will be addressed further in Chapters 2 and 4. But whether we call it revision or definition, the principle is the same, and it grows directly out of the idea of the historian's immersion in the sources as a path to understanding the people of the past, as people. Miles Fairburn put it this way: what I am calling unconditional historicism "does not impose exterior concepts or theories on the [historical] actors"; it instead seeks to "grasp the concepts and conceptual schemas of past people as they grasped them, and describe their values and beliefs with words that accurately convey the meanings that the values and beliefs had to the actors."[47] This means that when we discover that something was important to people in the past, we should investigate *that* – not something that *we* think *should* have been important to them.

Again, this is a very old idea, but not one that is dead. Jim Cullen offered a very practical formulation in 2009 (in a book subtitled "How to Read, Write and Think about History"): "Where do you get good questions? The answer is: from your sources . . . Only by delving into the sources . . . can a question really come into focus. And as often as not, a good question is the result of a *process*" of continual refinement as one deepens and broadens one's knowledge of the sources.[48] There are times when this approach can allow us to see what Michel-Rolph Trouillot calls "the unthinkable" – "that which one cannot conceive within the range of possible alternatives" because one does not have the categories that would permit one to ask

---

[46] Ludmila Jordanova, *History in Practice*, 2nd edition (London: Hodder, 2006), p. 62.
[47] Fairburn, *Social History*, pp. 25, 204.
[48] Jim Cullen, *Essaying the Past: How to Read, Write, and Think about History* (Malden, MA: Wiley-Blackwell, 2012), p. 35 (emphasis in the original).

about it – or "that which perverts all answers because it defies the terms under which the questions were phrased."[49] This is where History really becomes an adventure – when we discover that we do not have a map, that we do not have categories that people fit neatly into, that we have to do some more thinking and investigating before we will be able to understand what people were. As I suggested in the Introduction, that adventure can give us a new perspective on the present, as well, by forcing us to confront our own assumptions and categories, revealing to us our own historicity.

One great disadvantage of this approach is of course that as a rule there is very significant systematic bias in the sources themselves. The published record, archival collections, even, for example, the architectural record usually disproportionately reflect the interests, concerns, and perspectives of powerful and wealthy people. As Trouillot remarked, "the presences and absences embodied in sources ... are neither neutral nor natural. They are created ... They reflect differential control of the means of historical production" by people with differing degrees and kinds of social power. "Something is always left out while something else is recorded," and those inclusions and omissions reflect "uneven historical power."[50] Laura Doan put the point economically in 2013: "Archival materials come with their own agendas."[51] Middle- and upper-class people write and publish far more than poor people; colonial administrators and imperialist social scientists write and publish – or commit to archives – far more than colonial subjects; historically, in most societies women have been systematically excluded from the educated professions and administrative and government power, and therefore have left fewer published or archived traces; governments and nongovernmental organizations dominated by particular social groups have preserved records of their own activities or relevant to their own concerns, not those of people excluded from participation in them. If we simply follow the sources to our questions, it is easy to end up primarily writing the history of people with a disproportionate share of wealth and power. As Trouillot observed, historians must have "strategies for countering inequalities of power in knowledge of the past."[52] The unconditional historicist approach might predispose an historian to set aside that "doubt about the innocence of the archive" (including the published record) that, as Patrick Joyce pointed out in 2007, "is axiomatic to historical method."[53]

---

[49] Trouillot, *Silencing the Past*, p. 82.   [50] Trouillot, *Silencing the Past*, pp. 48–49.
[51] Doan, *Disturbing Practices*, p. 49.   [52] Doan, *Disturbing Practices*, p. xiii.
[53] Patrick Joyce, "The Gift of the Past: Towards a Critical Theory," in *Manifestos for History*, ed. Keith Jenkins, Sue Morgan, and Alun Munslow (New York: Routledge, 2007), pp. 88–97, here p. 89.

For this reason, again, this kind of unconditional historicism is often regarded as inherently politically conservative. While historicism was the primary theoretical orientation of academic historians up until the middle of the twentieth century, since then the historicist position has been questioned by scholars who regard it as not neutral or dispassionate at all. Instead, they see it as shaped by profound social bias, and by an unspoken desire to depoliticize investigation of the past. More activist critics – engaged historians – on the political Left have argued that it should instead be a function of History to call power and exploitation, discrimination, privilege, and injustice into question by using the tools of scholarship to show how current social arrangements were created, thereby proving that the commonsense defense of them ("this is just the way things are") is artificial and self-serving. This is sometimes called "denaturalizing" current social arrangements, revealing them to be ideological and created rather than inevitable.[54] To quote influential working-class historian Howard Zinn, History can "expose the ideology that pervades our culture" and our current social arrangements, by showing precisely how they came to be. John Tosh made the same point: History can benefit us by "overturning the belief that 'things have always been this way' … as a corrective to … static thinking, and especially any thinking with determinist or essentialist overtones. Confident assumptions … melt away when measured against the diversity of historical experience."[55] Of course the historicist approach can contribute to precisely this aim. Exploring the ways in which the past was quite different from the present can be the first step in understanding how the present came to be. Understanding how the assumptions and ideas of people in the past differed from our own can lead us to examine how people in our own time came to think as they do. Critics of historicism argue, however, that the focus on understanding the past "on its own terms" can too easily divert attention from topics that are relevant and lead the scholar or the student into "antiquarian" meandering without political purpose – again, it can "depoliticize" scholarship, rendering it effectively useless for our present.

For some on the political Right, similarly, History can be a tool for debunking the pious lies of the Left. History can be used to question a progressive story of the achievements of liberal democracy or of the

---

[54] Laura Doan discussed this approach in *Disturbing Practices*, pp. 2–3; there is a particularly clear statement in Jürgen Kocka, "Geschichte – wozu?" in *Über das Studium der Geschichte*, ed. Wolfgang Hardtwig (Munich: Deutscher Taschenbuch, 1990), pp. 427–443, esp. p. 438 – unfortunately not, to my knowledge, available in English.

[55] Quoted in Barton and Levstik, *Teaching History for the Common Good*, p. 74; Tosh, *Why History Matters*, p. 32.

welfare state or of racial justice; or to undermine heroic stories told by the Left about noble figures who have struggled for social justice and freedom. History can show us, for example, how murderous communist parties, regimes, and leaders have been; or how corrupt the people, events, institutions, or developments the Left celebrates actually were; or how creative and democratic free-market capitalism has been. In any case, both camps argue – as Jo Guldi and David Armitage did in a "manifesto" for History in 2014 – that we should "use history to criticize the institutions around us and ... return history to its mission as a critical social science."[56]

Even aside from this question of the wider purpose and social or political function of historical study, however, my own experience is that asking students to let their sources guide them to their questions can be demotivating. In the view of many students, it amounts to rendering History irrelevant. A History that ignores the present is likely to encourage many students to look for intellectual pursuits they believe to be more relevant to their concerns. Again, most students do not come to university to engage in detached intellectual labor. Most come to make sense of their world, to find their way in it (if they are older, to find a better way in it). Suggesting that their agenda should not be set by their interests is pointless.

In more positive terms, though, doing so would throw away one of the great strengths of History, which is that we all know that we are up to our necks in history. We all understand the validity of the historicist postulate that we, our lives, are the products of history. History is very often interesting to students because they understand that it has created the conditions in which they must live their own lives. I will return to this issue in Chapter 5; for now, I hope it is sufficient simply to say that a very great deal of the intellectual excitement that History classes can generate derives directly from their relevance to students' own concerns. This is of course not always true, nor true for all students. The two most intellectually exciting History classes I took as an undergraduate were on thirteenth-century China and medieval Russia. But current enrollments in college and university courses on, for example, medieval history do not lie. Most students want to learn about things that seem relevant to their interests, experience, concerns, and lives. Offering them the opportunity to do so makes more than just financial, "butts in seats" sense; it is pedagogically sound to engage students, as the saying goes, "where they live."

---

[56] Jo Guldi and David Armitage, *The History Manifesto* (Cambridge: Cambridge University Press, 2014), p. 85.

And yet immersing ourselves in the sources and listening to what seemed important to people in the past – rather than bringing to the sources our own list of topics that *we* have defined as important – can help us broaden our focus from matters that seem very important in our own society to take in matters that were important in the past. It can, in other words, prevent us from ignoring aspects of past historical situations that had significant influence on events and outcomes, including outcomes that shape the present. Focusing on what is of interest to us, not to the people of the past whom we are studying, can sabotage our understanding of them and of ourselves. I think this is a common problem, for example, for secular historians in our own time, who sometimes have a hard time understanding how profoundly religion shaped the thinking of people in the past. It can be very difficult for people who have no experience of religious faith to understand the language, the conceptual universe, the motivations, and hence the actions of people who understood their faith to be the center and purpose of life.

I can give my own work as an example of both the strengths and the weaknesses of the unconditional historicist approach, because I have largely followed it. I wrote my master's thesis on the law pertaining to children born out of wedlock in the 1920s. This was a subject I stumbled upon while reading German parliamentary debates in a desperate last-minute search for a topic for my master's thesis after several other topics proved not to be viable. I found it interesting largely because of the extraordinary vehemence of the debate. This was a matter that was clearly important to the politicians involved, particularly communists, Catholics, and women's rights advocates. That topic led me to the broader topic of policy directed at children generally, and I wrote my first book about child welfare policy in Germany between 1890 and 1960. In the course of my research for that book, I found that questions of sexual morality were of central importance to people concerned about the welfare of children; my second book was about that. While working on that project I was struck by the intensity of the debate over the moral status of modern dance in the two decades after 1900, and I wrote a book about that. In each case I followed the sources to new topics that were important to people at the time. The unfortunate result is that I have spent my career writing mostly about middle- and upper-class intellectuals, administrators, activists, and professionals. Even the socialists and the women's or homosexual rights advocates I have written about were primarily middle-class intellectuals, not working people. I have, in other words, fallen victim to – and arguably reinforced – the bias inherent in my sources.

On the other hand, the women who created the new cultural form of modern dance were not in positions of social power, and yet I believe I have been able to establish that they had a profound impact in the first three decades of the twentieth century on the way that people around the world thought about culture, art, the ordering of gender relations, and even colonialism. Further, they were extremely successful pioneers in one of the most important cultural and economic processes of the twentieth century, the emergence of commercial mass culture. Probably a substantial majority of my professional colleagues regard the history of dance as an ancillary or marginal topic, a sideshow to the main events of the early twentieth century – war, diplomacy, revolution, mass murder, nationalism, industrial growth, and so on. The story of those big, important events is often assumed to have been, and analyzed as if it was, dominated by men in positions of social power. I hope that if my colleagues were to read my book on dance they would not be so sure. In other words, following the sources led me to a topic that has the potential to subvert histories of the twentieth century that are obsessively focused on the thoughts, actions, and concerns of men with wealth and power.

As a matter of experience, then, I think the question of whether to adopt an unconditionally historicist approach to choosing what to investigate is not an "either/or," "yes/no" question. There have been attempts to strike a balance between these approaches. John Tosh, for example, argued in 2015 that "our priorities in the present should determine the questions we ask of the past, but not the answers."[57] I think this is a useful shorthand way to address the issue with students, and Chapter 4 will show that it has a long tradition in History.

As I have suggested in the Introduction, however, I believe the ultimately irreconcilable disagreement between advocates of engaged scholarship in History (History that responds to contemporary concerns) and advocates of unconditionally historicist History is an important resource for teachers. In my experience more students lean toward activist instincts, but most are also committed to the idea that the historian should be impartial. Addressing this question explicitly as a question of *method*, rather than

---

[57] Tosh, *The Pursuit of History*, p. 49. For interesting discussions, see Elizabeth Deeds Ermarth, "Beyond History," *Rethinking History* 5 (2002): 195–215, here p. 206; Oliver J. Daddow, "The Ideology of Apathy: Historians and Postmodernism," *Rethinking History* 8 (2004): 417–437, which offers a history of the idea of ideologically neutral History; A. Dirk Moses, "Hayden White, Traumatic Nationalism, and the Public Role of History" and Hayden White, "The Public Relevance of Historical Studies: A Reply to Dirk Moses," in *History and Theory* 44 (2005): 311–332 and 333–338.

simply of common sense or simple preference, can encourage them to confront epistemological issues that are of central importance for the discipline of History. I will address this issue at length in Chapter 4. For now, I want to suggest that in my experience it is fruitful to teach this problem (so to speak) of unconditional historicism in our History classes, and that a reasonable proportion of students find it to be a profound and interesting one.

1.3 How History Thinks II: Inductive and Idiographic Principles and Practices

While there is broad agreement among historians regarding the foundational historicist postulate that all human things are shaped by history, then, there is profound division regarding the more unconditional historicist position. A further divergence is less vehement, but still profoundly important in the discipline. Whether "unconditional" or not, historicists generally agree on a further fundamental characteristics of historical inquiry. They generally see History as almost uniquely committed to a particular form of *inductive* as opposed to *deductive* reasoning. Deductive reasoning proceeds by first developing a generalization or hypothesis, then developing a provisional prediction based on it, and then testing that prediction – through experimentation in the natural sciences, and in the social sciences often through quantitative statistical analysis or structured observation. If the prediction is correct (or the statistical correlation high), the hypothesis is supported; if not, an alternative hypothesis should be tested. In the sciences, formulating a hypothesis after performing the experiment is considered a fundamental methodological flaw – it is sometimes pejoratively called "HARKing" (hypothesizing after the results are known). In contrast, inductive reasoning begins with observations – in History, the sources – and derives its hypotheses and conclusions from analysis of them. Using the term "inductive" to describe what historians do is a bit confusing, because in the most common usage inductive reasoning leads to generalizations, and many historians do not do that. They reach conclusions, but do not generalize them. This is a point discussed in the next pages. But it is true that historicists usually rely, in constructing interpretations, on complexity, synthesis, and a standard often referred to as the "preponderance of the available evidence." They arrive not at yes/no answers based on decisive experimental or statistical results, but at more or less firm (or speculative) conclusions supported by a large body of suggestive evidence. Again, in History a persuasive conclusion is often one that rests on a holistic or integrative approach to the topic, drawing on multiple bodies and forms of evidence.

This is in practice true not just of historians particularly attached to the historicist tradition, but also of those more skeptical of it. The simple reason, of course, is that historians cannot conduct experiments or make direct observations. As the last section of Chapter 2 will discuss, many historians are very much committed to particular theoretical frameworks. But they cannot test them experimentally. They also very seldom have the quality or quantity of numerical data that would permit statistical testing. And they cannot directly observe historical events. Even historians committed to particular theoretical traditions, therefore, are largely confined to inductive methods. They examine the indirect, fragmentary, and often biased evidence that has survived from the past and interpret it with the help of their theoretical apparatus, or framework.

A further useful terminological contrast was developed in the late nineteenth century by Wilhelm Windelband, who characterized history as "idiographic" rather than "nomothetic."[58] In practice, historians more influenced by the historicist tradition devote themselves primarily to developing a full picture or description (*graphic*) of particular, unique, and individual (*idio*, as in idiosyncratic) phenomena, rather than to discovering or positing (*thetic*, as in "thesis" or argument) general laws (from the Greek *nomos*) that apply to a broad category of events, situations, people, or societies that are fundamentally "the same" or "similar." A nomothetic discipline seeks to find laws that govern how things work in general, consistently. Fundamentally, it *explains* a category of phenomena in the sense that it determines what causes things in that category to happen – whether the category is revolutions, wars, economic growth, bursts of religious innovation, or whatever. An idiographic discipline in contrast seeks to *understand* a particular and specific individual phenomenon. It aims to understand not "revolutions" generally but, for example, specifically the French Revolution; not "religious innovation" in general but specifically the revitalization of Buddhism in the late nineteenth century; not "what happens when differing human groups encounter each other" but nineteenth-century European racism. In History the aim is not to determine what causes things in a particular category to happen; it is to develop a detailed, multifaceted, descriptive analysis of an individual

---

[58] Windelband, "Rectorial Address," p. 175. See Christopher Lloyd, "History and the Social Sciences," in *Writing History: Theory & Practice*, ed. Stefan Berger, Heiko Feldner, and Kevin Passmore (London: Arnold, 2003), pp. 83–103, esp. pp. 90–92.

phenomenon, including an expansive multicausal analysis of what went into its making. As philosopher of History William Dray put it in 1993, the aim is to study phenomena "in their unique occurrence, in their particularity."⁵⁹

Nomothetic disciplines are primarily deductive. They posit hypothetical laws, and then test individual cases to see if the hypothesis holds up. Idiographic disciplines are primarily inductive. They explore a phenomenon through investigation in depth and detail, without necessarily arriving at generalizable conclusions – "laws" – at all. Philosopher Michael Oakeshott offered an extreme formulation of the historicist position in 1933: in History, "nothing ... is negative or non-contributory"; the entire historical context is relevant. Accordingly, "History accounts *for* change by means of a full account *of* change," and not by means of "an appeal to some external reason" or causal law. The "method of the historian is never to explain by means of generalization but always by means of greater and more complete detail."⁶⁰

A particularly uncompromising variant of the idiographic approach is generally called "nominalism." Nominalism is the view that general categories are merely convenient abstractions.⁶¹ They have no reality in and of themselves, independent of specific phenomena or cases. Rather, they are just ways of organizing our thinking about specific phenomena or cases. Specific phenomena, real things, are not examples of general or abstract categories ("class," "the state," "religion"); instead, each thing is unique. Specific phenomena therefore do not conform to general laws that govern all phenomena in the category in which we place them, when we organize our thinking about them. Such categories do not have any explanatory or "predictive" (in hindsight) power. There are no laws governing phenomena that we organize, for convenience, into categories, because those categories are not real things. Historians therefore cannot say: "this specific phenomenon is an example of general category X; we know how general category X behaves; therefore, we know how this specific phenomenon will behave."

---

⁵⁹ William Dray, *Philosophy of History*, 2nd edition (Englewood Cliffs, NJ: Prentice Hall, 1993), p. 13. See also Louis O. Mink, "The Autonomy of Historical Understanding," *History & Theory* 5 (1966): 24–47, here p. 28. The last widely cited attempt to persuade historians to look for "laws" of history appears to have been Carl G. Hempel, "The Function of General Laws in History," *Journal of Philosophy* 39 (1942): 35–48. Hempel was not an historian, did not publish his ideas in an historical journal, and as far as I can tell have had no measurable impact on the practice of historians. William Dray's *Law and Explanation in History* (Oxford: Oxford University Press, 1957) was an influential rebuttal.

⁶⁰ Michael Oakeshott, *Experience and Its Modes* (Cambridge: Cambridge University Press, 1933), reprint 1966), pp. 142, 143 (emphasis in the original).

⁶¹ For a particularly clear exposition, see Miller, *The Problem of Slavery*, pp. 25, 26, 27–28.

On the idiographic character of History there is even less agreement among historians than there is regarding the primacy of an inductive approach. Nominalism, moreover, at least as a matter of intellectual preference and practice, is not at all common today – in part because trying to reason without the convenient conceptual shorthand of categories like "state," "revolution," or "religion" is very difficult. The last section of Chapter 2 will address the importance of social science theory and the generalizations that social science generates – the categories and the "laws" it posits – for a large proportion of historians.

Nevertheless, again, in practice most historians do of necessity adopt an idiographic approach to their work. They go about investigating a particular historical phenomenon, not a range of historical phenomena that they hypothesize belong to a class or category, governed by common laws or principles. Some historians attracted to social science frame their work as an attempt to determine whether a particular social science theory describes ("predicts") the specific development they are looking at. A wonderful example is German historian Jürgen Kocka's *Facing Total War*, a book that posed an explicitly Marxist hypothesis about the impact of the First World War on German society, examined primarily quantitative sources (regarding employment and wages) in order to test it, and reached sophisticated, nuanced, and insightful conclusions regarding the degree to which Marxist theory seemed to account for the developments he found.[62] His book was exceptionally rigorous in its statistical approach, but the idea is common: Historians determine whether and to what degree a theoretical framework helps them understand the specific historical phenomenon they are investigating. And it is quite rare for historians to investigate multiple, much less many individual cases within the hypothesized class, to see whether the theory holds across multiple cases. There is a simple explanation for that: comparative the discipline is a gigantic amount of work. Writing a book about three revolutions, or three religious changes, or three encounters between different human groups, is three times as much work as writing about one. Given the expansive nature of historical research, it is just not very practicable.

Historians tend, then, not to think in terms of universal laws; more often, they think in terms of *patterns*.[63] They use general categories as follows: "this

---

[62] Jürgen Kocka, *Facing Total War: German Society, 1914–1918* (Cambridge, MA: Harvard University Press, 1985 [original 1975]).

[63] See, for example, William H. McNeill, *Mythistory and Other Essays* (Chicago, IL: University of Chicago Press, 1986), p. 5, and Paul Christianson, "Patterns of Historical Interpretation," in *Objectivity, Method, and Point of View: Essays in the Philosophy of History*, ed. W. J. van der Dussen and Lionel Rubinoff (Leiden: Brill, 1991), 47–71.

phenomenon seems to be similar in some nontrivial ways to a distinctive wider group of phenomena; it is useful therefore to think of this as part of a broader pattern." Each individual phenomenon can then be investigated with that broader pattern in mind, as part of what guides the historian's inquiry into its specific characteristics. In short, History is not like chemistry, physics, or Marxian sociology; it does not study phenomena that are "the same" and governed by universal "laws" of interaction or development. Historians are in practice not very interested in general rules governing all human societies across time or space. Their operating assumption is usually derived from the historicist view that each human society is subject to the unique conditions of a particular time and place.[64] British historian George Macaulay Trevelyan was particularly explicit about this: History, he wrote in 1913, has "failed to discover laws of 'cause and effect' which are certain to repeat themselves in the institutions and affairs of men" because an "historical event cannot be isolated from its circumstances ... none of which will ever recur ... no causal laws of universal application [can] be discovered in so complex a subject."[65] One hundred and four years later Sarah Maza, an historian of modern France, agreed: "Human behavior in a specific place and time is much too messy to be pressed into general laws."[66]

This fact that History is in practice primarily an inductive and idiographic discipline is a profoundly important resource on which History instructors can draw, and one of the characteristics that make History particularly pedagogically valuable. These characteristics make historical thinking and historical inquiry radically open, intellectually empowering, and liberating.

Of course in university and college History courses, particularly at the introductory level, students have to master factual material, the chronology of events, basic historical statistics. But most of the assessed work that students do in higher education History courses requires them to reach their own conclusions. In some classes, in some institutions, instructors cannot do without multiple-choice questions; I have used them myself. But most assignments at this level are not assessments of factual knowledge. Research essays, interpretation of documents, interpretive work with visual sources, reflection papers, class presentations, research journals,

---

[64] Still useful and thought-provoking on the nature of generalization in History: *Generalization in the Writing of History: A Report of the Committee on Historical Analysis of the Social Science Research Council*, ed. Louis Gottschalk (Chicago, IL: University of Chicago Press, 1963).

[65] George Macaulay Trevelyan, "History and Literature," *Journal of the Historical Association* 9:34 (1924): 82–91, here p. 89; *Clio, A Muse and Other Essays*, p. 144.

[66] Sarah Maza, *Thinking about History* (Chicago, IL: University of Chicago Press, 2017), p. 162.

annotated bibliographies, book or article reviews – all the primary forms of assessment used in higher education History courses ask students to analyze material for themselves and to develop and present their own conclusions from that analysis. Almost nothing students do in college or university History courses requires them to assume, or to confirm by demonstration, that certain theories or principles that they have been taught as general rules hold true in particular cases – experimentally in the chemistry lab, for example, or statistically in economic analysis.

History courses, therefore, essentially force students to adopt a posture of intellectual autonomy, because they are not given any "right" answers. They are not required to memorize and apply basic principles or laws; they are not tasked with testing the fit between their experimental or investigational results and general schema developed and validated by natural or social scientists. The historical cases they examine are not specific instances of general classes, categories, or rules. There are no right or wrong answers; there are only analyses and interpretations that are coherent or garbled, methodologically sound or flawed, insightful or trivial.

Studying History is therefore in important ways not just a critical but also a creative endeavor. Creative thinking is exciting and invigorating, and it requires students to be self-aware and self-critical, to decide for themselves whether they have got it right. Chapter 5 will discuss in some more detail how to maximize this potential benefit for students. For now, it is important simply to say that History as a holistic, inductive, idiographic practice is uniquely powerful training in independent thinking.

This can be psychologically difficult for some students.[67] In History there is no recipe, there are no fixed points of reference, and students never know if they have got the "right" answer. Their work is assessed with respect to its methodological and formal qualities – whether the research is thorough, whether the sources used are narrow or broad in variety and origin, whether the argument is well supported by evidence, whether the text is read "closely" (that is, with attention to multiple characteristics such as central concepts, rhetorical strategies, references, language, and values), whether multiple possible interpretations are considered, whether the writing is clear, whether the exposition of the interpretation the student has developed is well-structured and logical, whether the sources have been referenced to

---

[67] For research and theory on the cognitive development demanded by History, see W. G. Perry, *Forms of Intellectual and Ethical Development in the College Years: A Scheme* (San Francisco, CA: Jossey-Bass, 1970); P. M. King and K. S. Kitchener, *Developing Reflective Judgment: Understanding and Promoting Intellectual Growth and Critical Thinking in Adolescents and Adults* (San Francisco, CA: Jossey-Bass, 1994).

ensure transparency and verifiability, and so on. The answers cannot be found in the back of the book. This can be challenging for students, who may not be comfortable with the idea that they are not being offered "knowledge," or as many call it today "information" – authoritative, confirmed, validated, and reliable. In my experience, many students find this unsettling. Most students I encounter believe that knowledge of the past is important (obviously – they are in my History classes), but the discipline does not offer any certainty about that knowledge. Instead, they discover that they have been drawn into an endlessly expanding field of inquiry in which they deepen and broaden their understanding but never arrive at any proof.

The conventional language that historians have adopted to define for their students this open-ended character of study in History is that History is interpretive – that the student must make sense for herself of what she learns. History instructors also conventionally suggest that interpretation is perspectival. The sense one makes depends on the tools one has, the information one gathers, and the conceptual and experiential context one brings to bear on a problem. For many students, these qualities make History itself exciting. It is a place where one is never quite certain what might happen. History can be unsettling, even frustrating; but it is also an adventure.

But History poses for students still knottier problems. It confronts them also with difficult epistemological choices, with methodological questions for which there is no "right" answer but that they, rather, must answer for themselves. This chapter has laid out some fundamental characteristics of the discipline that are derived primarily from its early history. But as numerous qualifying statements in this chapter have indicated, the historicist tradition is only one of the traditions that have shaped History. Again, History today is a hybrid discipline that draws on the methods and epistemological assumptions both of the humanities and of the social sciences, and also on the endlessly ramifying field of critical social theory. There is no consensus in History on the inductive, idiographic, or holistic traditions of historicism. History not only asks students to decide what they know; it also asks them to choose between quite different ways of going about knowing it. This too can be challenging for some students, who may not be comfortable deciding for themselves what their own epistemological position is. Chapter 2 addresses these characteristics of the discipline, and some of their pedagogical implications.

CHAPTER 2

What Do Historians Do?

2.1 Interpretation and Inquiry

The expansive, inductive, and idiographic character of History defined in Chapter 1 gives work in History two qualities with which many students will not be familiar. History is interpretive and perspectival, and it is exceptionally driven by open-ended *inquiry* rather than by established, verified knowledge (or propositions). This means that History requires students to engage in a kind of thinking and encounter a concept of knowledge with which other disciplines are less likely to make them acquainted.

2.1.1 *Interpretation and Perspective*

A central reason for the first quality – History is interpretive and perspectival – is that students in History are rarely asked to generate and interpret a particular datum or finding, such as an experimental result or a statistical correlation. Again, they are asked instead to think in holistic or integrative fashion about complex subjects. They are asked to assemble (as far as possible and relevant for an assignment) a broad and varied range of evidence, to discern connections and relationships between and among a range of pieces of evidence or aspects of the available evidence, and to reach a plausible or persuasive conclusion. The product of students' work in university-level History classes is seldom a demonstration of factual knowledge, or a demonstration that a hypothesis is correct or an argument is right. Nor is it a theory or hypothesis that the student believes or hopes will hold in other, similar cases. Instead, students are asked to develop an interpretation they believe to be plausible, based on their own careful and expansive analysis of what evidence they have available. The expansive, ecological, web-like model of social reality that historians tend toward generates a form of knowledge that is too multifaceted and complex to yield hypotheses that can be subjected to yes/no, true/false, either/or tests.

Even if that were not the case, furthermore, the forms of evidence that students – and historians – have available to them would not permit such outcomes. Historians and History students rely on the sources that have survived from the past, which are often fragmentary, skewed or perspectival, incomplete, and/or only indirectly relevant. They cannot generate new evidence. As Henry Steele Commager put it in 1965, the "chemist or biologist can command whatever materials he needs for his experiments, but the historian works with what happens to come to hand," with whatever has survived from the past.[1] In the absence of experimental results (which historians cannot generate), statistical correlations (for which we seldom have sufficient data, of sufficient quality), or observation (impossible until time-travel is invented), historians have to rely on the principle of the preponderance of the available evidence. Based on a detailed exploration of an historical phenomenon and of its broader context, the historian offers usually not one key yes/no finding, but a broader, multifaceted, complex, more or less convincing *interpretation*. As Alan Booth put it, the task is this: "the structuring of evidence of different kinds into a coherent perspective."[2]

Such interpretations rely not on parsimonious logic but on amassing and analyzing an extensive body of evidence of various kinds, whether directly related to the topic under investigation or only indirectly relevant to it. And the analysis of these sources results not in a single clear and unambiguous result assigning a clear explanatory causal mechanism, but in a multifaceted – but necessarily partial – interpretive analysis presenting an *understanding* of a complex of dynamically related factors. Historians do not aim for parsimony and proof; they aim for depth and breadth of understanding. This is true not only of most research projects but also – for example – of close analysis of a single text, which will ideally draw on multiple forms of analysis (of language, references, the author's life situation or perspective, audience, etc.). Joseph Miller described this approach economically in 2012: Historians "assess contexts as fully as possible to identify all the aspects of them significant in motivating what people may be observed to have done ... historians do not prove anything but rather explain, in the sense of rendering others' actions plausible."[3]

---

[1] Henry Steele Commager, *The Nature and the Study of History* (Columbus, OH: C. E. Merrill, 1965), p. 44.
[2] Booth, *Teaching History at University*, p. 16.   [3] Miller, *The Problem of Slavery*, p. 26.

2.1 Interpretation and Inquiry

Usually, in doing so, historians must use what is often called their "historical imagination" – their ability to imagine how things *may* have been, on the basis of their knowledge of the context, of the people involved, and of similar cases in the same society and period. This allows them to interpolate, to fill in the gaps in the evidence, in order to arrive at an interpretation. As Simon Schama put it in 1991, given the kinds of evidence historians have, "even in the most austere scholarly report from the archives, the inventive faculty – selecting, pruning, editing, commenting, interpreting, delivering judgments – is in full play."[4]

The conclusions historians reach are therefore always subject to some degree of uncertainty. As G. J. Renier argued in a book on the "purpose and method" of History in 1965, historians "must be forever satisfied with possibilities and probabilities." Arthur Marwick argued in 1989 that "the historian is always offering an interpretation, some parts of which will be more substantable than others, some parts more open to challenge than others."[5] Both were merely voicing the near-universal view of historians for well over a century.

Because they offer neither experimental nor statistical proofs but the analysis of complex bodies of evidence, selected according to more or less clearly articulated criteria from the broader "web" of potential evidence, historians and History students develop interpretations that are distinctively *perspectival*. We can understand the same period, event, person, or problem in quite different ways if we examine it from the perspectives of different subfields of History, using different theoretical or interpretive frameworks, categories of analysis, or kinds of sources. Different historians will approach the same topic in different ways and arrive at different conclusions. In fact, individual historians often themselves offer multiple different interpretations, each from a different perspective, simultaneously. Each interpretation can offer a valid insight into the past, a useful way of thinking about or understanding the past. We might say that each can open a different window on the past, giving a different view of it. Adopting multiple perspectives can give us a much more complex and sophisticated understanding of an historical even, person, or development.

Even where individual historians do not deliberately adopt multiple interpretive perspectives, most will happily acknowledge the fruitfulness of alternative interpretations. The different interpretations that can be built

---

[4] Simon Schama, *Dead Certainties (Unwarranted Speculations)* (New York: Vintage, 1992), p. 322.
[5] G. J. Renier, *History: Its Purpose and Method* (New York: Harper & Row, 1965), p. 134; Elton, *Practice of History*, p. 87; Arthur Marwick, *The Nature of History*, 3rd edition (Chicago, IL: Lyseum, 1989), p. 24.

around alternate perspectives are, obviously, not necessarily competing or contradictory. Being convinced that one interpretation is persuasive and fruitful does not necessarily mean that we must conclude that another is not. As Murray G. Murphey put it in 1973, historians believe their interpretations "not to be exclusive of other and equally legitimate interpretations."[6] A generation later Mary Fulbrook reiterated the point: "there is no single true master narrative or metanarrative" (that is, interpretation); rather "there can in principle be an infinite number of 'partial narratives,' constructed as answers to particular questions phrased in specific ways about selected aspects of the past."[7] Again, such alternative interpretations often complement each other, so that considering multiple interpretations of the same topic can yield a richer, more nuanced understanding of it. As my colleague Ali Anooshahr has argued, any interpretation is likely not only to reveal or illuminate certain important aspects of an historical situation, but also to ignore, obscure, or downplay others.[8] Not only is there not one conclusively right answer, therefore; having multiple answers will often in fact be a distinct advantage. Adopting two different interpretations can help us see what we would have missed if we adopted only one. That will give us a fuller understanding, but it may also render our understanding more flexible and durable as perspectives change and debates and discussions evolve.

For all these reasons, as Kathryn and Luther Spoehr remarked in an essay of 1994 on the distinctive characteristics of History, "to think historically ... requires one to wrestle effectively with ... questions ... to which there is no single 'right answer.'" It encourages students to think "across categories of analysis." It demands that they develop a "densely textured analysis of the relations among ... facts" (and I would add, among interpretations). It requires them to understand that a "single set of facts is open to a variety of interpretations" depending on the perspective, interests, and methods of the historian.[9] James M. Banner put it more economically in 2021: The study of History can give students a greater capacity "to live comfortably with ... a suspension of the search for a single truth or a simple explanation," and to see "the existence of vigorous debates about

---

[6] Murray G. Murphey, *Our Knowledge of the Historical Past* (Indianapolis, IN: Bobbs-Merrill, 1973), p. 102.
[7] Fulbrook, *Historical Theory*, p. 29.   [8] Personal communication, June 25, 2020.
[9] Kathryn T. Spoehr and Luther W. Spoehr, "Learning to Think Historically," *Educational Psychologist* 29:2 (1994), pp. 71–77, here pp. 73, 74, 72. See also Todd Estes, "Constructing the Syllabus: Devising a Framework for Helping Students Learn to Think Like Historians," *The History Teacher* 40:2 (2007): 183–202, here p. 185.

interpretations of the past ... as pointing to the vitality, not the exhaustion, of the search for ... historical knowledge."[10]

Not infrequently, the results of the multi-perspectival approach History can cultivate may seem paradoxical. Thomas Jefferson, for example, is a heroic figure in the history of democratic thought and democratic institution-building. He was also a slave owner, a practitioner and de facto defender of that tyrannical and cruel institution.[11] There is one influential argument that holds that the former role was founded on the latter, because the inclusion of all white men in the polity, as active citizens, was made conceptually possible by the exclusion of other groups – African Americans, women, Native Americans – as unworthy of citizenship. The period in which Jefferson lived saw one of the first great democratic political revolutions of the modern era and the constitutional assertion of the Rights of Man and the Citizen in a whole range of societies in the Americas and Europe. It was also a period in which by many measures the rights of women became increasingly circumscribed and limited.[12] Or take an example on a much smaller scale from my own work. I have suggested in a book on the development of modern dance that from a psychological perspective we can see the women who pioneered that art form in the early twentieth century as suffering from neurotic compulsions and profound unhappiness caused by the patterns of interaction in their families of origin. From a feminist perspective we can also see them as courageous women who were able to make their own way in the world as independent entrepreneurs who treasured the joy of creative work, because the patterns of interaction in their families of origin gave them extraordinary strengths and unusual options. The evidence supports both conclusions; I feel reasonably confident both things were true.[13]

Even where alternative interpretations explicitly conflict with each other, then, they may not invalidate each other. Entertaining that possibility can train us in thinking with greater precision and discernment, and it can guide us to new questions. Precisely how, for example, was the expansion of political rights for one group of people (white men) related to the

---

[10] James M. Banner Jr., *The Ever-Changing Past: Why All History Is Revisionist History* (New Haven, CT: Yale University Press, 2021), p. 264.
[11] See Mark A. Smith, "Teaching Jefferson," *The History Teacher* 42 (2009): 329–340.
[12] Edmund S. Morgan, *American Slavery, American Freedom* (New York: Norton, 2003 [original 1975]); Clarence Walker, *Mongrel Nation: The America Begotten by Thomas Jefferson and Sally Hemmings* (Charlottesville: University of Virginia Press, 2010); Joan W. Scott, "Gender: A Useful Category of Historical Analysis," *American Historical Review* 91:5 (1986): 1053–1075.
[13] Edward Ross Dickinson, *Dancing in the Blood: Modern Dance and European Culture on the Eve of the First World War* (Cambridge: Cambridge University Press, 2017), pp. 108–116.

broad assault on the rights of other groups (women and people of color)? How could individual lives both defy and be determined by broader social structures and cultural patterns? Again: Human life is messy. The capaciousness of History encourages us to understand it in all its complexity and paradox. And paradoxes lead us to potentially fruitful questions – questions that lead us to more sophisticated, complex, and nuanced understanding.

As all these considerations should make clear, there is a quality to History that many students will find particularly difficult: Both historical inquiry and historical interpretation are *creative*. Historical inquiry proceeds not by eliminating variables to achieve falsifiable results, but by imagining where one might go next in one's research; and the final product is not a factual report but a reasoned interpretation. Many students have difficulty classifying what History "is." Is it a discipline in the social sciences, because historians don't just make stuff up? Or is it a discipline in the humanities, because historical inquiry and interpretation are creative endeavors?

Again, this is not a problem; it is an opportunity. History is a form of reasoning that many students will find unfamiliar. That is good; it can help foster intellectual flexibility – an important intellectual resource for anyone, not just for History students. It is intellectually beneficial for students to know that the same subject can be understood from multiple valid perspectives; that is an important antidote to narrow thinking. It is beneficial for students to be confronted with the fact that the world is not divided into neat categories, some of which can be ignored while one pursues understanding of others. (This is, of course, the unique value of the idea of the "university," where all branches of knowledge are pursued.) And History instructors can draw deliberately on the interpretive and perspectival quality of their discipline too, to cultivate intellectual flexibility – tolerance for uncertainty, openness to questioning, the disposition to pursue further inquiry.

2.1.2 *History and Inquiry*

The kind of knowledge that History produces, then, makes it a discipline that is uniquely driven not by *answers* but by *inquiry*. In the natural and social sciences, the aim of research is to identify a firm and decisive experimental result or statistical correlation. They narrow and focus inquiry in order to achieve unambiguous and practically usable results. In History, the aim is more often to broaden and expand inquiry to achieve

2.1 Interpretation and Inquiry

a more complex interpretation – or, again, to pursue the questions raised by the clash of alternate interpretations. Inquiry in History seeks less to achieve the closure of a defined, specific, and useful result than to open further avenues of research. As Robert B. Bain remarked in an essay of 2005, "History begins with – and often ends with – questions, problems, puzzles, curiosities, and mysteries."[14] The most valuable outcome of historical research is often not a confidently stated *answer* or *explanation*, but a productive question that challenges us to seek deeper and broader *understanding*. We might put it this way: The purpose of research in History is not so much to generate firm answers as it is to generate further questions, which drive further research – constantly expanding the breadth, depth, and complexity of our knowledge and understanding of the past.

Of course, this is a characteristic that History partly shares with the social sciences. In sociology, for example, an important finding of a study of one community is one that leads us to investigate the importance of a particular phenomenon in many other communities. And the same is to some extent true of the natural sciences. In chemistry or physics, a result can be powerful not only if it resolves a critical question, but also and particularly if it leads to further productive questions. For example, if we find that the presence of large predators increases species diversity in one environment, does that mean that it would in another environment – say one with more restricted resources, or less seasonal climatic variation? Does it mean that other factors limiting population densities of single species have the same effect – perhaps limited critical nutrient resources, or extreme cyclical instability?

Yet inquiry is distinctively important and valued in History. The "ecological" character of historical inquiry, its interest in *every* aspect of human experience, leads historians constantly to broaden and deepen their understanding of the historical context of the events, developments, or people they study. We can almost always expand our understanding of an historical phenomenon by viewing it from the perspective of another aspect of the human experience, another subfield of History, and by developing a further, complementary or contrasting interpretation based on a new perspective and on the different forms of evidence on which that subfield draws.

To give just one example: We understand the religious processes and commitments that led many Europeans to value family particularly highly

---

[14] Bain, "'They Thought the World Was Flat?'" p. 181.

in the nineteenth century, but perhaps that was related also to economic characteristics of Europe in that period. Or perhaps there were legal changes related to the expansion of the power of European states (or, to be consistent, of the people who organized and ran European political institutions) at that time that encouraged the idea that family was important. And was the same true, in the same ways, in all political settings – say, in both Russian autocracy and republican France, in monarchical Bavaria and republican Hamburg? Is it possible that changes in scientific understandings of heredity, or of individual psychology, played a role in shaping perceptions of "family"? Or were particular characteristics of family life – such as emotional intensity – fostered by developments in the arts, say the emergence of the novel as a popular literary form? And when we say "Europeans," are we referring to city people or to people in the countryside? Did "family" mean the same thing to aristocrats, middle-class shopkeepers or merchants, laborers in the mining industry, and peasant farmers? Perhaps family meant less and less to some of these people. Or perhaps all these people increasingly thought that "family" was important, but meant different things when they spoke of "family" – nuclear family or extended family, the family as an emotional context or as an economic unit, family created by religious sacrament or family created by cohabitation (e.g., with servants, or apprentices, or sexual partners), family as a sustaining tradition or as a refuge from oppressive tradition. For that matter, did developments in *all* religions in Europe encourage the identification of family as a particularly important social institution and context for the individual's spiritual development? Was this equally true in Jewish, Protestant, Catholic, Orthodox, Muslim, atheist, Mormon, or Waldensian families? When we have considered the phenomenon from all these perspectives, we can say that we have begun to understand it. This is how History works as a field of knowledge: by expanding inquiry.

This is one reason that historians often claim to advance historical knowledge not by proving competing interpretations *wrong*, but by building on, extending, modifying, or adding to the work of their colleagues. Historians do of course criticize and even debunk each other's work, but more often they build on it. This kind of intellectual posture toward the work of others in one's field is common in the social and natural sciences as well. But in History, again, there is only very rarely even any possibility of decisively "disproving" another interpretation. Historians can only very rarely *test* an interpretation. They can only offer a counterinterpretation, or a modification of an interpretation, or a complementary interpretation from a new perspective.

2.1 Interpretation and Inquiry

Some historians have suggested that History as an interpretive discipline is one in which *argument* has central and defining importance, and that this is one of the great benefits of the study of History. They suggest that the study of History is a particularly effective way to learn the difference between an individual *opinion*, which does not depend on any evidence, and an *interpretation*, which must be well grounded in the careful analysis of a substantial body evidence, be logically structured, and explicitly evaluate alternate interpretations. In an essay on pedagogical aims in History, for example, Joel M. Sipress and David J. Voelker held in 2009 that one of the greatest benefits of study in History is that it draws students into "evidence-based argumentative discourse about the human past" in which they have to apply a rational standard of evidentiary support in "making judgments among rival positions."[15] Todd Estes similarly suggested in the journal *The History Teacher* in 2007 that courses in History should focus on "conflicting interpretations"; they should teach students to develop "arguments of their own based on their readings of the evidence"; they should even cultivate an "argument culture."[16]

I believe this is true, and distinctively true of History because of the nature of historical interpretation. It is certainly essential that students learn that an interpretation is not a matter of opinion, but of structured rational discourse. Learning to marshal large, varied, and complex bodies of evidence to support or question an interpretation in the context of relative uncertainty is an extraordinarily valuable skill, and one that does not come naturally. What is more, the study of History requires the student to deal with kinds and forms of evidence that present particularly difficult challenges. That makes History an outstanding discipline for teaching how to handle evidence. Historians have developed many techniques and methods for dealing with the kinds of evidentiary problems they face, and those techniques and methods can be powerful and productive. Chapter 4 of this book will address some of those problems, techniques, and methods. For now, suffice it to say that learning how to establish a strong, logical, and convincing connection between evidence

---

[15] Sipress and Voelker, "From Learning History to Doing History," pp. 29–30, 32, 26. For examples of courses built around this principle, see Barbara E. Walvoord and John R. Breihan, "Arguing and Debating: Breihan's History Course," in Barbara E. Walvoord and L. P. McCarthy, *Thinking and Writing in College: A Naturalistic Study of Students in Four Disciplines* (Urbana, IL: National Council of Teachers of English, 1990), pp. 97–143, and Estes, "Constructing the Syllabus," esp. p. 186; Russell Olwell and Azibo Stevens, "'I Had to Double-Check My Thoughts': How the Reacting to the Past Methodology Impacts First-Year College Student Engagement, Retention, and Historical Thinking," *The History Teacher* 48 (2015): 561–572.

[16] Estes, "Constructing the Syllabus," p. 186.

and interpretation is certainly one of the central benefits of studying History.

But we can go further than this in defining the *distinctive* benefits of studying History. I think those distinctive benefits – the things that History teaches better or in greater depth than other disciplines – derive not so much from its character as an *argument*-driven discipline as from its character as an *inquiry*-driven discipline. Every field of knowledge outside the creative and performing arts is driven by argument founded on evidence. Writing a chemistry lab report requires the marshaling of evidence to support a conclusion. Macroeconomic analysis, sociological investigation, anthropology, communications – every analytical discipline requires the student to develop this skill. The most distinctive or important benefit of studying History is instead that students learn to question, explore, examine, consider, and reflect on arguments, conclusions, and interpretations specifically by expanding the field of their own inquiry, by bringing more perspectives, more information, more questions to bear on them. The most important pedagogical benefit of History is not that it teaches students to advance, support, evaluate, or critique arguments and counterarguments, or to debate issues effectively. The aim of History is not to win arguments. It is to expand and deepen inquiry by inviting discussion, sparking reflection, shifting perspective, and even, as Sam Wineburg puts it, "cultivating puzzlement."[17] History teaches us to ask further questions, from new perspectives, and to expand the mass and variety of evidence we use to answer those questions. To do that, the practitioner of History needs, in Dominick LaCapra's formulation, "to make argument as informed, vital, and undogmatically open to counterargument as possible."[18] To put it simply: A good argument in History is convincing; a great argument in History is thought-provoking.

History, then, does teach students to ask, "what does the evidence tell me?" But more importantly, and more distinctively, the expansive and interpretive character of inquiry in History teaches them to ask: What am I missing? What questions am I not asking? What questions do my sources guide me to ask? What other forms of evidence can I bring to bear? What other perspectives might there have been at the time? What other methods or perspectives might I adopt in evaluating the evidence? What else in the historical context might have influenced the behaviors, ideas, or outcomes

---

[17] Wineburg, *Historical Thinking*, p. 21.
[18] Dominick LaCapra, "Rethinking Intellectual History and Reading Texts," *History and Theory* 19:2 (1980): 245–276, here p. 256.

that interest me? These are certainly not questions that the natural and social sciences do not lead students to ask, but History does so with exceptional consistency. This is what the "messiness" of history teaches, in contrast to the "parsimony" of the sciences and social sciences. It asks us to look not for decisive answers, but for more questions. As historian of the French Revolution Richard Cobb put it in 1969, the ideal practitioner of History "should, above all, be endlessly inquisitive and prying."[19] The ideal of History is not the final answer or the winning argument, but dynamically evolving, flexible, expanding, multifaceted, complex, open-ended, deepening inquiry.

This inquisitive and open-ended quality of History is among its most important lessons. As G. J. Renier remarked in 1950, "credulity and certitude go hand in hand."[20] Both are stifling. History is an antidote to both. It teaches us to be skeptical, and to keep asking more questions.

2.2 Spooky Questions

But what *kinds* of questions do historians ask? Can we be more specific about what makes a *good* question in History?

Many recent and not-so-recent books on the study of History give us some good ways of thinking about this. Jim Cullen, for example, suggests in his book on "how to read, write, and think about history" (his subtitle) that a good question "invites consideration of broader historical issues." It is not limited to a simple matter of fact, but engages us in thinking about and investigating broader processes, patterns, and connections.[21] As another *Student Guide to Historical Thinking* suggests, "deep historical questions drive thought beneath the surface of things, forcing you to deal with complexity."[22] And because a good question engages with complexity, as Cullen points out it is also "open-ended," and can be answered in "more than one legitimate way."[23] Building an answer to a good question can be approached from more than one perspective, drawing on multiple sources or multiple kinds of sources, focusing on different aspects of the complex context of the phenomenon under investigation. In more technical terms,

---

[19] "Richard Cobb," in *Historians on History: An Anthology*, ed. John Tosh (Harlow: Pearson, 2000), pp. 39–45, here p. 44.
[20] Renier, *History*, p. 147.   [21] Cullen, *Essaying the Past*, p. 33.
[22] Linda Elder, Meg Gorzycki, and Richard Paul, *The Student Guide to Historical Thinking: Going beyond Dates, Places and Names to the Core of History* (Lanham, MD: Rowman & Littlefield, 2019), p. 18.
[23] Cullen, *Essaying the Past*, p. 32.

a good question in History is a question that plays to the specific strengths of History as a capacious discipline with a holistic and ecological way of thinking about issues. Of course the discipline of History is divided – and has become progressively more and more divided – into a vast array of subdisciplines and specializations. But the most fruitful historical questions build on the questions and perspectives of a number of specialized fields to pose puzzles of real breadth and depth.

A good question in History is, therefore, only the first of a series of questions that follow from it. How would I view this question from the standpoint of cultural History, or economic History, or urban History, or legal History, or social History? What sources might I use in approaching the topic from each of those perspectives? What would be the best approach to those sources – what should I be looking for? What would be the right time frame to adopt – should I be investigating a period of ten years, or a century, or ten days? Which further consequences or implications of my findings are particularly important, worth following up with further research? As G. R. Elton wrote in 1967, in History the "'right' questions" are "those that lead to further questions."[24] In short, a good question in History is a *productive* question – a question that produces deepening and broadening inquiry.

Consider a simple example. The history of the city-republic of Novgorod in northern Russia between the twelfth and the fifteenth centuries is a fascinating case of medieval urban history. There is a wonderful source for its history, the *Chronicle of Novgorod*, for the years from 1016 to 1471.[25] Novgorod was a vibrant commercial center, it had a complex social and political structure, and it was a center of political and military power. Over the centuries it had a complex relationship with other cities in the Baltic region and a complex political relationship with various princely states (e.g., Kiev, Muscovy, Poland, Lithuania, and the Teutonic Order). It was conquered in the 1470s by Muscovy. A question about this development that would be less likely to lead us into more complex and deepening inquiry might be "Why and how did Ivan II of Muscovy conquer Novgorod in 1478?" A formulation that would be more likely to lead us further might be "What had changed by the 1470s that allowed Muscovy to conquer Novgorod after some 300 years of efforts by various princely states to control the city?" This question is open-ended – it invites us to consider

---

[24] Elton, *Practice of History*, p. 19.
[25] *The Chronicle of Novgorod, 1016–1471*, trans. and ed. Robert Michell and Nevill Forbes (London: Royal Historical Society, 1914), https://faculty.washington.edu/dwaugh/rus/texts/MF1914.pdf.

2.2 Spooky Questions 73

what time frame to adopt, to consider multiple aspects of the history of the city, and to expand our inquiry at least to Muscovy and perhaps to other princely states.

Or consider a more complex example. Between the 1870s and the 1910s there were intense debates in Germany about public policy toward prostitution. A good open-ended question about this might be "why was prostitution a matter of intense political conflict in Germany in the early twentieth century?" That simple question would lead us to myriad further questions. Was the number of women selling sexual services growing? If so, why? Were more women in economically precarious situations? Did changes in the family deprive more women of forms of support important in the nineteenth century? Were more men unable to afford marriage, or unwilling to marry, or able to afford to pay for sexual services? Was prostitution encouraged by the emergence of commercial entertainments more broadly – modern "night life" in the metropolis? If there not more women selling sex, were the women who did sell sexual services more visible in the large cities that were forming at the time than they had been in the smaller towns of the nineteenth century? Were there political reasons for some people to raise alarm about prostitution – did the issue help some people get elected under the more democratic national suffrage law adopted in 1871, for example? Did some politicians use prostitution as a "dog whistle" issue, say to raise hostility to metropolitan society and culture? Did newspaper editors try to sell more papers by publishing spectacular and lascivious stories about prostitution and crime? Or perhaps the debates over prostitution originated with activists who sought to secure expanded social and legal rights for women more broadly. Did those activists use it as a "dog whistle" issue to suggest that women's legal and social disabilities were immoral? Did religious changes make some people more concerned about the general state of morality in their society? Was the issue of prostitution just one of a complex of such moral issues under debate? Or was there a public health reason for the heightened concern? Perhaps sexually transmitted diseases were becoming more prevalent. Or could it be that rising urban affluence expanded the tax base of cities, allowing them to hire more vice squad officers in police departments and generating a higher profile for the issue by arresting more women? In each case, what sources would we want to consult – police and court records, studies of the labor market, newspapers, studies by academic sociologists, census records on marriage rates, memoirs and autobiographies, legislative documents (e.g., the reports of parliamentary investigations and debates), medical journals, publications of the churches and their clergy, administrative records and reports of public health authorities? What would we look for in those sources? Statistical information? The frequency of press coverage? The language used? Would we want to investigate the professional positions and careers of the authors? And what is the relevant time frame – would we need to go back to, say, the 1880s and assess the situation at that time in order to be more specific about what was changing (or not) in the 1900s? Would we need to look at the 1920s in order to see whether longer-term trends seem to support one interpretation or another?

As an aside, a good *research* question in History – that is, one that engages with the sources available from the period rather than the scholarly literature produced in our own time – has another characteristic: it can be answered in the time the investigator has, using the sources available. This often means that a researcher interested in a particular topic must tailor their research question carefully to the time and sources available. For example, in an undergraduate research seminar I taught recently one student was interested in the impact of World War II on women's rights in the United States; she ended up producing a paper on policies regarding women's health at the Kaiser Shipyards in Richmond, California, based on material in the Kaiser archives. Another student was interested in the intersection of race and gender prejudices in Mexico between the colonial era and the present; she ended up writing about the practices and politics of wet-nursing in the eighteenth and nineteenth centuries, using primarily medical publications. A third was interested in the history of racial segregation in the United States; she wrote an essay based on the papers of a particularly influential lawyer and fair housing advocate in Sacramento, California. Each of these essays explored in manageable detail a particular case or instance of a broader pattern, building out from the particulars of that case to the broader context that it reflected and exposed.

Or consider again the example of Novgorod. A better *research* question – say, for an essay rather than a book, or for a reader interested in reading some of the available documents but not in devoting a year to the subject – might be this: "What caused the violent internal political conflicts that wracked Novgorod in the thirteenth and fourteenth centuries?" This question can be addressed in an interesting – certainly not exhaustive – way through a careful analysis of the *Chronicle of Novgorod*. Just from what we find in this one text we can build a complex analysis that includes certain economic and social conflicts; conflicts over the city's foreign policy; religious, regional, and ethnic conflicts; and dynastic conflicts between powerful rival families. In the case of prostitution in Germany, the stenographic records of the German parliament are available online,

2.2 Spooky Questions

and there is a marvelous study of the topic published in 1914 by influential American educational and social reformer Abraham Flexner.[26] A fruitful approach might be to ask "Did German politicians' concerns about prostitution in the early twentieth century arise from social changes or from political and cultural sources?" – using the independent external perspective of Flexner as a foil for parliamentary discussion and examining the evidence presented in parliamentary reports and hearings, and the language they used. This question would encourage us to investigate multiple possible answers, and also expand our frame of reference to include a transatlantic perspective.

But whether one is framing a specific research question or simply reading widely in the scholarly literature, the very best historical questions have a quality that derives from the interaction between the capacious, expansive nature of History and the interest in the particular and the individual motivated by its inductive and idiographic approach. At its best, the "ecological" ambition of History to understand many facets of an event, a development, a life, or a society, combined with its detailed and careful examination of particular topics and phenomena, yield questions that lead us understand deeper relationships that we would not otherwise have seen. It drives us to see connections and/or contradictions that energize the life and drive the development of societies across multiple fields of activity, endeavor, and conflict. In other words, the best questions in History are, in my view, questions in which depth of detail, pursued from multiple perspectives, yields an understanding not only of diversity and variety, but also of coherence.

I call this quality of a good historical question spookiness. A spooky question is a question that addresses the connections between things that might not, at first glance, seem to be related at all. It gets at what Goethe's Faust hoped for: to recognize "what holds the world together at its innermost core, to see all its forces and potentials."[27] A spooky question moves us to ask not what answer we need, but what *kind* of answer we would need. It makes us ask not only what kinds of sources we would need to answer it, but also what questions we need to ask *first*, before we can sensibly approach *this* question. A spooky question is not a path to an answer; it is a fountain of inquiry.

---

[26] www.reichstagsprotokolle.de/rtbiiaufauf_k13.html; Abraham Flexner, *Prostitution in Europe* (New York: Century, 1914).

[27] Johann Wolfgang von Goethe, *Faust, Eine Tragödie* (original 1828), p. 9, www.digbib.org/Johann_Wolfgang_von_Goethe_1749/Faust_I_.pdf.

To give one example, many years ago I taught a year-long undergraduate seminar course on "Imperialism and European Societies." I assigned readings on political economy – for example, on the class and business interests engaged by imperial expansion, the domestic politics of imperialism, and attempts to use imperialism as a strategy for reducing class conflicts by creating greater national unity or more economic growth. I also assigned studies of imperialism and culture – on the idea of race, imperialism and the social sciences, imperialism in working-class entertainments, the family lives of the British imperial ruling class, the psychology of imperialism, and so on. About two-thirds of the way through the year one of my students complained quite vehemently in class about the conceptual difficulty of bringing these two bodies of scholarly literature and the ideas and developments they discussed together as a coherent whole. The course seemed to be two courses, one on politics and the economy and one on culture. How could we bring some coherence to our reading? How could we understand the relationship between these two facets of what we were studying? For a moment after he spoke, the room was quiet. Looking around at the class, I caught a peculiar look on almost every face: We had all realized at the same moment that this was a powerful question. If we could answer it, we would understand something quite profound about the phenomenon we were studying, a deeper coherence and dynamic that we had not understood was there and that our readings had not captured. In short, we would understand something about what held imperial societies together at their innermost core.

A second example arose in a graduate research seminar I taught on "Europeans and the Conquest of Nature" a few years later. I assigned readings on what at the time seemed to me to be a range of examples of European efforts to control and command nature that were not directly related to each other. I wanted to give students a kind of survey of multiple different cases of what seemed to me to be a broad and amorphous phenomenon, to give them ideas for their own research. Among other things, I assigned some studies on mountain-climbing and changing understandings of the aesthetic qualities of mountains, and some reading about the burgeoning of bodybuilding and the broader "physical culture" and fitness movement. Both became important phenomena in European culture in the three or four decades before 1900. In one class discussion, a student asked, "Why mountains and bodies?" Why did these two themes gain importance in the same period? Were these really just two unconnected developments in the broad history of European recreation and mass culture? As the class discussed the connections and contrasts between these two sets of readings, we gradually came to realize that there *was* a profound connection between these two phenomena. These two activities were not just instances of changing recreational habits; they reflected a new understanding of the relationship between human beings and nature, including their own bodies. Put briefly, mountains had come to represent not the threat of wildness, but the transcendent potential inherent not in the realm of the spiritual, but in nature; and bodybuilding was an acting out of humankind's own movement toward that natural transcendence. Ideas about the beauty of landscapes and of bodies were in fact connected at a very deep level.

Moments like these are exciting. They reveal to students the potential power and depth of History as a way of thinking. They are proof that History is good, open-ended, spooky intellectual fun.

There is a more conventional way of describing a powerful question in History, one that History shares with almost every other field of knowledge – perhaps particularly in their academic varieties, though not exclusively so. In academic History as in any other academic discipline, a good book or article is a "definitive study" – the latest, potentially last, and certainly currently authoritative word on the subject. A great book or article, though, is one that opens a new field of inquiry. It identifies a new area of research. And it therefore inspires dozens of other historians to undertake studies investigating those questions. Academics call works like these "field-defining." Across the humanities, social sciences, and natural sciences, as in History, definitive studies are impressive and admirable. But field-defining studies are the ones that scholars find exciting. And what makes a field-defining study is a powerful question – often a spooky question.

I think that History as a discipline is particularly likely to generate such questions. History does two things, both of which have the potential to generate surprising results. On the one hand, it makes connections between phenomena – it is about everything human, and it can uncover surprising relationships and contexts. But on the other hand, it studies those phenomena in depth and detail, and it can uncover surprising characteristics that a more schematic and generalizing approach would not. As Dominick LaCapra put it in 1980, History cultivates "an interest in what does not fit a model and an openness to what one does not expect to hear from the past."[28] When we encounter the unexpected, sometimes things get spooky.

---

[28] LaCapra, "Rethinking Intellectual History and Reading Texts," p. 275.

2.3 Between the Social Sciences and the Humanities: History and Theory I

2.3.1 Social-Science History

The characteristics of History addressed thus far all derive specifically from the historicist tradition. But History has never been a discipline with a settled consensus as to its methods and aims. Some historians have since the inception of the discipline argued in favor of thinking of History as a nomothetic discipline, the aim of which should be to offer practical conclusions about – for example – public policy by discerning laws or principles that determine the course of individual action, organizational behavior, and/or societal development. Most importantly, History has evolved very significantly specifically since the middle of the twentieth century.[29] The decades since about 1970 have been a particularly dramatic period in the development of the discipline. Rapid change has been fueled by the growing diversity of the profession – the growing proportion of practitioners of History who are female, non-white, and/or from working-class backgrounds, rather than the white middle- and upper-class men who dominated the field well into the 1980s. Historians have also engaged much more systematically with other disciplines in the social sciences and humanities since the 1960s. Both processes have expanded the intellectual repertoire, resources, and options available to historians well beyond the historicist framework inherited from the nineteenth century. In particular, a sizable proportion of historians today argue that a more theoretically sophisticated approach to history is both more productive of significant findings and more intellectually honest. They argue that historians need to be guided in formulating research questions by the theories advanced by the social sciences and (more commonly in recent years) critical social theory – for example, by economics, sociology, anthropology, psychology, or by gender, queer, or postcolonial theory. The models these fields develop can be used to formulate explicit hypotheses, which can then be "tested" through research.

Those who favor this approach argue that it can help us avoid delving endlessly and in exhaustive detail into irrelevant trivia – into things that don't matter in any practical sense to anyone, are of interest only to a few dozen specialists, and don't tell us anything of practical or even purely of

---

[29] There are recent thumbnail summaries in James M. Banner Jr., *Being a Historian: An Introduction to the Professional World of History* (Cambridge: Cambridge University Press, 2012), pp. 1–33; J. Laurence Hare, Jack Wells, and Bruce E. Baker, *Essential Skills for Historians: A Practical Guide to Researching the Past* (London: Bloomsbury, 2020), pp. 10–29; and *The Sage Handbook of Historical Theory*, ed. Nancy Partner and Sara Foot (Los Angeles: Sage, 2013).

2.3 Between the Social Sciences and the Humanities

intellectual importance. They reject the "antiquarian" approach to History – just collecting a mass of detailed facts with no particular purpose. Theory guides scholars toward research on questions that are of interest to many people. Why do wars happen? How do bureaucracies work, and to what ends, and with what effects? What are the causes of genocide? What are the origins of economic growth? What is the role of psychopathology in political life? Why did the modern helping professions like medicine, social work, and psychiatry arise when they did, what forms of power do they exercise, to what ends and with what effects, and in what relation to other forms of power in modern societies? Those are questions of real current import and of broad interest.

The advocates of a more social-scientific approach to History also argue that it will produce superior scholarship. Every researcher, they suggest, starts their inquiry with a hypothesis – whether or not they admit it or recognize it. We choose particular research topics because we find them interesting and important, we find them interesting because we have particular assumptions about them or experiences with related phenomena that give us certain expectations or hopes of what we will find, and we choose what kinds of evidence to analyze based on those assumptions – that is, implicit theories. Moreover, even the most empirical approach eventually must give some *explanation* that goes beyond mere description. If we do not draw on social science in constructing those explanations, we are very likely to be constantly reinventing the wheel. What is more, we will be reinventing it as individuals and based on the *one* particular example of the event or development we are studying, rather than a broad range of examples studied by many scholars. This is not a very systematic approach, and it is unlikely to produce very sophisticated results. Our assumptions, premises, attitudes, and prejudices will constitute an unconscious and imprecise, ad hoc, idiosyncratic theory, not an explicit, sophisticated, and clear one that has been tested, refined, and elaborated by a community of scholars.

As Robert Berkhofer put it in 2008, then, historicists all too often resort to "armchair psychologizing" and "ad hoc theorizing and impressionism, supposedly justified by ... immersion in the sources."[30] Alun Munslow wrote in 1997 that while historicists argue in favor of "drawing un-biased inferences from the detailed evidence" (the method of "inductive inference"), in actual practice "deductively inferred theories are invariably employed, either consciously or unconsciously. It is impossible" for any

---

[30] Robert F. Berkhofer, *Fashioning History: Current Practices and Principles* (New York: Palgrave MacMillan, 2008), p. 56.

historian "to approach their evidence innocent of presupposition," of concepts, categories, and the theories from which they derive.[31] Ludmila Jordanova argued in 2000 that "no empirical activity is possible without a theory ... some are convinced that they are simply gathering facts, looking at sources with a totally open mind ... yet they are simply wrong to believe this."[32] This is not a new perspective on the practice of historians. In a radio broadcast debate held by the British Broadcasting Corporation in 1948 the great English historian Arnold Toynbee remarked that "Historians who genuinely believe that they have no general ideas about history are ... simply ignorant of the workings of their own minds ... The intellectual worker who refuses to let himself become aware of the working ideas with which he is operating seems to me to be about as great a criminal as the motorist who closes his eyes and then steps on the gas." His opponent Peter Geyl agreed: "The historian who imagines that he can rule out theory ... is obviously only deluding himself."[33]

Advocates of social-scientific History argue that the theories, categories, and concepts that every historian must work with will be used more effectively the more self-consciously they are articulated. Historians who formulate clear and precise hypotheses based on an established, recognized, and explicit theory, using well-defined and precise concepts and categories, will be more likely to test their assumptions critically and rigorously through research than those who are guided by vague and perhaps even unconscious assumptions or expectations – or by those they find in the sources themselves. This more self-conscious and critical approach, therefore, can guard us against simply finding what we set out – perhaps even unconsciously – to find. As John Tosh puts it, historians who do not make use of theory in formulating clear hypotheses too often "remain blissfully unaware of the assumptions and values that inform their own selection and interpretation of evidence." The "wishful thinking" this can lead to "is more likely to be controlled by the historians who approach their inquiries with explicit hypotheses."[34]

Beyond the question of the greater intellectual rigor of theoretically self-conscious History, however, this approach too – like the historicist

---

[31] Alun Munslow, *Deconstructing History*, 2nd edition (New York: Routledge, 1997), p. 44.
[32] Jordanova, *History in Practice*, p. 63.
[33] Peter Geyl and Arnold Toynbee, "Can We Know the Pattern of the Past? A Debate," in *Theories of History*, ed. Patrick Gardiner (New York: Free Press, 1959), pp. 308–319, here p. 318. For a classic statement, see Alan Bullock, "The Historian's Purpose: History and Metahistory," excerpts in *The Philosophy of History in Our Time*, ed. Hans Meyerhoff (New York: Doubleday, 1959), pp. 292–299.
[34] Tosh, *The Pursuit of History*, p. 218; see also, for example, Lloyd, "History and the Social Sciences," p. 84.

2.3 Between the Social Sciences and the Humanities　　　　　　81

approach – ultimately involves an important ethical commitment in two distinct senses.

First, central to this approach is the belief that historians should not treat their intellectual and political life as an exercise in purely academic, disinterested, socially irrelevant curiosity. Again: Explicit engagement with social science fosters engagement also with issues of contemporary relevance and importance because social scientists explicitly, as a matter of professional self-justification, seek to address those topics in ways that are relevant to public policy and public opinion. Explicit engagement with critical social theory fosters dialogue with wider communities of scholars, activists, and policy stakeholders who seek to understand and to address the problems of our own times. The critiques of Priya Satia and Michel-Rolph Trouillot, whom I cited in Chapter 1, are examples of what we might call the societal side of this ethical position – the belief that historians have an ethical obligation to make a positive contribution to their own societies, and not to deflect criticism of them.

But there is also a second important ethical implication to this position. Just as the historicist ethic holds that we should treat the people of the past as fully human beings, the argument in favor of a more theoretically self-conscious approach is also an argument that we should treat ourselves as fully human beings. History is not an exercise in self-mastery any more than it is an exercise in mastery over the people of the past. It would be unethical to try force ourselves to be pure, blank, neutral intellect. We are not; we are human beings with experiences, concerns, beliefs, and values of our own. In fact, for historians the attempt to reduce ourselves to pure objective intellect would also be a logical impossibility – the claim to being completely disinterested and neutral could only be a fiction, a pretense. Logically, historians cannot deny their own historicity, cannot refuse to acknowledge that they are what their history has made them. The demand that historians set aside their own interests, values, and concerns is not just intellectually austere or ascetic; it is ahistorical. The historian is not a disembodied mind, an intellectual "thing" outside of time, but an historical and social person; to deny that would deny the foundational postulate of History.

The importance of this ethical agenda is, I think, reflected in the fact that historians attracted to social science and social theory almost uniformly make use of theory in a very specific way. They do not claim to engage in what social scientists today would recognize as social science, in which explicit hypotheses are subjected to rigorous experimental or statistical testing. Instead, historians use social science theory or critical social theory as a guide in framing their initial questions; they develop interpretations built around those theories, but in between, they conduct their research according to the conventional norms, methods, and standards of historical investigation. They are more interested in drawing, for their own *interpretive* purposes, on the theories developed by social scientists than in themselves adopting social science *methods*.

In fact, far more historians are influenced by the interpretations of social systems and social dynamics produced by critical social theory than by the findings – much less the methods – of the social sciences. The most influential case in the past half century has been the discourse theory of Michel Foucault, which he derived very largely from his book-length interpretations of the histories of penology, psychiatry, and sexology (the study of sexuality). But this is true too of Marxist theory, psychoanalytic theory, postcolonial theory, queer theory, and so on, none of which are based on social-scientific investigation as it is currently practiced by economists, sociologists, cognitive psychologists, and so forth.

In short, historians attracted to theory use it not to develop testable *hypotheses* but to define *interpretive frameworks*. As Louis Mink noted already in 1966 (in a period of particularly intense interchange between the social sciences and History), "historians seem generally to regard generalized hypotheses not as potential laws but as *guides* whose services they employ." They do not really seek to confirm or falsify (disprove) these hypotheses; rather, they apply what Mink called "the commonly accepted criterion of 'fertility' for good hypotheses." A fertile hypothesis – or theoretical framework – leads us to interesting questions, questions that open up new topics; it offers us a new perspective; it guides us to new sources, and/or to new ways of interpreting sources. "A hypothesis" for an historian, then, "is not a tentative law but a rule for asking questions, a rule for delimiting the scope of inquiry, and a rule for determining the relevance of evidence" – and, I would add, a pattern around which to shape an interpretation.[35]

2.3.2 *Historicist Critiques*

Chapter 1 has already touched on the counterarguments of historicists opposed to a more theoretically driven approach to historical study. They argue, first, that if our hypotheses are defined by our own theoretical frameworks, we are very likely merely to project onto the past the problems

---

[35] Mink, "Autonomy of Historical Understanding," p. 35.

and concerns of our own times, and to understand them in the conceptual language familiar to us in our own times. We may either completely miss the problems, concerns, thinking, concepts, and motivations of the people we are investigating, or miss their importance and meaning in *that* time. And we may completely ignore aspects of past societies that were enormously important at the time but with which we are no longer familiar. Laura Doan used a vivid metaphor to define this problem in 2013: If we only ask questions defined by our own conceptual and theoretical frameworks, "it is as if we are sitting in a crowded courtroom amid hundreds of murmuring observers but can hear only one conversation." This approach is "limiting in reinscribing the way we know" (i.e., affirming the categories and assumptions that we are familiar with) rather than really engaging in "dialogue with difference, discontinuity, alterity, and rupture" (i.e., taking an open-minded approach to learning about people who are different from us [difference], who had unfamiliar assumptions [alterity], and with whom we no longer share an understanding of how the world works [discontinuity, rupture]). Many argue too that this approach would tend to be fundamentally boring and sterile. We already know what we think, and what we think *about*. There is no real adventure and no real learning in rehearsing or rehashing those ideas again. As Doan argued, "this approach is less adept at denaturalizing current categories or tolerating messiness"; it "has political purpose and meaning but yields few surprises."[36]

Genuine engagement with people whose ideas and concerns are unfamiliar, in contrast – *that* is interesting, and instructive. Influential English historian G. M. Trevelyan found in 1949 that "the chief and the peculiar fascination of historical study is to find out what people of the past themselves thought and felt and intended." That is both much more rewarding, he held, and "much more difficult than to spin guesswork generalizations" that are merely "the reflection of passing phases of thought or opinion in our own day."[37] James M. Banner, writing in 2021, was equally effusive: "Most historians reject the grim satisfactions of certainty in favor of the prospects of mystery and surprise" and "delight in seeing things anew and being forced to rethink our former views."[38] As one historian of modern France and Algeria wrote in 2022, approaching the

---

[36] Doan, *Disturbing Practices*, pp. 22, 11, 16, 132.
[37] George Macaulay Trevelyan, "Bias in History," in Trevelyan, *An Autobiography and Other Essays* (London: Longmans, Green & Company, 1949), pp. 68–81, here p. 77; George Macaulay Trevelyan, "Clio, A Muse," in Trevelyan, *Clio, A Muse and Other Essays* (Freeport, NY: Books for Libraries, 1913), pp. 140–176, here p. 151.
[38] Banner, *Ever-Changing Past*, p. 267.

sources from a particular theoretical standpoint, with a particular hypothesis, "encourages historians to stick with … contemporary certainties about what mattered in the past." French historian Arlette Farge similarly argued in 1989 that approaching the sources with a defined hypothesis derived from a particular theoretical framework can mean that the historian is "only drawn to things that will reinforce the working hypothesis she has settled on," unable to "notice things that were not a priori [i.e., at the start – ERD] of interest [to her]." That "stunts the imagination, inhibits the mind and stifles curiosity by confining reflection to narrow and suffocating paths." In contrast, Ethan Kleinberg argued in 2016 that "prospecting" more freely in the sources "allows us to challenge current certainties," offer "counterintuitive analyses," and generate new perspective not only on the past but on our own historical situation.[39]

From a pedagogical perspective, this is not merely a matter of intellectual pleasure. The task of focusing on what *other* people thought gives students systematic training in how to see things through other people's eyes. That is more interesting than once again seeing the same old things in the same old ways we usually do. It also cultivates the intellectual flexibility that – to return to the terms used in the Introduction to this book – can temper the narrowness and rigidity that more operational thinking encourages. It is, finally, a desperately needed skill in any society, and never more so than in the increasingly diverse societies of our own time – the more so because so many people increasingly live in a digital-media echo chamber, listening only to people who agree with them.

Historicists also often question whether the use of critical social theory or social science theory will really lead to a more critical and rigorous approach to research and to the sources. A research question defined by a hypothesis derived from social theory may be a narrowly defined and constricted one. We are looking for an answer – does the historical situation fit the theory or not? Once we have the answer, we may drop our inquiry. This is particularly true if the answer is "yes." If the answer is "no," we may then pose further questions that essentially ask "why not?" But if our research seems to confirm our initial hypothesis, we are likely to conclude that the case is closed. Since almost all historians attracted to theory in fact are not testing hypotheses but using theory as a guide

---

[39] Todd Shephard, "Practices Make Pertinent: Prospecting and Histories of the Present," *Modern Intellectual History* 20 (2023): 639–650, here p. 647; Arlette Farge, *The Allure of the Archives*, trans. Thomas Scott-Railton (New Haven, CT: Yale University Press, 1989), pp. 69, 71, 72; Ethan Kleinberg, "Just the Facts: The Fantasy of a Historical Science," *History of the Present* 6 (2016): 87–102, here p. 98.

2.3 Between the Social Sciences and the Humanities

to interpretation, however, the natural tendency is to draw on theories that offer explanations of what they have found in their research. So in practice the answer is virtually always "yes," and again the case is closed. But in the expansive and inquiry-driven discipline of History, the case should never be closed. From an historicist perspective, closing cases is not the point of History; expanding the investigation is.

John Tosh stated this perspective succinctly in 2008: "The merit of history lies in opening rather than closing questions, in revealing options rather than insisting on answers ... the most important feature of 'thinking with history' is that it resists closure." The problem of the social sciences is that "the rich particularity of context tends to be subordinated to a problem-solving agenda, often driven by theory." History, as a "holistic" discipline, avoids this kind of tunnel vision because it is "a synthetic discipline, centrally concerned with linkages between areas of human activity which are usually kept discrete."[40] To translate into the terms I have used in this book: The social sciences tend to be constrained by what I have called operational thinking and are therefore unlikely to ask spooky questions.

To be precise, the problem is not merely that a scholar or student will simply try to confirm their preformulated theory. That would simply be bad practice. The problem instead is that the method is bad. Preformulated theories constrain our questions. If we only ever investigate questions that we have already decided – on the basis of our theory – are important, we are only ever going to get answers to those questions. Our field of inquiry will be narrowed. What is more, an historian or a student guided by a particular theoretical tradition is likely to search out specifically and exclusively the kinds of sources that tradition defines as relevant to its interests, ignoring everything else. The social sciences tend to study one area of life in isolation – the economy, politics, the law, social behavior. Critical social theory is often concerned with a particular aspect of social relations – for example, race, class, gender, sexuality, imperialism and its aftermath – and more generally how the forms of power defined by all these categories shape social relations. But the particular benefit of History is that it trains students to consider many different aspects of an historical situation, simultaneously and as interrelated phenomena. It trains students and scholars not to give priority of interest or importance to just one, but rather to consider the interrelated contributions of each to a historical situation, development, or outcome. It pushes us to look for sources that do *not* seem relevant to our theory, to a particular narrowly defined

[40] Tosh, *Why History Matters*, pp. 23, 38, 39.

question. The distinctive value of History is that it trains us to look further and wider. Finally, if we are guided by the assumptions, aims, and categories imposed by a particular theory, we may limit our analysis of those already limited sources to those features that seem relevant to the theory – we may, as historicists sometimes put it, "cherry-pick" from or "ransack" or "mine" the sources for what seems relevant, rather than treating them as integral wholes to be assessed holistically.

The historicist view, then, is – to quote John Tosh again – that the more theory-driven approach "denies the very essence of the discipline." Human societies, cultures, and experiences are "so richly diverse that we can only understand man in specific epochs and locations."[41] The social sciences and social theory seek universal principles. History seeks to encompass the complex web of social, environmental, historical, economic, cultural (etc.) conditions in a particular place at a particular time, the whole ecology of a phenomenon. R. J. Collingwood put this argument economically in 1946: The "sciences of observation and experiment are alike in this, that their aim is to detect the constant or recurring features in all events of a certain kind ... But the historian has no such aim." History is the knowledge not of "the abstract and changeless" (how things behave in all times and places) but "of what is transient and concrete."[42]

Finally, for historicists change over time is of fundamental importance. The idea that medieval societies would operate according to the same "laws," or would have the same dynamics or conform to the same general patterns as ancient or modern societies is self-evidently ridiculous. One would have to be an absolute historical ignoramus to think that there would be any very meaningful parallels between, say, the Roman Empire in 200 BCE, the Mongol Empire in 1400 CE, and the British Empire in 1900 CE. Even aside from the question of geography and culture, the circumstances of those times and places were extremely different, whether we consider the history of technology, religion, population dynamics, the economics of global trade, or whatever else. Any theory that would bring these three phenomena together as "examples" or "cases" would be so schematic and general as to say next to nothing of any interest at all. John Gaddis sums up these problems neatly: Social science theories "tend to be static, neglecting the possibility that human behavior ... might change over time. They tend to claim universal applicability, thereby failing to acknowledge that different cultures ... respond to similar

---

[41] Tosh, *The Pursuit of History*, p. 219.
[42] R. J. Collingwood, *The Idea of History* (Mansfield Center, CT: Martino, 2014 [1946]), pp. 250, 234.

2.3 Between the Social Sciences and the Humanities

situations in different ways."[43] Again, he was echoing G. M. Trevelyan's dictum from a half-century earlier: History "cannot, like physical science, deduce causal laws of general application" because human societies are not only complex, but also change radically over time.[44]

There is, however, a deeper, epistemological reason for historicists to be skeptical of social science theory, and it is by far the most important one. From an historicist perspective, any social science theory is itself an historical phenomenon. People formulate their theories about how human societies work at particular historical moments, in particular historical circumstances. Those theories do not say anything about human societies in general. Rather, they tell us something about the particular historical moment (society, culture, context) in which they were formulated, and how that moment was experienced by the particular people who formulated them. The theories generated by the social sciences do not apply to history; they are history. Each one of the social sciences has its particular history, which has made it what it is, and so does each of the theories they produce. The historicist accused of ignoring their own implicit theories can answer simply that the social theorist is ignoring their own history – ignoring what Haitian anthropologist Michel-Rolph Trouillot called, in 1995, the "historicity of the human condition." And as Trouillot remarked, "we are never as steeped in history as when we pretend not to be."[45] When we deny the origins in a particular historical context of our own categories, assumptions, questions, perceptions, and theories, we cannot use them critically and reflexively, with self-awareness, and with an open mind. A mind open, for example, to the questions to which our sources might otherwise guide us and that escape from the expectations that we, for reasons that have to do with our own history, bring to our inquiry.

Take the example of Marxist social theory mentioned in Chapter 1. The conclusions that Karl Marx and Friedrich Engels reached in their *Communist Manifesto* of 1848 made sense in the specific social context of the social crisis of the 1840s in Europe – the "Hungry Forties," a period when rapid technological change was depriving millions of independent small-time producers of their livelihoods. The conclusions that Karl Marx reached in *Das Kapital*, finished in 1883, made sense in the specific economic and social context of the "Long Depression" of the 1870s and 1880s.

---

[43] Gaddis, *Landscape of History*, p. 57.
[44] Trevelyan, *Clio*, p. 144; see also Trevelyan, "History and Literature," p. 89.
[45] Trouillot, *Silencing the Past*, pp. 153, xxiii.

This was a period when advances in transportation and productive technologies drove expanding global competition, declining prices, instability of employment, a high number of bankruptcies, and rapid corporate consolidation (through mergers, acquisitions, and cartels). The consolidation of capitalist enterprise, the erosion of profit margins, the decline of self-employment, the concentration of wealth, and the immiseration of the working class seemed to be playing out before people's eyes. And it is not coincidence that one hundred years later, in the 1970s and 1980s, the Marxist focus on the control of the means of production came under growing assault from social theorists convinced that societies are structured instead by "discourses" – the ideas and practices that shape social behavior, particularly in the professions. That happened just at the moment that deindustrialization took hold with a vengeance in the developed world, and the consumer economy and service-sector employment (e.g., in the professions) took off.

For the historicist, then, social theory or the social sciences are not ways that we can make sense of history; rather, they are themselves historical artifacts. They do not explain; they need to be explained – that is, contextualized, understood as products of specific social, intellectual, social, economic, geographic, and cultural contexts. The fact that they arose or were influential in a particular period helps us understand *that period*, not the human condition or human societies generally. Determining whether a particular theory is right with regard to any particular historical development is not an historical question. Specifically, it is a category error. As Patrick Joyce remarked in an essay of 1995, the categories of social theory are "historically produced conventions" and it is "necessary to trace their origins and development."[46] Prominent historian of science Lorraine Daston observed that "History corrodes everything it touches."[47] I have sometimes put it this way: History is an impious discipline. It doesn't believe in anything; it sees everything as history.

2.3.3 Teaching a Divided Discipline

Every practicing historian is acutely aware of this fundamental division within the discipline between critical social theory or social or social-science theory and historicism, because it has been and continues to be

---

[46] Patrick Joyce, "The End of Social History?" *Social History* 20:1 (1995): 73–91, here p. 84.
[47] Lorraine Daston, "Die unerschütterliche Praxis," in *Auf der Suche nach der verlorenen Wahrheit: Zum Grundlagenstreit in der Geschichtswissenschaft*, ed. Rainer Marie Kiesow and Dieter Simon (Frankfurt: Campus, 2000), pp. 13–25, here p. 23.

2.3 Between the Social Sciences and the Humanities 89

a source of intense debate. I may have an exaggerated sense of that because I undertook my own graduate training in History at a time, in the late 1980s, of intense controversy between advocates and critics of the more systematic use of theory in History. Historians who lived through it sometimes refer to it as the period of the "Theory Wars." Things sometimes got heated. Influential historicist G. R. Elton, for example, in 1991 called on historians to "return to essentials," mocking the "overambitious dreams that afflict historians" who thought theory could explain everything and "do not see why they should not be gurus, like everyone else." They were mere "theory-mongers," "cocooned in their fictions" and suffering from the "conviction that the past must be constructed to coincide with the theory." This would "assuredly ruin the real historical enterprise," which was to understand the past "on its own terms."[48] John Tosh, in contrast, believed that the discipline of History was riddled with knee-jerk intellectual "conservatism." The "traditionalists" (like Elton) who "rejected" theory were "concerned to invoke the ... past in defense of institutions threatened by radical reform ... the study of the past often attracts those who are hostile to the directions of social and political change in their own day."[49] In 1995 Keith Jenkins referred to historicist method as a "servile version" of History used to defend particular social and political interests. The "study of the past 'for its own sake'" is "just the mystifying way in which a bourgeoisie conveniently articulates its own interests" by rejecting any critical function for the discipline. The "chronic antitheoretical nature" of mainstream History was a matter of class power, not scholarly method.[50] Manu Goswami, in contrast, in 2008 saw postmodernist history, focused on discourses and culture rather than on social structures, as eroding the "transformative, future-oriented vision" of social history and its "capacity ... to critically engage the historical present" with its "deep structures, durable inequalities, and persistent hegemonies" in favor of fragmentary, relativist, and depoliticized "representational forms specific to neoliberal capitalism."[51]

---

[48] G. R. Elton, *Return to Essentials: Some Reflections on the Present State of Historical Study* (Cambridge: Cambridge University Press, 1991), pp. 6, 13, 22, 15, 9.
[49] Tosh, *The Pursuit of History*, pp. 220–221, 48.
[50] Keith Jenkins, *On "What Is History?"* (London: Routledge, 1995), pp. 9, 176, 177, and see also *Rethinking History* (Routledge: New York, 1991), p. 20.
[51] Manu Goswami, "Remembering the Future," *American Historical Review* 113 (2008): 417–424, here pp. 418, 420. For related critiques, see Fredric Jameson, "How Not to Historicize Theory," *Critical Inquiry* 34 (2008): 563–582 and Arif Dirlik, *Postmodernity's History: The Past as Legacy and Project* (New York: Rowman & Littlefield, 2000).

The debate calmed considerably in the 2000s and 2010s, as more uncompromising historicism increasingly lost purchase in the profession, and the intellectual energy and excitement generated by greater engagement with critical social theory and social science theory became undeniable. In 2005 Patrick Finney celebrated the fact that it was sometimes hard to remember just "how entrenched aversion to [theory] once was" in History, since "theory is certainly now part of our disciplinary furniture."[52] By 2007 Dominick LaCapra suggested a kind of commonsense peace settlement: Historians should be trained to "combine the traditional skills of the historian with the acuity of a critical analyst," the "ability to do archivally based research requiring a painstaking concern for accuracy, lucidity and specific detail" with "a knowledge of critical and social-scientific theories that she is able ... to ... deploy ... in a careful, selective, thought-provoking manner." That could lead to a "mutually thought-provoking relation between historical research and critical theory."[53] This was clearly the direction the discipline was moving.[54]

Yet some critics have found the *way* greater openness to theoretically informed approaches has reshaped the discipline maddening. Rather than changing the way historians approach their work, they fear, ideas drawn from other disciplines have merely led to a proliferation of new avenues of research and new subfields and specializations – women's history, labor history, the history of particular ethnic groups, imperial and colonial history, gender history, and so on. As I remarked earlier in this chapter, most historians working in those fields still employ largely traditional methods. By 2012, in an article in the scholarly journal of the American Historical Association, Gary Wilder bitterly deplored this pattern. The "new optics" (i.e., new ways of looking at history) opened up by drawing on a wide variety of social theory had been "transformed into routine research topics," and now a "backlash" in favor of "descriptive realism and archival objectivism" was underway. Historians were still burrowing into the minutiae of archival research on very specialized topics. Even where the choice of those topics was guided by new theories, with regard to method it

---

[52] Patrick Finney, "Beyond the Postmodern Moment?" *Journal of Contemporary History* 40:1 (2005): 149–165, here p. 155. For an example of evidence to the contrary, see Richard E. Beringer, *Historical Analysis: Contemporary Approaches to Clio's Craft* (New York: Wiley, 1978).
[53] Dominick LaCapra, "Resisting Apocalypse and Rethinking History," in *Manifestos for History*, ed. Keith Jenkins, Sue Morgan, and Alun Munslow (New York: Routledge, 2007), pp. 160–178, here pp. 161, 162.
[54] A landmark reflection is *Theorie in der Geschichtswissenschaft: Einblicke in die Praxis des historischen Forschens*, ed. Jens Hacke and Matthias Pohlig (Frankfurt: Campus, 2008) – unfortunately not available in English.

was still true that "empiricism is entrenched as the disciplinary default." Wilder called on his colleagues to reject the "insidious logic" of the proliferation of new specializations and "reclaim the analytic space where history, social science, and critical theory once converged around large and pressing sociohistorical questions."[55] In 2018 another scholar observed a surprising "revival" of the "Rankean paradigm," a "return to prominence of empiricism" and the goals of "accuracy, impartiality, objectivity, fairness, attentiveness, perseverance, etc."[56]

Historians versed in the history of their discipline will find this story familiar. There was a similar cycle of critique, accommodation, and complaints about the failure of the revolution a generation earlier, when some had sought to turn History into a social science. A National Academy of Sciences report of 1970 advocating the use of social-science theory and method in History observed, for example, that the discipline had too often been "misused as a stick to beat reformers and to block change." But it too found that rising interest in social science method and theory over the previous two decades had had limited impact. To the extent that advocates of this development had "envisaged a metamorphosis of the discipline and an end to the more traditional kind of history, they have been utterly unrealistic." The report cited influential historian of the American South C. Vann Woodward: "'Far from being revolutionized by new techniques, transformed beyond recognition, or swallowed up by the social sciences,'" History had remained methodologically quite traditional. Most historians were guided by "'old fashioned canons and values: thoroughness of research, objectivity of view, and clarity of logic, together with lucidity and grace of writing.'"[57] The NAS panel that prepared the report was moderate in its rhetoric and aims, particularly compared to the debate of the 1990s. But the fundamental issues were strikingly similar.

---

[55] Gary Wilder, "From Optic to Topic: The Foreclosure Effect of Historiographical Turns," *American Historical Review* 117 (2012): 723–745, here pp. 723, 731, 744. For more recent and even more vehement perspectives, see Kalle Pihlainen, *The Work of History: Constructivism and a Politics of the Past* (New York: Routledge, 2017), esp. p. 65; Kalle Pihlainen, "The Distinction of History: On Valuing the Insularity of the Historical Past," *Rethinking History* 20:3 (2016): 414–432; Ethan Kleinberg, Joan Wallach Scott, and Gary Wilder, "Theses on Theory and History," *History of the Present* 10 (2020): 157–165; and, earlier, Joan Scott, "History-Writing as Critique," in *Manifestos for History*, ed. Keith Jenkins, Sue Morgan, and Alun Munslow (New York: Routledge, 2007), pp. 19–38, deploring, for example, the "superficial acceptance of the vocabulary of theory in the service of its domestication" (p. 22).

[56] Gabrielle M. Spiegel, "The Limits of Empiricism: The Utility of Theory in Historical Thought and Writing," *Medieval History Journal* 22 (2019): 1–22, here p. 2.

[57] Landes and Tilly, *History as Social Science*, pp. 6, 34–35.

History instructors cannot simply ignore this profound and persisting intellectual division. We have to address it with our students if they are to understand the discipline in depth. More important, though, addressing it can be outstanding intellectual training for our students. Doing so is intellectually honest, which is important in itself. But it is also consistent with the foundational postulates of the discipline. The discipline of History too is the product of history; its internal contradictions and debates are a quite striking illustration of the idea that everything is a product of history. History, in other words, is impious about itself too.

In my experience accepting and valuing this division, and this perspective on it, is not an easy step for students to take. Few students are comfortable with the idea that they are not being offered "the" correct method for learning about and knowing the past. If both historicist/empiricist and social-science/social-theory-driven History are products of the history of History, then neither of them is right, and if they are not right, what's the point? What use are they? This aspect of the adventure of History is not one that many students are inclined to embrace. They have generally been taught to want clear rules for how to do it right; they have been taught that the whole point of intellectual endeavor is to close cases, to get answers as the foundation for action. Again: Their instincts are usually operational, not strategic.

Wrestling with these characteristics of History, these "problems" it poses, can be exciting, however, because it can be liberating. Many disciplines teach students that there is a proper method of learning and knowing, and there are faulty methods. In History, instead, students encounter a discipline in which different ways of knowing are valid – or at least are regarded as valid by large groups of scholars. History encompasses not just multiple subfields, but multiple methods of inquiry. Each method offers advantages, each has drawbacks, and each can complement and enrich the other. Combining them raises new questions, draws us into further inquiry.

But most important: employing, considering, and assessing a multiplicity of approaches to the past is itself the most important *method* of the discipline. The "right" way of "thinking historically" is to think about history *in multiple ways*. This is true of the interpretive and perspectival nature of historical understanding, which presents students with the opportunity to deepen and expand their understanding of history by considering multiple interpretations, from multiple perspectives. And it is true of the epistemological complexity of the discipline, which presents them with the opportunity to ask fundamentally different *kinds* of questions, and to structure their inquiry into them in fundamentally – radically – different ways. In both respects, the study of

2.3 Between the Social Sciences and the Humanities

History is an opportunity for students to develop greater intellectual flexibility, greater methodological range, and openness to alternative ways of knowing.

How do we present this opportunity to students? With respect to the question of epistemology, of historicism or social science/social theory, there are three distinct but equally obvious answers.

The first is that History is a capacious discipline, and there is room in it for both heavily empirical approaches and highly theory-driven approaches. Each has its advantages and disadvantages, including the dangers that critics on each side assert. Limiting one's research only to the *kinds* of evidence likely to confirm one's theory is a real pitfall for social-science History. Vague, ad hoc, and amateurish theorizing is a real danger for historicists. The precision social-science method offers is a real strength; the open-ended quality of historicist enquiry is too. History pursued in different ways has different qualities. It is in the nature of History as a hybrid discipline that this is not an either/or dichotomy. Historians who take an approach explicitly defined by social theory or by social-science method produce outstanding and influential works of History. Again, Jürgen Kocka's *Facing Total War* (mentioned in Chapter 1) is an archetypal example. Historians who take a heavily historicist and hermeneutic approach also produce outstanding History. An archetypal example would be David Blackbourn's *Marpingen*, which decoded for the reader the meanings – political, religious, cultural, and social – of an apparition of the Virgin Mary in a small German town in 1876. And historians who draw on both traditions write superb history as well. A particularly influential example is E. P. Thompson's *Making of the English Working Class*, which explored in enormous empirical detail how working-class class consciousness emerged in the course of the early Industrial Revolution, just as Marxists argued it must, but at the same time explicitly rejected on empirical grounds the orthodox Marxist notion of how that process happened.[58] The point is not that students are free to choose which approach they prefer; it is that most students will appreciate the strengths of both.

The second obvious answer is that historicist and theoretically informed approaches are not in practice opposed or incompatible. They are complementary. There is a long tradition in History of the *heuristic* use of social-science and social theory. The term means simply that we use a technique

---

[58] David Blackbourn, *Marpingen: Apparitions of the Virgin Mary in a Nineteenth-Century German Village* (New York; Knopf, 1994); E. P. Thompson, *The Making of the English Working Class* (New York: Victor Gollancz, 1963).

or concept because we think it may be useful to us in immediate practical terms, not because we think it is ultimately or absolutely right. We are not asking whether it is correct; we are only seeing if using it as a tool is productive. Chapter 4 will explore in some detail how theory and empiricism complement each other in the practice of historical research and interpretation. For now, we can distinguish three ways in which historians commonly make heuristic use of theory.

First, History is inquiry-driven, and theory can help us develop fruitful questions. Historians are not likely to believe any social-science theory is *right*, since it is, again, a product of a specific historical context. But that doesn't mean that a particular theory is not *useful*. Theoretical perspectives from the social sciences and the humanities give us analytical categories, models of social dynamics, ideal-types (i.e., schematic general descriptions) of particular forms of social behavior, and relatively carefully defined vocabularies of concepts – such as class, cognitive dissonance, status anxiety, performativity, projection, and so on. Historians use these concepts as resources to help frame their research questions – to help define and direct inquiry. American historian Herbert Gutman, for example, remarked with respect to Marxism that "what is left when you clear away the determinist and teleological elements" (the great intellectual weakness of theory) "are good questions that direct your attention to critical ways of looking at … historical processes." For Marxism these included the evolution of class relations, the ways that social power is institutionalized, the emergence of popular opposition, and the "integration of subordinate or exploited groups" into a social order.[59] An historicist is not likely to want to stop with that list of questions, but they are a fine starting point.

Second, theoretical perspectives drawn from the social sciences or the humanities can also help expand historians' definition of the kinds of evidence they are looking for. If we adopt multiple theoretical perspectives, derived from multiple disciplines (economics, religious studies, women's studies, anthropology, sociology, literary theory), we will be encouraged to ask questions about multiple aspects of the society we are studying and to go looking for multiple kinds of sources. Engagement with the various social sciences and the kinds of evidence they rely on helps historians define a wide range of sources. In other words, self-conscious use of social theory can help to drive the expansive and "web-like" project of inquiry that the historicist and empiricist tradition values – not constrain it.

---

[59] "Herbert Gutman," in *Visions of History*, ed. Henry Abelove, Betsy Blackmer, Peter Dimock, and Jonathan Scheer (Manchester: Manchester University Press, 1976), pp. 185–216, here p. 201.

Finally, theoretical frameworks drawn from the social sciences or humanities can give historians guidance as to what to look for *in* the sources they have found. By offering explicit models of how societies (or individuals, or language, or documents, or institutions, or ritual processes etc.) work, they can make us sensitive to things in the sources that we might not otherwise see. In short, theory can enrich our empirical and hermeneutical approach to our sources.

Historians are universally familiar with these uses of theory, but perhaps it is worth offering two examples. One, regarding how we read sources, is the idea drawn from literary theory that *all* the stories people tell fall into a limited number of genres (i.e., kinds, or basic patterns). This is held to be true whether those stories are fiction, or about their own lives, about the past of their societies, or even, for example, in court testimony. According to theorist Hayden White, who has been very influential among historians, these genres include tragedy, comedy, romance, and satire.[60] Each of these genres has its own logic, its own rules of plot structure and requirements of character types, and its own implicit meanings. When one tells a tragic story, for example, one is claiming moral authority and there must be an innocent victim. When one tells a comic story, one is claiming that someone else has no moral authority and there must be a self-deluded fool. A romance gives its subjects moral legitimacy; a satire robs them of it. In a horror story there must be a monster. In a melodrama there must be someone struggling against their fate. People tell stories of these different kinds for specific purposes. It can be very useful to regard historical sources in this way – including, say, ethnographic texts, or psychiatric case reports, or autobiographies, or trial testimony. Doing so not only helps us see and make explicit the assumptions and biases of the authors (or speakers); it can also help us understand how and why the stories they told were convincing to other people (or were not).

Or consider a second example, that of the theory of complex systems, as formulated by German sociologist and social philosopher Niklas Luhmann. Luhmann argued that complex systems display not only particular forms of stability, but also specific forms of instability. Depending on the relationships between the many different parts of a complex society (e.g., institutions, groups, individuals, or traditions), relatively small changes in one element of the system may be subject to

---

[60] Hayden White, "Interpretation in History," in *Tropics of Discourse: Essays in Cultural Criticism* (Baltimore, MD: Johns Hopkins University Press, 1978), pp. 51–80.

amplification through feedback mechanisms. That can lead to major transformations in the whole system – say, to major legal reforms in central areas of social life like family law or business practice, or even to political revolution or regime change.[61] This can be a very useful way to think about why and how change happened in complex societies in the past – it can help historians discern causality and pattern even within a very complex, holistic, "web-like" understanding of a society in the past. But it can also be a fruitful alternative to the sociological theory of structural functionalism, which holds that societies tend toward stability by ensuring that many different practices, institutions, ideas, and groups work together in "functional" manner, mutually reinforcing assumptions, rules, and each other's power. Each of these theories, in inviting us to consider how *different* parts of a society work together, is congenial to the expansive and ecological agenda of History. And if we consider *both* theories simultaneously, we can begin to understand in a very complex way how it is that very divergent tendencies could have been present and interact dynamically, even reinforce each other, in the same historical society – toward disorder and discipline, toward stability and change, toward conformity and dissent.

Drawing on multiple theoretical frameworks in this way is a common characteristic of the heuristic approach to theory. Looking at a particular historical situation from multiple theoretical perspectives, using the concepts and models that each theory provides us, can help historians understand – even conceptualize, and therefore ask questions about – multiple aspects of an historical society or situation. Did people tell tragic or romantic stories about their identity and experience as members of the working class, or the middle class, or the aristocracy? Did the concept of class (including the kind of stories people told about it) create an inherently revolutionary potential, or did it also contribute to certain forms of social stability or social discipline? What was the nature of the interaction between class identifications and, say, religious, ethnic, or gender identifications? What if we combine with these three examples others, such as the theory of patriarchy, discourse theory, or anthropological theories regarding the common pattern of thinking in binary oppositions (raw or cooked, savage or civilized, light or dark, holy/sacred or sinful/profane)? When we study the emotional and psychological

---

[61] Niklas Luhmann, *Die Gesellschaft der Gesellschaft* (Frankfurt: Suhrkamp, 1997) and *Introduction to Systems Theory*, ed. Dirk Baecker, trans. Peter Gilgen (New York: Polity, 2011).

aspects of relationships between men and women, should we look at wills, divorce settlements, and bank records as well as letters and autobiographies? What role did religious concepts of the sacred and the profane play in defining either or both of those categories (class and gender)? Did men and women tell different kinds of stories about their societies, or about their class?

To take an example from my own research, I found that many middle-class white German professional men in the early twentieth century tended to see women, children, non-white people, and the working class as in some essential way similar – namely savage, unstable, dangerous, in need of guidance, authority, and supervision, and fundamentally not quite fully human. They often described them or their actions or ideas in comic or satirical terms. In contrast, from the perspective of women and working people in the same society the behavior of many white middle-class men – particularly and precisely toward people those men classified as not quite fully human – was visibly savage, dangerous, destabilizing, and not ethically fully human. They often told tragic stories, or horror stories, about the damage those men did. Because middle-class men held a near monopoly on financial, institutional, and educational resources, other people faced an uphill struggle to get their stories heard. To make things still more complex, middle-class women often themselves struggled to listen to the stories that working-class women could tell, or to sympathize with their critiques of class power. Until we understand that people saw each other through and in the terms of these stories, *and* the relationships of property and power within which this contest of stories played out, we cannot fully understand the depth of the divides that wracked Germany society in the early twentieth century.

When historians take this approach, the point is not to test a hypothesis. Instead, categories and models drawn from theoretical traditions give them a starting point for inquiry, some guidance as to what kinds of sources and evidence they might consider looking for, useful analytical concepts and categories, and a potential interpretive orientation. In short, theory assists them in pursuing more effectively the familiar agenda of History as an inquiry-driven, expansive, idiographic, and interpretive discipline.

From a rigorous social science perspective this approach can appear to draw us into very complex and shaky theorizing. Historians rarely construct a hypothesis derived from theory and then test it against their evidence. Usually they are simply reflecting on what insight a theory can give into a particular aspect of an historical situation as it is revealed in the sources they have already examined – again, a procedure sometimes called "HARKing" in the social sciences. Often that procedure, from a more austere social-science perspective, amounts essentially to creating a mishmash of different theoretical perspectives to generate a convoluted hypothesis – a model defining, for example, the literary qualities of bourgeois professional discourse in a capitalist patriarchy, or a theory that the quality of religious experience in nineteenth-century Latin America was defined by the experience of family in the context of informal colonialism and capitalist globalization. Theories of this kind generate propositions that are far too complex to be "tested" rigorously. How do we explain anything with any clarity and precision if we are considering multiple variables, with no clear procedure for sorting them into a hierarchy of significance? In short, this approach may be too ambitious and broad to produce meaningful results; it is unsystematic, scattershot, and lacking in rigor. It is "eclectic" (drawing on multiple sources and methods) and therefore prone to be amateurish in its use of any one theoretical perspective. An interesting insight or plausible argument, derived by considering a particular body of evidence in the light of one or multiple theories, is not a scientific result.

Nevertheless, the tradition of making heuristic use of social-science theory is a powerful one in History. Already in 1894 the originator of the distinction between nomothetic and idiographic disciplines argued that the latter, including History, "borrow – with perfect legitimacy – from the nomothetic disciplines."[62] In 1956 American historian Richard Hofstadter argued that the value of the social sciences for the historian "is in their addition to the speculative richness of history." Drawing on multiple theoretical and disciplinary perspectives might make the historian's conclusions "more tenuous and tentative, but this is a result to be welcomed. The closer the historian comes, with whatever aids, to the full texture of historical reality" the better. The result would not be "greater certainty, but greater range and depth."[63] More recently, in 2017, Sarah Maza observed quite happily that "historians opt for ... eclectic approaches" and "most academic works engage, analytically, in a little of this and a little of that."[64]

---

[62] Windelband, "Rectorial Address," p. 182.
[63] Richard Hofstadter, "History and the Social Sciences," in *Varieties of History*, ed. Fritz Stern (New York: Vintage, 1972 [1956]), pp. 359–370, here pp. 364–365.
[64] Maza, *Thinking about History*, p. 197.

2.3 Between the Social Sciences and the Humanities

In 2000 John Tosh, Tim Hitchcock, and Robert Shoemaker summed up with particular clarity the potential pedagogical benefits of this hybrid or eclectic approach in History. In an essay on teaching History at the university level, they asserted that the "methodological eclecticism of a history degree is one of its greatest strengths." The "history degree ... gives graduates a basic familiarity with a remarkably diverse set of approaches" and therefore competency in forms of analysis "which transcend disciplinary boundaries." They are "seldom expert in any of these forms of analysis," but they have the problem-solving ingenuity and the "peculiarly open-minded and flexible approach to knowledge" necessary to get to grips with "a uniquely messy object of study – the whole of a past society" undergoing "change over time."[65] It gives them, in other words, a uniquely large and varied set of intellectual tools, and comfort with – or even the habit of – employing them flexibly and pragmatically in the pursuit of open-ended and interpretive inquiry.

The great pedagogical benefit of History, then, is not just that it has room for people who think or inquire in different ways, from many different perspectives. It is that History asks individual students to make room in their own minds for different modes of inquiry. It asks them to develop not just interpretive flexibility, but also methodological flexibility. It demands that they confront fundamental epistemological questions and consider the benefits and drawbacks of their epistemological choices. But more than that, it can give them epistemological flexibility. Students in History get to decide not only what to learn about, and not only what they think about what they learn, but also how they want to go about learning it and thinking about it.

Having considered the relationship between History and social-science method in this third section of this chapter, I want to turn in the first section of the next chapter to considering an important aspect of the relationship of History to the humanities. For there is a third defining feature of a good historical question. It should lead us to explore the complexity of historical situations, it should lead us to further questions, it should ideally lead us to understand relationships and connections we might otherwise not have considered. But it should also enable us to tell a good story. For History is not only an idiographic and a social-scientific

---

[65] Tim Hitchcock, Robert B. Shoemaker, and John Tosh, "Skills and the Structure of the History Curriculum," in *The Practice of University History Teaching*, ed. Alan Booth and Paul Hyland (Manchester: Manchester University Press, 2000), pp. 47–59, here pp. 49, 50. For similar conclusions, see Jordanova, *History in Practice*, p. 4; Lynn Hunt, "Where Have All the Theories Gone?" *Perspectives on History* 40:3 (2002): 5–7, here p. 5.

discipline, but also in an important sense a literary one. It explains, deepens understanding, informs, and educates specifically by telling a story, usually about change. And it tells a story with certain literary qualities that, ideally, make it interesting, convincing, and even entertaining. History is expansively *analytical*, but it is also *narrative*. It deepens understanding through effective analytical storytelling. Chapter 3 will attempt to define what makes a good historical story.

CHAPTER 3

What Kinds of Stories Do Historians Tell?

3.1 The Literary Qualities of Historical Scholarship

As a field of knowledge History is exceptionally interested in the particular and specific rather than the universal and general – it is primarily idiographic rather than nomothetic. It is also centrally concerned with change over time. These two characteristics make History fundamentally a storytelling discipline. Its findings are most often presented in narrative form. Of course, many books do not follow one narrative from cover to cover. But research findings are most often presented as stories – not as reports of particular key results (as, for example, in a scientific lab report) or as the results of statistical analysis. Nomothetic disciplines tend toward examining a relatively narrow set of features of multiple cases in order to create generalizing theories and establish laws of regularity that define what will happen under a given set of circumstances at any and all times and places. History instead usually aims to organize into a coherent interpretation many features of a single case, exploring in detail what happened at a particular time, in a particular place. It often also aims to give us a complex, multifactor causal explanation of why it happened as it did, but usually that causal explanation is embedded in the narrative.

This is what we most often mean when we speak of an "historical interpretation." Most commonly, an interpretation is a kind of story – though it may be a complex and highly analytical story. As Leon J. Goldstein wrote in 1962, historical "interpretations are generally presented in narrative ... the function of a narrative account is to attempt to make sense of something by showing how it emerged in the course of events, and how it led to what followed."[1] This means that historians usually work at most with what John Gaddis called "limited, not universal,

---

[1] Leon J. Goldstein, "A Note on Historical Interpretation," *Philosophy of Science* 42:3 (1975): 312–319, here p. 313.

generalizations," not claiming "applicability for our findings beyond specific times and places." Historians may, for example, generalize about how nineteenth-century middle-class Egyptians thought about their families, and expect that a large proportion of them, if we examined the available evidence closely, would be found to think that way. But they would not think it very likely that nineteenth-century middle-class people in all societies (say, in China or in Argentina) thought about family in that way, or that middle-class Egyptians in other periods would (say, in the fifteenth century). In fact, they would be unlikely to think that any element of nineteenth-century middle-class Egyptian thinking about the family that is universal, that can be found in all social groups in all human societies, would be very interesting. Any such common characteristic would be so basic and so modified by circumstance in any specific historical case as to be effectively of no relevance in any specific historical situation. Again, they might be interested in comparative cases – say, nineteenth-century middle-class Frenchmen, Sri Lankans, and Chileans – that could help them determine what degree of similarity there might have been in the thinking and actions of middle-class people across the world in that period, and why. But few historians actually conduct that kind of comparative research themselves. They rely on the broader community of historians to conduct research on other societies. Frequently they draw on review essays summarizing multiple publications, synthetic treatments, or volumes of single-authored essays to do that. Broader generalizations tend to appear in those specific forms; most often, the books historians write focus on one story, told about one time and place. As John Gaddis put it, historians "normally embed our generalizations within our narratives," because it is the story in its complexity and uniqueness that is of interest. In contrast, social scientists tend to "embed narratives within generalizations" – that is, to see specific cases as interesting primarily because they confirm, modify, or invalidate generalizations.[2]

Historians "explain" the past, therefore, in a very specific sense. In general, historical interpretations or explanations are not sequential and generic. They do not follow the model "if X happens (at any place or time), it will cause Y to happen. X happened in this particular time and place, so therefore then Y happened there." Instead, they are chronological and localized. They follow the model "A, B, C, D, and E were happening at this time and place; each contributed in different ways to the complex of conditions that brought about F. F contributed to the

---

[2] Gaddis, *Landscape of History*, p. 63.

complex of conditions that enabled G, H, and I" and so on.[3] Clayton Roberts, in *The Logic of Historical Explanation*, distinguishes between social-science "theory," a term used to "refer to an explanation of a repetitive phenomenon," and historical "interpretation," which "refers to an assertion that some variable or number of variables are ... causal agencies in a particular historical development, that is, in a single sequence of events."[4]

A convincing historical interpretation, therefore, may well have some of the strengths of a powerful fictional story. It may have strong characters who illustrate or embody certain characteristics of the historical situation – heroic characters, or villainous, or tragically flawed, or complex and conflicted characters, characters who undergo development, whose flaws catch up with them, who experience redemption. The historian may use descriptive passages to establish a strong and interesting setting, a sense of the time and place, or a sense of character. Works of history may fall into a particular genre – mystery, tragedy, comedy, romance, horror. Many historical situations justify the use of multiple such genres. The Nazi invasion of the Soviet Union was a farce in the sense Hitler's generals told him that his army was not ready to win the war he wanted to wage, but he started it anyway with the help of toadying fools and suffered catastrophic but entirely predictable defeat. It is a tragedy in that his decision led to the deaths of tens of millions of human beings. The ways in which many of those millions of people died is a horror story more frightening and disturbing than any fiction. A good story of historical change may follow literary plot conventions – setting up the conflict, building toward crisis, resolution. Historians may use standard literary devices to etch their findings more clearly, to give them drama. For example, some historical developments lend themselves to the recounting of a surprising plot twist or change of fortune. Not a few histories of World War II make a point of the fact that in late 1941 the Nazi armies, apparently irresistible until then, bogged down in part because they faced the coldest winter in Russia in more than a century – a change of fortune. Many histories of feminism in the European world in the nineteenth century suggest that women were able to turn the stereotypes used to exclude them from public life into a source of public moral authority – an ironic plot twist. Finally, it can be useful to use literary devices such as shifts in perspective in illustrating the

---

[3] See, for example, Goldstein, "Evidence and Events in History," p. 185.
[4] Clayton Roberts, *The Logic of Historical Explanation* (University Park: Pennsylvania State University Press, 1996), p. 242.

complexity of an historical situation, analyzing what the situation looked like to different participants (or "characters"), or how their experiences of it differed. In this latter case, historians may even give rein to their imaginations to suggest on the basis of broader historical context how different participants *might* have seen and experienced historical events, rather than drawing on explicit reports by those participants. As G. M. Trevelyan remarked, a good deal of History writing "is a matter of rough guessing from all the available facts," or (in another text) "speculating about the past with the aid of a number of facts."[5] These are extreme formulations, but they are a useful reminder that (as will be discussed in Chapter 4) much or even most of our picture of the past is not archivally (much less experimentally) verified fact, but interpretation constructed from the preponderance of the available evidence.

The use of literary techniques is of course not a requirement of the discipline even in its more imaginative, speculative, and creative aspects. Trevelyan was a great advocate of the view that "the art of history writing" was a branch of literature, but he also wrote that "literary skill is a part of the equipment desirable at least in some historians, though not in all. There are diversities of gifts and diversities of tasks in Clio's temple" (Clio being the muse of History).[6] Still, most historians would agree on the importance for History – as Australian historian Greg Dening put it – of "creative imagination in telling a true story."[7]

Whatever the literary merits of a work of History, however, Dening's comment is a reminder that History is not fiction. Historians may use all sorts of literary devices or strain their imaginations – certainly even to the point of speculation and guesswork – to make as much as they can from the limited evidence they have. But the imaginative work of History is bounded by the evidence. This is why historians so frequently signal to their readers the degree of confidence they have in a given statement – whether they believe it is probably, likely, or possibly correct, or purely speculative but still useful in expanding our inquiry and our thinking. Leon Goldstein offers a good summary. "The past that the historian evokes," he suggests, "is not ... a free creation as in the writing of a novel, or a tendentious creation contrived for the purpose of propaganda, but a construction devised as the best explanation of the evidence he has."

---

[5] Trevelyan, "History and the Reader," in Trevelyan, *An Autobiography and Other Essays* (London: Longmans, Green & Company, 1949), p. 56; Trevelyan, "History and Literature," p. 85.
[6] Trevelyan, "History and Literature," p. 85; Trevelyan, "History and the Reader," p. 56.
[7] Greg Dening, "Enigma Variations on History in Three Keys: A Conversational Essay," *History and Theory* 39:2 (2000): 210–217, here p. 213.

3.1 The Literary Qualities of Historical Scholarship

The "narrative of the historian is . . . a creative and original act," but it is "at the same time restricted by the need to conform to historical evidence."[8] Historians sometimes speculate, they sometimes suggest how things might have been, but they do not invent stories or characters or plot twists or surprise developments just because doing so would make a good story.

Adherence to the evidence and powerful storytelling are not, however, incompatible. In fact, what makes History powerful as a form of literature is precisely that it is *not* fiction. It is about real people, real events. That gives it a power to move, inspire, terrify, and delight that is vastly superior to that of fiction.

I remarked earlier in this chapter that the Holocaust is a *more* frightening horror story than anything one could invent in fiction because it actually did happen. Hundreds of thousands of people actually did behave that way, were directly involved in that, really did do that; millions of people did lose their lives. Whole societies were complicit in the sickening lies, the grotesque cruelty, the animalistic violence, and the bottomless spiritual squalor of that. There is no fear that can compare to the fear of knowing that this is an historical reality and a real possibility. Nothing anyone could make up could possibly be as creepy as this. Very large numbers of human beings abased themselves to the level of committing acts like that; they organized themselves systematically and self-consciously and with virulent, unreasoning, and irredeemably corrupt malice to do that. That is true. That happened. We should shake with fear and shame knowing that. History gives us such horrors that we should all get down on our knees at least once a day and beg whatever higher power we believe in to give us all the strength and grace and decency not to let that happen again.

But the drama of history is not exhausted by the spectacular and the horrific – war, mass murder, slavery, injustice, cruelty, death. Personally, I find histories of those things dull. There are few surprises in stories like that, and the people who commit such abominable acts are generally stupid, boring, and pathetic. What is surprising is the seemingly endless variety of ways in which smart, creative, thoughtful, decent people have built their lives, art, ideas, relationships, knowledge, faith, wisdom, and foolishness. What is breathtaking is that they *really did that*. It's not just a story. We don't know the whole story because we build our stories out of fragmentary and imperfect evidence. But the evidence is enough to tell us that the creativity, tenacity, and diversity of humanity is astonishing. It is

---

[8] Goldstein, "Evidence and Events in History," pp. 177, 181.

fascinating, riveting, moving. I have spent my scholarly life exploring the lives of people who were for the most part neither victims nor perpetrators of atrocities, power plays, overt acts of rebellion or domination. Their passion, their creativity, and often their granite integrity take my breath away.

Consider, for example, Christian Jasper Klumker, the first professor of social work in Germany. Klumker spent his entire life fighting to protect the most vulnerable members of his society, he was the author of a profoundly humane and rational argument for the benefit to all of doing so, and he lost his job for rejecting the Nazis' firing of Jewish professors at his university.[9] Klumker's letters reveal that he was a stubborn, self-righteous, combative, and difficult man. He appears to have lost his cool during the Great Depression and questioned the value of his life's work in ways that may have contributed, in a very small way, to the crisis and collapse of German democracy. But he played a major part in creating social welfare institutions that saved at least tens and quite possibly hundreds of thousands of lives. This is not a fictional tale of heroism. He really did that.

Or consider Dai Ailian. A third-generation Chinese-Trinidadian, she studied ballet in London in the 1930s, joined the international movement to defeat Japanese imperialism, moved to China in 1940, helped found and lead the dance institutions of the People's Republic of China, worked to preserve and celebrate the many ethnic minority dance traditions of the country, was "sent down" to perform agricultural labor during the Cultural Revolution, was eventually rehabilitated, and in 1982 became vice chair of the United Nations Economic, Social and Cultural Organization's International Council for Dance.[10] Hers was a life of relentless creativity and courage. And, again, it is not a fictional romance. She really did all that.

I could go on for thousands of pages describing the lives of historical people I have studied whose accomplishments and character I admire. And while I try to steer clear of despicable people, I could certainly fill some pages with them too. As William H. McNeill wrote in 1985 in an essay titled "Why Study History?" "History offers innumerable heroes and villains," and learning about them "enlarges our sense of human capacities

---

[9] Franz Lerner, "Klumker, Christian Jasper," in *Neue Deutsche Biographie* vol. 12 (Berlin: Duncker & Humblot, 1986), pp. 144–145.
[10] Richard Glasstone, *The Story of Dai Ailian: Icon of Chinese Folk Dance, Pioneer of Chinese Ballet* (Alton: Dance Books, 2007).

for both good and evil."[11] What makes the lesson powerful is, again, that we know that these heroes and villains really lived and really did the horrifying and admirable things that they did. To return to the issue of judgment in historical study addressed in Chapter 1: This is one reason students take courses in History – because it is profoundly moving.

But again, History is not *just* a matter of heroes and villains. It is the complexity and diversity and sheer *difference* of people and their lives, as individuals and in aggregate, as "societies," that is consistently surprising. What is endlessly fascinating, as Leopold von Ranke put it, is "how man has perennially contrived to live."[12]

One does not have to pursue detailed research on individual people in the past to be overcome by wonder. I still remember the first time I realized that the ancient Romans really lived, really existed. It was 1981; I was in a movie theater, waiting for a film to begin (it was *Chariots of Fire*, to be precise), and thinking about ancient Rome. An odd feeling came over me – a spooky, elated sort of feeling. For a moment my world stood still as it hit me ... no, wait. That really happened. Thousands of years ago. Those were real people; they lived that just as vividly as I am now living this. Nothing could possibly be as dramatic as that. Except that so many things are, because the ancient Mediterranean was only one small corner of the human world, and every other part of that world has a history just as dramatic and extraordinary.

Much more recently, in 2014, I spent some hours in the Romano-Germanic Museum in Cologne, Germany. I worked my way through the display rooms moving backward in time, from the late Roman Empire back to the Stone Age. I was captivated by the complexity of the social, economic, and religious history the artifacts revealed. The ambition, sorrow, vanity, creativity, and sheer busy-ness of the people who had left behind those statues, mosaics, glassware, jewelry, buildings, inscriptions, and tools was moving. And the degree of change that took place over a period of some 300 years in Roman Cologne was remarkable. But I was particularly arrested by the display of stone axe-heads and other stone tools. Looking at the dates on display cases, it hit me that people living in that area made such tools for something like 10,000 years. Why? Why would people stick with such a rudimentary technology for literally hundreds of generations? It seems utterly implausible – a bad idea so bad that it seems

---

[11] William H. McNeill, "Why Study History?" www.historians.org/about-aha-and-membership/aha-history-and-archives/historical-archives/why-study-history-(1985).

[12] Leopold von Ranke, "A Fragment from the 1830s," in *The Varieties of History*, ed. Fritz Stern (Cleveland, OH: Meridian, 1956), 58–60, here p. 59.

unthinkable. I have no idea why they did it. But they really did. And it also made me wonder: Was it really a bad idea? It was sustainable for 10,000 years; maybe it was actually a very *good* idea. Compared to the current impending planetary catastrophe of industrial civilization after a mere two or three centuries, this was a monumental accomplishment. Were those people a lot stupider than we are? Or a lot smarter? But what was most striking to me was that whatever the reason, clearly they were not like us.[13]

That is what makes the stories that History tells powerful – that they are true. I do not mean "true" in the sense that any historical account or interpretation is absolutely and unquestionably correct. Rather, what I mean is that they are about real people and real events. What makes History moving, inspiring, funny, horrifying – what makes it powerful literature – is this: It's real. As G. M. Trevelyan wrote in 1924, "Truth is the criterion of historical study; but its impelling motive is poetic. Its poetry consists in its being true."[14]

In trying to capture the power of that entrancing realness of history, History sometimes has to resort not just to imagination, but to something approaching outright fiction. Where speculative or even fictional stories are *informed by* a knowledge of historical context and built on the available evidence, they can be very fruitful for historical understanding, particularly historical education. Simon Schama wrote a marvelous book that consists, as he described it, of two "historical novellas" about murders that really did happen. These stories are "pure inventions based, however, on what the documents suggest."[15] My colleague Ari Kelman wrote an illustrated novel about the American Civil War, incorporating numerous genuine historical documents and real historical characters.[16] Reviewers have praised both as useful pedagogical tools for History teachers, and for being true to what scholars know of the periods they treat – the broad context of social structures, cultural trends, and events. They can be useful, rather than merely entertaining, because they are not pure invention. Schama's and Kelman's books are fact-based fictions; they present historical interpretations in the form of fictional but plausible stories about real people. Where they are informed by deep expertise and research, as both these

---

[13] www.roemisch-germanisches-museum.de/Homepage.
[14] Trevelyan, "History and Literature," p. 91; see also G. M. Trevelyan, "Autobiography of an Historian," in Trevelyan, *An Autobiography and Other Essays* (London: Longmans, Green & Company, 1949), pp. 1–51, here p. 13.
[15] Schama, *Dead Certainties*, p. 322.
[16] Ari Kelman and Jonathan Fetter-Vorm, *Battle Lines: A Graphic History of the Civil War* (New York: Hill & Wang, 2015).

books are, such stories have a legitimate place within the discipline of History. Analyzing historical fictions of this sort with students can help pose and explore the question of how we know what we think we know, confronting them in particular with the central role of context in historical understanding. Figuring out how well-founded an historical fiction is, and what it is founded on, can be an effective way to sharpen our sense of what we can learn from limited sources, from context, from inference – of what the limits and potentials are of the use of "creative imagination in telling a true story" (Greg Dening).[17] Paradoxically, it can help students come to grips with the realness of the past by leading them to ask in greater depth what the sources might indicate, imply, and suggest, not just what they *show*. That can lead students to further inquiry and new sources.

3.2 Debates about Causation: History and Theory II

There is considerable debate among historians about whether the stories that they tell need to *explain* what happened, rather than only *recount* what happened. How important is causation, or cause and effect, in historical narrative? This is a debate that overlaps substantially with the debate over the role of social science theory and method in History. Historians who take a more theory-oriented approach to their work believe that "why" is the most important question historians must answer, and that getting an answer to that question requires an explicitly theoretical approach. John Tosh, for example, insisted that merely heuristic use of theory – "to raise interesting questions and to alert scholars to fresh source material" – overlooks the need to address "large scale problems of historical interpretation" such as "how to explain long-term processes such as the growth of industrialization or bureaucracy, and the recurrence of institutions such as feudalism or plantation slavery in widely separated societies. The broader the scope of inquiry, the greater the need for theory ... which actually attempts to *explain* the process or pattern in question."[18] In other words, again, History without theory is merely aimless antiquarian description. Without theory historians cannot explain *why* things were like that, or why things happened.

This view has been questioned from two very different positions. One is the more radically empirical and historicist standpoint, which holds that History does not aspire to explain things by reference to general principles,

---

[17] Dening, "Enigma Variations on History," p. 213.
[18] Tosh, *The Pursuit of History*, pp. 239–240 (emphasis in the original).

to universal regularities and laws – "X happened at this time and place because X happens whenever Y is true, and Y was true in that time and place." Instead, it explains by reference to the specifics of the historical situation – again, the historical context, broadly conceived. The aim is not to assess the validity of a general principle for a particular case by proposing and testing a hypothesis derived from a theory based on that general principle. Instead, the aim is to expand our knowledge and understanding of that specific historical time and place. As Madan Sarup wrote a generation ago, it seeks to "establish and preserve the singularity of events," rather than to fit them into a larger scheme of explanation.[19] Caroline Walker Bynum, a former president of the American Historical Association, even suggested that History is "perspectival, non-appropriative, and particular," respectful of the specificity of the world, and that "our job as teachers is to puzzle, confuse, and amaze" rather than explain – thereby obliging our students to generate answers for themselves.[20] In this view, History does not so much seek to explain in terms of cause and effect as rather to investigate, to explore, to inquire. It explains in the sense that it gives a detailed, complex, wide-ranging account. It aims to widen and deepen our understanding, not to establish general principles of cause and effect.

Those who hold this view sometimes argue – as discussed in Chapter 2 – that the application of theory sabotages understanding by leading the historian to adopt preformulated, overly simple, or downright false generalizations that do not actually capture the complex reality of an historical situation. As Martha Howell and Walter Prevenier put it in their book on historical methods, "generalizations sometimes disguise more than they reveal," and the kinds of "models" theory gives us "are just abstractions from selected data and are seldom transferrable to another historical situation. Human life is too complex" to be understood using such blunt tools. Instead of focusing on explanations of cause and effect, they argue, the historian should be "the caretaker of the memory of how different, how unique each moment in the past was. While historians must work with generalizations ('the bourgeoisie,' 'feudalism,' 'Christianity,' 'capitalism') … it is the historians' principal job to provide that kind of textured account of the past and the people who made it" that allows us to understand the past in detail and with precision, not in broad theoretical

---

[19] Madan Sarup, *An Introductory Guide to Post-Structuralism and Postmodernism* (Athens: University of Georgia Press, 1989), p. 64.
[20] Caroline Walker Bynum, "Wonder," *American Historical Review* 102 (1997): 1–26, here pp. 3, 26.

3.2 Debates about Causation

and general terms. In particular, Howell and Prevenier saw three intellectual dangers to the adoption of a social-science model. The first is anachronism, in which the experience of people in the past is misinterpreted in terms of the categories and assumptions of the present: "Scholars should not expect people of the past to have experienced or understood the world as they do." The second is "an overdose of conceptualizing, to the point that empirical detail is suppressed" in order to fit the historical account or explanation to the conceptual schema. The third is "the naïveté of too much model building on too narrow a database" – that is, cutting short one's inquiry when it has confirmed one's theory. In contrast, the more open-ended and hermeneutic approach "does not presume that the historian is in search of a grand theory or even of causal explanations, only of understanding." Rather than positing laws of causality, historians "formulate provisional causal statements ... on the basis of many observations" of a concrete, specific historical situation.[21] Historicism avoids these three pitfalls through openness to whatever is in the sources, even if it does not serve us in finding answers to our initial and particular question about causes and effects.

This is a very widespread and long-standing position. Leopold von Ranke regarded causal explanation as optional, writing already in 1824 that the aim of History is to understand the past "in its human comprehenibility, its unity, and its fullness ... our subject is mankind as it is, explicable or inexplicable."[22] G. M. Trevelyan, as we have seen, regarded historical explanation as speculative or even guesswork, but he was comfortable with that lack of certainty because, as he wrote in 1913, "[e]ven if cause and effect could be discovered with accuracy, they still would not be the most interesting part of human affairs ... The deeds themselves are more interesting than their causes and effects, and are fortunately ascertainable with much greater precision."[23] Ninety-nine years later, Joseph C. Miller was more radical: "'Cause' is ... an entirely false problematic for historians ... Causation may be possible to discern in defined scientific reactions, or mechanical processes, but among historians the word almost always attributes agency to abstractions" (e.g., the bourgeoisie, feudalism,

---

[21] Howell and Prevenier, *From Reliable Sources*, pp. 97, 95, 96, 102, 130.
[22] Leopold von Ranke, "Preface to the First Edition of Histories of the Latin and Germanic Nations (October 1824)," in Leopold von Ranke, *The Theory and Practice of History*, ed. Georg G. Iggers and Konrad von Moltke, trans Wilma Iggers and Konrad von Moltke (Indianapolis, IN: Bobbs-Merrill, 1973), pp. 55–58.
[23] Trevelyan, "Clio, A Muse," p. 147.

Christianity, capitalism).²⁴ Again: History is interpretive, and its aim is not closure but inquiry – to expand and deepen our understanding of the totality of an historical situation or development, to understand the "web" of connections and relationships that made it uniquely what it was. Historian of China Pamela Kyle Crossly remarked in a roundtable discussion in 2015 about causation in History that she was "puzzled by any historian who introduces the notion of parsimony into her or his methods," since for historians "everything explains everything." Historians aim for holistic understanding rather than laws of cause and effect.²⁵

The other source of skepticism about causal explanations is of more recent origin and derives from critiques of History itself. History, some critical theorists argue, is merely one of a whole range of disciplines that arose in the West (in Europe) as tools of nation-building and imperialism. The most influential advocate of this view is Dipesh Chakrabarty, who summarized his views in an essay of 1991. The discipline of History, he argued, was built around "metanarratives" (or "grand narratives") that explained the past on the basis of European theories that were derived from the European historical experience. These would include, for example, nationalism, racism, and the idea of progress in either its liberal/capitalist or its Marxist/socialist versions. The job of History was to produce "secular histories" that discount other ways of thinking about the human experience – for example, religious, mythic, or communitarian. It reduced the history of the rest of the world to an imperfect, laggard, or defective version of European development as defined by one or another European social theory. Causal explanations were "defining characteristics" of such secular histories, because the causes they posited always asserted Western superiority (Chakrabarty inserted the word "almost" before "defining," but I can see no reason for that qualifying word in his subsequent exposition). The message of History was that the nation arose because it embodied progress or "modernization" (i.e., becoming more like twentieth-century Europe), which is/are inevitable. European nations came to dominate other societies because they were racially, culturally, economically, or technologically superior. Pre- or non-capitalist modes of production and social organization were destroyed because they stood in

---

²⁴ Miller, *The Problem of Slavery*, p. 26. For an influential essay published midway between these two, see Arthur C. Danto, "On Explanation in History," *Philosophy of Science* 23:1 (1956), pp. 15–30, here pp. 15, 23.
²⁵ Pamela Kyle Crossly in "AHR Conversation: Explaining Historical Change; or, The Lost History of Causes," *American Historical Review* 120:4 (2015), pp. 1369–1423, here p. 1394.

3.2 Debates about Causation

the way of progress toward capitalism and democracy, or toward the dictatorship of the proletariat and socialism. The discipline of History, Chakrabarty held, "could die only if these institutions of power that feed upon it" (nation, market, empire) "were to disappear." Until then the "lethal grand narratives of freedom and progress" would continue, as he wrote (at the time of the First Gulf War), to pile up bodies in places like Baghdad and Kuwait.[26]

Chakrabarty's critique is particularly concise, but since the 1990s various versions of it have become a staple of postcolonial thinking in History. By 2019 Ibrahim Kendi could offer a pithy summary: Most social theory is "theories gleaned from European subjects masquerading as universal theories."[27] The conceptual vocabularies of academic disciplines like History, anthropology, economics, and sociology have come to be seen in this tradition as what Robert C. Young called "white mythologies." They serve the interests of class and imperial power by implicitly asserting the superiority of the West.[28] Partly as a consequence of such doubts, as the moderator of a roundtable discussion in the *American Historical Review* observed in 2015, the analysis of causation "has become rarer in recent decades in the discipline of history as a whole."[29]

These two critiques of the idea of causation in history are exact mirror opposites of each other. From the postcolonial perspective the empiricist is simply blind to her own implicit assumptions, refusing to ask why she thinks and works the way she does. That looks like a deliberate or unconscious effort to deny deeper structures of privilege and power. From the perspective of the historicist, in contrast, the postcolonial critique of History is a frenzy of overgeneralization. In much postcolonial scholarship the key actors in history are abstract categories – capitalism, imperialism, the nation-state, History or Economics or Anthropology as ways of thinking, Europe, the West, and so on and so forth. In a programmatic essay of 1992, for example, Chakrabarty delivered this astonishing sentence: "For

---

[26] Dipesh Chakrabarty, "History as Critique and Critiques) of History," *Economic and Political Weekly* 26:37 (1991): 2162–2166, here pp. 2164, 2166.

[27] Ibrahim X. Kendi, *How to Be an Antiracist* (New York: One World, 2019), p. 167. For an example of a critique of the categories of analysis central to a state world history curriculum for the schools, see Tadashi Dozono, "The Passive Voice of White Supremacy: Tracing Epistemic and Discursive Violence in World History Curriculum," *Review of Education, Pedagogy, and Cultural Studies* 42 (2020): 1–26.

[28] See Robert J. C. Young, *White Mythologies: Writing History and the West*, 2nd edition (London: Routledge, 2004).

[29] Mark Hewitson in "AHR Conversation: Explaining Historical Change," p. 1373; see also p. 1372. See also Maza, *Thinking about History*, pp. 177, 174.

'capital' or 'bourgeois,' I submit, read 'Europe.'"³⁰ That is abstraction on a truly epic scale. Historicists often refer to this kind of thinking as the "reification" of abstract categories – that is, thinking as if abstract general categories were concrete singular things. The term derives from the Latin "res," thing or matter; so reification means false conceptual "thingification." In fact, the postcolonial critique of meta-narratives is itself obviously a meta-narrative, in which just about everything is explained by the rise in Europe of capitalism, the nation, and the modes of thinking they favor, and by their imposition on the whole world.

Despite this divergence, the conclusions of these two critiques of the social-science model of causality are substantially the same. In postcolonial thinking the antidote to the lethal meta-narratives of social theory is precisely the radically nominalist and historicist conception of History. Commenting on the work of an esteemed colleague in an essay of 2004, for example, Chakrabarty wrote as follows: "Every human being and every human relationship is imbued with special qualities that shine forth in their uniqueness. Each radiates a past that is wondrous and multifarious . . . with myriad narratives and multiple realities of concrete human experience." To do justice to the people who inhabited this diverse past, historians would have to abandon the goal of "levelling them down to and labelling them with 'common' categories such as 'worker,' 'citizen,' or 'woman.'"³¹ In short, historians should abandon abstract sociological categories and immerse themselves in the world of the people they are studying. As German historian Carola Dietze pointed out in an assessment of Chakrabarty's most influential book, historically the discipline of History separated itself from the social sciences in the nineteenth century precisely by rejecting meta-narratives in favor of an historicist and nominalist approach. "Chakrabarty therefore has to be regarded as a thinker of radical historicism rather than as a critic of the discipline of history."³² Peter Seixas made the same point more generally in 2000: Postmodern theory, he wrote, "reinforces the mainstay of traditional historiography"; it "pushes historians further down the paths they have always traveled."³³

---

[30] Dipesh Chakrabarty, "Provincializing Europe: Postcoloniality and the Critique of History," *Cultural Studies* 6 (1992): 337–357, here p. 338.
[31] Dipesh Chakrabarty, "History and Historicality: Review of Ranajit Guha, *History at the Limit of World History*," *Postcolonial Studies* 7:1 (2004): 125–130, here p. 125.
[32] Carola Dietze, "Toward a History on Equal Terms: A Discussion of *Provincializing Europe*," *History and Theory* 47 (2008): 69–84, here p. 69.
[33] Peter Seixas, "Schweigen! Die Kinder! Or, Does Postmodern History Have a Place in the Schools?" in *Knowing, Teaching, and Learning History: National and International Perspectives*, ed. Peter Stearns, Peter Seixas, and Sam Wineburg (New York: New York University Press, 2000),

Where does all this leave us as teachers of History? What kinds of story should historians tell – and what kinds of stories should we ask our students to construct? How do historians think about causation? Is a "proper" historical story the kind that explains why, or the kind that recounts what? Should the work of historical scholars fall into the genre of mystery? Should the aim be to get the reader to think "Aha!" at the end, when everything is explained? Or should History be epic, or perhaps adventure? Should it aim to get the reader to think "Wow!" after reading a lusty sprawling tale with vivid characters, surprising plot twists, and dramatic events?

This question is meaningless. No one would think to ask writers of fiction to choose either mystery or epic. Why would we expect historians to do that? Some historians write epics. Others write mysteries. So what? Neither form is appropriate to *every* inquiry. What is more, it is an unanswerable question. The weaknesses and pitfalls of each approach, as pointed out by the champions of the other, are real. Antiquarianism, ad hoc theorizing, unconscious assumptions, and implicit bias in histories cast as factual narratives; or gross overgeneralization and reification, inappropriate narrowing of the field of inquiry, unconscious anachronism in histories cast as excursions into theory – these are all real problems. But again: So what? We do not judge a method by works in which it is applied clumsily. We judge it by what it can accomplish when done well. And plenty of historians use both methods well.

Further, the dichotomy between those who do and do not seek to explain causation is a false one. Not explaining causation through social science method is not the same thing as not explaining causation. As historian Caroline Arni remarked in 2015, what historicism rejects "is not explanation, but a specific *way of explaining*, namely through abstraction."[34] Historicists explain, but they do so in historicist fashion. They rely on what W. H. Walsh, in 1959, called the "the common historical procedure of explaining an event by locating it in its context"; they aim at "'making sense of' or 'understanding' their material," not discerning universal laws of causation.[35] In fact, historians sometimes regard social

---

pp. 19–37, here p. 30. See also Frank Ankersmit, *History and Tropology: The Rise and Fall of a Metaphor* (Berkeley: University of California Press, 1994), p. 238; Jörn Rüsen, *History: Narration – Interpretation – Orientation* (New York: Berghahn, 2005), esp. p. 139.

[34] Caroline Arni, in "AHR Conversation: Explaining Historical Change," p. 1375 (emphasis in the original).

[35] William H. Walsh, "'Meaning' in History," in *Theories of History*, ed. Patrick Gardiner (New York: Free Press, 1959), pp. 296–307, here p. 298.

science models of causation as incapable of "explaining" in an historical sense. Ross E. Dunn, for example, remarked in an influential volume published in 2000 that an account centered on "abstractions, not ... situated firmly in time and space ... disconnecting a particular type of phenomenon from the thick historical context of the times ... may be interesting sociological speculation, but it is not a satisfying explanation of change."[36]

The important point here is that History bridges these approaches – the social sciences and the humanities. As Chakrabarty himself conceded, "most important thinkers belong to both traditions at once."[37] His own work is a good case. He sought to debunk the meta-narratives that serve imperialism and capitalism by constructing a postcolonial counter-meta-narrative, but he recommended an empiricist and nominalist approach as the antidote to the forms of knowledge that power and its supporting ideologies impose. The whole exercise is rich in irony, but I don't mean to poke fun at it. Chakrabarty was advocating a more self-conscious historicist approach, one guided by an understanding of the intellectual legacies, within the discipline of History, of nationalism and imperialism. That is an important and intellectually beneficial agenda. This is what History does. It draws on multiple theories to pose fruitful questions. But it also makes historians conscious of their own place in history. The criticism that social theories are themselves historical artifacts (products of history) applies to the historicist approach as well.

The debate over causation in History really illustrates, then, one of the great pedagogical potentials of the discipline. It is capacious enough not just to accommodate both humanistic and social-scientific approaches to explanation or causation, but also to encourage the historian to engage with both simultaneously. It therefore confronts students with two radically divergent understandings of what constitutes "explanation," and forces them to consider the strengths and weaknesses of each. This can be a source of intellectual freedom in that it gives students two different approaches, two divergent conceptions of the nature of "understanding." It can also be a source of greater intellectual flexibility for students who are willing to entertain both. And it can impose a greater degree of reflexivity and self-awareness, not only by calling each into question, but also – if we explore with students how History came to be bifurcated in this way – by tracing the historical origins of these modes of understanding. History is a way of

---

[36] Dunn, "Constructing World History in the Classroom," p. 129.
[37] Chakrabarty, *Provincializing Europe*, p. 18.

thinking that applies to itself. Like social theory, historicism too is a product of a particular historical situation, in a particular place and time. I have found it fruitful to ask students why they prefer one or the other mode of explanation, or model of causation. That can sometimes be the starting point for awareness of the historicity of their own most fundamental intellectual commitments.

3.3 What Kinds of Causation Do Historians Consider?

The most pedagogically useful approach to disagreements over what kinds of stories historians tell, and hence over the nature of historical understanding, is precisely not to try to resolve them. Instead, they should be embraced and examined. The simplest way to do that, of course, is to ask students to both read and write historical accounts of both kinds.

Yet in one respect there is virtual consensus about a key characteristic of how historians think about causation. Virtually everyone agrees that historians think about *multiple* causes of any outcome. Historians think about multiple facets of historical phenomena, they consider issues of cause and effect with respect to all of those facets, and they consider how different causal factors interacted dynamically to form a complex of causation – and in an evolving, not a static historical context. As Sarah Maza put it in 2017, historians "often avoid putting their money on one type of cause over another, instead explaining how various factors accumulate over time," amounting to what we might call a causal complex.[38] John Gaddis agreed that historians "believe in contingent, not categorical causation. 'It all depends'" is their instinctive motto; they generally "think it irresponsible to seek to isolate ... single causes for complex events" and "see history as proceeding instead from multiple causes and their intersections. Interconnections matter more to us than does the enshrinement of particular variables."[39] Richard Evans argued that "all historians are used to the idea that historical events are frequently *overdetermined* – that is, they may have several ... causes" that operate in interaction with each other; they therefore seek to explain "the relationship of one cause to another."[40] Ludmila Jordanova was even more blunt: To historians, she observed, "an emphasis on single causes appears reductionist." Characteristic of how historians know the past, she believed, is "the ability to embrace

---

[38] Maza, *Thinking about History*, p. 173.   [39] Gaddis, *Landscape of History*, pp. 64, 65.
[40] Richard J. Evans, *In Defense of History* (New York: Norton, 1999), p. 135 (emphasis in the original).

complexities ... and to think flexibly about diverse phenomena at distinct analytical levels."[41]

In my experience this way of thinking about causation is counterintuitive for most university students. Most students are predisposed to think of causation in terms of human will and human action: Things happen because someone makes them happen. This tendency is so strong that students often have difficulty disaggregating collectivities in order to perceive multiple, divergent, conflicting, or even converging intentions. Wars happened because "the British" or "the Germans" or "Southerners" wanted them to; revolutions happened because "the people" were angry; prices went up because "the government" imposed higher taxes; suffrage was won because "women" wanted it. And students generally discern straightforward, familiar, and (they often presume) universal motives at the root of such intentions. People or collectivities were greedy, or wanted power, or thirsted for revenge or for justice, or yearned for freedom or for security.[42] Further, even where they do not personify causation in this way, students tend to think of causation as singular and determinative: One thing made another thing happen, and therefore it had to happen.[43]

Thinking about multiple causation is therefore a challenge for students. To help them develop their capacity to do so we need to give structure to causal complexity. Historians have three ways of doing that.

First, we can adopt the logician's terms relating to causation and distinguish between sufficient, necessary, and contributing causes (or conditions).[44] In an historical account a sufficient cause is one that the historian believes itself explains why something happened. For example,

---

[41] Jordanova, *History in Practice*, pp. 101, 171. For a theoretical position, see Jeroen van Bouwel and Erik Weber, "A Pragmatist Defense of Non-relativistic Explanatory Pluralism in History and Social Science," *History and Theory* 47 (2008): 168–182.

[42] See, for example, Ola Halldén, "On the Paradox of Understanding History in an Educational Setting," in *Teaching and Learning in History*, ed. Gaea Leinhardt, Isabel L. Beck, and Catherine Stainton (Hillsdale, NJ: Lawrence Erlbaum, 1994), pp. 27–46, here p. 35. Halldén was writing about schoolchildren, but in my experience this tendency has changed little by college age. Peter Stearns found much the same pattern; see *Meaning over Memory*, p. 158. There are similar findings in Avishag Reisman, "Teaching the Historical Principle of Contextual Causation: A Study of Transfer in Historical Reading," in *Interpersonal Understanding in Historical Context*, ed. Matthias Martens, Ullrike Hartmann, Michael Sauer, and Marcus Hasselhorn (Rotterdam: Sense, 2009), pp. 43–60, here p. 46. For an interesting discussion of causation and cognitive development, see Chris Husbands, *What Is History Teaching? Language, Ideas and Meaning in Learning about the Past* (Buckingham: Open University Press, 1996), p. 36.

[43] For a discussion of research confirming this view, see Arthur Chapman, "Causal Explanation," in *Debates in History Teaching*, 2nd edition, ed. Ian Davies (London: Routledge, 2017), pp. 130–143, esp. p. 132.

[44] I draw here from Fairburn, *Social History*, pp. 89–91.

a Marxist history of the French Revolution might hold that the expanding social and economic power of the French middle classes made revolution inevitable. An historian interested in disease biology might argue that the Aztec and Inca empires collapsed and were conquered by the Spanish conquistadors because European invaders brought with them devastating diseases like smallpox. An historian who believes that technology is the driver of historical events might argue that European empires expanded in the late nineteenth century because advances in European weapons technologies gave them overwhelming military superiority. In contrast, a necessary cause is one that the historian believes had to be present for the outcome to occur but would not have by itself caused that outcome. For example, an historian might argue that the growth of the middle classes was a necessary cause of the French Revolution, but not a sufficient one because other conditions had to be in place as well to bring revolution about – for example a financial crisis of the French state due to its long involvement in imperial wars. Finally, a cause that is neither necessary nor sufficient might nevertheless be important in shaping the course of events – it might be a contributing cause. For example, an historian might argue that the rise of the French middle class and the financial crisis of the French state together explain the outbreak of the French Revolution. These two necessary causes add up to a sufficient cause. But the historian could also argue that the precise timing and course of the revolution was shaped by other factors. Those might include the poor harvest of 1788, the ideas of the radical philosophes, the example of the American Revolution, the radicalization of the urban poor, the course of the military conflict with Europe's monarchies, and so on and so forth.

It should be obvious that in a sense the assumption of the historicist position is effectively that everything is a contributing cause. Every historical development is shaped by the entire "web" of the historical context. And rather than establishing a *hierarchy* of causes (most important, less important, least important), the historicist aims to understand the *complex interaction* of causal factors that shaped an historical development or event. What is important is not *degree* of causation, but *kind* of causation – that is, not "how much" a particular feature of the historical situation caused an outcome, but in what *ways* it shaped developments. For example, from the historicist point of view, the French Revolution is not "a" revolution, caused like other revolutions by some specific factor or condition or combination of factors or conditions. It is "the" French Revolution, one specific phenomenon with its own complex, intricate, specific history, or "story." To explain why it unfolded precisely in the unique way that it did one has to understand a vast array of relevant factors, forces, conditions, people, and events, all of which contributed to making it what it was, specifically and uniquely.

In contrast, an historian attracted to the social-science approach to History will likely be much more at home with this schema for dealing with multiple causation. For example, a Marxist historian might argue that all the "Atlantic Revolutions" of the late eighteenth and early nineteenth centuries in America, Holland, France, and Latin America are explained by the sufficient cause of the rise of the bourgeoisie to social power. Further, the Marxist position that all "bourgeois revolutions" (those caused by the rise of the middle class) result in the creation of a certain legal regime of property relations and ultimately in the creation of some form of representative government can be argued to explain much about the policy structure developed by postrevolutionary states in the nineteenth century. Similarly, our historian of disease might argue that imperial states cannot survive the dislocation caused by catastrophic epidemics – and argue, for example, that the Roman Empire collapsed because of a series of epidemics from the mid third century on, or that the decline of the Mughal Empire in India was caused by outbreaks of bubonic plague starting in the early seventeenth century. Our historian of imperial weapons technology would argue that imperial conquests will occur wherever stark differentials in military technology emerge, so that, for example, the conquest of the Americas was actually caused not by disease but by the superior armor and firearms of Europeans. In this kind of determinist scheme, contributing causes can be understood as merely helping to shape the particular *ways* in which events played out.

A second way of organizing our thinking about multiple causation is chronologically – into underlying, long-term, medium-term, short-term, and proximate (near-term) causes or triggering events. For example, we might view as long-term causes of the French Revolution the rise of the bourgeoisie; rural overpopulation and the gradual subdivision of peasant-owned land into smaller and smaller farms, closer and closer to the margin of subsistence; or the long-term drift of the nobility into cities, eroding social ties between elite and masses in the countryside. These processes can be traced back to origins or early stages perhaps as much as two centuries before the Revolution. The financial crisis of the French state would be a medium-term cause, brought on by almost constant imperial warfare that began in the late seventeenth century and intensified in the late eighteenth century. Profound shifts in political and social philosophy since the 1730s or 1740s – the Enlightenment – might be regarded as another medium-term cause. The poor harvest of 1788 would be a short-term cause. A triggering event would be the summoning of the Estates General to try to resolve the financial crisis of the monarchy. In the case of the conquest of Latin America, a long-term cause might be the emergence of traditions of crusade and conquest in Iberia in the course of the confrontation between Christian and Muslim states there since the seventh century; a medium-term cause might be the development of new weapons and military doctrines in Europe in the course of the late fifteenth and early sixteenth centuries; a proximate cause might be the catastrophic spread of epidemic disease shortly after first contact between Europe and the Americas. A long-term cause of decolonization after World War II would be the emergence of nationalist movements in European empires in the course of the late nineteenth and early twentieth centuries; a medium-term cause would be World War I and the Great Depression, both of which strained the administrative and financial systems of imperial rule; a proximate cause would be World War II, for example, the Japanese conquest of Southeast Asia, which gave nationalists unprecedented opportunities to consolidate their position in multiple different societies (e.g., the Philippines, Indonesia, Viet Nam).

As a third way of thinking about multiple causation, historians have developed their own complex informal vocabulary for discussing complex relationships among causal factors, one that encompasses most elements of these first two. The number of terms in this vocabulary is very large, and different historians use different terms; but we can give a few examples that will convey the purpose of this loose vocabulary, which is to allow us to speak about causation in complex ways, and without necessarily establishing a hierarchy of causes by importance. Again, it is the complex relationship between multiple causes that is important.

Historians speak, for example, of "underlying" causes, meaning stable, long-term conditions that made an outcome (a development, an event) possible, but did not in any direct sense "cause" it. An example would be the relative stagnation of agricultural technology in early modern Europe, which made raising productivity per acre of land difficult or impossible. This was what made population growth in the countryside a problem – "overpopulation." Another example might be long-term climatic cycles, which have been invoked as a cause of the "general crisis of the seventeenth century" in various parts of the world – a period of widespread political, population, economic, and cultural instability. Such underlying conditions do not determine that any particular thing had to or could not happen, much less happen the way it did, but they are often understood to be decisive characteristics of an historical situation.

"Enabling" causes, in contrast, are conditions that had to be present in order for something to happen, but again did not determine that it would happen, or that it would happen the way it did. Generally historians mean by this term that once certain other conditions were met, an enabling cause influenced the outcome in a particular direction. For example, the French Revolution started as a political conflict between the French nobility and the monarchy, caused by the king's financial needs and demands. Once that political crisis arose, important divisions within the nobility "enabled" the emergence of a popular revolution, a radical political movement among the Third Estate of non-nobles. To take another example, one could argue that political and social conflicts generated by the penetration of Christianity into non-European societies in many cases enabled European conquest, whether by weakening local states or by providing a reason/pretext for armed intervention to protect Christian populations. A good example would French intervention to protect Catholics in Viet Nam, which was a feature of the period of French conquest from the 1850s through the 1880s. On the other hand, the spread of Christianity in Korea was one factor enabling the emergence of nationalist resistance against the Japanese regime there, because Christians had religious reasons to be less able to reconcile themselves to Japanese rule.

Some historians speak of "conditions of possibility" that either prevent or permit developments. For example, the existence of the politically and socially radical lower- and lower-middle class sans-culottes of Paris was a condition of possibility for the emergence of the radical Jacobin revolutionary movement in the French Revolution; without them, the more middle-class Jacobins would not have been able to lever the more moderate revolutionaries out of government. Or perhaps we could regard the development of more advanced weapons technologies in the mid nineteenth century Europe as a condition of possibility for the rapid expansion of European empires from the 1860s onward. It made such conquests politically and economically feasible because it lowered the cost of imperial expansion. In neither case did these conditions of possibility make it inevitable that things would happen as they did, but they were elements of the constellation of causes that made it possible for things to happen as they did. In other cases, though, the absence of conditions of possibility limits possible outcomes. For example, the French Revolution could not have led to the emergence of a socialist regime because, despite the presence of some philosophical radicals and radical conspiracies, there was no powerful social constituency that would have favored such an outcome.

In other cases historians invoke "contingent" causes – effectively, influences external to the local historical situation that intervened to influence developments there. An example would be natural disasters such as epidemics or floods. Often the specific impact of such events is determined by underlying conditions. For example, limits on agricultural technology and productivity established permanent nutritional deficiencies that made disease more lethal. Enabling conditions may also play a role – for example, local wars disrupted food production and distribution, turning a challenging cyclical poor harvest into a food-supply disaster. Conditions of possibility may also come into play, for example, where the development of long-range transportation technologies and commercial networks permitted a very rapid spread of diseases, overwhelming limited available preventive methods. Arguments like these have, for example, shaped our understanding of the great influenza pandemic of 1918, which may have been enabled by gigantic troop movements during World War I, rendered more lethal by the nutritional deficits created in many parts of the world by the war's disruption of food supply and distribution, and encouraged by means of transport that outran the administrative capacity for containment of disease through quarantine measures. These factors don't explain why the pandemic happened, but they help us understand why it happened in the devastating way that it did.

It can be helpful to students to point out that these different organizing schema often articulate well with each other. "Long-term" causes are often "necessary" causes, or "conditions of possibility"; medium-term causes are often sufficient or enabling; short-term causes are often contingent or contributing. Further, I think it can be helpful to point out that complexes of multiple causation evolve over time. Historical explanation can be dynamic, in the sense that one constellation of causal factors can interact to create a particular change, which then becomes an element of a new complex of causal factors that lead to a further outcome, which creates new causal elements in a further complex or web of causation, and so on. In some cases outcomes may constitute "short-term" or even in a sense "contingent" factors – such as hyperinflation or the disruption of transport networks by war. In others they can become "long-term structural" factors such as the federal character of the United States.

The pedagogical purpose of familiarizing students with organizing schemes like this is to enable them to grapple with the complexity of human affairs – of societies – and of causation in them. More than that, though, it is to come to see their own understanding of the past as provisional, perspectival, and open-ended by inviting them to *refine*, *elaborate*, and *articulate* their understanding of causation in any historical context. Again, this is a defining characteristic of the discipline: that it seeks not closure but deepening and widening understanding. Each of these schema offers us guidelines for pursuing that broader and more precise inquiry.

3.4 Productive Uncertainties

In Chapter 2, I suggested that because History is an inquiry-driven discipline it often sees uncertainty as productive, in that it generates questions. Obviously, the way that historians usually think about explanation is directly related to this understanding of the usefulness of uncertainty. In the course of developing a complex, deeply contextualized account of an historical development, historians are very likely to find that they actually do not have a clear explanation for certain events. One of the great benefits of coming to know something in History is that in doing so we clarify what it is that we do not know. The more we learn, the more – and more precise – questions we have. In History explanation, understanding, is not an end point but a process. Often we learn that things happened a particular way, and we don't know why – because we lack the right evidence, for example, or because the situation was simply too complex to sort out the relative importance of causal factors, or because we do not yet understand what people thought they were doing. Because History as a discipline aims not primarily at actionable results but at deepening inquiry and understanding, this situation confronts students of History very frequently.

In order to make this kind of uncertainty or ignorance productive for our students, once again we need to give it some structure. Historians have developed several effective ways of giving structure to uncertainty.

One is to revert to the concept of the predominance of the evidence. We may not be absolutely sure what caused X to happen, but overall the evidence suggests that it was Y or a combination of A and B as necessary causes, Z as an enabling factor, the underlying condition M, and so on. This is often in effect simply to say that in the case of complex overdetermination we may not be able to sort out the *exact* relationships and importance of different factors, but by widening our research we can develop a more *complete* picture of those relationships. In widening our research to establish what the preponderance of the evidence suggests, we widen and deepen our inquiry and expand our knowledge. Uncertainty becomes the engine of discovery.

A very closely related approach is to refer back to the fundamental nature of History as an interpretive and inquiry-based discipline, not one that aims for closure. In effect the historian can argue as follows: This is what happened, and here are several factors that we know influenced that outcome. We may not be able to establish a clear hierarchy of causes or establish with certainty the relationships between them. But in exploring those questions we have developed a deeper knowledge and understanding of the historical context – of that society in that period and of the people who lived in it. And this deeper and broader knowledge has thrown up new questions – perhaps unexpected or even spooky questions. When we pursue them, we will further deepen our understanding. In doing so, we are not seeking the end point of a clear answer or causal explanation; we are seeking questions that produce greater knowledge.

A third closely related approach would be to explore the implications of alternative explanations – again with an eye to furthering inquiry. We may not be able to nail down causation with great confidence. But if we assume that things unfolded for one particular reason, what would be the implications of that, what questions would it raise? What findings, driven by those questions, would make our initial assumption seem plausible or justified – or not? What if we assume that things unfolded as they did for a different reason? What questions would *that* lead us to, and what research might they motivate us to pursue? Engaging in multiple speculative investigations can lead us to develop a particularly rich and dense understanding of historical contexts, of the interrelationships and interconnections between a wide variety of facets of an historical situation.

An example of this kind of use of uncertainty is my former colleague Willard Sunderland's book *The Baron's Cloak*, about an aristocratic ethnic-German officer in the Russian Imperial Army in the decades before and during the Russian Revolution. The man in question left behind very little written record of his life. But Sunderland was able to establish his itinerary over a period of decades – where he was at what time and in what capacity (child, student, officer, commander). Through careful reconstruction of the specific historical context at those places and times, Sunderland built a rich, detailed, and illuminating picture of the Russian Empire in the late nineteenth and early twentieth centuries. His book deepens our understanding of how that complex state and society worked as a military, administrative, and social system, and of the dynamics of its unraveling under the impact of World War I. Because Sunderland did not know exactly what the subject of his biography did or experienced at most places and times, he was able to offer multiple speculative explorations of what he *might* have done or experienced, on the basis of what we do know about those times and places. In this way uncertainty about his biography becomes a vehicle for exploring and understanding the context. The result is a wonderfully informative and thought-provoking book. It is a terrific story; it offers important new insights into the nature, strengths, weaknesses, and development toward disaster of the Russian Empire as a multiethnic state. It expands our understanding of the nature of the Russian Revolution as a crisis of that far-flung empire. And it does so by engaging with events, people, and forces in places far beyond the settings usually discussed in histories, in Saint Petersburg or Moscow.[45]

Another example is Marisa J. Fuentes's *Dispossessed Lives: Enslaved Women, Violence, and the Archive*. Like Sunderland, Fuentes uses a deep exploration of historical context to reconstruct the likely or possible courses of the lives of people for whom the written record is extremely thin – in this case Black women in Barbados in the eighteenth century. There are only fleeting and fragmentary traces of these lives because the archives we have were made by people – white slave-owning society – who not only regarded them as insignificant but actively sought to silence and erase their experience and intentions, both from their own contemporary world and from posterity. In exploring what the lives of individual women may have been like, Fuentes built a powerful, complex, multilayered picture of Barbadian society in the eighteenth century. That picture includes the social geography of Barbadian communities, the legal and institutional frameworks that structured them, the economic and labor relations that shaped individual existences, and in particular the pervasive violence on which this slavery-based society was founded. That violence is reflected both in what is, and also in what is not in the historical documentary record. In that sense, Fuentes was able to "read" even the gaps in the archival record as a source of understanding.[46]

A final approach to uncertainty is simply to entertain multiple interpretive possibilities at once, without deciding that one or the other is correct. Each may offer us a valid, plausible, and productive way of thinking about the past and of how people experienced it. As English historian Arnold Toynbee put it, "the same historical event often can be analyzed

---

[45] Willard Sunderland, *The Baron's Cloak: A History of the Russian Empire in War and Revolution* (Ithaca, NY: Cornell University Press, 2014).

[46] Marisa J. Fuentes, *Dispossessed Lives: Enslaved Women, Violence, and the Archive* (Philadelphia: University of Pennsylvania Press, 2016).

legitimately in a number of different ways, each of which brings out some aspect of historical truth which is true as far as it goes, though not the whole truth."[47] Historians who can construct more than one such partial analysis will gain a deeper and more complex understanding of their subject.

An example from my own work concerns the history of divergent branches of the homosexual rights movement in early twentieth-century Germany. One branch of that movement relied largely on scientific arguments regarding the biology of gender. It held that homosexuality was a normal variant of human sexual development – not a medical pathology, not a sin or immoral, but simply a normal biological variation that was unsurprising given the course of the development of the human embryo and fetus, in which sexual differentiation occurs rather late. Many of those who favored this view were attracted to democratic, socialist, and feminist political values, all of which were tolerant of diversity and favored equal rights and freedoms. A second branch of the homosexual rights movement argued, however, that men who loved men were superior to other men, because they were hypermasculine and therefore not interested in women. Associating reproductive love with the merely animal and biological side of humanity, those who held this view argued that bonds of affection between men were the foundation of all truly human values, institutions, and activities – social solidarity, citizenship, the state, the nation, the sciences, the arts, and so on. Men in this branch of the movement were frequently openly misogynistic, regarding women as inferior and as incapable and intolerant of the kind of spiritual love men experience for each other. Many were attracted to militarism and authoritarianism as "manly" values. Some were explicitly racist. There are two ways of thinking about this divergence. One is that men in the second branch of the movement were members of a sexual minority that faced vicious prejudice and persecution by people who regarded them as "effeminate" and corrupt. They therefore sought to compensate by developing an extreme "masculinist" self-concept and sense of superiority. Another would be, though, that educated, middle-class, white homosexual men in the patriarchal society and widely misogynistic culture of early twentieth-century Germany were just that – educated, middle-class, white men in a patriarchal society and misogynist culture. Some sought alternatives to that culture. Others were attracted to misogynistic, authoritarian, militaristic, and racist values. Was the way these men thought shaped by their membership in a persecuted sexual minority, or by their membership in a privileged social minority? Both things were

---

[47] Geyl and Toynbee, "Can We Know the Pattern of the Past?" pp. 315–316.

true. But considering both ways of looking at them helps us define more clearly the dynamics of sexual politics in that historical moment.

Writing in 1957, Charles Frankel gave a more stark example. A "sixteenth century American Indian's interpretation of the meaning of Columbus' discovery of America would be different from a sixteenth-century Spaniard's and this difference reflects a real and tragic clash of interests. But both can be equally true ... from the point of view of the facts they may not be in conflict at all, since they talk about different facts." Historians who write about a particular period in order to explain outcomes (he calls them "terminal consequences") that were not of interest to earlier historians are not "rewriting history, they are writing another history."[48] Of course, we may find one such legitimate history more complete and therefore better than another. Very early in my career, for example, I reviewed a book about the welfare state in New Zealand that argued that the state policy most effective in creating a society of prosperous and self-reliant citizens in that country in the nineteenth century was that of encouraging landownership by settlers. It seemed to me that this policy was made possible by the expropriation of the indigenous Maori population, many of whom became in consequence anything but prosperous and self-reliant – on the contrary, one aim of state policy was to reduce them to dependent wage labor. "The obvious question" about the book, I wrote, "is whether an approach that separates these two histories can give us a viable understanding of colonial social policy."[49] The book was not wrong, but it only told half the story.

We can return now to the title of this chapter: What kind of stories do historians tell? They are stories that are complex, multifaceted, provisional, and open-ended. They may be incomplete, they may be speculative, and they may even offer more than one narrative of the same events. Emmanuel Akyeampong summed it up economically in 2015: History is *partial*, it is fundamentally *perspectival*, and it is inherently *plural*."[50]

But how unusual is this? This is what all human knowledge is like. The central characteristics of History as a discipline simply confront us with these irreducible characteristics of human knowledge in particularly

---

[48] Charles Frankel, "Explanation and Interpretation in History," in *Theories of History*, ed. Patrick Gardiner (New York: Free Press, 1959), pp. 408–427, here p. 421.
[49] Edward Ross Dickinson, "Liberalism with a Vengeance? Three Books on Social Policy in New Zealand," *Kotare* 2 (1999): pp. 48–56, here p. 51.
[50] Emmanuel Akyeampong, "AHR Conversation: Explaining Historical Change; or, The Lost History of Causes," *American Historical Review* 120:4 (2015), pp. 1369–1423, here p. 1400 (emphasis in the original).

undeniable form. None of this is a problem – not even a pedagogical problem. These characteristics of the kind of knowledge and of understanding History produces are one of the great pedagogical strengths of the discipline.

Chapter 4 will expand on this point by suggesting that for the most part the classic problems of research and interpretation with which historians wrestle are in fact opportunities. The weaknesses of History are the strengths of History.

CHAPTER 4

What Kinds of Problems Do Historians Solve?

4.1 Some Common Problems of Historical Research and Interpretation

Historical research and interpretation pose a range of quite specific problems related to the nature of the discipline itself. History is neither an experimental nor an observational discipline. Unlike natural scientists (and some social scientists, for example, psychologists) historians cannot perform experiments to see how human societies work. And unlike social scientists (and some natural scientists, like ethologists who study animal behavior in the wild) they cannot observe history happening outside the laboratory either. As those interested in epistemology (the study of ways of knowing things) often say, History with a capital H has no direct access to history with a lowercase h. Instead, it has access only to traces left over from the past – most often documents, but also works of art, the memory of participants still alive, buildings, skeletal remains, and so forth. Translated into the terms I have adopted here: History is not history. While a few historians and philosophers of history certainly have hoped and longed for the creation of a scientific and objective History, this is how the overwhelming majority have understood their discipline.[1] History is an interpretive discipline and what it interprets is not the past, but the available evidence remaining from the past.

There has been remarkable consistency in this majority view for a century and a half. German historian Gustav Droysen wrote in 1868 that "past events lie before us no longer directly ... we cannot restore them 'objectively,' but can only frame out of the 'sources' a more or less

---

[1] For examples of the aspiration to create a scientific and objective History, see "Positivistic History and Its Critics: Buckle and Droysen," in *Varieties of History*, ed. Fritz Stern (New York: Vintage, 1972 [1956]), pp. 121–137, and, in the same volume, "History and the Social Sciences: Cochran and Hofstadter," pp. 348–359 and "History as a Science: Bury," pp. 210–223.

subjective apprehension [understanding – ERD] ... of them."[2] Ninety-nine years later G. R. Elton called History "not the study of the past but rather the study of present traces of the past."[3] Twenty years on from that, in 1987, C. Behan McCullagh refined the point: Historians "do not ... tell us about the past at all; rather, they tell us only what they find in evidence about the past" – and indeed not even that but rather "their inferences from the evidence."[4] After the passage of another three decades, postmodernist historian Alun Munslow wrote that History is "authorial," meaning that historians present their interpretation of the sources, not certain or objective knowledge about the past. The History that historians recount, therefore, "is not the past," and "the past is not history" (with a capital H).[5] In 1995 Simon Schama used a particularly striking image to make the same point: Historians study "the broken, mutilated remains of ... the documented past" and try to "restore it to life," always "painfully aware of their inability ever to reconstruct a dead world in its completeness," however thorough or revealing their documentation.[6] The density, kind, and character of sources available to historians will vary radically from period to period and society to society. But it will always be fragmentary and partial, specifically in the sense of having been produced by the limited number of people who played roles that left documentary or physical traces.

R. J. Collingwood used a particularly apt metaphor for the challenges History poses in a book on *The Idea of History*, published in 1946. The historian's knowledge of the past, he wrote, is "mediated or inferential or indirect," always "a web of imaginative construction stretched between certain fixed points" provided by the evidence. The historian always selects and interprets evidence on the basis of his/her own assumptions, hypotheses, hunches, or theories. The historian "is always selecting, simplifying, schematizing, leaving out what he thinks unimportant and putting in what he regards as essential."[7] And the "fixed points" of the historian's evidence are themselves always potentially biased or misleading because they were created and then also preserved by people in the past, who made their own selective choices based on their own interests and perspectives. As Christopher Blake pointed out in 1955, this "raises the possibility of

---

[2] "Positivistic History and Its Critics," p. 140.   [3] Elton, *Practice of History*, p. 9.
[4] C. Behan McCullagh, "The Truth of Historical Narratives," *History and Theory* 26:4 (1987): 30–46, here p. 43.
[5] Alun Munslow, "History, Skepticism and the Past," *Rethinking History* 21:4 (2017): 474–488, here pp. 476, 477.
[6] Schama, *Dead Certainties*, p. 319.   [7] Collingwood, *The Idea of History*, pp. 282, 242, 236.

a kind of double subjectivity in the material as finally employed" by the historian.[8]

Out of these fragmentary and biased sources and recognizing the potentially biased character of their own perspectives, historians must offer a coherent, plausible, persuasive perspective. That task presents daunting challenges. Many of those challenges are not unique to History – they are common problems of handling evidence and framing questions in any field. As a complex of interrelated challenges posed by the specific nature of History, however, they form a distinctive set of difficulties and imperatives for historians. This complex of problems is sufficiently common and familiar that historians have developed a range of ways of addressing them. In each case, the solutions that historians adopt are themselves important techniques of historical research and thinking; that is to say, again, that the solutions historians have developed turn these familiar problems into intellectual opportunities.

In what follows – drawing extensively on the work of my former colleague Miles Fairburn – I will describe five of these common problems of historical research and historical interpretation in order to illustrate that process of turning challenges into opportunities.[9] My aim here is to give a few examples of the central point: The particular problems of History are its particular strengths.

4.1.1 Problem 1: Availability Bias

A first very common problem that the fragmentary and partial nature of their sources creates is what historians call "availability bias," of which there are three distinct forms. One important form enters historians' work when the research questions they develop (regarding a particular development, topic, society, person, or period) are defined by the available sources. This is of course a pervasive and indeed almost unavoidable challenge. In the absence of adequate sources relevant to a topic, we may not even know what precisely to ask about it. As Paul Veyne put it, if fragmentary sources "dictate the questions to us," they may "not only leave us in ignorance of many things, but ... also leave us ignorant of the fact that we are

---

[8] Christopher Blake, "Can History Be Objective?" in *Theories of History*, ed. Patrick Gardiner (New York: Free Press, 1959), pp. 329–343, here p. 330.
[9] Miles Fairburn's *Social History* is one of the more useful practical discussions available; this chapter draws on it in some detail.

ignorant."[10] But even if we can formulate a clear question, it is very difficult to investigate a topic if we have no relevant historical evidence; and few historians want to undertake a research project that is likely to yield no significant or clear findings. Historians naturally tend to choose topics for which they know there will be adequate sources to support intensive research and interpretation. Yet it is of essential importance for a deep and broad understanding of past societies that we formulate questions about them that do require that we work harder and be more creative in generating answers. As just one very obvious case, urban society tends to generate more historical evidence (particularly but not exclusively documents) than rural society, and yet until the late twentieth century most societies on earth were primarily rural. If we want to understand those societies, we must find ways to develop and answer productive questions about what was happening in the countryside.

This brings us to a second form of availability bias, related not to the choice of topics to investigate, but to developing interpretations of those topics. Because historical interpretations need to be based on evidence, we naturally tend to become absorbed in research in the sources that are most rich and accessible. But in countless cases, those easily available sources will offer us only a very limited perspective on an historical development or period. Usually, they will tell us what privileged people thought, how they lived their lives, what they did, and how they understood their world. Less-privileged people do not produce as much historical evidence – and certainly not as much evidence that gets classified by governments, archivists, courts, libraries, and other institutions as worthy of preservation. To give an example, the urban poor left far fewer records than more privileged people. But they have always been the great majority of city dwellers; we need to know about them or we cannot understand cities at all. And this is true not only of cities. We know a very great deal about propertied families in the past because they left many kinds of records; we know a great deal less about the families of poor and working people because they did not. But most people in the past were poor. We really can't speak of "seventeenth-century family life," for example, unless we gain at least some understanding of what the families of poor people were like. Similarly, very frequently the most easily available historical sources will have been generated or preserved by national, regional, or local governments; by other major social institutions (such as religious or professional

---

[10] Paul Veyne, *Writing History: Essay on Epistemology*, trans. Minna Moore-Rinvolucri (Middletown, CT: Wesleyan University Press, 1984), p. 13.

organizations); by educated and well-to-do people in positions of power and responsibility (academics, functionaries of government, business leaders, aristocrats and plutocrats, religious officials); or by well-to-do people with the kinds of social connections that leave evidentiary traces – such as business accounts, private letters, diaries, wills and testaments, or buildings or artworks of sufficient value to preserve. But most of the lives of most people, in most of history, played out beyond the purview of these institutions. As American historian H. S. Commager remarked in 1965, in most cases "the record of the past, as we have it, is monstrously lopsided."[11]

To avoid having their understanding of the past shaped by these privileged perspectives, historians must assess their sources critically and with great care. They must consider who or what institutions produced the sources and what they were or were not interested in, what biases or prejudices or perspective might be reflected in them, what they might have left out of the story entirely, or what they might have interpreted in particular ways that conformed to their own purposes or interests or perspective. To give just one example, historians of crime have available to them for the most part sources produced by legal systems, or in more recent period by the media. Criminals themselves have in general left behind very little direct evidence. But to understand crime, we need to know about both.

To give a brief example of my own work, in writing about crimes against morality in nineteenth-century Germany I found that the national crime statistics reported numbers of convictions for offenses relating to prostitution as defined by the national criminal code. But they did not report on minor breaches of police regulations regarding prostitution. Those numbers are quite hard to find – some larger cities reported them, but they are not available for the whole country. The national crime statistics therefore create a completely skewed picture of the gendered enforcement of the law. In 1894, for example, in the city of Berlin alone there were twice as many women arrested for misdemeanor violation of police regulations regarding prostitution as there were people convicted of all other offenses against morality in the entire country (including public indecency, incest, child sexual abuse, sexual assault, etc.). If we were to judge by the national statistics, about three quarters of those convicted of morality offenses were men; if we were to include just the misdemeanor figures for Berlin alone, two thirds were women. It is true that penalties for most morality

---

[11] Commager, *Nature and the Study of History*, p. 44.

offenses reported in the national statistics were much more severe than for misdemeanor violations of police regulations. Nevertheless, the available statistics on these misdemeanors give us a completely different perspective on the gendered nature of law enforcement in the area of sexual morality in Germany in this period. Viewed from the perspective of the national statistics, the law in this area appears to have primarily aimed to control male misbehavior. Viewed from the perspective of the local misdemeanor statistics, it was used above all to harass, persecute, and (as we know from frequent vice-squad scandals) sometimes financially and sexually exploit women. But this is not all. Under German law abortion was categorized as a crime against life, not against morality. If we add convictions of women for this offense to our own category of crimes related to sexuality and reproduction (rather then using the contemporary category of crimes against morality), the picture skews even further toward the policing of women rather than of men – and for this crime, penalties were quite severe.[12]

(A small aside here: The concept of availability bias is quite different from the "availability heuristic." The latter holds that we can solve problems well enough for most practical purposes by relying on the most easily available and plentiful forms of information, since that information is likely to reflect common or pervasive patterns. The use of the availability heuristic is exactly what historians' concern with availability bias seeks to avoid.)

A third form of availability bias is less glaring but can be very important. Often the historical evidence most readily available relates to those aspects of an historical situation or of a life that were most politically charged, most publicly visible, most controversial, or have become over time most familiar to historians, and so have been preserved in greatest abundance and are most readily accessible. If we approach a situation or a person not from this better-known angle, but from another perspective, we not infrequently find quite surprising things. To give just one minor example from my own work, many years ago I investigated the puzzle of what seemed like a particularly odd relationship between women in Germany's liberal women's rights movement and women in that country's conservative Protestant women's movement. On the issue of the vote for women, these two groups were opposed – liberals for, conservatives against. On issues of sexual morality, though, they were in considerable degree aligned,

---

[12] See Edward Ross Dickinson, "Policing Sex in Germany, 1882–1982: A Preliminary Statistical Analysis," *Journal of the History of Sexuality* 16 (2007): 204–250, here p. 218.

in particular in their rejection of the sexual radicalism of some socialist women. To understand how the alliance between them could work and what its implications were, I had to look beyond the sources that most historians had examined and that most of their contemporaries had been interested in – which was what liberal women said in the journals and meetings of women's organizations and what conservative women said in religious journals edited by men. I looked instead at the less readily available and less extensive record of what liberal women said in their religious organizations and publications (and also in private correspondence and memoirs), and at what conservative women said in private meetings. In private, conservative women were often ambivalent or positive about women's suffrage. In their religious organizations, liberal women were not just liberal advocates of women's rights; they were liberal *Protestant* advocates of women's rights. Their understanding of the importance of women's rights was explicitly religious in nature. Once that became obvious, it also became clear that the women involved actually had not at all turned their backs on their liberal political principles when they allied themselves with more conservative Protestant women, as some historians had argued. They just understood those political principles in explicitly Protestant terms.[13]

It should be obvious that the challenge of availability bias – in all three forms – is particularly serious for historians attracted to the more uncompromisingly historicist approach to History. It is of course far easier to "immerse" oneself in a rich, plentiful body of sources than in sources that are scant, fragmentary, and only indirectly relevant to one's topic. This means that historians who think that such immersion is both the proper method and the greatest pleasure of doing History will gravitate toward topics and questions for which larger bodies of evidence are available. Obviously, this almost inevitably leads a narrowing of the field of inquiry to those topics that seemed relevant or interesting to those groups of people who produced and preserved the largest bodies of historical evidence.

The problem of availability bias thus very nicely illustrates the argument of historians more attracted to social theory – that a theoretically informed empiricism is actually a *better* empiricism. It is more exhaustive in its approach to the sources, not less so, and it is more open to a wider range of questions.

---

[13] Edward Ross Dickinson, "Dominion of the Spirit over the Flesh: Religion and Sexuality in the German Women's Movements before 1914," *Gender and History* 17 (2005): 1–32.

4.1 Some Common Problems of Historical Research

More empiricist historians of course argue that the methods they prefer offer their own forms of corrective for availability bias. One is that the empiricist tradition demands that historians – as E. H. Carr observed in 1961 – consider "all known or knowable facts [or sources – ERD] relevant, in one sense or another, to the theme" they are investigating.[14] That requires historians to go beyond the readily available sources, beyond the more obviously directly relevant sources, and beyond a narrow definition of the event, development, or life under investigation to consider its broad historical and social context. Informed by a broad understanding of that context, historians must be imaginative in thinking about where they might find sources that, though more scarce, fragmentary, and difficult to interpret, do reveal important aspects of the historical situation that the "easier" sources ignore or represent only from a particular, perhaps biased perspective. This can require historians to read a very great deal of scholarly work on their period in order to gain a broader understanding of the historical context. That may include reading not only about the society they are interested in, but about other societies, similar or different, in the same or different time periods, to expose them to the kinds of questions that historians of other places and times have asked. It most certainly will mean reading work from subfields in which they are not particularly interested – say, an historian of gender reading military history, or a military historian reading social history, or an urban historian reading religious history. An empiricist approach cannot be a narrow approach, and to be guided by what is in the sources requires that one be deeply informed about the context in which they were created.

Further, historians must use both their critical capacity and imagination to try to figure out what parts of the story are missing from the easily available sources. Whose perspective is represented in those sources – what social group, what institution, what cultural tradition, what intellectual community? What would they have ignored, discounted, been unaware of? Who might have had a different perspective, different experience and knowledge? Historians might need considerable ingenuity and imagination to figure out what people, institutions, or organizations *not* represented in the readily available sources might have left alternative documentary (or visual, or material) traces of *their* experiences and views, and where those traces might be preserved.

Beyond widening the search for relevant sources, though, it is often fruitful for historians to widen the search for productive topics. Historians with informed historical imaginations may arrive at relevant research

---

[14] Edward Hallett Carr, *What Is History?* (New York: MacMillan, 1961), p. 22.

questions by considering not only what is in the sources and in the scholarly literature, but also what is *not* in them. On the one hand, seeing what institutions, individuals, or organizations did *not* keep records of, or what elements of an historical situation or of a life are *not* reflected in the obviously relevant sources, can tell us something important about them and direct us to pursue research on *that* topic. We can adopt the landscape-gardening principle of "negative space," in which one's attention is drawn to the spaces left blank. Where the more readily available sources do *not* take us, and where the scholarly literature has *not* gone, is where we should go.

It is just here, though, that a more theory-oriented, social-science approach can help us most in avoiding availability bias – particularly where we draw on *multiple* theoretical frameworks or traditions. Theoretical approaches borrowed from other disciplines can lead us to formulate questions without regard to the availability of sources. Having identified such a question as important, we then must go digging for the sources that will allow us to build an answer – or go digging in sources seemingly only indirectly relevant for information that *is* directly relevant. Literary theory and literary analysis can help us read texts "against the grain" – that is, not for the information that the author sought to convey about a particular topic, but for the information on other topics that the author revealed without intending to say anything about them – topics such as (to give just one example), the biases of people in the author's class or social group, or the nature and sources of their knowledge of the world. Historians may be guided to alternative and less obvious kinds of sources by becoming familiar with the kinds of sources scholars in other disciplines use. For example, most historians are drawn primarily to texts, but quantitative sources of the kinds that economists or demographers use (price lists, census data, or financial data) may illuminate a question in ways the available texts cannot. Drawing on multiple theories, from multiple disciplines, can help make historians' thinking about what they are doing more flexible, and it can broaden their understanding of what they might investigate, what needs explaining. In short, again: Historians who are open to the usefulness of theory are likely to be better historicists, with a broader and deeper understanding of the specific historical contexts they are investigating.

4.1.2 Problem 2: Confirmation Bias

The concept of confirmation bias is deceptively simple. It refers to the tendency to find the evidence that one expects to find – the evidence that confirms one's hypothesis. But there are at least three different ways in which this can happen, ranging from the obvious to the more subtle.

The most obvious of these three forms is simply "cherry-picking" evidence that confirms one's expectations. One way to do that is by making use only of evidence produced from a particular perspective – say, only the current-events reporting and editorial views expressed in Catholic newspapers, or only the speeches at Socialist Party conferences. More common, though, is "mining" sources for what confirms one's expectations. An example would be an historian combing through texts for those quotes that perfectly summarize the point the historian has decided to argue, while not considering (or presenting to her reader) the whole content and import of the text. A third example would be consulting only data that confirms one's initial hypothesis. Our historian might, for instance, study only a case or cases (a community, region, or group) likely to confirm her assumptions or theories. Or she might look only at those particular categories of the available evidence that do so. To give a case already used in this chapter: If we examine only statistics relevant to those crimes classified under German law in 1900 as "crimes against morality" we might argue that the legal system was tilting steadily toward what Dutch historian Pieter Spierenburg called the "criminalization of men" in the late nineteenth and early twentieth centuries. By that he meant the intensifying use of the criminal law to discipline men's violent and antisocial behaviors, many of them long sanctioned by custom.[15] If we add crimes against life (abortion) and misdemeanors (breaches of police regulations regarding prostitution), however, this argument becomes untenable. A final variant of this form of confirmation bias has to do not with how one approaches the sources, but with how one approaches other historians' scholarly work. It is all too easy to read the work of historians whose interests and views are aligned with one's own and ignore or dismiss as boring or wrongheaded the work of those with whom one is less in sympathy or agreement.

A second pattern of confirmation bias is less obvious. When an historical question is too narrow, it can restrict the range of kinds of answers historians will arrive at. If one asks "was it A or B that caused C?" it is sometimes easy not to consider D, E, or F as possible contributing factors and instead do one's best to answer the question as posed. If one asks "was X an example of the broader category Y, or of the category Z?" it is sometimes easy not to consider that it was actually an example of A, or

---

[15] See Peter Spierenburg, *Men and Violence: Gender, Honor, and Rituals in Modern Europe and America* (Columbus: Ohio State University Press, 1998), pp. 198, 200, 201, 204, 206, 209.

that neither X nor Y really fit well. Having posed the question in this way, one does one's best to determine which is the best fit, X or Y. Yes/no questions in particular tend to create this kind of narrowing of inquiry and conceptualization.

To give an example from my own work, in 2016 I took part in a published debate regarding whether a conservative backlash against changes in the law concerning sexuality and reproduction contributed to the undermining of the democratic Weimar Republic and its replacement by the Nazi dictatorship in Germany. My response was that this yes/no question did not do justice to the complexity of that particular history. Multiple backlashes and revolutionary agendas were at work, I argued, reflecting the aims of multiple ideological and social groups – including communists, Catholics, fascists, trade-union socialists, and radical socialists influenced by anarchism. The cross-cutting conflicts they created cannot be read as simply as a matter of "democracy, for or against?"[16]

A final form of confirmation bias overlaps considerably with availability bias: looking at a limited set of sources that restrict the possible findings to a particular range. Suppose, for example, that our historian found that in Germany around 1900 many members of the Christian clergy believed that a decline in participation in organized religion was the cause of a decline in young people's respect for parental authority, resulting in more family conflicts and higher delinquency rates. She might then look at the publications of the Christian churches on the "youth problem," rates of participation in the sacraments (baptism, confirmation, marriage), membership in religious youth groups, and statistics on youth crime and participation in organized religion in particular communities in order to determine whether this were true. She would likely find confirmation of her hypothesis in such sources. With regard to the statistical sources, for example, probably she would find that youth criminality was rising in urban areas where religious participation was falling. But if she consulted statistics on youth employment and wages, she might posit a very different explanation for complaints about disrespect, rebelliousness, and disorder among young people. For example, probably youth participation in the paid labor force would also be highest in those same urban communities. Was it actually growing financial independence among young people that commentators

---

[16] Edward Ross Dickinson, "'Was There a Backlash against Weimar's Sexual Politics?' Some Further Reflections," Weimar Studies Network, May 12, 2016, https://weimarstudies.wordpress.com/2016/05/12/guest-post-edward-dickinson-on-weimars-sexual-politics-and-the-backlash-thesis/#more-1542.

4.1 Some Common Problems of Historical Research

found threatening? Was rising labor-force participation the cause of falling religious participation?

Whereas historicists are particularly susceptible to availability bias, obviously confirmation bias is a particularly important issue for historians who take a more theory-driven approach to their work. A scholar who has already formulated a reasonably firm expectation, based on a particular theoretical perspective, may well be inclined to find it confirmed by his/her evidence. It is very easy to see those quotations or telling statistics that will make one's point well, while overlooking those that make things more complicated. An historian who has formulated a very specific question derived from a particular theoretical framework is less likely to modify, broaden, or abandon that question when confronted with sources that lead in other directions – or never to look at them at all. And an historian with a deep interest in a particular theoretical perspective is likely to spend a great deal of time reading of works that elaborate and explore it and less time reading works guided by other theoretical perspectives.

How do historians try to correct for confirmation bias? One simple principle of historical practice is to treat documents and bodies of documents as wholes, not as "mines" from which the particular nuggets one likes can be extracted without reference to the whole. Historical documents must be understood in their entirety and internal coherence; one must understand the concepts in them, the relationships between them, their structure and organization, the hierarchy of importance of different elements within them, and so on. This is essentially the hermeneutic approach – historians must understand the sources on their own terms, not impose their own meanings on them. It is an important antidote to the most obvious and tempting form of confirmation bias, "cherry-picking" or "source mining" the helpful bits from sources and ignoring the rest.

Again, more uncompromising historicists would go a step further and argue that while it is fine for historians to start their research or reading of a document with a vague or provisional hypothesis, what they find in the sources themselves should guide them in reformulating, refining, or even completely changing their research questions. That would mean approaching whole bodies of documents in hermeneutical fashion, in their entirety and internal coherence. It also means following the trail of one's research to other bodies of documents – being open to following up curious leads that might prove merely tangential, but might also modify or refine our understanding by yielding a new and unexpected perspective on the issues. This is a corrective to the second form of confirmation bias, in which the research question itself restricts the range of possible answers. Following the sources to one's questions creates a more open-ended form of inquiry. It may be less precise and more time-consuming, but it is less likely to limit possible conclusions.

Finally, and closely related, it can often be helpful to examine different *kinds* of evidence. If an historian's initial research is in textual sources, it might be revealing to look also at some statistical evidence. Visual evidence – maps, photographs, cartoons – can sometimes transform our understanding of the statistical or textual sources. Or, even considering only textual sources, consulting "ego-documents" such as letters, diaries, or memoirs can radically alter the perspective one gains from publications in professional, political, or advocacy venues.

To give just one example from my own work, I studied a particular advocate of sexual radicalism, Helene Stöcker, for some years before I gained access to her personal papers. Stöcker was a passionate, principled, vehement radical, an advocate of the right of people to have unconventional relationships and lives. She devoted her entire life to the causes of individual freedom, peace, and nonviolence, forgoing every conventional life path, whether domestic or professional. The person I encountered in her personal papers was completely unfamiliar. She was a conventional bourgeois woman living a very privileged life. She spent a month at a spa almost every year, traveled regularly all over Europe apparently without any concern for cost, and lived a settled and comfortable domestic life in a large apartment in a very nice neighborhood in Berlin.[17] Suddenly I understood how it was that Stöcker remained throughout almost her entire life an incorrigible idealist and optimist.

There is a fourth corrective to confirmation bias, and that is simply to widen one's reading, to broaden one's "conversation" with History. Read History written from perspectives that you find objectionable. Read History shaped by theoretical approaches that you think are irrelevant, wrong, or boring. Again: The eclectic approach most historians take to social theory is not a rejection of the usefulness of theory, but a corrective to one of its potential weaknesses. Both historicists and those attracted to theoretical models – whether they are practicing historians or just people interested in history and History – need to read the work of historians on the *other* side of the historicism/theory divide. Read works in subfields you have no interest in – if you are interested in military history, read some economic history; if you are interested in social history, read some diplomatic history; if you are interested in the history of sexuality, read some art

[17] Helene Stöcker Papers, Swarthmore Peace Collection, Swarthmore College, DG 035, Boxes 1 and 10.

4.1 Some Common Problems of Historical Research

history. Wide reading will open new doors of inquiry; it will encourage a critical approach to one's own assumptions; it will alert one to the different ways that historians analyze sources and to the different sources they analyze. That in itself is a fine corrective to confirmation bias – which is, in some part, simply a form of intellectual rigidity. There is no excuse for intellectual rigidity in an historian. Rigidity is not what History does; it is not what it does for the mind.

4.1.3 Problem 3: The Environmental Fallacy

The name of this problem is a little confusing. It has nothing to do with the natural environment. Instead it refers to the potentially flawed assumption that there is a causal relationship between an historical development or event and some element in the broader historical context of the time. If the specific nature of the connection between these two elements is not determined, then we actually do not know and should not assume that they are causally connected. A third factor might have caused them both; in that case, they might be highly correlated (both present in an historical situation) without one having a causal relationship to the other. For example, the fact that consumer debt was rising in the United States in the late 1920s does not *necessarily* mean that consumer debt played a role in causing the Great Depression. We would need to establish a causal connection between the two. Alternatively, one could take the social-science approach of examining a large number of cases in which consumer debt was rising in a society. If we found multiple cases in which recession or depression did *not* follow from a rise in consumer debt, then we would not be justified in *assuming* that consumer debt played a role in causing the Great Depression in the United States.

From the standpoint of social science, in a sense the historicist approach is one giant omnidirectional environmental fallacy – what David Hackett Fischer called the "fallacy of indiscriminate pluralism."[18] Historicism assumes that it is the sum total of factors and features of any given historical situation that determines – in dynamic interaction – the outcome of that historical situation. But why make that assumption? What if we can determine that actually there was just one decisive factor? More realistically, a social scientist might argue that we arrive at a more precise understanding if we can rule out as causal or influential factors some elements of

---

[18] David Hackett Fischer, *Historians' Fallacies: Toward a Logic of Historical Thought* (New York: Harper & Row, 1970), p. 175.

the political, economic, social, or cultural context of the time, and focus on those we can actually show to have been important. In the social sciences it has become quite common to rely on coefficients of statistical correlation to tell us which factors were important and which were not. In the example of consumer debt in the Great Depression, one could build a database of economic crises and establish whether there is a strong statistical correlation between high debt levels and the likelihood of economic crisis. If not, then the notion that default on private debt caused the financial crisis in just our one particular case is questionable or at least needs to be further investigated. Short of that kind of statistical approach, however, social theory can help guide the historian in selecting which of the overwhelming number of *possible* factors and features of a given historical situation to investigate to try to uncover actual mechanisms. Theories built around multiple cases (e.g., episodes of recession or depression, or periods of rising consumer debt) can help in making the empirical approach of the historicist more targeted and efficient. For this reason, a simple counterweight to the environmental fallacy is to read more broadly in the historical literature – read about more cases of similar developments, in many different societies, perhaps even in many different periods. This will not only increase the number of cases that might call one's assumptions into question; it will also expose one to competing theoretical and interpretive frameworks, increasing the likelihood that one will think more broadly and precisely about the relationship between a particular development and the broader social context of the time.

For an historicist, the problem is simpler: Again, what was the *mechanism* that linked two elements of the historical situation? For example, if a wave of private bankruptcies and defaults precisely preceded the collapse of the financial system in 1929 and the preponderance of the evidence – such as business journalism, or government inquiries – supported the idea that default on private debt brought about the financial crisis, then it is perfectly reasonable to suppose that this was probably a decisive factor. But that would need to be established in concrete terms, for example, by examining the records of particular failed banks to see whether their bankruptcy was in fact caused by a spike in defaults on private debt.

Obviously, in the case of the environmental fallacy the advantage of engaging in both kinds of inquiry – historicist and social scientific – is particularly clear. The historicist's concern with minutiae is a fine method for discovering concrete causal mechanisms, helping eliminate the "correlation equals causation" fallacy. The social scientist's goal of establishing some rational criteria for measuring the importance of particular factors, or at the very least the potential for social-science theory to refine the scope of empirical inquiry, is a good corrective to the historicist tendency to assume that "everything explains everything" without actually *showing* that it does.

4.1.4 Problem 4: Categorization

A problem that particularly highlights the differences between the social-scientific and the historicist approach to History is that of the use of appropriate categories for analysis of the sources. This question is particularly difficult for the historian attracted to social-science approaches. If we want to understand how particular kinds of societies work, or how particular kinds of people define their interests, react to crises, or structure their lives, we have to assume the existence of general categories applicable across various times and places. For example, if we want to understand "peasant societies," or how peasants manage risk in different social and historical contexts, or whether peasant societies can be innovative and under what conditions, or what the dynamics of peasant revolutions are, we have to assume that "peasant" is a category that describes people in many different societies.

The same is true of the "middle class" or "bourgeoisie" and of bourgeois societies, bourgeois families, or bourgeois revolutions. Historians refer to the feudal ruling class, feudal societies, political and social crises of feudalism. These are terms central to various social theories (particularly but not exclusively Marxist) that historians have found useful in developing hypotheses and interpretations about developments in various societies in the past. We might refer to these as prefabricated categories of social analysis.

The obvious problem with such categories – a problem central, for example, to Dipesh Chakrabarty's critique of History as a discipline, referenced in Chapter 3 – is that they are almost all derived from European history. Their use in the analysis of other societies can all too easily bias the historian in the direction of finding that other societies were "*almost* like" European society, but not quite. That in turn all too easily creates a bias toward finding something lacking in them. Java, for example, didn't really have peasants the way France or Russia did, so it didn't have a peasant revolution. India didn't have a proper bourgeoisie, so it never had a bourgeois revolution. The Middle East *might* have started down the path to modern democracy that led through the representative institutions developed in feudal societies, but it didn't quite have a real feudal nobility, so that didn't happen. The problem with such a perspective is that what matters is not what didn't happen, but what did. Being predisposed by our theoretical apparatus to think about what was *not* there is a great way to stop ourselves from seeing what *was*.

A closely related problem with the use of such prefabricated categories is that they may not actually fit the social realities of non-European and/or non-modern societies very well. For example, I began my historical training with a primary interest in medieval Europe, and when I switched to modern history, I was stunned to find some Marxist historians describing nineteenth-century peasants as members of the "bourgeoisie" because they owned the means of production (land). This, it seems to me, is to confuse peasants with farmers – the latter a social group produced through a centuries-long and profound process of legal, cultural, economic, and social change, stretching from the sixteenth century (or perhaps the fourteenth) through the twentieth. That process included the enclosure of land and the dissolution of the legal rights and self-governing mechanisms of the peasant community, the development of regional and national markets in agricultural products, the integration of rural people into regional and national cultures, and so on and so forth. Similarly, to refer to eighteenth- or nineteenth-century Zulu or Matabele agriculturalists in South Africa simply as peasants would be to deny the specificity of social, political, and economic organization and the cultures of those societies.

In purely practical terms, further, a particularly knotty problem of historical analysis is that our prefabricated categories are very often too general to capture the dynamics of the phenomena we are investigating. Take the example of "peasant society" again. According to an influential intellectual tradition, this is a thing that exists. It is characterized by largely subsistence agriculture, limited exposure to capital and commodity markets, tightly knit local social and political organizations, highly localized or regional cultures, risk aversion and highly developed mechanisms to contain and distribute risk (e.g., land distribution, kinship ties, religious institutions), often high levels of violence (e.g., against women, children, vagrants, or neighboring villages), and so on. We can find societies in which many people fit this description all over the world, in many different centuries. And yet many people we can identify as "peasants" according to such criteria defined their own social position and roles, interests, and motivations according to quite different criteria.

For example, to what extent are a Muslim, a Catholic, and a Buddhist peasant "the same" in their interest, motivations, and thinking? To what extent are peasants in a relatively poor hill community with low degree of social stratification the same as peasants in a rich agricultural lowland with a high degree of social stratification? Development experts have discovered that giving small amounts of capital to peasant women can have a transformative impact on peasant communities, whereas giving the same money to peasant men changes little. To what extent, then, are men and women "peasants" in the same way? To what extent are peasants who are bound by law and custom to the land and required to contribute labor service to their landlords the same as peasants who are not? Are peasants who are tenants (renting the land they far for cash or as sharecroppers) the same as peasants who own some land and sell their labor to local farmers or industrial enterprises?

Historians who use the term "peasant society" are aware of all of these distinctions. But if they are layered on top of one another, one does start to wonder: How useful is the *general* concept of a peasant society? Many of the characteristics that we use to define the concept of a peasant society may be present in a given historical situation. But it can easily come to seem that those characteristics are just parts of a wider complex of contributing factors. If that is so, how helpful is it to call the society in question "a peasant society"?

A third, closely related issue is that the categories of analysis that social theory uses may not be present in the sources. This can lead historians into tortured readings of sources in order to ferret out, from the terms and categories they do use, the characteristics that interest them. Tomoko Masuzawa's *The Invention of World Religions* gives us a wonderful example.[19] The category "religion" is a specifically modern and Western one. European scholars of religion posited the existence of coherent (often "true" or "original") dogmatic structures constituting, for example, Hinduism, Islam, or Buddhism. But that was not the lived reality of those faiths, which were very diverse across broad geographies and evolved substantially over time. Of course, the same was and is true of Christianity, with its myriad so-called sects or confessions. Something similar applies to many of the basic categories by which social theory organizes its understanding of the world. The assumption that there is a distinction between something called "religion" and something called "politics," for example, is not valid for most societies and times. Neither is the assumption that there is a distinction between both of those spheres and "economics" or between all three and "private life."

To give an example from my own research, conservative Christians in late nineteenth- and early twentieth-century Germany did not make any of

---

[19] Tomoko Masuzawa, *The Invention of World Religions* (Chicago, IL: University of Chicago Press, 2005).

these distinctions. That is why, when the Great Depression came, they did not perceive it as merely an economic upheaval. They saw it as a moral crisis, a political moment of reckoning, an economic disaster, and a turning point in the history of Christianity in their society. They did not see those facets of the situation as distinct. They saw them as one integral, coherent whole. If we don't understand this, we don't understand the collapse of German democracy in 1933.

Finally, being overly committed to the importance or interest of a particular category may lead historians to ignore the ways in which many other categories interacted in a particular society. In fact, societies are so complex and our thinking about social categories is structured by so many different factors that adopting just one as one's primary conceptual tool seems foolhardy on the face of it. We can think of people as members of a regional culture, an ethnicity, a class, a gender, a nationality, a religious community, a professional group, a family network, a generation; we can classify them by education, language, health status, recreational interests, by the size of the community they live in, by the landscape they inhabit (mountains, plains, swamps, deserts), their membership in organizations, their legal status (free or unfree, noble or not, with special privileges or not), their places of origin and citizenship status, and so on and so forth. There are so many ways of thinking about people that to assert that just one outweighs all the others in importance seems not very plausible.

For the historicist and hermeneutic traditions the solution to these problems is simple. We should describe any society in the terms that people in it used to describe it, after studying in depth and detail what those terms meant to them. As G. M. Trevelyan put it in his autobiography, "we are hampered in our attempt to find out what our ancestors really thought and felt, if we try to fit them into some modern category which did not exist in their time."[20] So we should use the categories that *did* exist in their time. This can help us avoid the problem of anachronism because we do not apply to past societies terms that were developed to describe our own society and only imperfectly fit the real social circumstances of the past.

An example would be that the term "middle class(es)" was developed to describe a range of social groups in nineteenth-century European societies, including members of the professions (doctors, lawyers, some engineers, and clergy), mid-level managers and merchants, mid-level civil servants, and so forth. The middle classes are also generally held to have included the

---

[20] Trevelyan, "Bias in History," p. 77.

"bourgeoisie" or "upper-middle class" (bankers, heads of major mercantile firms, industrialists, high-level civil servants) and a "lower" or "small middle class" (office employees, small-time retailers, better-off artisans, lower clergy, etc.). But even employing this complex range of meanings does not give us categories that would adequately describe, say, the middling groups of eighteenth-century French society with its poor nobility, its village priests, its guild masters, its urban patriciate, its administrative "nobility of the robe," and so on. Even less would it give us a terminology adequate to describe the societies of nineteenth-century India, Persia, or Sumatra. The historian should therefore seek clearly to define what people meant when they used the terms *they* used, and then use *those* terms. A *zamindar* in the Mughal Empire in North India in the eighteenth century was a member of neither a "middle class" nor a "nobility" nor a "gentry"; he was a *zamindar*. The gentry of seventeenth-century England were not middle class, not aristocrats, and not "farmers" in the twenty-first-century meaning of those terms; they were gentry.

The adoption of such a radically historicist approach, however, may not actually be possible. A critically important conceptual mechanism by which we routinely identify what things are like is comparison. Marc Bloch, in his essay on *The Historian's Craft*, even argued that "there is no true understanding without a certain range of comparison."[21] Whether such a categorical statement is correct or not, certainly bringing a comparative apparatus to our examination of the available sources is an efficient way to begin to identify the characteristics of the phenomenon we are studying. Every student of history who has done any appreciable amount of reading comes to the books and the sources with a rich store of cases and categories in mind. Most professionally trained historians have also the categories and concepts central to a whole array of social theories. It may actually be impossible *not* to use that store of cases and categories as one's starting point. And why would one not? As long as one uses them heuristically, rather than imposing them on what one finds in the sources, they are useful tools. A useful tool for historians in beginning to make sense of their findings is to establish what is distinctive about those findings, relative to the available categories and cases – even if their aim is the purely historicist one of understanding the past in its own terms.

This does not mean that historians automatically assume that what they are examining falls into a familiar category or is like a familiar case. Rather, it is simply useful to begin our inquiry by comparing what the sources tell

---

[21] Marc Bloch, *The Historian's Craft* (New York: Vintage, 1953), p. 42.

us to specific cases and general categories familiar from other contexts. General categories or "ideal types" (abstract models) like "peasant" or "middle class" or "gentry" or "nobility" are useful starting points. So is our knowledge of other societies that we think are perhaps similar, or different. These are conceptual resources; they can tell us what to look for and help us identify what we are seeing. As Alun Munslow points out, without such "concepts and categories ... the complexities of the past would be inexplicable, remaining at the level of lists."[22]

This kind of use of general categories and comparative cases can also help historians widen their perspective and develop broader interpretive frameworks. To give an example, the concept of a peasant society may be very general and encompass many societies that are in important ways quite different. But that does not mean that it is not a useful category. There may have been important shared characteristics that established common dynamics among "peasant societies" in a particular period, despite the differences between them. Understanding those similarities *and* differences can then help us understand why different "peasant societies" responded in both similar and divergent ways to broader forces affecting many of them at the same time.

An example of the conceptual benefits of such an approach is an important interpretation of the violent social and political upheavals of the early twentieth century. Those violent upheavals (revolutions, wars, totalitarian violence) were partly the product of the revolutionary response of small-scale agriculturalists ("peasants") in many different societies to the economic stresses and changes the increasing integration of the world economy imposed in that period. Partly they were social-engineering attempts to transform the social and economic roles of such rural producers. Seeing this pattern can help us understand both the connections and the distinctions between the Mexican, Russian, and Chinese revolutions of the 1910s; their course in the 1920s, 1930s, and 1940s; and some of the most lethal policies of totalitarian regimes between the 1930s and the 1950s.[23]

Using conceptual categories in this way can enrich our understanding of broader patterns and geographies (such as world history, the history of Latin America, the history of Southeast Asia). It can make our understanding of *particular* societies productive for our understanding of those *broader* geographies. On the other hand, it can also enrich our

---

[22] Munslow, *Deconstructing History*, p. 51.
[23] See Edward Ross Dickinson, *The World in the Long Twentieth Century: An Interpretive History* (Berkeley: University of California Press, 2018), esp. chapters 5 (pp. 129–162) and 9 (pp. 263–333).

understanding of the specific characteristics of particular societies by posing fruitful questions. Why did the Mexican revolution not lead to a titanic outbreak of mass murder, whereas those in Russia and China did? Why did the Bolshevik totalitarian regime turn its violence primarily against its own population, while the Nazi totalitarian regime turned its violence primarily against foreign populations? When done carefully, the use of general categories and comparative cases does not impose a particular narrative on our sources ("they failed to do X because they were not like Europe"). And neither does it lead us to neglect careful empirical research. On the contrary: It gives us a more nuanced understanding of the relative significance of specific empirically discovered characteristics of societies and periods, both by giving us coherent points of comparison and by posing useful questions.

Here again, then, on careful examination it appears that theory-driven and historicist approaches are not contradictory at all; they are complementary. The epistemological conflict between them – the fact that they make divergent claims about how we gain knowledge of the past – is not a problem for the discipline, but one of its great strengths.

4.1.5 Problem 5: Fragmentary Sources

One final problem characteristic of historical study is a common factor in the four other problems discussed here: the problem of limited evidence. We can discover sources that have not been used before or use familiar sources in new ways, but historians are limited to the evidence that has survived from the past. This means that historical evidence is very often fragmentary, incomplete, indirect, and suggestive rather than conclusive. This is as true of tree rings and pollen counts in lake-bottom mud as it is of medieval texts. It is a particularly acute problem for ancient history, but modern historians encounter it constantly as well. And again, it is often a major issue specifically for the history of people who were not literate or did not have time or reason to write much, or in cases where it was not in the interest of powerful people and institutions to preserve the voices of particular groups.

To give a few minor examples from my own research, I have encountered many cases in which relevant records in German archives were destroyed by Allied bombing in World War II. The notation "lost in the war" appears with demoralizing frequency in entries for books and periodicals in the catalogue of Germany's greatest public library, the Staatsbibliothek preussischer Kulturbesitz in Berlin. In other cases I have been able to find only the edited, "cleaned-up" versions of the minutes of important committee meetings within private charitable organizations, from which most signs of controversy – which I knew from other sources had been intense in those meetings – had been removed. In one case the police files on a legal case of particular interest to me are simply missing, for no known reason (and only those files, not the ones directly adjacent to them in the catalogue of the archive in question).

A constant problem in my own study of the history of sexuality is that we have very little direct information about what people actually did in their sexual lives. For Germany in the early twentieth century the available sources include a few surveys by academic sexologists, some troves of letters written to them, a few fragments from autobiographies, memoirs, and diaries, and court records. Indirect sources include some case notes by psychologists and psychiatrists; a great number of usually critical or alarmist observations by jurists, police officials, and morality campaigners; and here and there comments, for example, from military officers about the habits of the men under their command. Even more indirect are demographic statistics and statistics on crimes against morality (e.g., the display sale of contraceptives or of pornography, or statistics on sexual coercion and violence).

This list makes the empiricist's answer to the problem of fragmentary sources clear: If the available sources in any one category are patchy, multiply the number of categories, the *kinds* of evidence used. If we expand our investigation of the context (social, political, cultural economic, etc.), we can draw on a wider range of indirect evidence to construct a more convincing interpretation. If the few directly relevant scraps of evidence we have point to a conclusion, if the available secondhand reports seem to suggest it, if the indirect evidence concerning outcomes (e.g., demographic patterns) supports it, then we have a reasonable case for advancing it as part of our interpretation. We may not be able to draw a strong conclusion from any one kind of evidence, but if we have multiple different kinds of evidence that seem to support an interpretation, that interpretation can at least become plausible, or persuasive, or even convincing.

Miles Fairburn calls this "maximizing the weight and variety of observations" and gives the example of a history of the aristocracy in the English Revolution in the 1640s that uses "an extraordinary variety of positive examples, a large range of different types of evidence, that converge on the same conclusion." Though the author has in each case "only a few examples of unknown typicality ... taken as a whole they enhance the weight of the overall hypothesis." What is more, precisely because it does consider so many different types of evidence, the argument has the advantage from an historicist viewpoint that it "wonderfully illuminates the whole environment of [the] social elite" it analyzes.[24] In short, the historicist approach is to cast one's research net more broadly – to expand one's inquiry.

But the social science approach obviously offers us equally useful tools. One approach is to extrapolate from cases that appear comparable. If we have direct evidence that something was happening in a nearby or related community or in a society that was in some important way similar, it may be reasonable to posit that something similar was happening in the case we are interested in as well, even if we do not have *direct* evidence for that. The historian can then test that supposition against available *indirect* evidence. If we can establish that in one society for which we have very extensive records murder statistics reflect police department budgets more than they do actual levels of violence (because when the money for investigations runs out deaths are classified as "accidental"), then there is good reason to suspect that the same might be true in another society for which we do not have such extensive records. If we find, for example, that in the mid nineteenth century homicide rates in poor states in the South, for which we have sparse statistical sources, were lower than in Massachusetts, which was wealthy and gathered more extensive statistics, we might want to compare demographic data more closely to see whether the death rate for men in their twenties was inexplicably higher in the South.

A second alternative is to make use of social theory either as an interpretive tool or as a guide to research. On the one hand, social theory can give us interpretive alternatives that we would not otherwise have developed – ways to understand our findings that plausibly fit the limited available evidence, even if we cannot confirm with absolute certainty that the general models they posit are correct for the case we are considering. In my own work, for example, I have argued that "moral entrepreneurs" interested in building their own influence and their own careers helped cultivate a sense of moral and sexual crisis in Germany in the late nineteenth and early twentieth centuries. This is a concept British sociologist Stanley Cohen developed in the early 1970s to explain intense negative reactions to popular culture, particularly rock and roll.[25] It has since become influential as a way of understanding "moral panics" of all kinds, because it helps to explain how social "problems" or issues get defined in

---

[24] Fairburn, *Social History*, pp. 61, 74.
[25] Stanley Cohen, *Folk Devils and Moral Panics* (London: MacGibbon & Keen, 1972).

new ways and rise in public profile, even when we cannot find evidence that the social behaviors they address were actually radically changing, or becoming more common. This concept is often combined with the older sociological concept of "status anxiety," a negative responses in particular social groups to a perception of declining social influence, which can help explain the broader motivations of such moral entrepreneurs.

For example, concerns about the declining influence of particular social groups appear frequently to have been transposed onto gender relations, giving rise to a "moral panic" about sexual decadence and disorder, even where there is little evidence to justify that panic. In the case I examined the direct evidence concerning actual sexual practices was extremely limited, but certainly did not point conclusively to the kind of "crisis" that the people I was studying insisted was going on everywhere around them. Indirect evidence concerning the relative social influence of the groups most strongly represented in the organizations committed to combatting the alleged moral and sexual crisis (particularly the Christian clergy) suggested that they had very good and concrete reasons to be suffering from status anxiety. I could not *prove* that the concept of the moral panic gives us the best explanation of what was going on, but the evidence certainly *suggested* that the broader theory described this specific situation.

Finally, using social science models in this way can suggest new avenues of empirical research – new *kinds* of evidence that we might look for. In other words, it can assist us in making intelligent and productive choices about *how* to expand our inquiry. The use of social theory as a guide to research does carry the risk that we might go looking only for the kinds of evidence that confirm our theory. But the opposite danger is that we will miss potential lines of inquiry that are, so to speak, right in front of our eyes. The idea of status anxiety, for example, led me to look at the changing proportion over time of university students in Germany who took degrees in theology as opposed to other disciplines. That offered a telling bit of indirect evidence for the declining social influence of the clergy.

4.1.6 Summary

The message of each of these examples is clear by now: The historicist approach improves the quality of theory-driven inquiry, and theory-driven approaches improve the quality of historicist inquiry. What is more, in each case the specific weaknesses and problems of History as a discipline are the sources of some of its greatest strengths. The limitations of historical evidence are often what drive historians to broaden and deepen both their empirical inquiry and their conceptual reach. Awareness of the pitfalls of the use of theoretical models drives the kind of skepticism that leads historians to entertain multiple models and to pursue the multiple empirical questions that arise from doing so. But the same is true of the wide-ranging and capacious nature of History in its historicist practice: The consideration of multiple facets of an historical situation drives historians to reach for a *range* of conceptual tools developed by social theorists and humanists working in multiple fields (e.g., sociology, literature, economics, anthropology, philosophy, religious studies, women's studies, communications).

For the discipline as a whole, the tension between these approaches is productive – it is a challenge, a motivator, and a resource that gives History much of its analytical range and its intellectual vigor. Arthur Marwick wrote that in the debate between so-called naive empiricists and theory mongers "there is no perfect approach, no perfect paradigm."[26] My point here is more than that. It is not simply that these are in principle alternative ways to conceive of History. It is that the great strength of History is that in practice we conceive of it in both ways simultaneously. When pursued simultaneously each makes the other better.

Students can benefit enormously from confronting this paradox – that epistemological and methodological conflict or "confusion" strengthens the discipline as a whole and enriches the practice of individual historians. Of course, it does give students choices – they can focus on the approach that most fits their own intellectual affinities. But more important, considering both approaches – perhaps even experiencing both in their own historical work – can help cultivate a greater degree of intellectual flexibility than the study of any other discipline by giving them the opportunity to reflect on the benefits of two discrete ways of knowing, two *different* modes of inquiry. At the very least, this can give them multiple ways of approaching any given problem. Ideally, it can also enable and encourage them to ask questions that escape the constraints of particular epistemologies – questions that are, in a word, spooky.

4.2 The Objectivity Question: Postmodern Doubts about History

Many of the characteristics of History explored in this book so far make it a particularly challenging discipline for those with an interest in epistemology – the study of how we know things, or the philosophy of knowledge.

---

[26] Marwick, *Nature*, p. 72.

History is an interpretive discipline and every interpretation sees its subject from a particular perspective. Historians do not have direct experimental or observational access to their subject matter. The fragmentary, indirect, and partial forms of evidence that historians have available to them permit only degrees of plausibility, rather than certainty. Interests derived from historians' own ideological commitments, experiences, and concerns guide their choice of topics.[27] There are no objective criteria to establish what is potentially interesting and important – such as "will the bomb work if we build it this way?" or "will the computer be faster if we build it this way?" Historians routinely draw on concepts, categories, and theoretical or interpretive options developed in other disciplines, usually without a very rigorous assessment of their applicability, following the simple principle that if it seems to offer us an interesting or fruitful perspective or to generate interesting questions, we should use it. Historical analysis usually considers multiple factors contributing to an historical situation, development, or outcome, and rarely can or seeks to identify the statistically measurable relative importance of those factors. History is driven by the logic of expanding and multifaceted inquiry rather than by the imperative of finding "right" or actionable answers.

All these considerations put together have led more philosophically inclined observers to question whether History ever produces reliable knowledge. Is any History accurate, or "true"? Does any History capture the reality of history?

A close examination of multiple works of History on any specific topic will often confirm this doubt because the conclusions scholars reach can be radically different. A marvelous case is Norman F. Cantor's *Inventing the Middle Ages* (1991), which examines the ways in which twentieth-century historians' personal experiences, ideological commitments, and contemporary concerns shaped the histories they wrote. Reading the book is like immersing oneself in a world of gossip, as Cantor analyses the concerns, experiences, assumptions, personalities, and beliefs that guided the research and interpretive work of each of twenty historians, from French Jews and Christian Oxford professors through Nazi Germans and nostalgic

---

[27] See Gaea Leinhardt, "History: A Time to Be Mindful" and Stuart Greene, "Students as Authors in the Study of History," both in *Teaching and Learning in History*, ed. Gaea Leinhardt, Isabel L Beck, and Catherine Stainton (Hillsdale, NJ: Lawrence Erlbaum, 1994), pp. 137–170 (esp. p. 142) and 209–255 (esp. pp. 239–240). This was a central point Max Weber had made already in 1904: "What is made the object of study, and how far this study expands into the endless realm of causal relationships, is determined by the values that guide the investigator and his times." Max Weber, "Die 'Objektivität' sozialwissenschaftlicher und sozialpolitischer Erkenntnis," *Archiv für Sozialwissenschaft und Sozialpolitik* 19 (1904): 22–87, here p. 58.

American Southerners to liberal triumphalist Cold Warrior Yankees. The gossip is corrosive. One could all too easily end up wondering whether we *know* anything about the Middle Ages at all, or whether it is all just a lot of subjective junk.[28] Similarly, in the sixteen chronologically ordered chapters of his influential book on the history of the idea of objectivity in the historical profession in the United States, Peter Novick analyzed the formative influence on historical interpretations exercised by racism in the aftermath of the Civil War, the mobilization of historians for propaganda in World War I, a second mobilization for cultural combat in the Cold War, and so on and so forth.[29]

Or take a third example, from my own experience: As a graduate school exercise I undertook an analysis of some two dozen biographies of Henry Ford written between 1917 and the 1980s. In some of these books Ford appeared as the embodiment of American individualistic and democratic entrepreneurialism. In others he was a cunning corporate strategist and builder of the enormously successful American industrial system. One or two presented him as a small-town tinkerer with narrow horizons and a narrow mind, who happened to hit the technology cycle just right. Still more critical were those that portrayed him as a ruthless exploiter of labor and opponent of democracy for working people. And in some he was a bitterly racist Nazi sympathizer who contributed to the emergence of a genocidal regime in Germany and posed a danger to democracy in his own country. These books seemed to reflect the concerns of particular biographers, shaped by particular current events and by their own ideological commitments. Perhaps all these things were true of Ford. But even if so, each of these biographies is very partial.

Historians consider primarily two quite different kinds of bias. One derives from their personal experiences and characters, the other from their political, ideological, religious, and social commitments. Both influence how individual historians work in two ways: by guiding their choice of topics and sources, and by guiding their interpretation of their findings.

The influence of ideology is relatively straightforward. Marxist historians, for example, tend to be interested in the history of class relations, perhaps particularly in the experience of working people, even perhaps of the labor movement specifically. They seek to understand historical situations and developments in terms of the dynamics of class struggle, the

---

[28] Norman F. Cantor, *Inventing the Middle Ages: The Lives, Works, and Ideas of the Great Medievalists of the Twentieth Century* (New York: Quill/William Morrow, 1991).

[29] Peter Novick, *That Noble Dream: The "Objectivity Question" and the American Historical Profession* (New York: Cambridge University Press, 1988).

exploitative requirements of capital, the overriding interest of the ruling class in maintaining control of the means of production and the profits it generates. They interpret social relations as part of either of the ruling-class system (the universal conspiracy of class power) or of the resistance against it. Conservative historians are interested in the acts and thoughts of statesmen, generals, and philosophers. They regard revolutionaries and reformers as misguided, pernicious, and/or only relevant insofar as they were able to disrupt the stability and peace of society. Liberal historians are interested in the ideas and deeds of constitutional moderates, bold entrepreneurs, and rational reformers. They regard conservatives and radicals alike as unreasonable and power-mad. Catholic historians are interested in the history of the Catholic Church, the Catholic community, Catholic organizations, and their faith. They regard anti-Catholic Protestants and socialists as intolerant, unreasonable, and destructive. Nationalist historians may assume that the history of their own country is unique, failing to see (or to care) that it is part of broader regional or global patterns. Nazi historians were interested in the greatness of the German people and interpreted Germany's history in racial terms.

The influence of individual experience and character is more subtle, but often important. Historians who have lived lives of privilege often do not have deep interest in or understanding of the experience and ideas of those who have not. They will likely be drawn to topics familiar to their class – military strategy, economics, high politics, diplomacy, the struggle for world power. People who have established themselves as scholars (inside or outside the academic world) in the face of the privilege of elite institutions and their predominantly white, male, and middle-class graduates will be more likely to question widely accepted historical interpretations. They may be more inclined to investigate topics closer to their own experience and less common in the discipline thirty or fifty years ago – race, slavery, working-class life, genocide, food, recreation, gender relations, the politics or culture of empire, anticolonial resistance. There is a fairly clear division of interest among historians along gender lines – the emergence of women's and gender history as an important subfield, for example, was largely the work of women historians. It has been in large part non-Western historians who have driven the growing influence of postcolonial perspectives in the discipline.

As for character, historians are – as one manifesto for social-scientific History put it in 1970 – often people "of caution and moderation who do their best to avoid extremes."[30] Such people favor a highly empirical and

---

[30] Landes and Tilly, *History as Social Science*, p. 9.

4.2 The Objectivity Question: Postmodern Doubts about History 159

hermeneutic approach. Those with urgent political or ideological commitments may regard the work of such scholars as inherently conservative. Historians with the ambition to play a leading or formative role in the collective intellectual life of the discipline of History may favor the excitement of the interpretive options and the claim to higher intellectual authority that one or more social theories offer. More intellectually or politically conservative or liberal colleagues may regard interpretations based on such theories as politically biased, or even as implicitly totalitarian because they put scholarship in the service of politics. More contrarian historians may seek constantly to confound their colleagues by calling prevailing views into question, offering "revisionist" interpretations that may seem, from the point of view of the cautious and painstaking, idiosyncratic and one-sided, or even contentious (i.e., seeking controversy for the sake of controversy).

Professional historians are mostly not overly troubled by these forms of bias. Most are comfortable with the idea that History does not produce objective knowledge or absolute truth. This is particularly true of those whose conception of the discipline is more historicist. The reason for that is obvious: The most fundamental assumption of the historicist approach is that everything is historical, conditioned by the context of its specific time and place. The same applies to historians themselves. We can assume that historians' choice of topics, of source materials, of concepts and categories and theories, and of interpretation will be conditioned by the specific historical contexts in which they work. Any other finding would explode the entire foundation of the discipline of History because it would establish that there is at least one human being who is *not* shaped by historical context. Reassuring, then, that we find no such thing. Instead, we find that medievalists "invented" the Middle Ages, or that historians have viewed Henry Ford from myriad different perspectives, depending on the circumstances, ideas, issues, and problems of the times in which they wrote.

One prominent historian of race in the American South, Nell Irvin Painter, put this point with particular clarity in a roundtable discussion in 2003 on how historians think: "In no case is history cut off from the political economy or the personal interests and demographic characteristics of each historian. What goes on in our institutions, our polity, and our experience affects our thought. Who we are as people enters into what we see as important historically."[31] Her comment elicited no response at all

---

[31] Drew Faust, Hendrik Herzog, David A. Hollinger, Akira Iriye, Patricia Nelson Limerick, Nell Irvin Painter, David Roediger, Mary Ryan, and Alan Taylor, "Interchange: The Practice of History,"

from the eight other roundtable participants because it summarizes historians' conventional understanding. That has not changed in the two decades since. In 2021 James M. Banner remarked that historians do not try to "put themselves outside history itself. All historians are implicated in their own histories; none of them, no more than any other individuals, can escape being the product of his or her own circumstances."[32] The president of the American Historical Association remarked in 2022 that there is a "consensus that every generation writes its own version of the past."[33]

This is a view of very long standing among professional historians. In 1985 David Lowenthal observed that no historian "however immersed in the past, can divest himself of his own knowledge and assumptions . . . Our hopes and fears, expertise and intentions continually shape the historical past . . . the historian reaches an understanding distinctively of his own time . . . bias is inescapable."[34] Henry Steele Commager advanced this position with gusto two decades earlier. "Consciously or unconsciously," he wrote, "all historians are biased; they are creatures of their time, their race, their faith, their class, their country – creatures, even prisoners." What was more, we are prisoners of our own modern ways of thinking and speaking. "If we speak, we must speak with words; if we think, we must think with thoughts"; but since we "are moderns, our words and thoughts cannot but be modern," and therefore potentially blunt tools for grasping the past.

The choice of topic too is often dictated by what Commager called "present-mindedness," for "we almost instinctively assume that the past . . . is interesting only insofar as it caters to our current interests, and significant only when it has ostentatious consequences for us." All this "helps explain," he concluded, "why each generation rewrites the history of the past; the view depends on the point of view."[35]

Edward Hallett Carr was scarcely less vehement in *What Is History?* (1961). "We can view the past, and achieve our understanding of the past, only through the eyes of the present. The historian is of his own age . . .

Journal of American History 90 (2003): 576–611, here p. 578. See Lionel Rubinoff, "Historicity and Objectivity," in *Objectivity, Method, and Point of View: Essays in the Philosophy of History*, ed. W. J. van der Dussen and Lionel Rubinoff (Leiden: Brill, 1991), 133–153.

[32] Banner, *Ever-Changing Past*, p. 268. See also Iggers, "Historicism," pp. 134–142.

[33] Jacqueline Jones, "Presidential Address: Historians and Their Publics, Then and Now," *American Historical Review* 127 (2022): 1–30, here p. 9.

[34] David Lowenthal, *The Past Is a Foreign Country* (Cambridge: Cambridge University Press, 1985), p. 216.

[35] Commager, *Nature and the Study of History*, pp. 44, 46, 53, 59.

4.2 The Objectivity Question: Postmodern Doubts about History 161

The historian, before he [sic] begins to write history, is the product of history."³⁶

Both were echoing American historian Charles Beard, who offered an influential statement of the same principle in an essay titled "Written History as an Act of Faith" in 1934. It had, he asserted,

> been said for a century or more that each historian who writes history is a product of his [sic] age, and that his work reflects the spirit of the times, of a nation, race, group, class, or section ... Every student of history knows that his colleagues have been influenced in their selection and ordering of materials by their biases, prejudices, beliefs, affections, general upbringing, and experience, particularly social and economic; and if he has a sense of propriety, to say nothing of humor, he applies the canon to himself, leaving no exceptions to the rule.

Beard enthusiastically endorsed the "scientific method" of research in History as "the only method that can be employed in obtaining accurate knowledge of historical facts," on which historical interpretation is founded. But the interpretation itself was necessarily subjective, shaped by the values, beliefs, and preferences of the historian. The "selection and arrangement of facts ... is an act of choice, conviction, and interpretation ... Facts ... are known, but they do not select themselves or force themselves automatically into any fixed scheme of arrangement in the mind of the historian. They are selected and ordered by him as he thinks." That process of selecting and ordering, the construction of an interpretation, was "controlled by the historian's frame of reference" – by the values, concepts, interests, categories, assumptions, and of course blind spots imposed on or made available by the historian's own history.³⁷ The best defense against unconscious bias and narrow-mindedness is therefore not pretended objectivity, but awareness of our own assumptions, limitations, and interests.

We might call this notion – that historians must understand themselves as part of history – the historicist doctrine of self-reflexivity. It continues to be the operating assumption of most historians. Martha Howell and Walter Prevenier remarked in their handbook of historical method in 2001 that "historians must learn to recognize that they can read sources only from the standpoint of their position" in society and history.³⁸ Jorma

---

³⁶ Carr, *What Is History?* pp. 19, 34, 38.
³⁷ Charles A. Beard, "Written History as an Act of Faith," *American Historical Review* 39 (1934): 219–231, here pp. 220, 228.
³⁸ Howell and Prevenier, *From Reliable Sources*, p. 148.

Kalela, writing in 2011, offered a pithy formulation of the central epistemological assumption derived from this awareness: The fundamental assumption of the historicist is that the challenge for historians is not achieving objectivity, but "managing their present-mindedness."[39]

Obviously, this doctrine is in a sense a paradoxical one. If everything is historically conditioned, then logically the belief that everything is historically conditioned must also be historically conditioned. It arose at a particular time, in a particular region, in a particular context, and out of particular historical developments.[40] Again, most historians are untroubled by this paradox. We strive to understand history in a historically conditioned way. That historically conditioned way of understanding history makes it impossible for us to believe it is in an epistemological sense the "right" way, the "objective" way. But it is the way we do it – for good historical reasons. That is paradoxical, but it also makes sense. It is consistent.

In recent decades a number of postmodernist thinkers have carried this fundamental historicist position a step further – while, ironically enough, seeing themselves as critics of historical knowledge and practice. Alun Munslow's *Deconstructing History*, first published in 1997, summarizes their arguments admirably. Munslow pointed to the fact that individual historians will bring their own perspectives, experiences, and commitments to their work. Historical knowledge, he pointed out, "is not objective but has upon it the fingerprints of its interpreters . . . History cannot be written as if it were in some way entirely removed from the experience of the present, of our everyday life or the dominant ideas within the broader intellectual community."[41] But he was not referring here to individual bias or perspective. His argument instead was that the conceptual tools and the language that historians work with are the product of "socially encoded and constructive discursive practices that mediate reality so much that they effectively close off direct access to it."

In other words, the very terms in which we think are determined by our historical social context. What is crucial is not that every person has an individual perspective, but rather that "the notion that understanding emanates from the independent knowledge-centered individual" is false. Historians do not have individual thoughts, ideas, perspectives. Rather,

---

[39] Kalela, *Making History*, p. 15.
[40] For a thoughtful intellectual history of the emergence and development of historicism, see David D. Roberts, *Nothing but History: Reconstruction and Extremity after Metaphysics* (Berkeley: University of California Press, 1995).
[41] Munslow, *Deconstructing History*, pp. 9, 25.

4.2 The Objectivity Question: Postmodern Doubts about History 163

they work with the tool kit – the words, concepts, ideas, and perspectives – that their society and their culture make available to them. *This*, and not any individual bias, is why they are incapable of "the accurate representation of [past] reality."[42]

A central element of this argument is that historians do not discover or "reconstruct" the past from the evidence. They impose a story on the past – again, not because they are biased, but because they have to. "'Facts,'" Munslow argues, "are literally meaningless in their unprocessed state of simple evidential statement. The evidence is turned into 'facts' through the narrative interpretations of historians." In short, "facts emerge from analysis, not analysis from facts."[43] While Munslow and others sometimes asserted that this was a new insight, in fact it was a long-established – and again, logically necessary – tenet of historical thought. It echoed, for example, E. H. Carr's assertion forty-six years earlier that "[t]he facts are really not at all like fish on a fishmonger's slab. They are like fish swimming about in a vast and sometimes inaccessible ocean; and what the historian catches will depend ... mainly on what part of the ocean he chooses to fish in and what tackle he chooses to use ... By and large, the historian will get the kind of facts he wants. History means interpretation."[44] Carr's observation in turn echoed that of J. M. Trevelyan thirty-seven years earlier again: To "collect the evidence and the facts you must previously have arrived at a certain interpretation – otherwise you would not know which class of facts you want to collect."[45]

What *was* new in postmodern discussions of how History creates knowledge, however, was the argument that historians' interpretive work, and therefore their selection of facts/evidence, is dictated not only or primarily by individual historians' individual choices but by a set of linguistic and cognitive structures, conventions, and rules. These structures and rules are inherent both in the *nature* of thinking itself and in the *form* that historical interpretation takes – primarily narrative, or storytelling. As Munslow put it, there are "pre-existing or generic mental structures located in the mind of the historian" from which no one can escape. The "data do not possess inherent and discoverable empirical truths"; rather, we construct meanings from the data in accordance with these generic structures. They constitute the "infrastructure of consciousness ... that ultimately

---

[42] Munslow, *Deconstructing History*, pp. 11, 10, 2.
[43] Munslow, *Deconstructing History*, pp. 28, 7, 49. [44] Carr, *What Is History?* pp. 18, 84.
[45] Trevelyan, "History and Literature," pp. 85–86.

determines how historians elect to explain the facts explored in their narratives."⁴⁶

Munslow borrowed his understanding of the rules and structures that shape historical understanding from an essay on "Interpretation in History" by literary theorist and philosopher of History Hayden White, which I touched on briefly in Chapter 2. According to White, in Western cultures all stories fall into four patterns, four basic plot structures, or what White calls "emplotments" or in other places "*mythoi*" (mythic patterns): comedy, tragedy, romance, or satire. Stories that do not fall into these patterns are not recognizable as meaningful stories. Any historical interpretation therefore must adopt one of these "emplotments"; otherwise it would be incoherent. As White put it, "the historian must draw upon a fund of culturally provided *mythoi* in order to constitute the facts as figuring a story of a particular kind ... to endow his account of the past with the odor of meaning or significance."

Further, there are "four different concepts of explanation" that all interpretations have to rely on: "the idiographic, the contextualist, the organicist, and the mechanist." Usually there is some alignment of emplotment with explanatory mode (romance tends toward the idiographic; tragedy tends toward the mechanistic, etc.). Third, all authors adopt four fundamental ideological orientations: liberal, conservative, radical, and anarchist. And finally, all historical interpretations rely on one or more of four ways that people (or perhaps people in the West?) integrate new information into their understanding, or as White put it, "dominant tropological strategies by which unknown or unfamiliar phenomena are provided with meanings": metaphor, metonymy, synecdoche, and irony.⁴⁷ These are the basic and inescapable forms of narrative – the tools with which we build stories that have meaning, rather than being a simple listing of facts or events.

The symmetry of this model – four sets of four – seems suspiciously arbitrary (in fact in early passages of his essay White actually referred to a fifth mode of emplotment, "epic," which he dropped later in the essay). And not all postmodern critics of History embrace exactly these sixteen basic elements. But most do share White's belief that some "infrastructure of consciousness" like this is embedded in language itself – that rules govern the way we construct meaning, independent of conscious thought. Our very vocabulary is a web of interconnected and mutually reinforcing

---

⁴⁶ Munslow, *Deconstructing History*, pp. 13, 37, 29, 77.
⁴⁷ White, "Interpretation in History," pp. 59, 60, 66, 68, 72.

4.2 The Objectivity Question: Postmodern Doubts about History 165

meanings; those meanings impose themselves on our understanding when we use words. As Elizabeth Ermarth argued in 1991, "language is not neutral"; words do not simply name things but rather have particular connotations, histories, and associations. They make up functional parts of a "coherent system" that dictates what we think and say when we use them. The word "revolution," for example, has a whole army of associations; so does "crisis"; so does "tribe." It matters whether we use the word religion, faith, belief, sect, confession, or church, because each has a different meaning and a different field of associations and connotations. And it matters that we have only a limited roster of such words, with a limited range of meanings, to choose from. Not only do the associations, connotations, and histories of the words we use shape the meaning of what we say; we also struggle to say things for which we do not have words. Language constrains our interpretive options, limits our ability to escape from our own infrastructure of consciousness. As French linguistic theorist Luce Irigaray put it in 1977, "if we continue to speak the same language ... we will only reproduce the same story" (or at least the same *mythoi*).[48] All of this mattered to Munslow in part because he believed that recognizing that the way we think is prestructured by cognitive rules and by language can be liberating and empowering. If "we can find no objective certainty in the past," there is nothing to "validate the authority of those in power over us." Drawing on social theorist Michel Foucault, he argued that the very idea of "Truth" is simply a tool of power. Truth is a product of discourses (systems of ideas and practices and the institutional arrangements built on them, and in order to propagate them) that both reflect and help to constitute (by constraining thought) power relations within a society. These include legal discourses, gender discourses, medical discourses, religious discourses, scientific discourses, and so on. When we believe the "truth" that they impose, we are locked into the structures of power that they define and dominate. The idea of truth is by its nature confining, repressive, and a tool of power, which aims to assert control over our thoughts and actions.

History is no different. The idea that historians find their interpretations by analyzing the evidence and arriving at the truth about the past is a false

---

[48] Elizabeth Ermarth, "Sequel to History," in *The Post-modern History Reader*, ed. Keith Jenkins (New York: Routledge, 1997), pp. 47–64, here p. 48 and quotation p. 53. For important corollary ideas, see Fischer, *Historians' Fallacies*, p. 244; Kevin Passmore, "Poststructuralism and History," in *Writing History: Theory & Practice*, ed. Stefan Berger, Heiko Feldner, and Kevin Passmore (London: Arnold, 2003), pp. 119–126.

claim to authority, to expertise, to power, because "all judgments about what to include or exclude are based on ideology, preferred narrative structures," formal arguments, and so on. Therefore, the "organized study of the past" – as long as it rests on the claim that historians discover the truth about the past – "is itself founded on the dispensation of authority/power in contemporary society." History as professional historians practice it is "about the will to gain power." (Munslow prefaced these last six words with the word "perhaps," but his text gives no reason to do so.)[49] Implicitly, then, Munslow clearly agreed with Keith Jenkins, whose view I cited in Chapter 2: History is a tool of bourgeois power.

Again, much of this postmodern critique was a restatement of the postulates of historicism. The great majority of historians have never claimed that they knew the absolute and objective truth about history. As Christopher Blake observed in 1959, that claim has "nothing whatever to do with the way in which historians credit each other with objectivity and a respect for the facts."[50] The historicist view is that History is an interpretive discipline. Every interpretation is built from a particular perspective. The evidence is biased, fragmentary, and is not the past but only what survives of the past. Historians must select from the available evidence in order to build an interpretation of the past. Their selection of evidence will be guided by their own assumptions, theories, and interests (intellectual, but also social and professional). Historians' thinking is shaped by their society and culture, including by the structures of power that prevail in it – that is, historians are themselves a product of history, not outside it. The language that they use is the language of a particular time, place, culture, discipline, tradition, and society, with peculiarities, limitations, and biases built into it – that is, our language is also a product of history, not outside it. History with a capital H is not history, is not the past. In fact, as English medievalist V. H. Galbraith put it in 1963, the "longer one studies history, the harder it gets to arrive at results which even the author, let alone the reader, can decently consider the truth."[51] These are all fundamental assumptions of History in the historicist tradition.

Beyond that, though, from the perspective of an historian of the twentieth century the idea that a commitment to the idea of "Truth" is a tool of power seems politically naïve. This may be a useful way of thinking about claims to professional expertise in well-functioning liberal societies, but it

---

[49] Munslow, *Deconstructing History*, pp. 14–15, 65.   [50] Blake, "Can History Be Objective?" p. 340.
[51] V. H. Galbraith, *An Introduction to the Study of History* (London: Watts, 1964), p. vi.

does not appear very useful beyond that specific context. Judging by the political history of the twentieth century it seems at least as accurate to argue that what powerful people want to establish is that there is no Truth, but only competing political claims. They want to persuade others that words are merely instruments of power, not tools for building knowledge or understanding. That way they can tell whatever lies might be convenient at any given moment, without anyone having the category of "lie" to apply to their words. This is the epistemology of all totalitarian regimes: There is no such thing as true or false, but rather everyone must *act* as if whatever the regime is saying at any given moment is right (or pay an unbearable price). And when the regime changes course and says the opposite, everyone will have to pretend *that* is right. The practice of open inquiry structured by established standards of evidence and argumentation is the epistemological opposite of this technique. As Charles Beard remarked in the heat of the early twentieth-century confrontation with totalitarianism, the "inquiring spirit of science ... is the chief safeguard against the tyranny of authority, bureaucracy, and brute power."[52]

It is not surprising, then, that relatively few historians have cared to engage deeply with the epistemological questions posed by postmodern theorists. "Most simply do not think about them," Munslow observed; the "vast majority of historians are just not interested in that undertaking."[53] Patrick Joyce, another prominent theorist of postmodern History, similarly remarked in 1991 that "rank indifference rather than outright hostility" was the "dominant response" of historians to the arguments of postmodernism.[54] Thirty years later James M. Banner concurred: "Historians continue to proceed more or less as always to seek plausible knowledge of the past as if mounting doubts about objectivity do not exist." They "still hold to the conviction that they can and do make progress in closing the gap between historical ignorance and historical understanding" and "still try to arrive at reasonably impartial knowledge of what happened and why it did so."[55]

This indifference is not the product of intellectual laziness, but of the central epistemological assumptions of historicism. Historicism does not rest on a claim to have access to objective truth; but it is also not founded

---

[52] Beard, "Written History as an Act of Faith," p. 227. For a similar view, see Perez Zagorin, "Rejoinder to a Postmodernist," *History and Theory* 39 (2000): 201–209, esp. p. 208.
[53] Munslow, *Deconstructing History*, p. 32.
[54] Patrick Joyce, "History and Postmodernism," in *The Post-modern History Reader*, ed. Keith Jenkins (New York: Routledge, 1997), 244–250, here p. 245.
[55] Banner, *Ever-Changing Past*, p. 263.

on what Bruce A. Vansledright has called "naive relativism or subjectivism" and John Tosh "lazy relativism" – the assumption that History is just opinion, or propaganda, or a particular form of fiction.[56] History does not claim to speak "Truth," but it does establish criteria for rational dialogue about the past. Historians have clear criteria for gauging the relative plausibility, persuasive power, and productivity or usefulness of historical interpretations. As Dipesh Chakrabarty put it in 2007, "Historical truths are broad, synthetic generalisations based on research collections of individual historical facts. They could be wrong but they are always amenable to verification by methods of historical research."[57] Wulf Kansteiner made the same point seven years earlier: Historians have a "concrete epistemology of historical practice" defining "standards which help both practitioners and readers make ... discriminations" between strong and weak interpretations, persuasive and fruitful or unpersuasive and flawed historical analysis.[58]

How do we do that? First, we assess the limitations of an historical interpretation, the conceptual constraints within which it operates. We can, for example, examine historians' political commitments and cultural background, training, assumptions, use of language, reliance on or ignorance of particular theoretical frameworks, even their experiences in life, their biography. We assess the nature of the categories and the terms they employ and the discourses from which they are drawn (e.g., economic, psychological, gendered, etc.). This allows us to read historians' work critically and skeptically, sensitive to the forms of bias that it may present. The point is not to dismiss their views as subjective or biased; it is to understand the perspectives that inform their analyses.

Next, we can assess the technical quality of historians' work: their conceptualization of the topic, research process, and the thinking applied in establishing their findings from the evidence they gathered. Are the questions they framed as the starting point for their inquiry open and historically appropriate, or do they impose interpretive constraints or blinders, or rely on historically inappropriate categories? Are they preemptively constricted or predefined by a particular theoretical perspective, or by some form of explicit or implicit bias, and if so what specifically was the

---

[56] Bruce A. Vansledright, *Assessing Historical Thinking and Understanding* (London: Taylor & Francis, 2013), p. 30; Tosh, *Why History Matters*, p. 6.
[57] Dipesh Chakrabarty, "History and the Politics of Recognition," in *Manifestos for History*, ed. Keith Jenkins, Sue Morgan, and Alun Munslow (New York: Routledge, 2007), pp. 77–87, here pp. 77–78.
[58] Wulf Kansteiner, "Mad History Disease Contained? Postmodern Excess Management Advice from the UK," *History and Theory* 39 (2000): 218–229, here pp. 220, 218.

effect on the quality of their research and thinking? Did the historian adequately consider the limitations of their sources – including the perspective, motives, knowledge, assumptions, and biases of those who produced or preserved them? Did they neglect or ignore specific relevant bodies of evidence, or broad categories or kinds of evidence? Did they respect the integrity of their sources, or selectively "mine" them for the bits useful to them?

With respect to their interpretive work, did they consider multiple relevant aspects of the subject of their research? Were they sufficiently widely read to have enriched their own thinking through their understanding of the findings and the reasoning of other scholars on their topic, or related topics? Did they address alternative perspectives and interpretations?

Beyond these more technical criteria, we can assess the quality of historians' thinking as well. New Zealand historian Miles Fairburn has given us a useful list of criteria for doing so. Some of his criteria are, again, technical: We should examine "the quantity of the supporting evidence; the weight of the counter evidence; mastery of the primary source material ... ; accuracy in quotation, referencing and so on ... ; use of novel primary source material." But he goes on to suggest that we look for higher-order intellectual characteristics, including "imaginative handling of apparently unpromising source material; the degree of analytical rigour; the amount of ingenuity applied to the tackling of inherently difficult evidential problems; the logicality of the arguments; the crudity or sophistication of the concepts; readability and the quality of prose style." Finally, we can look at the qualities of the interpretive apparatus historians use – for example, the "originality of theory" presented, "breadth of subject-matter; the failure or otherwise to discuss key works in the historiography; the capacity to open up new fields of enquiry; the use of a novel and interesting approach; avoidance of anachronism and sensitivity to the specificities of context ... ; a good feel for the period; the capacity to empathise with the actors."[59]

Obviously, some of Fairburn's criteria are subjective and even aesthetic ("quality of prose" or an "interesting approach"), and of course there is no accounting for taste. Yet an important step for anyone seriously interested in assessing the quality of an historical interpretation is precisely to account for their *own* taste – to examine their own response to it. Do we find an interpretation plausible because we share the bias of the author? Because it

---

[59] Fairburn, *Social History*, pp. 239–240.

appeals to some aspect of our own perspective or experience? Because romance, or irony, or farce are aesthetically or emotionally satisfying to us? Because we enjoy sober and unadorned prose? Because we love the poetic quality of the historian's writing? Not just the historian but the historian's reader should try to avoid confirmation bias. Readers too are a product of their history. Not infrequently, the best book to read is the one that one enjoys the least. It may turn out, on closer inspection, to be the better History.

Finally, we can assess works of History against the central aim of the discipline – to deepen understanding by expanding inquiry. In an essay published in 1994 Mark Bevir offered a set of criteria centered precisely on this disciplinary agenda. Bevir focused not on individual interpretations but on the "webs of interpretations" developed by communities of scholars working within broader interpretive traditions, and on the conversation between and among those traditions. A good web of interpretation, he argued, is one that encourages and fosters inquiry because it is "progressive, fruitful and open." By this he meant that it offers conceptual tools that allow those engaging with it to develop new questions, projects and interpretations "not previously connected with that web of interpretations." It "consists of clearly defined propositions, thereby facilitating criticism," which is the engine of further inquiry. A fruitful interpretative community is, in fact, one that shows "willingness to take [such] criticism seriously," to respond to it directly and in depth and detail, not by ignoring it or dismissing it on political or epistemological grounds but through further research and argumentation. It is open in the sense that it engages in productive debate, rather than "merely blocking off criticisms of our existing interpretations." It is one that operates according to "established standards of evidence" and applies "consistent criteria of evidence and reason" rather than relying on authoritative assertions or reiteration of its assumptions.[60]

In short, we measure the quality of historical interpretation against what the first three chapters of this book described as the fundamental characteristics and aims of the discipline. Again, criteria like these will not produce a judgment as to the absolute truth of an historical interpretation. As Bevir put it, historians "make sense of the past as best they can; they do

---

[60] Mark Bevir, "Objectivity in History," *Theory and History* 33 (1994): 328–344, here pp. 335–336. For similar assessments, see James T. Kloppenberg, "Objectivity in Historicism: A Century of American Historical Writing," in *American Historical Review* 94 (1989): 1011–1030, esp. pp. 1018, 1030; Vansledright, *Assessing*, pp. 25, 30; Chris Lorenz, "Historical Knowledge and Historical Reality: A Plea for 'Internal Realism,'" *History and Theory* 33 (1994): 297–327, here esp. pp. 306–307.

not discover certainties."⁶¹ History is not a discipline that is in the business of pursuing certainty. But these criteria do give us ways to measure the quality, coherence, and fruitfulness of interpretations, and their contribution to furthering the central intellectual agenda of History – deepening and widening inquiry and understanding.

4.3 Epistemological Doubt and Historical Practice

Of course this epistemological position was familiar to postmodernist critics of History; in fact, most explicitly shied away from actually asserting that History is effectively fiction. Alun Munslow, for example, repeatedly reiterated that History is "literary" and even "primarily a fictive enterprise," but ultimately he conceded that historians are "still constrained by what actually happened (historians do not invent events, people or processes)." Any historical interpretation is "a fictionalized version that plays with the real events and real lives of the past," and historians therefore have "little of the imaginative freedom exercised by writers of fiction." His conclusion: "Hopefully the narrative in a deconstructionist essay will be coherent and sensible, but it will not be epistemologically self-assured."⁶² In other words, historians should tell us what they think happened, and how and why it happened, but they should anchor their interpretation in specific evidence, and they should not pretend that they are certain about it or that they themselves are absolutely objective or impartial. Again, this is a fundamental assumption of un-deconstructed, historicist History.⁶³

But the postmodernist critique offered more than simply a restatement of historicist tradition. On the one hand, the discipline of History has been enormously energized by postmodern theories that powerfully deepen and expand the hermeneutic tradition and method. Particularly important have been new understandings of how language works to establish an "infrastructure of consciousness," or cognitive infrastructure, and new conceptions of the nature of meaning-making, such as that advanced by Hayden White. Both have enriched historians' understanding of their own interpretive process.

---

[61] Bevir, "Objectivity in History," p. 337.
[62] Munslow, *Deconstructing History*, pp. 187, 13, 79, 80, 74.
[63] Zoltán Simon argues that postmodern critiques of History could not transform the practice of historians because they actually merely described it. Zoltán Bolizsár Simon, "Do Theorists of History Have a Theory of History? Reflections on a Non-discipline," *Historia da Historiografia* 12 (2009): 53–68, esp. p. 63.

A particularly important contribution to the depth and precision of historical understanding has derived from the concept of "discourse," which in postmodern theory means not just knowledge as constructed by language but also the practices built on it – for example, "medical discourse," which includes not just medical science but the institutional and professional practices built on it. These concepts have given historians new and more sophisticated ways to approach the familiar task of establishing what worlds people inhabited in the past, what they saw, and what they meant when they talked about it.

Postmodern theory has also given historians more sophisticated and powerful ways of examining assumptions and biases not in their sources, but in their own thinking. It gives us new ways of examining our own ideas critically, of understanding with greater specificity and concreteness how our own history has shaped our thinking.

This is a problem for which the historicist tradition offered only very blunt tools. Effectively, what historicists proposed as the solution to the problem of bias was that historians try not to be biased. Leopold von Ranke, for example, argued already in the 1830s that for the historian the "first demand is pure love of truth ... Intelligence, courage, and honesty in telling the truth are sufficient ... if in his studies he remains free of prejudice and retains his humility."[64] G. M. Trevelyan echoed him a century later, arguing that "Inaccuracy is inevitable," but "dishonesty alone cannot be pardoned. If an author withholds the evidence against his side; if he chooses out one part of a document, which by itself bears a meaning it did not bear in the context; if ... he relates only what is creditable to one party, and only what is discreditable to another," then he is a bad historian.[65] Dominick LaCapra argued in 1980 that the historian "must attend to the facts, especially when they test and contest his [sic] own convictions and desires," and not reduce writing History to a "pretext for his own inventions or immediate interests."[66] And Ludmila Jordanova, writing in 2006, admitted that there is "no such thing as unbiased history, but there is such a thing as balanced, self-aware history" in which the historian is "judicious" and maintains "critical distance from their work," and in which her "passions" are "tempered by evidence." The historian must simply commit to

---

[64] Ranke, "On the Character," pp. 39–40.
[65] Quoted in Cannadine, *G. M. Trevelyan*, pp. 197–198.
[66] LaCapra, "Rethinking Intellectual History and Reading Texts," p. 274.

"weighing up and considering carefully a wide range of evidence," and to being "realistic and honest."[67]

The problem with these recommendations is that the more common issue is not dishonesty but the way that our infrastructure of consciousness shapes our inquiry and our interpretations. No amount of careful and judicious weighing of evidence will correct bias in the choice of what to investigate and what not to investigate – the choice of what to weigh up evidence *about*. No amount of careful and judicious weighing of evidence will help us if the categories of analysis available to us prevent us from seeing certain features of or patterns in the evidence we are interpreting.

A classic illustration is Joan Scott's essay on "Gender: A Useful Category of Analysis." By examining the lives of women in various historical periods, Scott was able to argue that a number of the great ages of emancipation and progress in Western history (e.g., the Enlightenment) were not ages of emancipation and progress for more than half the population. Because historians, who had historically overwhelmingly been male, did not pay much attention to the lives of women, because they did not have the analytical category "gender," they had got the big picture quite wrong.[68]

An opposite case, in which a category we *do* have skews our interpretations, is presented in Tomoko Masuzawa's book *The Invention of World Religions*, discussed earlier in this chapter. Again, Masuzawa argues that the very category "religion," used to denote a coherent body of doctrine and practice, was an invention of nineteenth-century academics. It does not adequately capture the cultural and institutional dynamics of the ways people shape their spiritual lives, because even among people who consider themselves members of a single religious tradition (Islam, Christianity, Buddhism) beliefs and practices vary radically from place to place and region to region.[69] If we rely on this artificial category, we will get the big picture quite wrong.

Historicists did offer some practical methods for addressing bias. Again, an important assumption of the historicist tradition is that while interpretation is necessarily subjective, research methods can limit that subjectivity in decisive ways. Historians can adopt a conscientious and careful approach to the question of bias in the sources. The historian should be thorough and wide-ranging in seeking out sources, and careful and critical in assessing their limitations, their potential biases, their strengths, the context in which they were produced, the perspective and motivations of

---

[67] Jordanova, *History in Practice*, pp. 3, 89. [68] Scott, "Gender."
[69] Masuzawa, *The Invention of World Religions*.

the people who produced them, the concepts central to them, the language and rhetorical devices they use, and so on. John Tosh gives a good thumbnail sketch:

> [The] procedure ... is to amass as many pieces of evidence as possible from a wide range of sources ... In this way the inaccuracies and distortions of particular sources are more likely to be revealed, and the inferences drawn by the historian can be corroborated. Each type of source possesses certain strengths and weaknesses; considered together, and compared one against the other, there is at least a chance that they will reveal the true facts – or something very close to them.[70]

And Ludmila Jordanova offered a concise set of criteria for assessing the work of historians: "Of any piece of historical writing we need to ask what sources have been used, how they have been selected, whether they have been used in their entirety or only in part, if they have been interpreted in a plausible manner, if the result is derivative or original, and whether the limitations and specificities of sources have been taken into account."[71]

In fact we can construct a long list of such techniques and desiderata – and I draw here on excellent books by Martha Howell and Walter Prevenier and by Miriam Dobson and Benjamin Zieman. Historians should assess the "genealogy" of the source (the history of its production and preservation). They should know the context in which it was created (in what institution? Under what circumstances?). They should be aware of the intended meaning or purpose of the source. They should understand the competence of the person or persons who created it – their knowledge, their interests, their prejudices, the influence over them of experience, need, or authority. They should know their experience, including their social and cultural background and their distance from or proximity to the events or developments that they are interested in. They should have a knowledge of the conceptual tools and cultural codes they had available to them, and understand their likely or apparent assumptions. They should know their language intimately, in depth and in its varieties (e.g., "officialese," working-class dialects, religious metaphors and associations, regional dialects, its languages of intimacy and hostility, not just the meanings but the connotations of words). They should assess the demonstrable degree of their truthfulness. They should seek out and compare multiple bodies and kinds of sources (we might call this listening to many voices or perspectives). They should draw on multiple theoretical frameworks, drawn from

---

[70] John Tosh, *The Pursuit of History*, 5th edition (Harlow: Longman, 2009), p. 134.
[71] Jordanova, *History in Practice*, p. 95.

4.3 *Epistemological Doubt and Historical Practice*

multiple disciplines, to extract the broadest understanding they can from their sources. At the same time they should not be blinkered by the generalizations those theoretical frameworks rely on, or drawn by them into anachronism – that is, relying on concepts and assumptions drawn from the period of the theory's creation or use but not appropriate for the time period they are studying. They should understand the central concepts used in a text, their associations and connotations. They should pay close attention to the literary and rhetorical devices used – images, metaphors, analogies, stories, turns of phrase. They should pay attention to the references the text makes. They should analyze the forms of emplotment it uses.[72] And we can add that historians should be aware of some of the common pitfalls of historical analysis, of the type addressed in the first part of this chapter.

But what about the biases of the historians themselves? Historicists claim that there is a mode of research that can correct for our *own* bias or subjectivity: the hermeneutic and unconditionally historicist method of immersion in the sources, and of allowing the sources themselves to guide one's formulation of questions. To some extent, they suggest, this method *can* allow historians to step outside of their own history. They do that by suspending their own categories, judgments, concepts, theories, and narrative preferences, and coming to know those of the people they study.

Gertrud Himmelfarb offered a summary of this approach: The historian must make "strenuous efforts to enter into the minds and experiences of people in the past, to try to understand them as they understood themselves," and in doing so "intrude his own views and assumptions as little as possible." He must strive "to transcend his own present in order to recapture the past." That is a task "requiring a great exercise of self-restraint, even self-sacrifice."[73] English historian Richard J. Evans suggested what this kind of approach might mean in practice. The "first prerequisite of the serious historical researcher," he held, "must be the ability to jettison dearly held interpretations in the face of the recalcitrance of the evidence ... Evidence running counter to the argument cannot be omitted or distorted, even at the cost of amending the argument or abandoning it altogether." And this is standard practice. Historians "are perfectly used to trying out ideas on the evidence and throwing them away

---

[72] Howell and Prevenier, *From Reliable Sources*, pp. 60–68; "Introduction," in Miriam Dobson and Benjamin Ziemann, eds., *Reading Primary Sources: The Interpretation of Texts from Nineteenth- and Twentieth-Century History* (New York: Routledge, 2009), pp. 1–18.

[73] "Gertrude Himmelfarb," in *Historians on History*, ed. John Tosh (Harlow: Pearson, 2010), pp. 290–298, here p. 291.

when they don't fit."[74] Again: Historians' relationship with the sources, with the past, is not a struggle for power; it is a dialogue. Historians not only talk; they also listen. Both Himmelfarb and Evans were arguably echoing, again, E. H. Carr, who in 1961 quoted nineteenth-century English historian John Acton's argument that "'History must be our deliverer not only from the undue influence of other times, but from the undue influence of our own, from the tyranny of environment.'"[75]

Himmelfarb and Evans were both bitter critics of postmodernism. But obviously the postmodern epistemology of knowledge offers an excellent starting point for precisely this kind of self-sacrifice, for delivering ourselves from the tyranny of our own environment. We can't sacrifice ourselves until we know who we are. We can't enter into the minds of other people without understanding how their assumptions, categories, expectations, conceptual language – their "infrastructure of consciousness" – differ from our own. Postmodern epistemology helps us understand our own assumptions, categories, language, and premises, as well as those of people in the past. This is a prerequisite for self-restraint. We can't stop thinking in a particular way until we know we are thinking that way. As Carr put it, "the historian who is most conscious of his own situation is also the more capable of transcending it."[76] Charles Beard probably intended something quite similar in 1934, writing that the historian should "examine his [sic] own frame of reference, clarify it, enlarge it."[77] Postmodern theory gives historians invaluable tools and a far more rigorous and systematic method for doing that.

These epistemological considerations create a difficult challenge for students in History, and for teachers as well. The predominant epistemological position of History is paradoxical. As Keith Jenkins observed in 1991, historians know that "history is a shifting discourse constructed by historians and that from the existence of the past no one reading [i.e., interpretation – ERD] is entailed: change the gaze, shift the perspective and new readings appear. Yet although historians know all this, most seem to studiously ignore it and strive for objectivity and truth nevertheless." They continue to go about the mundane business of what Leopold von Ranke called "documentary, penetrating, profound study" in the archives.[78]

---

[74] Evans, *In Defense of History*, p. 104.   [75] Carr, *What Is History?* p. 38.
[76] Carr, *What Is History?* p. 38.   [77] Beard, "Written History as an Act of Faith," p. 228.
[78] Jenkins, *Rethinking History*, pp. 13–14; Ranke, "On the Character," p. 39. For a similar formulation, see Kalle Pihlainen, "Narrative Objectivity versus Fiction," *Rethinking History* 2 (1998): 7–22, here p. 16.

4.3 Epistemological Doubt and Historical Practice

Why? Historians assume, as James Banner put it in 2021, that "historical inquiry is ... always provisional, partial, and perspectival ... Historical knowledge is ineradicably incomplete and uncertain."[79] Our understanding of the past is always being renegotiated, reshaped, and revised, as perspectives change, as social theory evolves, and as inquiry not only deepens or broadens but shifts direction entirely, often in response to events in our own times. Our knowledge of the past does not achieve fixed forms. All History is not just open to debate, critique, and question by people with different experiences, commitments, and perspective; it is guaranteed to be superseded as our own historical context changes. The most fundamental postulate of the discipline of History means that – as the subtitle of Banner's book asserted – all History is revisionist History.

Most historians do not want it not to be this way. They do not want History to achieve certainty. They want inquiry to continue, knowledge to evolve. Change over time is what History is about. If there is any lesson of History, or of history, it is that things change. Why would History not change too? Logically, historians must assume that as the social and historical context of their discipline changes, understandings of the past will change too. Or, rather, the conversation – or debate – about how to understand the past will change.

Coming to understand this model of what "knowledge" is can be very difficult for students, but it can also be enormously exciting for them. Most university students are very familiar with a quite different model of what knowledge is, one drawn from the natural sciences. They understand knowledge to be a coherent body of experimentally or statistically verifiable propositions. That body of propositions evolves over time (as new scientific findings require, e.g., perhaps made possible by new instruments), but it retains the character of coherence and verifiability. That is a very powerful way to define knowledge. Among other things it is the foundation of the astonishingly dynamic technological civilization that has transformed human life over the past 200 years and more. But it helps us relatively little in understanding human affairs, because in human affairs propositions generally cannot be experimentally verified, and can only infrequently and provisionally be statistically tested. The enormous benefit of the mode of understanding that History offers is precisely that it gives students criteria and methods by which we can arrive at plausible and productive assessments of human affairs – or to put it another way, at meaningful questions about human affairs and productive answers to those

[79] Akyeampong, "AHR Conversation," p. 1400; Banner, *Ever-Changing Past*, p. 234.

questions. For the sciences, there are questions for which there are true or false answers, and then there are questions for which there are no true or false answers; there are matters of verifiable fact and matters of opinion. History is a mode of inquiry, a way of knowing, that offers neither verifiable facts nor opinions. Instead, it offers methods for building plausible, coherent, and productive interpretations and arguments in answer to questions for which we know we cannot develop verifiably correct answers.

I have found that confronting this way of knowing is difficult for students. Many make one or both of two assumptions about our knowledge of human affairs. One is that knowledge of human affairs is essentially immune to discussion: If people have different opinions that is the end of the matter. The other is that when people see things differently they have an argument and one wins. Usually, in the context of discussions in class, one side wins by persuading more of their peers to agree with them than with their counterpart. It can be a powerful and inspiring intellectual experience – an intellectual adventure – for a group of students instead to examine their own assumptions and interpretations, together, collectively, through a reasoned and critical discussion, and arrive at a surprising conclusion. I recently took part in such a seminar discussion in a course on the history of terrorism in Europe. In that day's discussion, we compared the thinking of an outright reactionary and of an influential radical feminist. Toward the end of the three-hour seminar, one participant remarked, "isn't it hard when you realize that the most objectionable person you've read actually has a point?"[80] It is hard, but it is also what is called "learning" – not only learning something new about history, but also learning something new about how we learn from others, both scholars and fellow students.

This too may sound paradoxical: History, which assumes that all understanding of the past is perspectival, is also our best antidote to naïve relativism – to the view that, in human affairs, one opinion is as good as another and argument is therefore a zero-sum game in which one opinion wins and the other loses. The model of understanding that History cultivates can be the foundation of reasoned discussion rather than argument, of shared inquiry rather than debate.

Because it is such a capacious discipline, moreover, History is a discussion about everything – politics, economics, religion, philosophy,

---

[80] The readings for that seminar were Moshe Amon, "The Phoenix Complex: Terrorism and the Death of Western Civilization," in *Perspectives on Terrorism*, ed. Lawrence Zelic Freedman and Yonah Alexander (Wilmington, DE: Scholarly Resources, 1983), pp. 13–18, and excerpts from Robin Morgan, *The Demon Lover: On the Sexuality of Terrorism* (New York: Norton, 1984).

science, medicine, gender, sex, war, art, music, hiking, dance halls, coffee shops, books, automobiles, nations, cities, the environment, murder, love, grief, ideas, food, drugs, architecture, farming, stock-breeding, wine, childbirth, and so on endlessly. There is something for everyone and everyone views things from their particular perspective. Many people from many backgrounds want to stick their oar in. Some of them will champion one or more of a wide range of theoretical perspectives drawn from the social sciences, from critical social theory, or from the humanities; that makes the discussion yet more complex. Historicists will not be constrained by any theory and will be comfortable coming up with an interpretation that is idiosyncratic, ad hoc, possibly even original. That creates still greater diversity.

This diversity creates breadth and depth of understanding. Human problems, historical problems, are enormously complex. They cannot be fully understood, productively understood, from one perspective, by one person. As G. M. Trevelyan put it, given the complexity of historical issues and the partial and interpretive character of historical interpretation, the "only way in which a reader can arrive at a valuable judgement on some historical period is to read several good histories ... written from several different points of view, and to think about them carefully." And if those points of view are argued with passion and vehemence, that is fine. The "dispassionateness of the historian is a quality which it is easy to value too highly"; what really matters is "accuracy and good faith."[81] Given those qualities, diverse perspectives and intense disagreements are productive of deeper understanding.

This was not a new view when Trevelyan advanced it in the early twentieth century. Writing in 1828, the great English historian Thomas Babington Macaulay even went so far as to suggest that the "practice of distorting narrative into conformity with theory is a vice not so unfavorable as at first sight it may appear," since "conflicting fallacies ... correct each other."[82] One hundred and sixty-one years later the great English Marxist historian Eric Hobsbawm made a "case for the benefits of partisanship ... insofar as it provides an incentive to change the terms of scientific debate, a mechanism for injecting new topics, new questions and new models of answer."[83] One year after that Thomas Haskell wrote in an essay on the

---

[81] Trevelyan, "Clio, A Muse," p. 173.
[82] "History and Literature: Macaulay," in *The Varieties of History*, ed. Fritz Stern (New York: Vintage, 1972 [1956]), pp. 72–89, here p. 82.
[83] "Partisanship," in Eric Hobsbawm, *On History* (New York: New Press, 1997), pp. 124–140, here p. 136. This essay was originally published in 1979.

objectivity question that it is through the "collision with rival perspectives" that "our thinking transcends both the idiosyncratic and the conventional." History is "essentially a communal enterprise," a field of inquiry both riven and driven by disagreement. Disagreement is not chaos; the fact that there are competing interpretations does not mean that we do not know what we are talking about. Rather, precisely "by doing what we can to multiply the perspectives brought to bear on a problem, we can achieve higher levels of completeness" of understanding, by seeing a topic from multiple perspectives.[84]

Indeed, as Chapter 2 pointed out, the existence of multiple competing interpretations does not necessarily invalidate any one of them. As Stefan Berger wrote in 2018, because historical reasoning is interpretive and perspectival, there is always "a possible plurality of true statements" about any particular history.[85] In fact, given the nature of historical evidence, the enormous complexity of any given historical situation (including our own), and the perspectival nature of both historical interpretation and most historical evidence, a plurality of true statements and of plausible, productive, empirically justified interpretations is not just possible but guaranteed. The same evidence, viewed from a different perspective, will support different interpretations. The same topic can be illuminated using different bodies of evidence, and that will likely yield different interpretive conclusions. Different historians will investigate different aspects of a given – inevitably complex and multifaceted – historical phenomenon, development, or place and time.

Diversity of perspectives is not a problem or a weakness of History, then; it is a strength. The discipline of History is not sabotaged by lack of objectivity. It is energized and enriched by diversity of perspectives. As Trevelyan put it in 1913, "There are indeed, and there ought to be, many kinds of historian and many kinds of history."[86] One hundred and nine years later the president of the American Historical Association, Jacqueline Jones, concurred: "Today the wonderful kaleidoscope of methodologies, time periods, archival sources, and topics indicates a vibrant discipline that needs no heavy-handed advice from any one person or group in order to

---

[84] Thomas Haskell, "Objectivity Is Not Neutrality: Rhetoric vs. Practice in Peter Novick's *That Noble Dream*," *History and Theory* 29 (1990): 129–157, here pp. 134, 136.

[85] Stefan Berger, "A Plea for Renewing a Left-of-Centre Engaged History Writing," in "Conversations: What Is History? Historiography Roundtable," *Rethinking History* 22 (2018): 500–524, here p. 501.

[86] George Macaulay Trevelyan, "The Present Position of History," in Trevelyan, *Clio, A Muse and Other Essays* (Freeport, NY: Books for Libraries, 1913), p. 194.

thrive."[87] This is why a tremendous number of people read History, despite the fact that it is of no immediately apparent practical use to the great majority of them: because it is so interesting. If you don't find an interesting book about history on the shelf in a bookstore or library, there is a simple solution: Move along the shelf a bit, and you will find a topic or a perspective or an argument or a story that *is* interesting to you.

Historians must hold each other to a high standard of methodological rigor. They must be expected to formulate well-informed and open-ended questions; be thorough in their search for evidence; read carefully and with respect for the integrity of sources; remain open to evidence that contradicts their expectations, theories, and ideological preferences; bring to their sources a variety of theoretical frameworks and methodological tools; avoid or find ways to compensate for availability bias, confirmation bias, anachronism, source mining, and other common pitfalls of historical inquiry; examine their own assumptions, language, preferences, and experience, and so on. As long as they do, the inevitable bias of individual historians – what they, for historical reasons, find interesting and important – is a useful starting point for inquiry and for interpretation. "Biases" in this sense direct different historians to different questions, sources, and interpretive resources. That is a strength, not a weakness. The diversity of historians' motives and perspectives is a positive benefit. Political agendas, religious beliefs, life experiences, even quirks of character guide historians to formulate *many* and *varied* questions.

If History were a matter of opinion, political and personal motivations would be a problem. In fact, if that were the case, History would not exist; only people with opinions about history would. But History is not a lot of people with opinions. It is a lot of people with interpretations. Interpretations are based on evidence and analysis. History with a capital H has standards of evidentiary support, standards for the use of evidence, standards of analysis, standards of exposition. The discipline of History cannot ask for objectivity because it cannot ask historians to erase their own historicity. History just asks them to pose interesting questions and to address them through methodologically sound inquiry. History as a discipline embraces the irreducible variety, diversity, and particularity of the human condition. Logically, therefore, it also embraces the specificity and the irreducible variety of its practitioners.

Again: This view is not a pious politically correct celebration of diversity. It is a restatement of the fundamental assumption of historicism – that

---

[87] Jones, "Presidential Address," p. 22.

knowledge is historically conditioned. Knowledge, understanding, and meaning come from a particular place and time. History never yields certain, verifiable, objective findings, except on very narrow factual matters. It does not generate certain conclusions or reproducible results. That is fine. It is not supposed to. History is not about knowing things for certain. It is an inquiry-driven, critical, interpretive discipline. It is not about knowing; it is about thinking. It is not about certainty; it is about reasoning. This is not an epistemological problem or crisis of History. It is the epistemology of History. G. R. Elton wrote in 1967 that the task of history teachers is to give their students "a real sense of the fluidity inherent in enquiry, debate, disagreement ... it is his [sic] function to cast doubt upon the possibility that in historical studies anyone will ever be finally 'right.'"[88] Why? Because that is what History is for. Not answers but inquiry, discussion, debate, thinking and rethinking, with others, so that we continue to deepen our insight and our understanding – so that we continue to learn. Chapter 5 will turn to the subject of what we learn when we learn to learn in this way.

[88] Elton, *Practice of History*, p. 165.

CHAPTER 5

What Does History Teach Us?

5.1 History as a Way of Thinking

The discipline of History employs a particular way of thinking, unique among the academic disciplines. As Michael Oakeshott put it, it is a "distinct mode of inquiry and understanding."[1] It is a particular way of defining questions, of pursuing knowledge and understanding, and of building answers. The most important thing History teaches is this unique mode of inquiry and the habits of thought that guide and support it.

The foregoing chapters have defined historians' modes of inquiry and have discussed some of the benefits of learning them. As a starting point for thinking about what History teaches and how to teach, it is helpful to think about why it is useful to us more broadly in life, not only as students of History.

First, History is a capacious, expansive, and holistic discipline. It encourages us to look at multiple aspects and dimensions of any problem or puzzle. It asks us to place human phenomena in broad social context (economic, political, cultural, historical, environmental, etc.). It encourages us to examine the ways in which different aspects and dimensions of any problem or historical situation were interrelated with each other and with their context. It gives us a holistic and dynamic rather than a hierarchical model of such connections and relationships. It predisposes us to accept and understand complexity and indeterminacy. Historians are trained not to ask what "the" cause was, or what "the most important" cause was, but to ask how a complex web of causal factors interacted. History may, therefore, help us avoid the habit of developing narrow solutions. More important, it may also help us avoid the habit of developing narrow definitions of the puzzles or problems we want to solve.

---

[1] Michael Oakeshott, *On History and Other Essays* (Camel, IN: Liberty Fund, 1999 [1983]), p. 49.

The second section of this chapter will address why all of this is important. For now, we can simply say that vanishingly few of the puzzles and problems that we face in our individual and collective lives resemble those addressed in the lab by the natural sciences, or through datasets in the social sciences. We do not usually have much reliable data, and we cannot usually generate it by experiment. We usually cannot identify the one question that would reduce the puzzle to a straightforward, clear yes/no problem. So we need to do the best we can to develop a plausible and useful understanding of things on the basis of the information we do have. We have to piece together as much information as we can, with a sharp eye for possible sources of bias, from the greatest practicable variety of sources and perspectives, keeping an open mind and an awareness that the evidence may show us that we have been asking the wrong question, or that our premises or assumptions were incorrect. Then we have to develop as comprehensive and plausible an interpretation as we can, still remaining open to the idea that it may turn out that we were wrong, or that it would have been equally or more fruitful to think of the problem in a different way. In most human affairs the only available approach is to get our problem surrounded by examining it from many angles, and develop a solution that seems likely to be successful on the basis of that broader contextual understanding.

Sam Wineburg has given us a concise statement of this argument: "History," he wrote, "offers a storehouse of complex and rich problems, not unlike those that confront us daily in the social world."[2] William H. McNeill had much the same view a decade and a half earlier, in 1985: "We have to learn to live with uncertainty and probabilities, and act on the basis of the best guesswork we are capable of." As a discipline that not only lives with uncertainty but often makes it a virtue, using it to open new avenues of inquiry, History is "the very best introduction we can have to the practical problems of life."[3]

Second, History is a nominalist and idiographic discipline. It asks us to set aside preconceptions, expectations, assumptions, and even experience. Specifically, because it is capacious and expansive, it encourages us to weigh great masses of evidence, of many different kinds, to consider how different forms of evidence are correlated, how they contradict, confirm, or complement each other, and to examine that evidence critically. It does not limit

---

[2] Wineburg, *Historical Thinking*, p. 51.
[3] McNeill, "Why Study History?" For a similar statement, see Reisman, "Teaching the Historical Principle of Contextual Causation," pp. 44–45.

us to consideration only of those kinds of evidence that appear most directly relevant to our definition of the problem. Historians are in the habit of searching constantly for more and different kinds of evidence. They are in the habit of thinking self-consciously about how they might interpret different forms of evidence. Moreover, History can teach us respect for the integrity of our evidence – it can teach us not to "cherry-pick" or "mine" evidence for those elements that confirm our assumptions or our perspective, or that appear to speak most directly to our concerns. Instead, historians are trained to examine both particular pieces of evidence (e.g., texts) and larger bodies of evidence as coherent wholes. To use the language of the American Historical Association's definition of the skills History education should impart, History teaches "a disciplined, skeptical stance and outlook ... that demands evidence," it teaches students to "seek a variety of sources," and it teaches them "a methodological practice of gathering, sifting, analyzing and ordering" that evidence.[4] Finally, and not less important, in its more uncompromisingly historicist mode History can teach us to be attentive to the questions that the evidence opens for us, rather than the questions that we – initially – wanted answered.

In short, at its best History can teach a specific form of intellectual rigor. This is not the logical rigor that enables natural scientists to develop experimental programs that will lead to clear, unambiguous answers. It is the empirical rigor that forces us to assess the evidence in its full mass, coherence, and expanse, and to follow where it leads us. This is the rigor of intellectual flexibility; perhaps we might call it rigorous open-mindedness. The natural and social sciences tend to cultivate the habit of asking "does the evidence confirm my expectations?" History cultivates the habit of asking "what do my sources tell me?" But beyond that, it cultivates the habit of asking "what have I missed?" What evidence – and what kinds of evidence – have I missed? What have I missed in the evidence I have? More still, what *questions* have I missed, and what forms of evidence would help me to get *those* question surrounded? Is my question too narrow? Is my thinking biased by particular assumptions? An historicist, in particular, might put it this way: Historians do not expect the evidence to conform to their own definition of what the important questions are. They are inclined to follow the evidence to the important questions – and to define "the evidence" expansively, not limiting it to what is relevant to the first question they pose, or the second, or the third, or the fourth. This is of

---

[4] American Historical Association, "History Discipline Core" (2016), www.historians.org/teaching-and-learning/tuning-the-history-discipline/2016-history-discipline-core.

enormous importance because the world is a tremendously complex place. It is not always at all easy to understand what our problems really are. It is very often difficult to define what we need to know to address our problems and opportunities effectively. History, as a discipline that asks open-ended and strategic rather than operational questions, can help us do that.

Third, History is inquiry-driven. It is driven by and to not answers but questions. Historical inquiry does not reach an endpoint. It reaches a provisional conclusion on the way to the next question. Again, this is a characteristic that History shares with all fields of knowledge, all forms of inquiry. Obviously, historians have to reach conclusions. Equally obviously, the natural and social sciences too advance by deriving new questions from recent results. But because History is so capacious, so expansive, because it is a holistic and integrative discipline, investigation in History can often generate a richer, more varied, more open field of questions than investigation in other disciplines.

This is one reason that the standard measure of historians' scholarly accomplishments is the number of books they publish, whereas in the natural sciences (and to a lesser extent in the social sciences) the number of "papers" – that is, articles in scientific journals – is the appropriate measure. The kinds of inquiry that History most values cannot be addressed in an article; they are complex and wide-ranging, and answering them requires book-length publications. But even for the student of History, who will not be publishing any books, History teaches a specific form and *habit* of inquiry. The natural sciences seek to refine and narrow the question until it is answerable by an experimental result. Most of the social sciences, increasingly, seek to refine and narrow the question until it can be answered by statistical analysis. History instead teaches us to get our problem surrounded by broadening the question, by asking more questions, by seeking not the decisive experimental or statistical result but the new perspective, the angle not yet considered, the body of evidence not yet examined.

This is how History can teach its students to think strategically. We might put it this way: The sciences and social sciences ask their students to put their eye to the microscope or to the telescope and zero in on the subject; History asks its students instead to sit up and look around as widely as possible. The issue for an historian is not: What is the right question to yield a result? Historians ask themselves instead two closely related questions – each of them appropriately complex. The first is: Have I asked enough questions so that I can present an analysis that is comprehensive enough to be convincing? The second is: Do I know enough now

5.1 History as a Way of Thinking

to present my findings in a way that is coherent, that is interesting, that expands understanding, sparks reflection? In all these ways, History helps broaden thinking, to counteract narrow and overly simple understandings of human problems.

Fourth: History is self-consciously eclectic and pragmatic in its use of theories about human societies and human affairs. It cannot be other than that, because it sees such theories as themselves historically conditioned – as not true or false, right or wrong, but as products of the experiences of particular people in a particular time and place. History is a natural antidote to dogma. Historians cannot commit themselves, intellectually, to the rightness or correctness of any one particular theoretical or interpretive framework because all such frameworks are themselves historical artifacts. That means that historians can draw on insights and on questions generated by many different theoretical approaches without being constrained by any of them. Indeed, because History is so expansive, historians really *must* draw on multiple theoretical resources, in order to do justice to the multiple aspects of any historical situation or problem that they are very likely to consider in the course of their research and of constructing their own interpretations.

This approach to theory can cultivate the intangible but very important quality that I call *active* intellectual flexibility. Historians are not trained only to consider multiple perspectives, multiple points of view, the possible questions that might derive from multiple theoretical approaches and the possible answers that such approaches might generate. They are trained, rather, actively to go in search of new perspectives, of alternative theoretical approaches. Again, the question for the historian is not: Is this the right theory? It is rather: Are there more theories that could help illuminate this complex historical situation?

Fifth: History is interpretive and perspectival. Because it builds not on decisive results but on holistic and integrative answers, History produces a form of understanding that is always approximate and provisional. Further, the fundamental postulate of historicism (that everything is historically conditioned) makes it impossible for historians to see their own conclusions as anything but themselves artifacts of history. Historians know they are not "right." We are all children of history. We think the way we do for good historical reasons. So do other people, who think differently. Historians become accustomed to the assumption that there may be multiple plausible and productive perspectives on an issue, or interpretations of a question. They understand that there are multiple valid views on what the really important and meaningful question is. They are aware of – as the American Historical Association put it – "the value of conflicting narratives and evidence."⁵ Or consider Mary Jo Festle's conclusions from speaking to her students about the benefits of studying History: "The interpretive nature of the discipline," she observed, is "a fundamental and striking lesson."⁶ In History we do not just expect, we actively hope that there will be multiple competing interpretations on any issue – because multiple perspectives deepen and enrich our understanding of an historical period or situation. Even better, a multiplicity of perspectives can yield a multiplicity of questions; and in an inquiry-driven discipline, that is gold.

History not only presents us, self-consciously, with interpretations rather than proofs, however. It also explicitly demands that we understand the very different ways that people in the past saw their world. Again, the hermeneutic tradition – energized and enriched by postmodern discourse analysis – asks us to understand the conceptual world of the people we study. It asks us to set aside our own ideas, assumptions, terminology, and views and understand how *other* people saw things.

Because it is committed not to any particular social theory but to the eclectic and pragmatic use of social theories (and in recognition of their character as historical artifacts), History also teaches us to be agnostic regarding the truth and the value of theories, ideologies, perspectives, dogmas, and beliefs. The point of History is not to determine whether such intellectual formations are right or wrong (because we know they are instead simply historical), but to understand their origins and to consider what productive questions they raise. Again, this does not mean that historians do not have moral standards, or that they do not find the beliefs of people in the past to have been deplorable or admirable. It means instead that the first job of historians is to understand how people came to have those beliefs, or how they came to have moral standards different from ours. Doing that also forces us also to consider why we think differently than they did.

In short, the study of History can be exceptionally good training in open-mindedness, in tolerance for multiple viewpoints, in willingness to learn from others who do not think as we do, and in critical self-awareness. Again, this is not a fashionable plea for diversity or tolerance; it is in the bones of the discipline. G. M. Trevelyan was not making a fashionable plea for diversity when, already in 1913, he urged the student of history to "read

⁵ AHA, "History Disciplinary Core."
⁶ Mary Jo Festle, "How They Change: Students Tell Us How History Transforms Them," *Perspectives in History* 53:9 (2015), www.historians.org/publications-and-directories/perspectives-on-history/december-2015/how-they-chaged-students-tell-us-how-history-transforms-them.

several good histories" about any topic, "written from several different points of view, and to think about them" carefully, or in 1949 to "get inside the minds of the people" of other times "and see their problems as they saw them, not as we see them now."[7]

Sixth, one reason that History produces holistic and integrative interpretations rather than decisive results or proof is that the evidence historians must use is almost always fragmentary, incomplete, and perspectival or biased. The discipline has developed sophisticated ways to deal with these problems, but historians are forced to develop the habit of thinking of the conclusions they draw in degrees of certainty and uncertainty. Historians are accustomed to regarding their own conclusions as possible, plausible, likely, fairly solid, or pretty well convincing but not certain. That can be further training in open-mindedness, but it can also excellent training in how to think effectively about the real situations that human beings face. We almost always have only imperfect, partial, fragmentary, and biased evidence. We can almost never perform experiments or gather statistics; even where we can gather statistics we usually know that they are likely to be the product of imperfect data-gathering mechanisms, and not infrequently of self-serving lies. In business, in politics, in policy, in diplomacy, in our personal affairs, we do not get the chance to put our hypotheses to decisive experimental or statistical tests. In real life we have to get our problems surrounded as best we can with evidence that we do have, try to understand them in broad context, and come to provisional conclusions with varying degrees of confidence, in awareness of the limitations of what we know. Marc Bloch put it this way in 1941: "It is always disagreeable to say: 'I do not know. I cannot know.' ... But there are times when the sternest duty of the savant [i.e., scholar – ERD], who has first tried every means, is to resign himself to his ignorance and admit it honestly."[8] History teaches us that stern duty with some regularity.

The potential benefits of learning History, with a capital H, can be summed up as follows: Because of its fundamental characteristics as a field of inquiry, History can be uniquely effective in fostering:

- breadth of thinking
- depth of inquiry
- rigor and imagination in the use of evidence
- intellectual flexibility

---

[7] Trevelyan, "Clio, A Muse," p. 173; Trevelyan, "Bias in History," p. 77.
[8] Bloch, *The Historian's Craft*, pp. 59–60.

- open-mindedness in the face both of diverse perspectives and of the limitations of our knowledge
- sophistication in reasoning from imperfect information

There are certainly skills and habits of mind that History is less good at fostering than some other disciplines. The natural sciences are often better at training us to think with precision. Mathematics and philosophy are often better at training us in logic. The social sciences often give us better training in deductive reasoning. The humanities (literature, theater, the arts) are better at fostering our creativity. But the things that History does teach are extraordinarily important, and it can teach us those things extraordinarily well.

There are two further, more economical ways to summarize the benefits of History education. First, many teachers make a distinction between *information* and *analysis*. Higher education does involve absorbing information, even simply memorizing it, but it also involves learning to analyze the information one has. As Keith C. Barton and Linda S. Levstik write, analysis "involves breaking material down into its constituent parts, detecting the connections and interactions of those parts, and identifying the arrangement or organizational structure that holds them together."[9] To analyze is to make connections, to establish relationships, to compare, to organize information into coherent patterns and coherent interpretations. This is what enables both critical evaluation and the creation of a coherent perspective – an interpretation, insight, or understanding.[10] It is a common experience among university instructors that university students have little training in analysis. They can find information or evidence in a text. They can understand it – they can read a text and understand what it says. They can apply the information they have gathered, for example, by answering factual questions. But they do not have the habit of developing a structured analytical understanding of what they learn – of examining connections, making comparisons, seeing relationships.

In fact, in my experience (and it is confirmed in some of the literature on teaching history at university) most students arrive at university with the habit of viewing the texts they read either as "information" or as "opinion,"

---

[9] Barton and Levstik, *Teaching History for the Common Good*, p. 69.
[10] Many teachers derive their understanding of this distinction from some variant of Bloom's Taxonomy, a theory of educational objectives developed in the 1950s. See, for example, Patricia Armstrong, "Bloom's Taxonomy," https://cft.vanderbilt.edu/guides-sub-pages/blooms-taxonomy or "Bloom's Revised Taxonomy," www.celt.iastate.edu/teaching/effective-teaching-practices/revised-blooms-taxonomy.

but not as analysis or interpretation.[11] They have a hard time grasping, as one 2008 study found, "such unfamiliar mental operations as analysis, interrogation, interpretation, subjectivity, and argumentation." They are accustomed to "looking for information to be extracted," but they "have difficulty slowing down enough to allow a complex explanation to emerge," much less present it in the form of a reasoned, structured argument or interpretation.[12]

Alternatively – again, in my experience – they are accustomed to agreeing or disagreeing with a viewpoint, but not to analyzing it in depth or detail. How does an author's conclusion follow from her assumptions, and where do her assumptions come from? How are different features of a text related to each other? How do the characteristics of one text relate to the characteristics of another? How is language being used in a text, and how does that compare to the use of language in another text? Passive scanning of information and statement of opinion they "get." Active construction of understanding, they do not "get."

This is not because students cannot analyze, interpret, or ponder. It is because they have not been taught to do so. My own impression from three decades of teaching is in fact that the emphasis on testing in schools has encouraged students coming into higher education to think that the purpose of education is to test their ability to absorb information. The central place of testing in schools does not tell them that the aim is to teach them how to think analytically. Exactly that is what History does teach them. History asks students not to memorize theorems, apply equations, or reproduce key experimental results, but to analyze, to establish relationships, to make connections, if possible even to develop spooky questions.

Second, for some decades "critical thinking" has been the gold standard for higher education. Critical thinking is valued because it is more applicable to real-world situations than, for example, the kind of thinking involved in recognizing what theorem or equation to apply to a problem and applying it correctly. Definitions of critical thinking uniformly identify as its elements many of the skills and habits of thought that History

---

[11] See, for example, Peter N. Stearns, "Getting Specific about Training in Historical Analysis: A Case Study in World History," in *Knowing, Teaching, and Learning History: National and International Perspectives*, ed. Peter N. Stearns, Peter Seixas, and Sam Wineburg (New York: New York University Press, 2000), pp. 419–436, esp. pp. 422–426; Stuart Greene, "Students as Authors in the Study of History," in *Teaching and Learning in History*, ed. Gaea Leinhardt, Isabel L Beck, and Catherine Stainton (Hillsdale, NJ: Lawrence Erlbaum, 1994), pp. 137–170, esp. pp. 155–157; Diaz et al., "The History Learning Project," here esp. pp. 1214, 1219.
[12] Diaz et al., "The History Learning Project," pp. 1213, 1215.

cultivates. One influential review of the subject defined critical thinking for example as

> a rational response to questions that cannot be answered definitively and for which all the relevant information may not be available. It is ... an investigation whose purpose is to explore a situation, phenomenon, question, or problem to arrive at a ... conclusion about it that integrates all available information and that can therefore be convincingly justified. In critical thinking, all assumptions are open to question, divergent views are aggressively sought, and the inquiry is not biased in favor of a particular outcome ... Because conclusions cannot be tested (as they can be in problem solving), the arguer must demonstrate their plausibility by offering supporting reasons.[13]

That is pretty precisely what History does, and can teach. But History can also be a useful way of teaching a particular subgenre of critical thinking, what Patricia M. King and Karen Strohm Kitchener defined in 1994 as "reflective judgment." This term means the ability not only "to make defensible arguments about vexing problems," but also to "recognize that a problem exists" in the first place. This is a talent that is cultivated precisely by the very broad and open-ended approach the discipline relies upon.[14]

There is another useful definition of "critical thinking," however, that is also relevant in History pedagogy. As Suresh Gunasekaran has defined it, critical thinking is the ability to understand that in any system of thought truths – or at least conclusions – derive from assumptions, and that if the assumptions are changed the truths will be too.[15] As a discipline, History can train us to examine the unfamiliar assumptions that historical people had and to analyze how their conclusions derived from those assumptions and guided their actions. This too can foster intellectual flexibility – the ability to understand ideas unlike our own and to analyze the logic of systems of thought that we do not subscribe to. Ideally, doing that fosters self-awareness – the ability to consider what the consequences of making different assumptions would be; to examine our own assumptions, and how our own truths and decisions derive from them; and to see the logic of other people's views.

---

[13] Joanne Gainen Kurfiss, *Critical Thinking: Theory, Research, Practice, and Possibilities* (Washington, DC: Association for the Study of Higher Education, 1988), p. 20.

[14] Patricia M. King and Karen Strohm Kitchener, *Developing Reflective Judgment: Understanding and Promoting Intellectual Growth and Critical Thinking in Adolescents and Adults* (San Francisco, CA: Jossey-Bass, 1994), pp. 1, 3.

[15] Personal communication, June 18, 2022.

5.2 History and the Present

I believe that the potential benefits of studying History are of particular importance in the present time, for three specific reasons. First, globalization is rapidly advancing all over the world. Interactions between societies, and between people from different societies, are becoming more frequent and more intensive at an enormous rate. And almost every society on the planet is becoming rapidly more diverse. In my own lifetime I have lived in three moderately homogenous societies – far Northern California, Germany, and New Zealand. All three of those societies have been transformed by a tidal wave of globalization and diversification. This is true of a very large proportion of early twenty-first-century societies.

In this context, intellectual flexibility is of enormous importance. The ability to understand the perspectives, values, and assumptions of other people; the ability to understand difference; the ability to accommodate and profit from diverse perspectives; the ability to understand and analyze complexity – these skills have never been more important. History can teach them. In particular, a discipline that can give people the concrete experience of understanding that other people do (or did) not think the way we do, have no reason to, and are never going to, is of enormous relevance today. It can help us avoid making ignorant and self-referential assumptions and doing arrogant things that fuel conflicts.

Second, the deepening romance of technology, in a global society being transformed by innovation, has generated rising momentum toward purely operational thinking. "There's an app for that" has become a not-so-humorous commentary on how we deal with the opportunities and problems we face. There is a growing obsession in discussions of policy with data-driven decision-making, as if data alone could give us perspective that allows us to evaluate it with intelligence, or could dictate the values that we try to realize in our lives, institutions, and societies. There is a growing obsession in the social sciences with big data, as if we will find the right answers if we can just amass enough data. It is true that masses of data, if gathered on the basis of sufficiently broad definitions of our problems and analyzed in sophisticated and open-minded ways, can correct our assumptions and broaden our perspective. But historicism tells us that data are generated by people in specific historical contexts, on the basis of assumptions and aims shaped by those contexts, often in the service of interests defined by those contexts. As Ethan Kleinberg wrote in 2016: "Data is a 'given,' but by whom and to what purpose?"¹⁶ And data generated on the basis of narrow criteria can give people the illusion that they have posed the right question and that by answering it they have mastered problems that actually they have not even begun to understand or even perceive. If our questions are too narrow, if our models are too simple, if our assumptions are skewed, no amount of data and processing power can save us from doing stupid things. As a discipline that can teach people to examine assumptions, to widen inquiry, to embrace not just the power of "information" but the complexity of the contexts in which it is generated and in which we use it, History has never been more needed than in the age of "big data." History can teach us to broaden our questions, to make our models more complex, and to examine our assumptions more critically and with greater self-awareness.

Third, the internet is enormously corrosive of community, of reason, and of critical and analytical thinking. It is a universe of echo chambers in which people are told that they are right and everyone who does not agree with them is stupid, dishonest, or crazy, and in any case certainly contemptible. There seems to be no limit to the cultivation of moral outrage about and intolerance of difference on the internet. The internet endlessly repeats the message that people have the right and even the duty to be narrow-minded. Because of this the internet has become a giant petri dish in which simplistic thinking proliferates like a well-fed bacterial colony. It is a thermonuclear explosion of spur-of-the-moment "hot takes" and vehement assertions, the overwhelming majority of them grossly simplistic and completely unfounded. Almost everywhere on the internet single-factor explanations thrive – in particular, conspiracy theories. As Henry Steele Commager remarked already in 1965, "the most useful lesson the student of history can learn is to avoid oversimplification, to accept the notion of multiple causation," and to avoid the tendency to "find the explanation of prodigious events in some fortuitous occurrence, in some lurid conspiracy."¹⁷ A generation later a group of scholars concerned with History education warned that "nothing is more poisonous to whole societies than a simple, monocausal explanation of their past experiences and present problems," which can "stir unwarranted pride or shame or fury, raise up scapegoats," and "hopelessly tangle public debate on the most critical issues at hand."¹⁸ The kind of thinking that History fosters can be

---

[16] Kleinberg, "Just the Facts," p. 98. [17] Commager, *Nature and the Study of History*, p. 88.
[18] *Lessons from History: Essential Understandings and Historical Perspectives Students Should Acquire* (Los Angeles: University of California Press/National Center for History in the Schools, 1992), p. 20.

an antidote to that. It asks students to broaden their perspective, consider more aspects of the problem, inquire further. It pushes them to develop a complex, nuanced, dynamic understanding of the puzzles and problems they consider. It requires them to adduce substantial evidence, of multiple forms, cross-checked and weighed against each other.

In short: Thinking in the ways History teaches us to think – strategically, flexibly, and critically – has never been more important than it is right now. This is anything but an original thought – it is something professional historians have argued for decades. There is a long tradition in liberal democracies that argues that the forms of critical thinking History fosters are essential skills for democratic citizenship. An excellent example is a study published in 1992 by the National Center for History in the Schools in the United States, titled *Lessons from History*. The authors argued that the study of History can help give people the "ability to distinguish between fact and conjecture," to understand "the complexity of causation," to understand "how human intentions matter, but also how consequences are shaped by the means of carrying them out." History "inculcates an understanding of paradox," it helps train us to "detect bias, to weigh evidence, and to evaluate arguments ... to distinguish between anecdote and analysis," and gives us "wariness about quick, facile solutions, which have so often brought human suffering in their wake." History is also "conducive to the kind of mutual patience and civic courage required to bring to life those values that are so much needed in our pluralistic, multicultural society," because it acquaints students with "people of other cultures and other eras" and confronts them with the unfamiliar ideas, values, assumptions, traditions, and habits those people had. It teaches students not to lodge "an indictment of them for not thinking and behaving as we do," but to "explain why they thought and behaved as they did." And History can even offer us the "dignity of free choice" by revealing to us the "immense range of approaches people have taken to political, economic, and social life, to personal integrity and salvation, to cultural creativity" as potential alternatives to the approaches our own traditions, values, and ideas offer us.[19]

Hopes like these continue to thrive. Keith Jenkins argued in 2003, for example, that the fact that all History is interpretive, that no History is ever "literally true, objective, fair ... non-positioned" (i.e., not written from the perspective of historians as themselves historical persons) "is a positive democratic value" because it means that "there is no credible authoritative

---

[19] *Lessons from History*, pp. 14, 15, 19, 6.

or authoritarian historicized past that one has to defer to."[20] What is more, if History is always in "interpretive flux ... even the most marginal [people in a society – ERD] ... can at least make their own histories even if they do not have the power to make them other peoples' ... a space exists for the desirable outcome of as many people(s) as possible to make their own histories such that they can have real effects (a real say) in the world." Beyond this, and independent of any particular group interest or identity, History fosters "an approach designed to develop a democratising critical intelligence."[21] In 2004 Keith C. Barton held that the "unique 'way of knowing'" distinctive to History "engages students in a process critical to democratic pluralism: that of reaching conclusions based on evidence." By requiring us to make carefully reasoned judgments on the basis of often complex and ambiguous evidence, History teaches us the ability to "distinguish between a myth and a grounded assertion," between a slanted opinion and a reasoned conclusion, and this, according to Barton and Levstik, is "the foundation for participatory democracy."[22] Sarah Maza wrote in her 2017 book *Thinking about History* that "exploring and accepting the strangeness of the past on its own terms is a lesson in tolerant relativism" as well as "an invitation to critique the present" – both important aspects of democratic citizenship.[23]

In short, there is a long tradition of arguing that the study of History in higher education can teach students a democratic way of thinking. Or perhaps we can be more precise: The study of History in higher education can give students the *experience* of a democratic way of thinking.

I believe, though, that hopes like these should be kept modest. In sketching them out, I have used the word "can" a great deal – History "can" teach this or that, or it "has the potential to" teach one thing or another. That is because I have only anecdotal evidence that it *does* teach these things. That anecdotal evidence is extensive, and sometimes striking. One student told me many years ago that he came into my class thinking that Hitler was a great national leader and left it understanding that he was a racist criminal who brought disaster to his own country and the world. Another stopped me in the hall to tell me that my classes taught him to think through answers for himself, "and no one can ever take that away from me." A student told me recently in a seminar on terrorism that the

---

[20] Keith Jenkins, "On Disobedient Histories," *Rethinking History* 7 (2003): 367–385, here p. 367.
[21] Jenkins, *Rethinking History*, pp. 66, 67, 68. For a similar argument, see also Lynn Hunt, *History: Why It Matters* (Cambridge: Polity Press, 2018).
[22] Barton and Levstik, *Teaching History for the Common Good*, pp. 82, 189.
[23] Maza, *Thinking about History*, p. 196.

5.2 History and the Present

most important thing she felt she had learned in the class was to be critical in her use of abstract terms like "terrorism," "revolution," "totalitarianism," and so forth. More prosaically, students have told me that they learned to write analytically in my classes, and that this has been important in their subsequent professional success – in the military, in the State Department, and in the marketing division of a cosmetics company, to give three examples. I don't mean to trumpet my own pedagogical achievements; I believe responses like these are common for any History professor. They have convinced me that History *can* yield extraordinary intellectual benefits for students, including helping prepare them for participation in a democratic society.

But it is not clear that it reliably *does* these things. I have touched on the reason for that already: It is easy to show that historians in the past have embraced a great multitude of profoundly objectionable ideas and values and have often acted as apologists for and servants of vicious and grossly self-defeating regimes and social systems – imperialist, slave-holding, dictatorial communist, fascist, and racist ones, for example. To refer again to my own intellectual experience, I was originally trained as an historian of Germany, a country in which a large proportion of professional historians in the early twentieth century embraced chauvinistic and aggressive nationalism, and in most cases happily accommodated themselves to Nazi totalitarianism (and some of them, later, communist totalitarianism too). The record does not particularly suggest that historians are better than others at warning against moral turpitude, false assumptions, stupidity, and self-destruction.[24]

Once more, however, this unfortunate fact is not a problem but a resource for college-level instructors in History. It is an outstanding way to get the central message of History across: that we are all creatures of our history. What is more, the awareness that historians do not have superior insight into human affairs is an important part of the democratic message of History pedagogy. What could be a more democratic message from a teacher than acknowledgment that people very much like her, loyal to much the same intellectual tradition that she values, using much the same intellectual tools that she uses, have often turned out to have been egregiously wrong? The point of teaching History is not to persuade students that "if you think like me, you'll get it right." It is to give them

---

[24] See, for example, Herbert Butterfield, "The Dangers of History," in Herbert Butterfield, *History and Human Relations* (New York: MacMillan, 1952), pp. 158–181, here pp. 162, 164; William Appleman Williams, "Introduction," in *History as a Way of Learning* (New York: New Viewpoints, 1974), pp. 3–23, here pp. 7–8.

effective tools for thinking like – and for – themselves and the ability to recognize that they are doing so as historical persons, persons shaped by their own time, place, and experience.[25]

5.3 An Aside: History Pedagogy and Civic Education

In addition to seeing the intellectual habits cultivated by History as having important democratic potentials, some historians have argued that the *content* of historical instruction should inculcate democratic values as well. This has been particularly true of thinking about History education in the schools. Again, *Lessons from History* (from 1992) is a good example. After enumerating the ways in which History can cultivate democratic habits of thought, they also suggested that the history curriculum should familiarize students with and build their loyalty to Anglo-American legal and constitutional traditions and the historical struggles to defend them – including, for example, both the philosophical and political traditions central to the thinking of the framers of the American Constitution (Montesquieu, Locke, the Glorious Revolution of 1688, the common law tradition) and the alternatives championed by early twentieth-century totalitarians and the titanic struggle to defeat them.[26]

Learning about all of these things is unquestionably important, but the exclusive focus on them in a History curriculum would be a profound error. There is a long history, reaching back into the nineteenth century, of efforts to use the schools to inculcate specific beliefs – in this case a sense of national belonging, of shared citizenship, of patriotic loyalty to a country and its institutions. Recent debates in the United States (as well as in Australia, Great Britain, and many other countries) have made clear how strong the hold of this idea still is on the imaginations of many people. In those debates some proponents of anti-racist education have argued that History and/or Social Studies education in the schools should contribute to American democracy by giving pupils an understanding of the ways racism is engrained in American institutional structures, economic arrangements, social practices, public policies, and cultural forms. If we fail to address these systemic injustices and their origins in our national history, they argue, we are tacitly supporting systemically racist

---

[25] There is a very cogent discussion in Alberto Rosa and Ignacio Brescó, "What to Teach in History Education When the Social Pact Shakes?" in *Palgrave Handbook of Research in Historical Culture and Education*, ed. Mario Carretero, Stefan Berger, and Maria Grever (New York: Palgrave MacMillan, 2017), pp. 413–428.
[26] *Lesson from History*, pp. 5, 10, 11, 12.

5.3 An Aside: History Pedagogy and Civic Education

outcomes.[27] Opponents have argued instead that History and/or Social Studies instruction should not focus on developing a critical eye for the injustices suffered by some and inflicted by others or teach pupils to dismiss important American traditions, such as respect for the Founding Fathers and their ideas and values. Instead, it should focus on inculcating the traditions, values, and goals that underpin a shared democratic civic culture and our shared democratic aspirations.

Whether History education in schools can really be used in these ways is open to question. The heyday of nationalist education in the late nineteenth and early twentieth centuries was also the era in which revolutionary socialist internationalism was most influential, in some cases (such as Germany) precisely in those societies where public education was most widespread. Some recent international studies suggest that efforts to indoctrinate school pupils may backfire, leading them to reject the ideas and values teachers attempt to impose on them. Others suggest that in practice History teachers in the schools are primarily focused not on instilling values but on teaching cognitive skills – in other words, that teachers simply will not teach to national History curricula in the ways curriculum commissions think they will.[28]

In any case, whatever the merits of values-oriented approaches in school-level History instruction, they are largely irrelevant for higher education, the primary concern of this book. There are two reasons for this, one less important, the other more important.

The first reason is that historians study – and History departments teach – a great many subjects that do not have any *direct* relevance to current developments in our own society, but are enormously valuable in part precisely for that reason. If we really want people (to quote again from *Lessons from History*) to gain a "comprehensive understanding of their ... world" in the early twenty-first century, they really need to learn about *other* times and places. They need to study, for example,

---

[27] A particularly influential example is Kendi, *How to Be an Antiracist*.
[28] See, for example, James V. Wertsch, "Is It Possible to Teach Beliefs, as Well as Knowledge about History?" in *Knowing, Teaching, and Learning History: National and International Perspectives*, ed. Peter Stearns, Peter Seixas, and Sam Wineburg (New York: New York University Press, 2000), 38–50; Ronald W. Evans, "Educational Ideologies and the Teaching of History," in *Teaching and Learning in History*, ed. Gaea Leinhardt, Isabel L. Beck, and Catherine Stainton (Hillsdale, NJ: Lawrence Erlbaum, 1994), pp. 171–207, here esp. pp. 203–205; Sakki, "Aims in Teaching History," esp. pp. 75–79; Arthur Chapman and Terry Haydn, "Teaching History in Changing and Challenging Times," *History Education Research* 16 (2020): 1–3; Symcox, "Internationalizing the U.S. History Curriculum," p. 41; and Joan Middendorf, David Pace, Leah Shopkow, and Arlene Diaz, "Making Thinking Explicit: Decoding History Teaching," *National Teaching and Learning Forum* 16 (2007): 1–4.

medieval European history, ancient Chinese history, the history of seventeenth-century Thailand, or the history of the Kingdom of Kongo between the fifteenth and nineteenth centuries. No one who lacks knowledge of at least one politically decentralized society can have a full understanding of the modern centralized bureaucratic national state. No one who has not studied at least one colonial society can really understand any imperial society. No one who knows nothing of how subsistence economies have worked really understands the history of capitalist or socialist economies. We come to understand any phenomenon not only by studying it in great detail but also by studying contrasting phenomena, so that we can grasp with depth and clarity what it is *not*. In this sense, the least relevant education in History is also the most relevant education in History. As John Tosh put it in 2008, "the value of the past lies precisely in what is different from our world. By giving us another vantage point, it allows us to look at our own circumstances with sharper vision."[29]

The second, more important reason that the goal of teaching a specific set of beliefs is irrelevant for History instruction in higher education is that teaching a particular historical interpretation, much less a particular political perspective or civic orientation, will not work in History instruction at that level. For one thing, students in university and college classes are adults with already formed political views and loyalties. Again, they are not interested in being told what to think. The understanding that pupils arrive in the classroom with their own ideas about the past, and about how we know about the past, is central to the recent literature on History in the schools as well. The focus in that literature tends to be on the problem of what one group of authors in 2005 called "preexisting but inappropriate knowledge." I do not think that way of framing the issue can be useful for college or university educators. Students arrive in university and college classrooms with ideas. We can ask them to adopt new methods of arriving at their own ideas, we can ask them to examine the origins of the ideas they already have, but telling them their ideas are "inappropriate" is not an option.[30]

---

[29] Tosh, *Why History Matters*, p. 28.
[30] See Rosalyn Ashby, Peter J. Lee, and Denis Shemilt, "Putting Principles into Practice: Teaching and Planning," in *How Students Learn: History in the Classroom*, ed. M. Suzanne Donovan and John D. Bransford (Washington, DC: National Academies Press, 2005), pp. 79–177, here p. 79. See also Lévesque, *Thinking Historically*, p. 171; Alan Sears, "Trends and Issues in History Education in International Contexts," in *Debates in History Teaching*, 2nd edition, ed. Ian Davies (London: Routledge, 2017), pp. 42–51, esp. pp. 46–48.

5.3 An Aside: History Pedagogy and Civic Education

But beyond that, the nature of the discipline itself means that it would be self-defeating to try to use History instruction in this way. To attempt it would contradict many of the essential intellectual characteristics of the discipline, including specifically the very ones that make it, as a way of thinking, potentially a great contributor to the political and social competence of democratic citizens – and therefore a great benefit for the civic culture of any democratic society. That would include, for example, its holism, its interpretive character, its fostering of critical and analytical thinking, its drive toward expanding and open-ended inquiry. These characteristics subvert any prescriptive program of content-oriented civic education.

Educational researcher Peter Seixas offered a brilliant summary of this point in an essay of 2000. The discipline of History, he wrote, "is public, subject to debate, and falsifiable. Its truth claims rest on historical method and the historical record through documentary and artifactual sources." Instruction in History aims to teach students how one applies historical methods to historical evidence in order to construct interpretive claims. In teaching that, History "should help them to develop the ability and the disposition to arrive independently at reasonable, informed opinions" (I would say instead, interpretations). It "provides students with standards for inquiry, investigation, and debate. History taught through this approach exemplifies the liberal, open society and should prepare students to participate more fully in one."[31]

At the university and college level in democratic societies young people already participate fully in a liberal and open society, and they are acutely aware of that. To repeat: They will not sit quietly and be told what to think. To use the example of *Lessons from History*, it is easy to imagine the kinds of critical responses students in any substantive course in History would oppose to the approach advocated in that study. No one familiar with the traditions of continental European Christian Democracy or Social Democracy would be likely to agree that the Anglo-American tradition is the only legitimate or viable democratic tradition. No one familiar with the histories of British or American imperialism would be likely to take celebrations of Anglo-American legal and constitutional traditions at face value. There are unlikely to be many young people today who would consider it appropriate to study the political vision of the Founding Fathers in isolation from the fact that many of them held Africans and African Americans in slavery or advocated dispossessing or exterminating

---

[31] Seixas, "Schweigen!" pp. 24, 25, 34.

Native Americans. The use of college or university History courses for the kind of instruction proposed for the schools in *Lessons from History* simply would not work.

Something similar can be said of the debate over anti-racist education at the college and university level. I have taught at only three universities, in New Zealand, Ohio, and California. Nevertheless, this is experience broad enough to convince me that there is probably not a university-level History classroom in any democratic society on the planet in which it would be a good idea for an instructor to gloss over the history and legacy of racism – certainly not in a course on modern history, whether of the United States or any other place. The history and legacy of racism is a topic that a large proportion of young adults around the world today regard as central to their own lives and interests. Any History instructor who tried to ignore it would be giving away one of her most effective tools for engaging student interest. She would also surrender a major part of her pedagogical and intellectual authority, since a large proportion of students would regard her approach as not intellectually legitimate. I would expect, further, that if she failed to address the subject in her classroom her students might very well step in and address it themselves. In higher education, we cannot ignore the interests of our students; they will not let us do that.

By the same token a highly directive approach to anti-racist education might backfire as well, because many students object to having *any* intellectual agenda imposed on them by their professors and will vote with their feet if that is attempted. This is of course particularly likely to be true in more conservative and less diverse educational settings. In that social context, again, History instructors can easily throw away a good share of their pedagogical authority if they are perceived to be using their teaching position to pursue a political or social agenda. Having taught in a department of History with predominantly quite liberal faculty and predominantly quite conservative students (in southern Ohio), I can say this as a matter not of speculation but of direct experience.

In short, I repeat once again: Students do not take university-level courses in History (or in any social-science discipline) to be told *what* to think, but rather to learn *how* to think things through for themselves. The function of higher education is to give them the intellectual tools with which to do that. At the college and university level education in the social sciences and humanities is not something that we do to people. We offer them our support and guidance in their pursuit of their own education. It may be that this is not true in authoritarian and totalitarian societies, which have more extensive means of limiting the amount and kind of information and the number of perspectives accessible to their young citizens. But in democracies students arrive at university with well-defined interests and convictions, and with an acute sense of their right to be respected and to pursue their own intellectual agendas. Any effective pedagogical approach must accommodate this simple fact.

There is a further important consideration concerning education in History as civic education. What we say to students in History classes – certainly in higher education, arguably at any level – is less important than how we treat them. The kind of relationship we establish with students is more important than the outcomes we aim to pursue. Talking *at* students, telling them what to think, treating them as a captive audience, is disrespectful. Ignoring their concerns and focusing solely on our own is disrespectful. Trying to make students instruments of our own purposes is disrespectful. Students who feel disrespected are very likely to reject what they are being told as the narrow-minded and arrogant opinions of a person who is ignorant of and indifferent to their lives, experiences, and values. If we treat students as independent people with their own views, perspectives, needs, and goals, rooted in their own history, if we do that consistently and visibly with all our students, then we are not only establishing our own pedagogical and intellectual authority, but also teaching democracy.

But we are also teaching the foundational ethic of the discipline of History. It should be obvious that what I am suggesting is that to teach History effectively we must establish with our students a relationship quite similar to the kind of relationship historians have with the people of the past whom they study. We must engage with them as fully human beings. It is good historical practice to be interested in the values, thoughts, experiences, and perspective of the people we study, to "immerse" ourselves in *their* world. It is good historical practice to "listen" to them, just as it is good pedagogical practice to listen to our students. It is good historical practice to respect the integrity of our sources, not to "cherry-pick" the parts of them that interest us, or fit our preconceptions, just as it is good pedagogical practice to respect the integrity and independence of our students rather than viewing them as useful instruments for our own aims. It is good historical practice to be willing sometimes to set aside our own interests and questions and be guided to *new* questions by our sources, and it is good pedagogical practice to sometimes be guided to new questions by our students. It is good historical practice to expand our horizons by reading books written by scholars who disagree with us, or who have quite different interests from our own, just as it is good pedagogical practice to support the intellectual aspirations and listen to the ideas of students whose interests and values are not our own. It is good historical practice to understand that our perspective is peculiar to our own time, place, and experience, just as it is good pedagogical practice to address our students from an acknowledged interpretive position, rather than posing as all-knowing, objective, and "right."

To teach History effectively, we must give our students the same respect we give to the past. Our intellectual ethics and our pedagogical ethics are one and the same. If we focus on mastery and outcomes – on controlling what our students learn and what it means to them – we will often be working both against them and against the foundational logic of History. Doing that, we are very likely to fail in four ways. First, we will fail in our goal of control. Second, we will fail to learn from – and with – our students. Third, we will fail to convince our students that History offers them a powerful way of thinking. And fourth, we will fail to give our students the benefit of that way of thinking specifically in their civic lives – for example, the understanding that people are complex historical beings, that causation is complex and dynamic, that understanding why our society has a problem is more powerful than having a "solution," that every solution will have unintended consequences, that they themselves are historical beings who think the way they do for historical reasons, and that getting the process right is more important than controlling the outcome. We are most likely to succeed at all these things if we engage our students in a spirit of open inquiry, with respect for them as historical persons and acknowledging our own historicity as well.

5.4 Lessons of History

Beyond this fundamental ethical posture, does the study of history, as it is undertaken by the discipline of History, offer us practical lessons? Does it give us concrete knowledge about how human societies and systems work, knowledge that can help guide our individual or collective decision-making? As prominent historian Marc Bloch pointed out already in 1941, an intellectual pursuit "will always seem to us somehow incomplete if it cannot, sooner or later, in one way or another, aid us to live better."[32] If we

---

[32] Bloch, *The Historian's Craft*, p. 10. For a more recent argument, see Leo Goarke, "Teaching History: The Future of the Past," in *The River of History: Trans-national and Trans-disciplinary Perspectives on the Immanence of the Past*, ed. Peter Farrugia (Calgary: University of Calgary Press, 2005), pp. 59–75, esp. pp. 61, 71.

use the methods and approaches of History, can we draw lessons from history that help us do that?

This question may be becoming more urgent as the emphasis on practical education and return on educational investment (for individuals and societies) grows. Some critics now argue that History needs to start proving that it offers concrete benefits. David Armitage, in an essay of 2021, argued that historians need to consider "what the discipline of history can contribute to human flourishing," or they might "put ourselves out of business by failing to justify our craft and our profession to publics starkly confronted by the challenges of the present."[33] In 2022 Daniel Steinmetz-Jenkins observed that "the history profession is experiencing a turn to the present" because "long-standing anxieties over presentism have crumbled under the weight of recent events" like the election of 2016 in the USA, mounting climate catastrophes, and the global upheaval over the legacies of colonialism and racism.[34] The concerns of the present are so urgent, these authors suggest, that History has to contribute to addressing them or become irrelevant.

Yet the idea of deriving generalizable lessons from history runs counter to many of the most enduring characteristics of History. The self-consciously expansive nature of the discipline creates a powerful presumption that human affairs are so complicated, and the webs of dynamically interrelated causes and influences so dense, that no historical situation can be "the same as" any other historical situation. There may be important similarities between two historical situations; we may be able to identify common forces at work in them. But given the complexity of the webs of causation History explores, stating that societies "have a tendency" or people "have an instinct" is not even a useful starting point for inquiry into any specific historical or present situation.

In fact, the historicist conception of History in particular has often predisposed its adherents to argue that there are no lessons of history. Many, across the political spectrum, do argue that professional historians have the important function of puncturing the convenient lies that many people tell about history. As Canadian historian Margaret MacMillan put it in 2008, their "proper role ... is to challenge and even explode national myths"; in this she agreed with English historian Eric Hobsbawm, who observed in in 1994 that the "deconstruction of political or social myths dressed up as history has long been part of the historian's professional

---

[33] Armitage, "In Defense of Presentism," pp. 59, 79.
[34] Steinmetz-Jenkins, "Introduction," p. 559.

duties."³⁵ But the idea that history offers us positive "lessons," as opposed to the argument that History can be a check on politically motivated lies, has not attracted much support among historians. G. M. Trevelyan summed up a well-established position in 1924, for example, when he suggested that "the study of history has often disproved the universal applicability of supposed laws laid down by political or other theorists with an insufficient range of observation" to understand the true complexity of human societies.³⁶

Historians drawn to postmodernism have restated this view with a new theoretical sophistication by rejecting the structural-functionalist notion that human societies behave in coherent and determined ways at all. The most influential statement of this view is that of Michel Foucault, who argued in the 1970s that careful analysis of any historical situation would reveal "several pasts, several forms of connexion, several hierarchies of importance, several networks of determination, several teleologies" or possible outcomes.³⁷ This irreducible complexity makes it impossible to retroactively predict what happened next. By extension, all an historian could say about any present situation would be that a number of different things *might* happen, but we can't be sure which things *will* happen. Every historical outcome is so complex that it is fundamentally open and indeterminate. The search for clear causation "assumes the existence of immobile forms that precede the external world of accident and succession," but in truth the "forces operating in history are not controlled by destiny or regulative mechanisms, but respond to haphazard conflicts."³⁸

More recently historians influenced by queer theory have made similar arguments in favor, as Valerie Traub put it in 2013, of a "queer analytic that encompasses a range of relations that do not aspire to any intelligible identity [i.e., unity – ERD] ... continually exposing identity's contradictions and indeterminacy."³⁹ Historical outcomes emerge not from determining causes, but from complex and open-ended dynamics; history is not

---

[35] Margaret MacMillan, *Dangerous Games: The Uses and Abuses of History* (New York: Modern Library, 2008), p. 39; Eric Hobsbawm, "Identity History Is Not Enough," in Eric Hobsbawm, *On History* (New York: New Press, 1997), pp. 266–277, here p. 273.

[36] Trevelyan, "History and Literature," p. 89. See also Theodore S. Hamerow, "What Is the Use of History?" in *Reflections on History and Historians*, ed. Theodore S. Hamerow (Madison: University of Wisconsin Press, 1987), pp. 205–243, here p. 208.

[37] Michel Foucault, *The Archaeology of Knowledge* (New York: Pantheon, 1972), 5.

[38] Michel Foucault, "Nietzsche, Genealogy, History," in *Michel Foucault: Language, Counter-Memory, Practice*, ed. Donald F. Bouchard (Ithaca, NY: Cornell University Press, 1977), pp. 139–164, here pp. 142, 152, 154.

[39] Valerie Traub, "The New Unhistoricism in Queer Studies," *PMLA* 128:1 (2013): 21–39, here p. 29 – but note that Traub did not agree with this position; she was merely characterizing it.

governed by laws like those that govern the behavior of matter or living systems. It is irreducibly complex.

Despite my own appreciation for the historicist tradition, I do not think that this apparently logical conclusion is logical at all – and for two quite divergent reasons. The first is that (as I suggested in Chapter 2) while historians do not discover "laws" that govern human societies, they do discern patterns – sometimes independently, sometimes with the aid of social theory. Recognizing such patterns does not allow us to predict with certainty what will happen in any given situation, but it can give us a sense of the likely potentials and dynamics of that situation. As Louis Gottschalk put it, "historical analogies present us most often with clues to *possible* rather than *probable* behavior, with the ability only to *anticipate* rather than to *predict*, to *take precautions* rather than to *control*."[40]

To give just one example, the history of the twentieth century gives us a pretty good idea how leadership cults work in totalitarian movements. Those movements aim to abolish popular sovereignty and legality as the source of legitimacy for political and social action, replacing them with the will of the Great Leader or of the Party. That requires that they posit that the Great Leader or the Party is not merely human but godlike – unerringly wise, infallible in judgment, irresistible in willpower. Because the criteria totalitarians use for the selection of leadership, administrative and scientific personnel are not integrity, expertise, and ability but loyalty to the Leader or the Party, they are exceptionally incompetent and corrupt. Because loyalty is often expressed in them as ideological extremism or extremist activism, they are commonly subject to constant, progressive radicalization of rhetoric, dogma, and practice at the expense of realism and rationality. Since their legitimacy rests on the idea that the Leader or Party determines everything (and is infallible), they therefore need scapegoats for their inevitable corruption, inefficiency, failures, and excesses. They usually therefore resort to widespread persecution of scapegoats, not infrequently escalating to mass murder. They frequently start wars, either to distract from their failures or to justify mass murder of scapegoats alleged to be "internal enemies" in league with the external enemies they have created for themselves. What is more, there is a correlation between the depth of the corruption and the viciousness of the crimes such regimes indulge in, and the degree of loyalty they inspire. The supporters of such a regime are complicit in its corruption and crimes and are therefore motivated to attribute infallibility to the Great Leader or Party and to grant them

---

[40] Luis Gottschalk quoted in Hamerow, "What Is the Use of History?" p. 210.

absolute authority. The Leader or the Party can then be seen as the real author of those crimes; he becomes both a justification and an alibi for their follower's criminal complicity. For this reason, the leadership of such regimes has a positive incentive to engage in corrupt and criminal action, in order to consolidate the loyalty of their supporters. The more blatantly and extravagantly criminal their actions, and the more obviously dishonest their excuses for them, the greater the loyalty they inspire, until the Leader or the Party is free of any constraints of at all – except the constraints of reality, which ultimately catch up with them and implode the whole edifice of criminal stupidity.[41]

The specific history of every totalitarian movement is different. Some avoid war with external enemies, some are relatively modest in their persecution of internal enemies, in some a dictatorial Party can serve as a check on a Great Leader, and some are even able, once they have consolidated near-total control, to abandon a policy of murder because they develop the capacity to cover up their failings in other ways. Historians attracted to the social-science method would want to reduce the pattern I have laid out here to something measurable and defined. They would draft up a definition of totalitarianism (determined by statistical measures, organization charts, or legal principles); develop statistical measures of policy outcomes (persecution, murder, war); define a roster of contextual or internal factors that might influence such regimes (ethnic diversity, religious division, inequality; degree of participation in international trade relations, degree of ideological isolation). Statistical correlations would then tell her which such regimes will behave in which ways and under what conditions. An historicist would regard all of that as indulgence in an inadmissible degree of reification and generalization. Regardless: If we are looking for useful lessons of history, even the most rudimentary pattern recognition should warn us that any such regime is quite likely to be an exceptionally ineffective, aggressive, and destructive one; that probably nothing said by anyone who participates in it can be trusted; and that ultimately it will either impose on its neighbors the necessity of defeating it, or else destroy itself by its incompetence.

The second – and more important – reason I find the idea that we cannot draw any lessons from history unconvincing is that this is in itself arguably the most important lesson of history. As G. R. Elton remarked in

---

[41] For an effort to present "lessons" about tyranny based on patterns in the history of twentieth-century dictatorships, see Timothy Snyder, *On Tyranny: Twenty Lessons from the Twentieth Century* (New York: Duggan, 2017).

1990, what history "will teach above all is the unpredictability of the human animal."[42] Unlike most historicists, however, I regard this as a lesson of the most profound and enormous practical significance. It is in fact the most important lesson that any person can learn about human beings and human societies. People and societies are stubbornly, irremediably complex. Outcomes are therefore not determined, nor can we determine them. We do not know what people are going to do, or what is going to happen in any given society at any given time. And we cannot make people do things, or make things happen in societies as we wish. People are not things. They are not governed by the kinds of laws that govern things. People are people, they are complex, they are not reliably or predictably governed by anything – in fact, not even by their own specific and particular histories, because both people and their histories are so complex that people can make many quite different uses of the resources their histories give them.

Empirically, it appears that this is not self-evident. Historically, many people have failed to understand this.[43] Their failure has often had disastrous consequences. Generations of theorists of capitalism have argued that markets will regulate themselves. But they don't. Generations of theorists of capitalism have also believed that people will act in their own rational economic self-interest. But they don't. Generations of theorists of socialism have argued that people will behave in their own best social and economic interests as defined by their class position in society. But they don't. Generations of theorists of socialism have also argued that planned economies will be more efficient and provide a better standard of living for the vast majority of people. But they aren't, and they don't. For millennia, the champions of nearly every religion known to humanity have argued that faith would make people better – more moral, less violent, more compassionate. But it doesn't. Generations of racists have thought that they understood how relations between different ethnic groups "had to" work. But they didn't. Slave-holders in the American South believed that they could dominate and exploit African Americans with impunity, but they couldn't. They faced relentless and ineradicable resistance. Nazi planners believed that the Slavic peoples of Eastern Europe were racially inferior "herd people" who were uncreative and weak and unheroic, and that therefore it would be easy to defeat, dominate, exploit, and

---

[42] "G. R. Elton," in *The History Debate*, ed. Juliet Gardiner (London: Collins & Brown, 1990), pp. 6–12, here p. 9.
[43] For an influential study centered on this point, see James Scott, *Seeing Like a State: How Certain Schemes to Improve the Human Condition Have Failed* (New Haven CT: Yale University Press, 1998).

exterminate them. But it wasn't. By 1942 the Nazis faced perhaps half a million partisans in arms in occupied Eastern Europe and were being slowly crushed by an army of Soviet soldiers who were indomitably courageous and resourceful.

Every theory that has claimed to be able to predict how people will act has been wrong – often disastrously wrong. But sometimes the opposite is true. Human beings and human societies are so complex that we cannot even reliably predict the failure of our own predictions of their behavior. Sometimes people do act in their own rational economic self-interest. Sometimes they do behave in the way we would expect members of their class to behave. Sometimes people of faith do rise above the average of human character and behavior, and show a degree of kindness, decency, self-sacrifice, and wisdom that are extraordinary and inspiring. Some people are crushed by oppression. Sometimes markets do work the way they are supposed to. Sometimes economic planning does pull off what people later call economic miracles – for example, in South Korea between the 1960s and the 1990s, or in Western Europe between the 1950s and the 1980s. And sometimes people accurately predict the future. The brightest scientific minds in the USSR told their political leadership in 1970 exactly why and how the Soviet economic and social system would – and nineteen years later did – fail. Vaclav Havel told the leadership of the Czech Communist Party that the entire system they presided over would one day suddenly implode, and fourteen years later it did.[44]

There is an important corollary that I believe is a further lesson of history. Political and social systems that treat people as if they are things are very likely ultimately to fail. Sometimes that failure will come quickly and be catastrophic, like the explosion of death, blood, and destruction in which National Socialism, Italian Fascism, and Japanese militarism destroyed themselves. Sometimes it will be slow and grinding, as it was in the case of the Soviet Union's long, miserable decline into economic and social meltdown. Sometimes it will be a combination of both, as in the case of nineteenth-century imperialism, which ground on for decades, relentlessly failing to create stable and self-sustaining imperial societies before imploding after 1945. Sometimes failing systems, like slavery in the Americas, can be mercilessly clamped onto social and political orders for centuries. The end can come in a tidal wave of blood, as it did in the United States, or in

---

[44] Andrei Sakharov, Roy Medvedev, and Valentin Turchin, letter to Brezhnev, Podgorny, and Kosygin, March 1970, in *An End to Silence*, ed. Stephen F. Cohen (New York: Norton, 1982), pp. 317–327; Vaclav Havel, "Letter to Dr. Gustáv Husák" (1975), in *Václav Havel, or Living in Truth* (London: Faber and Faber, 1986), pp. 3–35.

a whimper of legal reform, as it did in Brazil. And sometimes there never seems to be any end at all, and failure must be measured by persistent outcomes rather than by a change of regime or legal order. Racism and sexism are based on the false premise that people are, first and foremost, things, bodies. Every society afflicted by them pays a gigantic and obvious price in conflict and in opportunity costs that impoverish everyone in them. Still they persist, despite those costs, despite their obvious ongoing failure.

A second corollary lesson is that it is not possible to make people. Societies and people are too complex to be shaped, sculpted, molded. Italian Fascists were convinced that they would shape a New Fascist Man who would recreate the ancient Roman Empire, but they didn't. German National Socialists were convinced that they would generate the Aryan master race that would conquer the world, but they didn't. Soviet communism was convinced that it would give birth to the New Soviet Man who would build a utopian society, but it didn't. Liberals were convinced that the liberal capitalist order would create a rational, moral, and civically responsible *homo economicus*; but it didn't. Evangelical Christianity claims that it delivers people who are born again pure in heart and upright in action, but the long history of financial and sexual scandals involving televangelists shows that it doesn't. Some people believe that Buddhism will foster peace and tolerance, but the long histories of conflict and upheaval in Myanmar and Thailand (for example) do not indicate that it does. No human contrivance can so effectively control the endless complexity of human life, or so obliterate historical experience, as to make people predictable.

A third corollary lesson is that nothing is ever free, nothing ever comes without cost. Human societies and human histories are so complex that any action will always come at a price. There are consequences to everything; every action impacts the entire complex pattern of human society – human relationships and connections. Human societies are dense webs of interconnections. When we exert force on one part of that web, that force will reemerge somewhere else in it. When we change one part of it, we change the whole network of relationships that make it up. Everything we do in one area of human life, of a society, will have consequences in multiple other areas. And we are almost never fully aware of what those consequences will be because they emerge from the dynamic interaction of myriad factors at play in any given social and historical context. My colleague John Smolenski, an historian of early America and the transatlantic world, calls this the "iron law of unintended consequences." As Joseph C. Miller wrote, History's "epistemology is richly ironic, filled with unpredicted outcomes, consequences of actions unintended by the initiators of the changes to which they ended up having contributed, indirectly, through the reactions of others that they provoked."[45]

Historians sometimes offer pithy formulations of such lessons in unpredictability. Take, for example, this insight from historian of Russia Alexander Etkind: "Human grammar distinguishes between subject and object, while human history does not necessarily do so."[46] In other words, people with power (subjects) do not act with predictable effect or with impunity on people without power (objects). No people are without power; privilege is a ceaseless struggle, and it exacts a terrible price. This is an insight that is simple to state; but its implications are enormous. Or consider the reflections, in a history of the Brazilian musical form samba, of Hermano Vianna: "Movement toward homogeneity can coexist with movements toward heterogeneity. They are not necessarily opposing forces." When societies strive to create greater uniformity and conformity, they generate resistance and difference. When societies become more diverse, they generate pressure toward unity. Vianna argued that in fact some disorder, disunity, conflict, or division – some "entropic heterogeneity" – is a social necessity. Without it "the system cannot create anything new. It becomes static and eventually 'dies.'"[47] This was exactly Vaclav Havel's prediction about communism in Eastern Europe in 1975: It regarded all human spontaneity and creativity as a threat; it was therefore blighted by a "death principle" hostile to the essential nature of human beings, and it would eventually collapse.[48]

Lessons like these are not actionable knowledge. They do not give us a particular course of action. Instead, they can (again that word!) make us think more carefully about what might happen if we do choose a particular course of action. As a capacious and expansive field of inquiry, History can help us define the *range* of possible outcomes and of possible costs by developing the habit of seeing situations in their full complexity and context. It can encourage us to spend some more time reflecting on how we have come to have the problem that we are trying to solve. It can persuade us to pursue the kind of open-ended and eclectic inquiry that can help us understand our problems more fully and precisely. It can train us to consider what kinds of biases might compromise our understanding of it,

---

[45] Miller, *The Problem of Slavery*, p. 28; John Smolenski, personal communication, April 2018.
[46] Alexander Etkind, *Internal Colonization: Russia's Imperial Experience* (Cambridge: Polity Press, 2011), p. 6.
[47] Hermano Vianna, *The Mystery of Samba: Popular Music & National Identity in Brazil*, ed. and trans. John Charles Chasteen (Chapel Hill: University of North Carolina Press, 1999), p. 112.
[48] Havel, "Letter," p. 24.

what kinds of solutions we might be predisposed to adopt, and what potential consequences we might be predisposed to ignore. It can give us a better understanding of where we might look to find intelligent critique of our own unconscious biases and of our preferred solutions. It can encourage us to understand that we do not have *the* answer, but only *an* answer, and to reflect on the strengths, weaknesses, advantages, and drawbacks of that answer. History can remind us that we are very likely to fail to foresee the full range of consequences of our actions, that we need to be prepared to be flexible, and that we need to have mechanisms and "signposts" or indicators in place that tell us when we are failing and should exercise that flexibility. Above all, it can train us to look further than the answers we already have, further even than the questions we already have – because it trains us in *inquiry*. Dominick LaCapra has offered a pithy formulation: History trains us in habits of thought that "are not narrowly utilitarian but instead allow one to intervene in, or contribute to, an open, questioning, and self-questioning process of inquiry."[49]

Perhaps it is useful to put it this way: History is training in deliberation. Deliberation has three meanings. One is careful reflection. The second is slowness to take action, founded on the understanding of the need to have a care about the consequences of what we do. The third is discussion, debate, thinking together with others who may disagree with us, but with whom we weigh considerations, objectives, perspectives, costs and benefits, and thereby work toward what is appropriately called "collective wisdom." As Jim Grossman, the president of the American Historical Association, put it in a 2016 *Los Angeles Times* opinion piece on the decline in the number of History majors in recent years: "To think historically is to recognize that all problems, all situations, all institutions exist in contexts that must be understood before informed decisions can be made."[50] History can teach us how to go about achieving an understanding of those contexts, in breadth and depth.

This is not at first glance a very inspiring message, particularly for people who seek practically useful lessons from History. But if we think a little more carefully about it, it is very inspiring. Again: History is uniquely valuable precisely because it asks us to think broadly, not narrowly; it requires us to think and to ask about complex contexts. We can hope that thinking in this way can be the foundation for important decisions that are

---

[49] Dominick LaCapra, *Understanding Others: Peoples, Animals, Pasts* (Ithaca, NY: Cornell University Press, 2018), p. 156. LaCapra is speaking here of the humanities as a whole.
[50] James Grossman, "History Isn't a 'Useless' Major," *Los Angeles Times*, May 30, 2016, www.latimes.com/opinion/op-ed/la-oe-grossman-history-major-in-decline-20160525-snap-story.html.

more grounded, more realistic, and therefore less likely to go catastrophically wrong. But equally important, we can hope that it can help mitigate the ongoing, grinding, petty, paltry, stultifying, humiliating, squalid, cumulative disaster of narrow-minded, simplistic, unrealistic, fumbling, ill-informed, hasty, oblivious, and self-defeating patterns of decision-making across the whole range of public policies and private actions, trivial as well as momentous, that affect our lives from day to day. It can do this not least by training us to think systematically about the complexity, and the history, of the problems and the opportunities we face – and about how our own history influences our understanding of them.

Almost four decades ago, I spent some months doing research in an archive in a small provincial town in what was then communist East Germany. One Sunday afternoon while out for a ramble in the countryside around the town, I made the acquaintance of a gentleman of advanced years, a Baltic German who had fled the Soviet advance into Latvia in 1944, gotten sick, and not made it all the way to the West. He was bitterly anticommunist. After some initial chitchat, he proceeded to explain to me in some depth and detail what was wrong with communism. At one point in that explanation, for some reason I can't recall except that it had to do with repairing his roof, he jabbed me in the chest with his forefinger and said, "Listen up, young man: *First* think; *then* work." History teaches us *how* to think in a uniquely powerful way, and it encourages us to believe that, having thought, we should perhaps think a little more before getting to work.

CHAPTER 6

Principles and Guidelines for Teaching History

6.1 Respect for Our Students and for Our Discipline

In an essay on History pedagogy published in 2009, Joel M. Sipress and David J. Voelker remarked that "in a discipline renowned for its freewheeling intellectual diversity, it may not be possible (or even desirable) to define a single distinctive approach to" teaching.[1] This is certainly true, and it is one of the great strengths of History as a subject of study in higher education. Nevertheless, approaching History in ways that build on the particular and unique strengths of the discipline will maximize the benefit to those studying it. I have six suggestions for how to do that. These suggestions are founded on two general principles that I believe can guide effective teaching in History.

The first principle is respect for our students as people, as products of their own history and choices, and not as things that we make. Again: Education in History is not something that we do to students; it is something that we do with them.[2] This is an approach to teaching that is focused not on *message* and *outcomes*, but on *ethics* and *process*.

The second principle is respect for History – for the power and distinctiveness of this particular way of thinking. We can have faith that History, as a way of thinking, will be fruitful for our students. We do not need to – and cannot – control outcomes. Instead, we should aim to establish a process through which students can experience the costs and benefits of

---

[1] Sipress and Voelker, "From Learning History to Doing History," p. 25. For an account of how History is taught at universities, see Hitchcock, Shoemaker, and Tosh, "Skills and the Structure of the History Curriculum," pp. 50–56. For a study of the range of teaching approaches in the schools, see Evans, "Educational Ideologies and the Teaching of History."

[2] For a similar point, see Heidi Eskelund Knudsen, "History as a Designed Meaning-Making Process: Teacher Facilitation of Student–Subject Relationships," *Historical Education Research Journal* 17 (2020): 36–49.

the different ways in which historians pose questions, pursue inquiry, analyze evidence, and formulate interpretations.[3]

Obviously, this is the ethical position of historicism itself. We encounter our students as fully human beings with their own experiences, histories, beliefs, values, and lives. We respect the ways their histories have shaped them and the ways History can empower them. We recognize our own limitations and our own positive potentials as fully human and historical people. In this chapter I propose six ways of thinking about how to approach teaching in History, founded on these two principles.

6.2 Pedagogical Reciprocity: Teach Things Students Want to Know

In college and university History courses we can often assume that students want to know about the topic of the course because they have options – they are not required to take a fixed curriculum. But History is so expansive that almost no course topic puts many constraints on the subjects addressed. Students in my twentieth-century world history courses clearly want to know something about world history, otherwise they would not enroll in them. But what do they want to know about the twentieth-century world? Learning to think, to analyze, to pursue inquiry in the ways that historians do is very difficult and often not at all intuitive for students. To learn something that difficult, they need to be motivated by genuine interest. The instructor's agenda in any university History course is unquestionably in part to guide students' acquisition of knowledge about the past, and as Angela Bermúdez and Rosário Jaramillo found in a study of 2001, the complexity and sophistication of students' understandings "depends in great part on the richness and precision of the information that the student may possess."[4] But the consensus among historians is that the goal of teaching students the modes of inquiry, analysis, and interpretation that constitute the distinctive nature and the unique value of the discipline is both more challenging and more important. We can, then, take a flexible approach to the specific topics we address within the range of possibilities the broader course topic offers. It will help us in teaching

---

[3] For a similar view, see Christine Gutierrez, "Making Connections: The Interdisciplinary Community of Teaching and Learning History," in *Knowing, Teaching, and Learning History: National and International Perspectives*, ed. Peter Stearns, Peter Seixas, and Sam Wineburg (New York: New York University Press, 2000), pp. 353–374, esp. p. 358.

[4] Angela Bermúdez and Rosário Jaramillo, "Development of Historical Explanation in Children, Adolescents and Adults," *International Review of History Education* 3 (2001): 146–167, here p. 163.

6.2 Pedagogical Reciprocity: Teach Things Students Want to Know

students about History (as well as history) if we give them the opportunity to engage with historical topics that are of great interest to them.

This approach does introduce an important element of bias. Our students' interests are shaped by their own histories, by what their history has made them. They may not think of the relative importance of some topics in the same way we, as professional historians, do. It may be appropriate to ask them to examine topics that are not "top of mind" for them. But I have found it very fruitful to shape course content at least partially to engage the explicit, self-conscious interests my students bring with them to my classes.

That has worked well for students because it has made my courses more interesting than they were when I first started teaching and was much more rigid in my approach to subject matter. But it has worked well for me too, on a purely intellectual level. I have learned a tremendous amount of history by exploring topics of interest to my students. To return to an observation I made in the last section of Chapter 2: I already know the history that I know and that I am interested in. What is really exciting is the history that I *don't* know and that *other* people are interested in. The principle of reciprocity has become one of the most important foundations of my approach to teaching. I think there are useful things that I can help my students learn, but I know for a fact that there are exciting things that they can help me learn – if I listen to them.

Again: This is an approach that conforms to the ethical imperative of historicism. Historians learn most when they listen to their sources and when they listen to their students. But it also aligns with the ethical position of the more theory-driven approach to History, particularly in the more activist mode favoring an approach to History that enhances its contemporary relevance. History instructors are not depersonalized intellects; the people in our classes are not generic "students." We and they are people, with concerns and interests specific to our own time and place and histories. Pretending this is not so is intellectually dishonest, and it can suck the life out of the History classroom. Seeing it as an opportunity can help make the learning that students and professors do there exciting and satisfying.

I have found several ways to identify topics that will spark students' curiosity and interest. One has been to ask students in introductory courses what historical topics they would like to take courses on and then develop new courses that address those interests. I have tried both free-form questions ("what topics interest you?") and ranked preference lists ("please rank the following list of topic areas in order of your interest in taking a course on that topic"). That approach (not solely on my initiative) contributed to curriculum development efforts in my own department, which appear to have had some success in building enrollments.

A second approach, which I have taken in my world history courses, has been to speak to students' regional identification by using the history of California to illustrate central themes in world history. This has included, for example, the nineteenth-century history of land appropriation and genocide in settler societies, the history of mass migration and resource development, the history of transnational socialist and labor movements, and the history of the development of grassland and river-delta agriculture. California history offers a rich field of case studies that can be used to explore processes central to twentieth-century world history.

Finally, I have adopted the practice of asking students at the beginning of each academic term (at my current university, each quarter) what topics they would like to examine in the course. I ask students to brainstorm a list of potential topics and ask students who proposed them to explain why they think they are important. Once we have a list of twenty or twenty-five topics and rationales for studying them, I ask the class to vote on them (I find it helpful to give each student three votes in order to get a clearer sense of relative levels of interest). I then devote a class period at some point during the quarter to each of the top few most popular topics – five to eight, depending on how much time I have available to devote to this process that quarter and whether I have already prepared material on some of the topics they have chosen. Where I have time, I develop essay questions and find sources relevant to each of these topics, so that students can write their essays about them, or pursue their own research on them. This approach can be stressful because it sometimes requires that I devote considerable time to research and thinking not only about the topics students choose but also about how to use those topics to address particular skills important for the discipline. It is not something that I have found it practicable to do in more than one course each academic term. But it is a way to draw students into the process of inquiry and interpretation in concrete ways in the classroom. It is also a way for me to maximize the learning I do while teaching.

With regard to classroom discussions that ask students to take an interpretive approach to course topics and course readings, I have found it fruitful deliberately to engage students' interest in the present. Most students in History courses are not History majors and are not interested in the past for its own sake. They want to learn things that help them understand their own world, their own time. Historicists tend to be allergic to this orientation as superficial and oversimplifying, since it means we will pluck out of the past only those topics and questions that seem relevant to our own time. Some dismiss it as "presentism," a term that can mean, for example, a refusal to try to understand the people of other times on their own terms (by ignoring their values and judging them instead by our own), or a failure to understand the complexity of the past because one sets out to "plunder the past for convenient stories for present ends," cherry-picking topics and evidence to support our particular political, moral, or social aims and preferences.[5]

I do not think these concerns are justified, for three reasons. One is that these forms of "presentism" are simply obvious forms of bias and poor method, and students easily understand that. The second is that if we refuse to address students' current interests and ideas, we deprive ourselves of one of the central appeals of History – which is that it *can* illuminate and inform our thinking about the present. The third is that we can use students' present concerns to give them a better understanding of the past. In fact, these two functions of History are inextricably interrelated. When we juxtapose the ideas of people in the past with our own, we understand both better.[6]

To give an example: In my courses on twentieth-century European history, I have often assigned a scholarly article on the mail-order trade in consumer goods related to sexuality in postwar Germany.[7] One of the trends the article discusses is the growing importance of pornography in that business and conservative Christian responses attempting to limit or contain it. After the class discusses the argument presented in the article, I ask students which is more democratic: a society in which people are free to consume whatever media products they want (as long as crimes of sexual violence or coercion were not committed in producing it), or a society that tries to suppress the circulation of images or videos that encourage some people to view other people as merely sexual objects, as instruments of their own pleasure. The discussion inevitably yields a majority in favor of individual choice. Once that majority has emerged, I ask students to think about what assumptions might lead to a preference for the maintenance of community standards of morality over individual freedom of choice. Finally, I ask what historical factors and experiences might have

---

[5] Peter Lee, "History Education and Historical Literacy," in *Debates in History Education*, 2nd edition, ed. Ian Davies (London: Routledge, 2017), pp. 53–65, here p. 57.
[6] For a similar view, see Iber and Ratner-Rosenhagen, "The Present Is a Foreign Country."
[7] Elizabeth D. Heineman, "The Economic Miracle in the Bedroom: Big Business and Sexual Consumption in Reconstruction West Germany," *Journal of Modern History* 78:4 (2006): 846–877.

made those assumptions plausible to some Germans in the 1960s. This can encourage students to grapple with what it meant to live within a vital and authoritative religious tradition and community in the mid twentieth century and how people living in such a tradition and community might have experienced National Socialism.

Or take another example: Toward the end of the same course, I point out that both certain aspects of European public policy and survey data regarding fundamental social values suggest that Europeans tend to value stability, harmony, and security more highly than Americans, who instead favor innovation and open expression (even where it leads to conflict). I then ask students which orientation they favor. Again, once that discussion has yielded the inevitable majority preference for innovation and free expression, I ask students what historical experiences of Europeans in the twentieth century might have predisposed them toward a preference for security and stability.

I use this technique frequently in my courses, not just because many students appreciate the chance to think about their own views and to think them through, together, but also because it is an exercise in critical historical thinking. It helps students understand that different assumptions lead to different truths and that different historical experiences lead to different assumptions.

Beyond speaking to what students generally identify as their own interest in particular topics, however, I believe courses in History should generate interest by offering students a new and powerful way of thinking. In this respect, I do tend to be more directive, to try to develop student interest in something that very few of them would otherwise have thought about. It is important and almost always fruitful to tell students what it is that you want to teach them. There are various ways to do this; I have tried more dialogic and more directive approaches and found both fruitful. Particularly in introductory classes I often ask my students what the scientific method is, and then ask them what the historical method is. Uniformly, without exception, they can define scientific method but have never heard of the idea that History has a method, and they draw an absolute blank in trying to imagine what it might be beyond reading some old stuff in libraries or archives. I then ask them what chemistry is about, what biology is about, and what History is about. They soon conclude that History is about everything. So History is about everything, but they do not know what method it uses for studying everything. This is a great starting point. From there we can begin to discuss how one *does* go about studying everything – with no laboratory and no instruments. We can start

6.2 Pedagogical Reciprocity: Teach Things Students Want to Know 221

to build a collective conception of what historical *understanding* is like. Alternatively, often in more advanced classes, I have found it useful to devote a class period early in each academic term to telling students that I want to give them the opportunity to become familiar with a particularly powerful tradition and mode of inquiry. I try to give them a sense for the nature and complexity of that tradition, the kinds of questions historians ask (and do not ask), the kinds of analytical problems they face and how they try to solve them, and the distinctiveness of these features of the discipline of History. I also indicate how each of the forms of assessment I use in the course aims to develop their skill in the distinctive modes of inquiry and analysis that History employs. Whatever the approach taken, many students find the idea of learning a new way to define problems and to seek answers, and a new way to conceive of "understanding," to be interesting and even exciting.

There is one final step that I think is appropriate particularly in many seminar classes, and that is to ask students to think of themselves as historical persons, as products of their own history, and to ask them what intellectual preferences, what assumptions, what experiences, what institutional codes and expectations, even what subconscious biases might shape their experience of higher education. I do this for two reasons. One is that it is sometimes an effective way to get students to think about the central assumption of historicism – that all human affairs are historically conditioned. The second is that while in my experience students are almost universally interested in the history and legacies in the present of racial, class, and gender injustice, they are often not very attentive to the dynamics of race, class, and gender in the classroom. This is true in any discipline, but I think that the specific nature of inquiry in History can make those dynamics particularly visible and pernicious in History classes. History classes are often built around relatively open discussion, open collective inquiry; that can make them particularly susceptible to the interpersonal dynamics of social privilege. To put it bluntly, in my experience middle-class white males from schools in affluent communities are very accustomed to being asked for their views and to having them taken seriously; and they often assume that their views must be the universal views of all rational people. People from less privileged backgrounds quite often do not have those experiences or assumptions.

It is important that History instructors use concrete and practical techniques to counteract the tendency of some students to dominate discussion and of others to "switch off" or "check out" and remain quiet. That can include assignments that draw out each students' perspective and voice – for example, interpretive oral presentations, or circulating student "thought pieces" for discussion, or discussing thesis statements for essay assignments. It can include simply calling on some students, and even sometimes suggesting to more talkative students that it is time to hear from others. Writing the names of students who have signaled that they want to contribute to discussion on a whiteboard, and calling on them in order, can help the more exuberant avoid talking over their peers.[8]

But I think there is a more fruitful way of thinking about how to handle interpersonal dynamics than as counteracting the distortions introduced by privilege. This problem too is an opportunity. Encouraging students to see themselves and their classmates through historicist eyes, as products of their own individual histories and of the histories of their society, can open intellectual doors for them. It can give them a very concrete, immediate, and visceral understanding of the aim of the hermeneutic approach central to History as a discipline – to understand what *other* people think, not what *we* think. It can give them a very "tactile," immediate sense for the meaning of the idea of "listening" to the perspectives of the people they encounter in the sources, even of "immersion" in the sources. We are asking students to listen to each other, to immerse themselves in the class, as a group of people from whom we have something to learn. It can give them a very immediate understanding of the intellectual gains that can be made by considering a question from multiple perspectives – or from considering what questions about a topic different perspectives might yield. That can give them a new *kind* of sense for what we mean when we say that History is "inquiry-driven" – that we inquire not only about the past, but also about our own perspective on and perceptions of the past. It can encourage them to consider that being right might be less important than learning something new. It is an opportunity, in other words, to encourage students to understand themselves as authentically part of what Peter Seixas calls a "community of inquiry in the classroom."[9]

What I am suggesting, obviously, is that the ethics of interpersonal interaction in the History classroom are the same as the intellectual ethics of the discipline of History. It is not easy to bring students to make this connection; I have not always succeeded. But when I have, some have found it inspiring. It gives a whole new depth of meaning to the idea that History is "a way of thinking." History is not just a way of thinking that we

---

[8] For a still useful perspective, see Lynn Weber Cannon, "Fostering Positive Race, Class, and Gender Dynamics in the Classroom," *Women's Studies Quarterly* 18 (1990): 126–134.

[9] Peter Seixas, "The Community of Inquiry as a Basis for Knowledge and Learning: The Case of History," *American Educational Research Journal* 30 (1993): 305–324, here p. 312.

apply to understanding the past. It is a way of thinking about our place in the human world. It is a way of thinking about what we are, and what it means that we are here with others who are not what we are.

6.3 Teach the Sources

Second: Any History course should introduce students to the central disciplinary task of analyzing and interpreting historical sources, materials, documents, and data with care and precision. A central goal of History instruction is to develop students' capacity for careful and critical hermeneutic analysis. Further, because History thrives on breadth and on variety, and both fosters and depends on intellectual flexibility, we should ask them to analyze different *kinds* of sources.

To give the example of my own courses on the history of terrorism in Europe, I ask my students to read late nineteenth- and late twentieth-century novels about terrorism; late nineteenth- and late twentieth-century autobiographies of terrorists on both the political Left and the political Right; terrorist tracts and "how to" essays; and interviews with terrorists from the 1980s. Toward the end of the course, we look at statistics available from the Global Terrorism Database.[10] (I also assign scholarly discussions of whether "terrorism" exists or is a fiction useful to powerful interests, but that is a different aspect of the course.) In my courses on European history I ask my students not only to read scholarly books and articles but also to analyze novels and short stories, autobiographies, eyewitness accounts, essays in political philosophy, election statistics, opinion polls, advocacy and opinion pieces (such as pamphlets presenting arguments for and against women's suffrage), political speeches, texts by Hitler, Lenin, Mussolini, and English novelist E. M. Forster, papal encyclicals, and party programs. We look in depth at statistics available in Palgrave MacMillan's *International Historical Statistics* database. We spend a good deal of time analyzing visual sources – particularly photographs, also paintings and cartoons.

It is essential, further, to assign such primary sources not merely to confirm, exemplify, or illustrate broader themes in the course material, but to give students hands-on experience in the forms of analysis that are fundamental to the discipline of History. Historical documents should be used not just to consolidate or deepen an understanding that has been presented to students "prepackaged." Students should be required to

---

[10] www.start.umd.edu/gtd.

develop their own understanding. They should be asked to approach texts analytically and to develop their own interpretations of them. This means that assignments making use of primary sources should not ask students to explain the broader context in which they were produced (and which they have learned about, e.g., from a textbook or lectures), or how that context explains what they say. Instead, they should require students to read the documents themselves with great care.

Each instructor will develop their own agenda for textual analysis, but I would recommend as possibilities that students be asked to do the following.

- Assess when, where, and by whom, with what purpose, and under what circumstances a text was created.
- Examine in depth what a text says, what is written in it.
- Wrestle with the author's unspoken assumptions and with the fundamental categories of his/her thinking – for example, class, morality, virility and femininity, nature, justice and injustice, honor and abasement, society and individual, the sacred and the sinful, rights, science and superstition, freedom and authority, and order and chaos.
- Analyze the logical structure of the text and the relationships between key concepts in it. What set of steps does it make to advance an argument or view? What relationships of cause and effect does it describe? What motives does it ascribe to the people it depicts?
- Grasp the author's scale of values – what he/she considers good, what bad, what important, what trivial, even what he/she considers not worthy of mention or consideration.
- Examine the language used. What specific words does the author use, and what function do those words serve in the text? What kinds of verbs does he/she use, and what connotations do they have – for example, of violence, seduction, judgment, desire?
- Consider the narrative or storytelling strategy of the author. What incidents does he/she recount, and what does he/she not recount? What purpose, within the text, do those incidents serve?
- Identify the genre to which the author appeals. Is the explicit or implicit narrative in the text a tragedy, farce, melodrama, romance, satire, or horror story?
- Examine the author's use of literary and rhetorical devices. What metaphors does he/she use, with what implications or connotations? What images does he/she present, and what anecdotes or instances?

What emotions does he/she seem to want to stir – for example, anger, pity, disgust, pride?
- Examine what position the author claims – for example, as ironic observer, authoritative arbitrator, reluctant combatant, or impassioned patriot.
- Identify what authorities the author appeals to, what texts or ideas or thinkers he/she references. What ideas or people does he/she regard as wrongheaded or evil?
- Reflect on what the text/author does *not* consider – what blind spots he/she may have had, what contemporary events or ideas he/she ignored, what he/she did not know that we do about the historical context.

Beyond this kind of close analysis of the text itself, students should be asked to apply the hermeneutic principle that we understand what historical persons said and did and thought only when we understand what words, actions, or ideas meant to people in the place and time they were produced. Again, this does not mean only that we determine how the document "fits" a broader narrative that has already been presented in prepackaged form. Instead, it requires that we examine the text itself closely and compare its content to our broader knowledge. What traditions does it evoke or denigrate? What contemporary audience does it address and for what contemporary purpose? How does it differ from or resemble other texts from the period? What issues or events of contemporary importance does it ignore?[11]

For example, what did it mean when a Muslim Indian soldier fighting in France in World War I wrote home that he had experienced something like the Battle of Karbala (in the year 680 of the Western calendar and 61 of the Islamic calendar)? What would the implications of that statement have been at the time? What did it mean, in historical context, when a British professional soldier with experience in India, recalling the same war, wrote of a particular incident that he and his fellow soldiers shot German soldiers "like rabbits"?[12] What did it mean, for readers in 1929, when Ernst Jünger wrote in his account of the experience of combat in World War I that he believed that one day people would look back on him and his comrades in arms as he looked back on the Christian martyrs of the first centuries after

---

[11] For incisive discussions of how to approach documents, developed for teaching in the schools but relevant for university instruction as well, see Gutierrez, "Making Connections," pp. 369, 345, and Bain, "Into the Breach."

[12] *Indian Voices of the Great War*, ed. David Omissi (New York: St. Martin's, 1999), p. 56; Frank Richards, *Old Soldiers Never Die* (London: Faber & Faber, 1933), p. 40.

Christ? What would it have meant in 1929 to claim that just as in his own time people "cannot understand the martyrs who threw themselves into the arena in a transport that lifted them even before their deaths beyond humanity," so in future "we shall be envied, as we envy the saints their inward and irresistible strength"? What did it mean in contemporary context when Erich Maria Remarque wrote of soldiers in combat in World War I addressing the Earth as follows: "Earth! Earth! Earth! Earth with thy folds, and hollows, and holes, into which a man may fling himself and crouch down ... O Earth, thou grantest us the great resisting surge of new-won life"? What would it have meant in 1929 to write that "By the animal instinct that is awakened in us we are led and protected," and that soldiers going into combat "become on the instant human animals"? Or what did it mean in context when Sukarno remarked at the opening of the Bandung Conference in 1955 that the whole of humanity was threatened by nuclear war and that "We, the peoples of Asia and Africa ..., can demonstrate to the minority of the world which lives on the other continents that we, the majority are for peace, not for war"?[13]

Students in History should also be trained not to "cherry-pick" or "source mine" for convenient evidence, but to treat historical documents as integral wholes. To give a disturbing example, frequently my students are very attracted to Adolf Hitler's contempt for parliamentary politics, as expressed in the early sections of *Mein Kampf*. Unfortunately, that sort of antidemocratic attitude is widespread in popular culture in many societies. It is only as they read further into the text that students begin to understand that Hitler's hatred for parliaments was founded specifically on his hallucinatory anti-Semitism – which students sometimes have a hard time noticing at first reading. Eventually they are able to make the connection between Hitler's homicidal racism and his contempt for democracy. It is often only then that they can go back and take note of the grotesquely misogynistic, racist, and violent language in which Hitler couched his account of the alleged weaknesses of democracy in earlier chapters of the book. Or take a more positive example: I had the privilege of working with a student who was examining the history of Nazi youth organizations in the 1930s by analyzing their newsletters. She developed a fine, insightful written analysis of the topics, language, and tone of the articles in these publications. But one of the most revealing sections of her essay presented

---

[13] Ernst Jünger, *Storm of Steel* (Garden City, NY: Doubleday Doran, 1929), pp. 282–283; Erich Maria Remarque, *All Quiet on the Western Front* (New York: Fawcett Crest, 1982), pp. 55–56; www.fordham.edu/Halsall/mod/1955sukarno-bandong.asp.

instead a quantitative analysis of how the mix of advertisements for various categories of goods and services in those magazines changed over time. Again, this student examined the whole publication, not just those parts of it that she thought might most directly answer her questions.

Despite my earlier comments about the pernicious influence of the internet, one of its great benefits for History instructors is that it makes an astonishing variety of historical sources freely available and easily accessible to anyone with a computer. The possibilities for engaging students in analysis of historical source material are effectively limitless today. A little research will turn up such a wealth of freely available material that History instructors are really no longer even minimally constrained by the availability of material for use in the classes. Let me offer just a few examples.

- The New York Public Library has made a wealth of video clips of the history of modern dance freely available.[14]
- A vast range of news photography from the entire twentieth century (and some from the late nineteenth) is freely available through the US Library of Congress.[15]
- The Bracero History Archive offers access to interviews with participants in the Bracero Program that brought Mexican workers to work in the United States from 1942 when wartime labor demand skyrocketed until the reform of US immigration law in 1964.[16]
- Firstworldwar.com makes a vast collection of World War I diaries accessible.[17]
- The *Hawaiian Almanac and Annual* for the years 1875 through 1925 is available in digital form through the Hathi Trust.[18]
- City guides for San Francisco are available in electronic form for almost every year from 1850 to 1982 through the San Francisco Public Library.[19]
- Historical maps of all kinds can be found at oldmaps.org.[20]
- The little illustrated cards placed in cigarette and chocolate packaging in the early twentieth century, which can tell us all kinds of things about how people in that period thought about or were directed to think

---

[14] https://digitalcollections.nypl.org/collections/jerome-robbins-archive-of-the-recorded-moving-image-original-documentation#/?tab=navigation.
[15] www.loc.gov/pictures/collection/ggbain. [16] http://braceroarchive.org.
[17] www.firstworldwar.com/diaries. [18] https://catalog.hathitrust.org/Record/008866808.
[19] https://sfpl.org/locations/main-library/magazines-newspapers-center/bay-area-city-directories-and-phone-books/san-o.
[20] www.oldmapsonline.org.

about their world, are preserved in digital form by the New York Public Library and the National Library of France.[21]
- Historical data on global inequality are made available by the World Inequality Database and by the University of Texas.[22]
- Historical land-use data are made available by the University of Wisconsin.[23]
- Estimates of per capita incomes worldwide and reaching back several centuries are produced by the Maddison Project and maintained by the University of Groningen.[24]
- Estimates of arms expenditures are available from the Stockholm International Peace Research Institute.[25]
- Historical data on patents are made available by the World Intellectual Property Organization.[26]
- Data on tourism are maintained by the European organization Eurostat and by the OECD.[27]
- For more recent decades survey data on public opinion are published by the Pew Research Center.[28]

These are merely examples I have found interesting and useful; one could go on endlessly listing such materials. The internet, approached with care, is an absolute playground for historians and their students. This is particularly true for the modern era, but sources abound for others as well – I cited, for example, in Chapter 2 the medieval *Chronicle of Novgorod*, also available online.

Instructors do need to be sensitive to potential student responses to disturbing and offensive material in the primary sources they assign or point their students toward. Approaching our students as fully human interlocutors includes taking their emotional responses, their religious and ethical values, and the state of their knowledge of the human condition into account. Again, we should not try to impose an abstract, objective, or distanced perspective on our students or expect it of them; neither should we strike such a pose ourselves. I warn my students before they read excerpts from Hitler's *Mein Kampf* that it is a mendacious and offensive

---

[21] See https://digitalcollections.nypl.org/collections/cigarette-cards#/?tab=navigation and https://gallica.bnf.fr/ark:/12148/btv1b525123332/f1.item.
[22] https://wid.world; https://utip.lbj.utexas.edu/data.html.
[23] www.nelson.wisc.edu/sage/data-and-models/global-land-use/index.php.
[24] www.rug.nl/ggdc/historicaldevelopment/maddison/releases/maddison-project-database-2018.
[25] www.sipri.org/databases/armstransfers/background. [26] www.wipo.int/ipstats/en.
[27] https://stats.oecd.org; https://ec.europa.eu/eurostat.
[28] www.pewresearch.org/topics/social-values.

document; I warn them that eyewitness accounts of the Holocaust are horrifying and disturbing; I warn them that the misogynist views of Almroth Wright or of Filippo Marinetti are offensive and insulting; I warn them that the autobiographies of working-class women are full of accounts of sexual harassment. Beyond that, I also warn students in my classes that our class discussions and my lectures treat terrible, tragic, offensive, and disturbing topics. In short, I issue what are commonly called trigger warnings. I think this is constructive and important for two reasons – one ethical, the other more purely pedagogical.

One important consideration is that the ideas, values, and actions of many people in the past are reprehensible by the standards of most people in our time, and it is potentially dismissive and disrespectful to tell students (or to imply) that they should not be troubled by them. Beyond that, it is important not to discuss ideas in isolation from contexts and consequences, but rather to acknowledge the harm or benefit they have caused. To discuss the fantastical racist fantasies presented in Hitler's *Mein Kampf* without acknowledging the consequences of such ideas would be both nonsensical and irresponsible. What is more, a substantial number of our students have themselves passed through traumatic experiences, and the memories and feelings of some will be stirred by the material addressed in my classes. It would be cruel and disrespectful of their lived experience for me to surprise them with such material. Finally, it is important that students understand that their instructors do not pretend to be purely intellects – that they are aware of and acknowledge their own status as fully human people, with values, feelings, and a moral sense.

Second, using trigger warnings can remind students that history is real, that the things they are reading or discussing really happened, that people really thought and said and did those things. This can enhance their sense of the seriousness of what they are doing in studying History. I have been struck by the long-term growth of ironic distance among a large proportion of my students, a sense – or at least a pretense – that every belief is just someone's opinion, that politicians are all just liars, that ideas are cheap and words just noise, and that all of it is not really worth thinking about a lot. Acknowledging the ethical and moral gravity of the material they are engaging with can help awaken in students a more realistic and urgent spirit of intellectual engagement. But it is also important for students to consider the problem of how to navigate their encounter, as themselves historical persons, with the past. What role do our own values, feelings, and experiences play? What do we do with them when we work toward formulating an historical question or an historical interpretation, or when we wrestle with the problems of analyzing a text, when we seek to understand the thinking of someone whose ideas we encounter in an autobiography, letters, a treatise in political philosophy, a pamphlet? Chapter 1 discussed the "reflexive" character of historical thinking – the understanding that historians are not objective intellect and must "manage" (as Jorma Kalela put it) their relationship, as fully human and historical persons, to the past. Confronting our own responses to the ideas, words, and actions of historical persons is important training in doing that.

Finally, as I remarked in Chapter 3, I do not mean to suggest that the encounter with people in the past is *only* potentially disturbing or traumatic, or that only horror is serious. It is certainly not appropriate for historians to suggest that students should view particular historical persons as heroic and virtuous. But I think it is appropriate to acknowledge students' appreciation for people who did and said things that they regard as admirable. Students can be inspired by the courage, integrity, brilliance, wisdom, humanity, faith, and creativity of people in the past. As historians, I believe we are often tempted to point out to students that historical people are complex, that people they (or we) admire may also have done, said, and thought things we find reprehensible. Doing that can serve our pedagogical purposes because it can lead our students into deeper inquiry and deeper understanding of the historical context in which those people lived. But I do think that history instructors should avoid falling into the habit of *always* saying "yes, but." We should not seek to negate or dismiss our students' positive judgments any more than their negative judgments. Instead (again, as I have argued in Chapter 1) we should regard the fact that our students find people in the past inspirational as a pedagogical resource. Our job is to encourage our students to learn more, for themselves, motivated by their own interests, feelings, and values. Admiration for the real achievements of people in the past can be such a motivation.

6.4 Teach the Breadth of the Discipline

History instruction at the college level can draw on the great breadth and scope of History as a discipline by giving students exposure to a wide range of topics drawn from a wide range of subfields. The aim here is to make evident to students how History contextualizes any subject – how it grasps the complex web of relationships and connections of which any historical phenomenon (event, person, incident, institution, document, life) is a part. To give an example: An instructor creating a course in military history should focus not just on the narrative of campaigns and battles, or on the uses of weapons, or on the decisions that shaped a conflict. To understand military history we need to understand the history of technology – whether armaments or industrial or communications or transportation or agricultural technology. We need to know the culture and social makeup of military institutions (armies, officer corps, ministries of war). We need to understand the economics of production for war, whether of armaments for the combatants or of food for civilians. We need to understand the traditions and ideas of gender identity that shaped how men and women understood their role in wars and the impact that war had on such ideas. We need to understand class relations in the combatant societies and how war affected them. An understanding of religious traditions may be absolutely essential to our understanding of the origins and course of a war, and some wars have profound impact on religious life. We need to understand the influence wars can have on artistic life, on philosophy, on popular culture, and so on.

I can give the example of my own courses in twentieth-century world history as an illustration of what this approach looks like in practice. Those courses are built explicitly around a particular interpretation, which is that technological change drove the comprehensive transformation of the world over the past 150 years. I ask my students to examine the consequences of those developments for economic, political, social, cultural, religious, military, and environmental history. We examine the history of the banana industry and of totalitarianism, of multinational corporations and of genocide, of terrorism and of the space age, of postcolonial Asia and of the welfare state, of the Arab-Israeli conflict, and of development aid.

Often individual lives are a wonderful way of drawing together multiple topics and illustrating what they meant in human terms. The course draws on the example of Turkish revolutionary and feminist Halide Edib Adivar, who left an account of what it was like to live through one of the great revolutions of the early twentieth century, and through the ethnic violence inflicted by the dictatorial state created by that revolution. It draws on the life of Sri Lankan nationalist Buddhist Anagarika Dharmapala, who inspired people in his own society and across the globe to explore the meanings of Buddhism for the contemporary world. It draws on the example of Japanese communist Sen Katayama, who converted to Christianity in California and to communism in New York and played an influential role in global communism into the 1930s. It draws on the biography of American labor activist, anti-fascist, communist, Manzanar internee, US military intelligence officer, and chicken farmer Karl Yoneda.

I try to illuminate the history of globalization by examining the lives of the Jamaican anti-racist musician Bob Marley; Nigerian musician and critic of corrupt military regimes Fela Anikulapo Kuti, who was trained in music in London and – as he put it – "Africanized" by the American Black Power movement in Los Angeles; early twentieth-century Indian musician and spiritual teacher Inayat Khan, who moved to London in 1913 and founded the Universal Sufi Order; Ali Akbar Khan, the extraordinary virtuoso sarod player who founded a music school in California in 1967 and influenced a generation of California musicians; Indian dancer Uday Shankar, whose fusion of Indian dance idiom with European variety theater performance influenced the earliest roots of the Bollywood musical film tradition; and American dancer Ruth St. Denis, who appropriated Indian dance idioms and hired Indian sailors in New York and London for her variety-theater performances and was welcomed with open arms by Indian nationalists when she toured that country (then still a colony of Britain) in the mid-1920s.

We do not understand the transformation of the twentieth-century world if we do not understand the lives of people like these. And to understand them, we must approach them in two opposed and complementary ways. We must grasp them in their specificity, uniqueness, and particularity. And we must grasp how they fit into, illustrate, and illuminate broader patterns.

But teaching the breadth of the discipline means not only giving students a sense for how the discipline generates expanding inquiry. As I argued in Chapter 2, it also means introducing them to the methodological diversity of the discipline – introducing them to what one essay of 2000 called History's "eclectic approach to theory" and to the value of intellectual flexibility and "adaptability."[29] In the previous section of this chapter I suggested students be asked to take an essentially hermeneutic and historicist approach to texts. But they should also be asked to take a more theoretical approach to the same texts. This can be done by giving them a brief introduction to a range of social and social-scientific theories and asking them whether the historical documents they have read appear to conform to what those theories would lead us to expect. I have found it useful, for example, to ask students to consider whether the rhetoric of political figures like Adolf Hitler, or communist critiques of American economic and cultural imperialism after World War II, is illuminated by the psychological concept of projection, or by feminist analyses of patriarchal violence. I ask students to consider

---

[29] Hitchcock, Shoemaker, and Tosh, "Skills and the Structure of the History Curriculum," p. 59.

whether anthropological theories concerning the ritual process, or the cultural function of binary oppositions (raw/cooked, healthy/pathological, masculine/feminine, civilized/savage) can help us understand autobiographies or political theory. I ask students to consider whether sociological concepts such as status anxiety or cognitive dissonance help us understand debates about women's suffrage. I ask students to examine the autobiographies of terrorists in light of feminist theories regarding male identity formation in patriarchal societies, and in light of the classical sociological theory of anomie. I find it best not to ask whether such theoretical frameworks are "right," but rather whether they appear to throw up useful questions, questions that lead us to a deeper analysis of historical materials.

We can also ask students to consider the kinds of evidence that might be more common in the social sciences – in particular quantitative evidence. It can be particularly useful to juxtapose qualitative sources with quantitative, to see, for example, whether the narratives or claims made in the former are confirmed by the latter. I do this consistently in my own presentation of material in my classes; I find it a useful way to speak to multiple kinds of students (e.g., in the sciences and the humanities) who take my courses, but also to "layer up" a more complex, multifaceted context for the historical sources I ask the students to engage with. But we can also ask students to engage directly with multiple forms of evidence themselves. As one example, a reading of working-class biographies in the late nineteenth and early twentieth centuries can leave students with the sense that people in that period had lives of unrelieved and unrelenting misery. And yet historical statistics on wages, household consumption, education levels, and the like indicate that working-class lives were improving at least from the 1890s onward. Examining sources like that can help explain the differences between the diagnosis of capitalism's terminal illness in *The Communist Manifesto* at the end of the 1840s and Eduard Bernstein's revisionist view in *Evolutionary Socialism* at the end of the 1890s.

As a discipline, History builds complex and multifaceted understandings, in depth and breadth, drawing on multiple methodological approaches and theoretical frameworks, to give us a flexible and expansive understanding of human affairs. That is the strength of the discipline; we should teach to that strength.

6.5 Pattern and Specificity: Case Studies

One of the great attractions of studying History for university and college students is that it gives them the opportunity to explore in depth the lives and thoughts of individuals, the complexities of very particular and specific historical events, the day-to-day affairs of local and regional societies. For many students History is attractive specifically not as the study of "people," but of particular persons. And the same is true of the discipline's approach to everything – for example, institutions, organizations, ideas, forms of exchange, forms of artistic expression, whole societies. The attraction of the particular and of the dramatic can be used to appeal to students' interests. But History also offers students the satisfaction of making sense of those particulars and dramas because it asks them to put particularity (specific persons, institutions, art forms, etc.) in broad historical context and to identify common *patterns* across those contexts. This relationship – between pattern and specificity, between different "scales" of analysis, between phenomena and their broad social and historical context – is central to the way History as a discipline constructs understanding. History identifies large-scale patterns, trends, and developments and explores the particular ways in which those patterns manifested in individual locations (towns, societies, families, regions, religions, organizations, etc.), how those broad developments played out in unique but related ways in specific instances.

Case studies are an effective way to pursue both aims, the study of particularity and the identification of pattern.[30] I teach both world history and European history, so I constantly confront the task of giving students a concrete understanding of very broad patterns in very large contexts. I do that by exploring the particularities of specific cases and establishing relationships between those particular cases and broader patterns and events. For example, in the first week of my course on world history I ask students to read a textbook chapter and two scholarly articles on mass migration, settler frontiers, and resource "bonanzas" in the second half of the nineteenth century. Again, individual lives are a wonderful way of exploring the human implications of such very broad patterns. I devote class time then to examining the lives of a German military adventurer who was drawn to participate in the gold rushes in California, Australia, and New Zealand in the 1850s and 1860s, and of a Chinese immigrant who took part in New Zealand's gold rush in that period. These lives illustrate the

---

[30] This is a suggestion advanced by Peter N. Stearns a generation ago; see *Meaning over Memory*, p. 165. Peter J. Lee and Jonathan Howson called this a model of "depth studies nesting within themes" in "'Two Out of Five Did Not Know That Henry VIII Had Six Wives': History Education, Historical Literacy, and Historical Consciousness," in *National History Standards: The Problem of the Canon and the Future of History Teaching*, ed. Linda Symcox and Arie Wilschut (Charlotte, NC: Information Age, 2009), pp. 211–263, here p. 247.

prevalence of racial violence in the period (one of these men was a perpetrator, the other a target). They are examples of the global demand for specific forms of skilled labor with which to develop the resources of settler colonies (including military "labor" that played a key role in genocidal land appropriation). They illustrate the complex interaction between public and private institutions in organizing both violence and labor recruitment.

But regional case studies can be a powerful "magnifying glass" to apply to broad trends, as well. In the second week of my course, alongside a textbook chapter devoted to patterns of resource extraction and economic globalization, we examine the history of the banana trade in the late nineteenth and early twentieth centuries, focusing on Central America. That industry illustrates central features of the process of accelerating economic globalization in that period. It is also an excellent way to investigate the political consequence and the environmental impacts of globalization. Another marvelous case that illustrates the ways multiple broad global trends interconnected in the decades around 1900 is the history of the sugar industry in Hawaii. That history illustrates the complex interactions between and among economic change and state policy, here a trade agreement between the Kingdom of Hawaii and the United States; the reshaping of local economies and populations, here through the importation of Portuguese sugar workers, Mexican ranch hands, and Chinese plantation workers; and the relationship between those processes and imperialism, ending in the annexation of Hawaii two decades after the crucial trade treaty was signed. I use this as an example too of processes of cultural globalization and cultural appropriation, specifically with respect to the important influence of Portuguese instruments and musical forms in modern Hawaiian music, and to hula dance, which was an important aspect of Hawaiian religious life before annexation and became a tourist attraction and cultural export commodity in the early twentieth century.

This kind of case-based approach can help give students models of the way in which History approaches coherence and deepen their understanding of what it means to analyze a problem in History. In many disciplines in the sciences and social sciences, the project of analysis is fundamentally oriented around causality. Again, the aim is to understand those laws or principles that explain why things are the way they are. In History, the project of analysis is aimed as much at *relationship* as at causation. The aim is to understand how things were connected. The question, for example, is not to discover what price differential was necessary to make Hawaiian sugar competitive in the US market, or what wage differential would lure sugar workers from Madeira to Hawai'i, or what price would permit wages to reach that level. Rather, it is to understand how the development of trade policy, immigration and demographics, politics, and religious and cultural life were all interconnected. The aim of case studies is not to determine and specify what causal mechanisms determined outcomes; it is to understand the multiplicity of ways in which complex concatenations of local, regional, and global factors could interact dynamically to create patterns both of similarity and of difference in varying contexts. It is to apply a microscope to particular regional or local or even individual examples in order to tease out the ways in which developments were "overdetermined" in multiple divergent and convergent ways in different historical contexts.

I have found it useful to cast entire university courses essentially as "case studies" built around particular themes. For some years, for example, I have built my courses in world history around the question of the related roles of violence and innovation in shaping the twentieth-century world. The process of economic, political, and social globalization that fundamentally shaped the history of the world in that century (e.g., the integration of agricultural and mineral resources into the world economy, the creation of a global labor force, and the creation of gigantic imperial politics) rested on a foundation of tremendous technological, organizational, and intellectual innovation. It also relied on and incubated a horrifying explosion of (often genocidal) violence. How did they interact? What were the relationships between them? How did people understand those relationships? My twentieth-century European history courses are built around an examination of the ideas of modernization, modernism, and modernity. These courses examine the technological, economic, social, political, cultural, and demographic changes were reshaping European societies between the 1870s and the 2020s. But they ask students to consider how various Europeans understood those processes, what they saw as the dangers and opportunities they posed, how they sought to construct understandings of their implications and meaning. What did different people imagine a "modern" society would, could, or should be like? What were the consequences of such ideas?

I have found these themes particularly helpful, but I have experimented with others (capitalism and socialism, race and citizenship, democracy and dictatorship, unity and diversity), and I do not think the stakes are high in the choice of such themes. The aim of adopting them is not to impose a particular story but to use them as heuristic devices. They can give students a starting point for thinking and discussion – a coherent set of questions they can begin with and build on. They can also make more visible to students the *interpretive* and perspectival nature of the discipline of History. The aim of the juxtaposition of violence and innovation is to give students the opportunity to construct competing and/or complementary interpretations of world history in the twentieth century – and to see for themselves how the choice of values, questions, and interests shapes interpretive approaches.

6.6 Teach Interpretation and Analysis

History is interpretive and perspectival, and it is important both to read competing interpretations and to gain practice in constructing them. Students should be asked not only to read divergent and conflicting scholarly interpretations, but also to think critically and analytically about the divergences and conflicts between them. What are the fundamental assumptions underlying two (or more) divergent interpretations? What biases do they exhibit? What choices did they make regarding kinds of evidence to analyze, or modes and methods of analyzing them? What are the strengths and weaknesses of each approach? What fruitful questions does each open up for us, and what questions does each neglect? Students may reach the conclusion that one interpretation is superior to another, or even that one is right and the other wrong, but again, right or wrong should not be the automatic focus of discussion. The quality of analysis and argumentation, the costs and benefits of particular approaches, the implications of differing perspectives, the drawbacks and advantages of different modes of analysis, the specific insights that different interpretations offer – all these are more important than the question "who is right?"

Appreciation of the interpretive nature of historical knowledge should not be reduced to a "debate" model, to binary comparisons. Any course in History should give students multiple ways of thinking about the topic and ask them to think about how they complement and/or contradict each other. In my courses on the history of terrorism, for example, I ask students to read historical texts influenced by feminist critiques of the mythic structure of terrorist thinking; by neoconservative critiques of Soviet support for terrorism; by anti-capitalist critiques of the antiterrorist security establishment and its role in fostering terrorism. I ask them to read analyses built around criminological theories focused on individual psychology, around sociological theories focused on life histories, around understandings of sectarian conflict developed by historians of religion, and by reactionary critiques of Western liberal individualism as it has evolved since the sixteenth century. What are the advantages and disadvantages of each? What assumptions drive them? What biases shape them? What evidence do they use and how? It is not enough to read a work of History and then move on to the next work of History. Pull it apart, see how it works as an interpretation, check some of the sources, figure out how it confirms or confounds other interpretations, think about how to reconcile different interpretations or to make useful irreducibly conflicting ones, and think about how to make sense of the full range of histories of different aspects of an historical situation or event.

It goes without saying, further, that we should take the same approach to the primary documents we ask students to analyze. Students should be given a concrete sense for the breadth of the spectrum of views present in any society, at any point in time. In my classes on modern European history, for example, I assign classic works of liberalism – for example, by nineteenth-century social theorist of classical liberalism Herbert Spencer; anti-totalitarian English novelist E. M. Forster, writing in 1939 on the eve of World War II; post-war German-English sociologist Ralf Dahrendorf, writing in the aftermath of the revolt of the 1960s; and Czech dissident playwright and philosopher Vaclav Havel, who diagnosed the self-subversion of communism in 1975. I assign classic works of socialism such as Karl Marx's *Communist Manifesto* and Eduard Bernstein's revision of Marx in *Evolutionary Socialism*, and of radical socialism, communism, and the New Left, including Vladimir Lenin's theory of communist dictatorship, Rosa Luxemburg's rejection of the Leninist fantasy of democracy through dictatorship, and Herbert Marcuse's critique of the functional "totalitarianism" of consumer capitalism. I assign classics of Catholic social teaching, for example, *Rerum novarum* of 1890 and *Mater et magistra* of 1961, but also of conservatism, such as Heinrich Treitschke's theory of the absolute sovereignty of the state, Margaret Thatcher's neoliberal celebration of individualism, and the grudging recognition of the contribution of the welfare state to the substantive freedom of the citizen by the One Nation Group within the Tory Party in Britain.

It can also be very useful if History teachers acknowledge to their students their own position as interpreters of history, not purveyors of absolute truth. By this I absolutely do not mean that instructors should explain their own values and beliefs or even their own preferences with regard to historical interpretation. Just the opposite – I think it best if instructors do not do that so that students do not feel any pressure to conform to their instructor's views. I mean we should make it clear to students that we too are fully human beings, products of our own history, engaged in the same kinds of analysis of the same kinds of evidence that we are asking them to embark on. This can be done even where students are entirely aware of what their teachers think about the history they are studying.

In my introductory-level university world history course, for example, I use as a textbook a history of the world in the twentieth century that I wrote myself and gave the subtitle "An Interpretive History." The second word in the subtitle really ought to be redundant because every work of History is interpretive. But I wanted it on the front cover. At the beginning of the course I ask students to consider the significance of the interpretive choices the book makes. At the end of the course I ask them whether they think the interpretation is persuasive and what other interpretations might be superior. Perhaps we shouldn't understand the twentieth century as fundamentally shaped by technological transformation. Maybe something else was driving that technological transformation. Perhaps focusing on technology obscures something else that was more important, more fundamental – the transformation of religious or spiritual life, say. After all, the implications and impact of technological change are not automatic. Societies make choices about whether they will adopt and how they will use technologies, and about what technologies to develop in the first place (e.g., in the modern era, through government research funding, or through corporate research and development budgets). What guides those choices – culture, class power, the priorities of institutions, political agendas and capacities, religious traditions? For example, is it really coincidence nuclear and thermonuclear weapons were first developed in societies in which the image of fire raining down from the sky, or an inescapable inferno, have been features of religious life for many centuries?

This approach is important not least because History teachers should require their students to pursue their own analyses and develop their own interpretations. This can be done at the level of individual documents by asking students to make sense of them for themselves. In some cases such questions can be very specific, or "leading." Should we understand Mohandas K. Gandhi's perspective in *Hind Swaraj* (1921), in its contemporary historical context, as radical or as conservative? In what sense radical, and in what sense conservative? What if we compare it to Hu Shih's perspective in "Our Attitude toward Modern Civilization of the West" (1926)?[31] We can be more open-ended or broader too. To take an example from my courses on the history of terrorism: why were authors

---

[31] Mohandas K. Gandhi, *Hind Swaraj* (Madras: G. A. Natesan, 1921); Hu Shih, "Our Attitude toward Modern Civilization of the West," in *Modern China: From Mandarin to Commissar*, trans. and ed. Dun J. Li (New York: Charles Scribner's Sons, 1978), 163–173.

who wrote fantastical or science fiction novels about terrorism in the late nineteenth century fascinated by the image of death raining down from the sky? What did those images mean in their contemporary context – how might they have been related to the history of terrorism itself, or to perceptions of contemporary technological development, to perceptions of the development of states and policing in the period, or to specific Western cultural patterns and traditions?

We can also do this at the level of the entire topic of a course. Final examinations in all my university classes ask students to present their own coherent interpretations of the history we have explored in depth, breadth, and variety. What were the most important developments? What were the most important changes and/or continuities? Was the twentieth century a century of violence or of creativity – or how were violence and creativity related in the twentieth-century world? Was the history of the world in the twentieth century shaped by racism, or was the history of racism shaped by the major developments of the twentieth century? Is the story of twentieth-century Europe a story of continuity or discontinuity? How were the two related? These are not factual questions; they are interpretive questions, and it is essential that students understand that their instructors are aware that their own understanding of the period is one plausible interpretation, not the "right" one, and that students are tasked with developing their own plausible interpretation.

History professors have developed numerous specific kinds of assignments that help students develop the habit of and capacity for interpretive analysis of this kind. Short essays that require analysis of a particular issue or document are common. I have found it particularly useful to ask students to write "thought papers" reflecting on particular interpretive questions, sometimes posed in deliberately provocative ways (e.g., a response to the proposition "There is no such thing as terrorism; there are only people for whom it is convenient to assert that there is such a thing as terrorism"; or to the proposition "Hitler didn't have political ideas; he had racist ideas with political implications"; or "Imagine you are a female Futurist living in 1909. What might *your* 'Manifesto' say?"). Giving feedback on the logic and presentations of such shorter papers and then requiring students to revise them can help develop analytical precision and ambition – as well as fostering intellectual dialogue with students.[32]

---

[32] There is a useful short discussion of this kind of writing in Ira Lee Benjamins, "Writing and Thinking: History inside the Classroom," www.teachingushistory.co/2019/writing-and-thinking-history-inside-the-classroom.html.

6.6 Teach Interpretation and Analysis 241

Longer research essays that ask students to pursue analysis through several investigative steps – by requiring them to think through what questions their preliminary findings raise, and how to go about answering those questions, and then repeating that process – are somewhat less common, but invaluable as training in the kind of expanding inquiry historians particularly prize. Review essays that require students to discern the analytical structure of scholarly books or articles can develop their sense for the nature and potentials (and weaknesses) of historical analysis – ideally, of multiple modes of historical analysis. Asking students to compare, contrast, and assess competing scholarly interpretations, or competing perspectives as revealed in historical documents, can be particularly productive. Requiring students to keep a "thinking journal" in which they write about what they have learned in a course each week can help them focus on the coherence and significance of the interpretive priorities and conceptual framework implicit in any course syllabus. A "research journal," in which they write about what they have found in the course of working on a larger inquiry-based essay, can help them track the development of their own thinking and to refine and expand it. I have found it useful to ask students to write a short essay or presentation explaining the meaning, in historical context, of visual sources such as photographs, cartoons, and maps. Students often abhor collaborative assignments because of the free-rider problem (some students do most of the work, but all get credit for it), but if structured carefully they *can* encourage students to consider problems from multiple analytical and interpretive perspectives. Asking students to present their work (individual or collaborative) can create opportunities for the same sort of productive intellectual exchange.[33]

Developing coherent interpretive responses to questions like those posed in History courses requires *analysis*. Again: History is not "about" information; it is about understanding. The aim of inquiry in History is not to report results; it is to make sense of them. Above all, therefore, I ask my students to make connections and to think about relationships. For example: Are there similar ideas or attitudes about violence in the reflections of a German general's reflections on war in 1912, in the novel *A Princess of Mars* by

---

[33] The American Historical Association's newsletter *Perspectives* is a trove of suggestions for assignments in History courses; there is a collection of short essays from that publication on teaching approaches in *History Anew: Innovations in the Teaching of History Today*, ed. Robert Blackey (Long Beach: California State University, Long Beach Press, 1993). For discussions of various forms of informal writing, see the essays in Teresa Vilardi and Mary Chang, *Writing-Based Teaching: Essential Practices and Enduring Questions* (Albany: State University of New York Press, 2009).

Edgar Rice Burroughs, published in the same year, and in Almroth Wright's misogynistic anti-suffrage essay of 1913? What about in Filippo Marinetti's "Futurist Manifesto" for modern art of 1909?[34] In my courses on twentieth-century Europe, I ask students to decide whether the implications for gender relations of the early twentieth-century development of shopping and of recreational swimming were similar, or whether and in what sense the organization of publicly mandated vacations in the 1920s and in the 1960s was democratic.[35] I ask them whether there are similar themes, assumptions, attitudes, or vocabularies in the writings of Lenin, Hitler, and Mussolini, and how those writings contrast with those of Pius XII in the encyclical *Summi pontificatus* of 1939 or of Christian Jasper Klumker, one of the leading theorists of social policy in the early twentieth century.[36] I ask them to consider whether terrorists on the radical Left and the neo-fascist Right in the 1960s shared similar motivations, or a similar understanding of their actions, and whether either shared anything with early theorists of terrorism in the mid nineteenth century. I ask whether punk music in Hungary, Britain and Spain in the 1970s was "the same" phenomenon or not, and what the broader implications of the answer to that question might be for our understanding of European culture and politics in that period. I ask them to think about what it means that the Sex Pistols' anarchist punk anthem "God Save the Queen" and Abba's "Dancing Queen" came out within about a year of each other. In my world history courses I ask them to consider what it would have meant in historical context, in 1976, when Bob Marley quoted extensively in the song "War" from a 1963 speech to the UN General Assembly by Haile Selassie, and what it might have meant in 1990 when the New Zealand band Moana and the Moahunters put out "AEIOU/

---

[34] Friedrich von Bernhardi, *Germany and the Next War* (London: Arnold, 1912); Edgar Rice Burroughs, *A Princess of Mars* (New York: Dover, 2005 [1912]); Filippo Tommaso Marinetti, "The Futurist Manifesto" (1909), in *Italian Fascisms*, ed. Adrian Lyttleton (London: Cape, 1973), pp. 209–215.

[35] Erika D. Rappaport, "'A New Era of Shopping': The Promotion of Women's Pleasure in London's West End, 1909–1914," in *Cinema and the Invention of Modern Life*, ed. Leo Charney and Vanessa R. Schwartz (Berkeley: University of California Press, 1995), pp. 130–155; Catherine Horwood, "'Girls Who Arouse Dangerous Passions': Women and Bathing, 1900–1939," *Women's History Review* 9 (2000): 653–673; Laura Lee Downs, "Municipal Communism and the Politics of Childhood: Ivry-sur-Seine 1925–1960," *Past and Present* 166 (2000): 205–241; Ellen Furlough, "Making Mass Vacations: Tourism and Consumer Culture in France, 1930s to 1970s," *Comparative Studies in Society and History* 40 (1998): 247–286.

[36] Benito Mussolini, *Fascism: Doctrine and Institutions* (Rome: Ardita, 1932), pp. 7–14, 20–23; Adolf Hitler, *Mein Kampf*, www.hitler.org/writings/Mein_Kampf; "Summi Pontificatus," www.vatican.va/content/pius-xii/en/encyclicals/documents/hf_p-xii_enc_20101939_summi-pontificatus.html; Christian Jasper Klumker, *Fürsorgewesen* (Leipzig: Quelle & Meyer, 1918).

Akona te Reo," with lyrics that instructed their audience on the proper pronunciation of vowels in the Maori language.

Some of these examples may seem trivial, and while students enjoy thinking about music or art, some do feel that they are a bit of a sideshow to the presumed major events that they feel constitute "real" history, like wars, elections, revolutions, economic crises, mass murder, or technological innovation. My aim, though, is to point out that things do not "just happen" – that, in fact, *no* things just happen. Everything happens for historical reasons; everything is historically conditioned. It is not enough to set students the task of understanding why World War I, or the Holocaust, or the French Revolution, or any other grand, epic event happened. Understanding that there are historical reasons for that kind of thing is relatively easy and therefore it does not really drive home the central message of History. When we understand why we order the food we do at restaurants, why we like particular musical forms, why people buy the automobiles they do – that's when we begin to understand History as a way of thinking.

6.7 Teach through Inquiry

Finally: History is driven by inquiry – specifically by open-ended inquiry. Any student of History should, therefore, gain the experience of independent, self-directed research. The goal of the study of History is not getting answers; it is learning about *asking* questions, and *seeking* answers. Again: The outcome is not the aim; the process is the aim. Learning to ask questions encourages students to get to grips with the question "what is a fruitful question?" Engaging in the open-ended search for answers confronts students with the classic evidentiary problems of the discipline – the problem of fragmentary and biased sources, the problem of appropriate categories, the problem of confirmation bias, the possibilities of considering multiple different forms and bodies of evidence, and so on and so forth. It confronts them too with the necessity of developing complex models of causation, not simple monocausal explanations. It encourages them to consider multiple theoretical frameworks and approaches as potential sources of good, productive questions.[37] This is why the "pyramid" curriculum is undesirable at best. As F. M. L. Thompson put it in 1990, "there is not, in the study of

---

[37] There is an excellent argument regarding this function of inquiry in Scott M. Waring, "Escaping Myopia: Teaching Students about Historical Causality," *The History Teacher* 43 (2010): 283–288.

history, any division between a junior period during which rules and answers are simply taught, and an adult period in which independent thought and criticism are permitted and encouraged." Independent thought, criticism, and inquiry is the essential point.[38]

It can be difficult to build such inquiry into a college or university course in History. History is drastically neglected in high school curricula in the United States, and in most of the rest of the world as well. Most students arrive at university with so little historical knowledge that they have no idea what kinds of questions to pursue in a research project, no idea what to make of the sources when they encounter them, and no ability to reach meaningful conclusions from their research. A university course in History must begin by giving students knowledge of the historical context for their research interests, sufficient to allow them to do those things. There is no point in teaching students how to "think historically" if they don't know enough history to think about anything coherent.

Yet university History curricula should not be structured to give students some accurate historical knowledge in introductory courses and then teach them how to think historically in later courses. The knowledge History generates is by its nature perspectival and interpretive, so teach it that way from the ground up. Further, only a tiny minority of students will ever take a course in which they are asked to focus exclusively or primarily on a major independent research project (e.g., an honors thesis). Most students who take history courses are not History majors and will take at most one or two History courses. If they are not required to practice the ways the discipline thinks in those courses, they never will be. Of course it is unquestionably hard to strike a good balance between the various aims of History courses, particularly at the introductory level. In those courses, but also in more advanced courses, an essential aim has to be to expose students to many different aspects of a particular historical place and period, and many different interpretive perspectives on them. That limits the amount of time students have for their own, more focused individual or collaborative research projects.[39]

But there are ways to address this problem. The most basic one is to give students models of productive historical questions – again, assignments

---

[38] "F. M. L. Thompson," in *The History Debate*, ed. Juliet Gardiner (London: Collins, 1990), pp. 74–80, here p. 76.
[39] Bruce A. Vansledright offers a good discussion of this problem, focused on high school History instruction, in *Assessing*, pp. 16–17, 33–37. In my experience, everything he writes about this problem applies to most university students as well. See also Jeffery D. Nokes, "Recognizing and Addressing the Barriers to Adolescents' 'Reading Like Historians,'" *The History Teacher* 44 (2011): 379–399;

that ask them, for example, to analyze a document or a limited number of documents in multiple ways. In my experience, this effectively expands students' conception of the kinds of questions it is possible to ask and it gives them a more concrete sense of the breadth of the conceptual resources historians can draw on in framing the research enterprise.

A more involved, more demanding method might be to create research assignments that require multiple analytical steps, with consultation built into the process of designing next steps. For example, students can be asked to analyze an historical dataset of their choosing in order to come up with a perspective on a particular proposition, such as "lower taxes spur economic growth," "less religious societies are more technologically innovative," or "greater inequality is associated with higher fertility." Once they have an initial answer, they can be asked to develop a second question building on that result. Do different kinds of tax structures (more reliance on income taxes, or on business taxes, or on consumption taxes, or on taxation of imports) have different consequences for economic growth? Are less religious societies more creative in other areas of endeavor besides technology – for example in the arts? Is the relationship between inequality and fertility the same in predominantly rural and in predominantly urban societies? Once they have developed an answer to that second question, they can be required to develop a third – so that they pursue a deepening and widening process of inquiry.

Since students are often more interested in people than in broad trends, an approach that can be more appealing to many is to ask that they place a particular historical personage in broad historical context – for example, by reading an autobiography, then exploring through self-directed reading how that person's life was shaped by or contributed to broader historical events. Once students have done that, they could be asked to do the same with another person who appears in the original biography or autobiography, but experienced the same events in quite different ways – or, to put it more poetically, encountered a very different fate.

Yet students can also find it very instructive – and satisfying – to take their own investigative path through a "canned" or predefined "archive" assembled by an instructor.[40] One form of such archive might be

---

Barbara Stipling, "Teaching Inquiry with Primary Sources," in the Library of Congress' *Teaching with Primary Sources Quarterly* 2 (2009): 2–4.

[40] For an example, see Jennifer L. Cote, "'None of My History Classes Were Like This': An Experiment in Mastery Pedagogy," *The History Teacher* 4 (2017): 597–627. On learning History by doing it, see also particularly Scott T. Barksdale, "Good Readers Make Good Historians," *The History Teacher* 46 (2013): 231–252; Linda Sargent Wood, "Hooked on inquiry: History Labs in the

a collection of letters – for example, letters from European immigrants to the United States and Brazil. Students might be asked to search through such a collection to discover how immigrants defined their own experiences, how they preserved, broke, or formed social ties, how they thought about the possibility of integration into a new society.[41] Another such "archive" would be a particular newspaper. The *New York Times* or the *London Times*, for example, are widely available in searchable electronic form. Students can be asked to find a person or event of interest to them, search for them or it in that particular database, and construct an interpretation based on what they find in that particular source.[42] Another such "archive" might be a defined run of a particular magazine – *Scientific American* between 1900 and 1914, for example, or the British medical journal *The Lancet*, or perhaps even a fashion magazine (e.g., how did the way fashion magazines discuss relationships and sexuality change or not change over time?). The documents on US foreign policy (including many memos from the diplomats of other countries) available through the Office of the historian of the US State Department might give students insight, for example, into incidents like the 1956 Suez Crisis.[43] Even where students do not themselves choose the broader research topic or the kinds of sources used, a course focused on an exercise like this can, as one recent example suggests, "fully immerse students in the real hands-on practices of historians" in analyzing sources and developing interpretations.[44]

Assignments like these should be framed carefully to lead students beyond superficial findings such as "what happened," "who was to blame," "who was right," or "this event caused the Mexican Revolution." Usually, moreover, an assignment like this should be progressive – that is, the student should undertake research and present their provisional findings, then be given feedback by the instructor and by their peers regarding both the quality of their interpretation and what next research steps they need to take to broaden and deepen their understanding. Ideally, the

---

Methods Course," *The History Teacher* 45 (2012): 549–567; Christopher R. Corley, "From Mentoring to Collaborating: Fostering Undergraduate Research in History," *The History Teacher* 46 (2013): 397–414.

[41] Witold Kula, Nina Assorodobraj-Kula, and Marcin Kula, eds., *Writing Home: Immigrants in Brazil and the United States, 1890–1891*, ed. and trans. Josephine Wtulich (Boulder, CO: East European Monographs, 1986).

[42] See Kyle Jantzen, "Teaching the Practice of History with the *New York Times*," *The History Teacher* 49 (2016): 271–284.

[43] See, for example, https://history.state.gov/historicaldocuments/frus1955-57v16.

[44] Elizabeth S. Manly, Rien Fertel, Jenny Schwartzberg, and Robert Ticknor, "Teaching in the Archives," *The History Teacher* 53 (2019): 67–105, here p. 69.

student should be required to reach some preliminary conclusions on the basis of one form of historical evidence, and then revise those conclusions on the basis of research with a different form of evidence, a different "archive." For example, how does the account of a particular event in a mainstream newspaper differ from an account of it in the autobiography of a participant? How did coverage of a particular event differ in Protestant and Catholic newspapers? How does the extent of discussion of a particular disease in a medical journal compare with the importance of that disease as reflected in public health statistics?

Projects like these are of course merely "exercises"; the aim is not to generate new and original historical insight. Such exercises may not succeed in moving students beyond familiar myths and conventional oversimplifications. It is difficult to get to grips with the way that History thinks, and it is difficult to reach coherent conclusions in History. Regardless, there is value simply in giving students the opportunity to confront the problems of historical research and interpretation.

Ideally any curriculum for a degree in History would make room for at least one major research undertaking, one that requires active, self-directed, hands-on analysis and interpretation of an open field of historical materials. In many university History departments every History major is required to write a senior thesis; in others only selected students write an "honors" thesis. My own view is that ideally any History major should write a substantial thesis requiring independent research over an entire academic year. A project of that size gives the student time to wrestle with the availability of sources; to develop, revise, and refine a research question, or even discard it and start over afresh; to consider multiple interpretive options, multiple theoretical resources, and multiple problems of bias in the evidence; perhaps even to confront biases and assumptions, and to put sufficient time into developing an interpretation to be confronted with the problems of selection of evidence and interpretation of sources.

A project like that can begin with something as simple as getting access to a long run of a newspaper or magazine (or ideally more than one) and reading through it to see what was being reported on, how, and by whom. A survey of a source like that can yield wonderful historical questions that can then be pursued further. Another approach would be to immerse oneself in the published letters of a figure of interest. That can lead one to further published letters, or to published autobiographies, or diaries. Simply poring over an historical dataset, analyzing some statistics in spreadsheets, and generating some charts can yield exciting questions to be pursued in the same or other datasets. University and public libraries' special collections sections, local historical societies, and online sources all offer a world of possibilities for students of History to begin open-ended, expansive, holistic archival inquiry – an inquiry that will present them with at least some of the challenges and opportunities for learning History generates.

But any student of History should, finally, take the next step as well: that of developing and then also *presenting* an interpretation. Historians are often thought of as solitary scholars burrowing into archives and datasets and emerging years later with articles or books. There is a great deal of truth to that. But History is also a gregarious discipline, a very social one. I have remarked that History teaches deliberation. Deliberation means not only slowness to action, imposed by careful reflection; it also means discussion. The two are, of course, directly connected. Because History is not action-oriented, because there is nothing that urgently needs to be decided or done about the past, the historian has time to think. And no one thinks very clearly if they think alone. History is perspectival; it therefore teaches us that no one perspective is exhaustively and conclusively right. Critical discussion will always make History better – more thoughtful, more complex, broader, more self-aware, more analytical. In discussion, debate, and deliberation we cultivate intellectual flexibility and openness.[45]

6.8 Concluding Thought

Whatever the pedagogical or investigative approach or methods one adopts, there are two important and distinctive characteristics of History as a way of thinking that can and should be central to teaching and learning History. First, History can teach us to expand our thinking. Independent individual research should play a central role in History courses and curricula because it exposes students to the characteristic openness and boundlessness of inquiry in History. But whether the method is independent research, "canned" research exercises, close examination and analysis of particular texts, careful reading of scholarly articles, or an examination and

---

[45] For discussions of how to approach teaching through independent research projects in History, see Keith A. Erekson, "From Archive to Awards Ceremony: An Approach for Engaging Students in Historical Research," *Arts & Humanities in Higher Education* 10 (2011): 388–400; James W. Loewen, *Teaching What Really Happened: How to Avoid the Tyranny of Textbooks and Get Students Excited about Doing History*, 2nd edition (New York: Teachers College Press, 2018), pp. 91–111; Elizabeth Belanger, "Bridging the Understanding Gap: An Approach to Teaching First-Year Students How to 'Do' History," *The History Teacher* 49 (2015): 35–62; and, still usefully, Carol Toner, "Teaching Students to Be Historians: Suggestions for an Undergraduate Research Seminar," *The History Teacher* 27 (1993): 37–51.

6.8 Concluding Thought

critique of the interpretive framework presented in a textbook, the greatest value of learning how History thinks is that it encourages us to inquire further. History draws students into exploration of multiple different aspects of any historical phenomenon and of the historical context in which evidence can be placed. It draws us into open-ended, unbounded exploration of a web or network of connections between different elements in a broad social and historical context. It asks us to expand our conceptual apparatus by considering any particular topic from the perspective of multiple theoretical frameworks or traditions. It asks us to look at more cases, and more different cases, in order to refine and expand our understanding of specific phenomena and of broad patterns. It encourages us to expand our conception of the relevance of evidence bearing on a particular question by asking that we examine multiple different kinds of sources – either as a formal requirement of an assignment, or, even better, because we have to find ways to compensate for the limited quantity and quality of any one body of sources. It does so too by encouraging us to approach our evidence holistically, apprehending and analyzing not only those aspects of the sources that appear to have been most directly relevant to our hypotheses or interests, but also those aspects that seem *not* to be directly relevant, or those that appeared most important to the people who produced them. In doing that, it expands also our capacity to question our own assumptions, biases, and interests. It asks us to expand our conception of what it means to understand and to interpret evidence by encouraging us to dig deeper into the sources or into multiple interpretations, to adopt multiple different modes of analysis, multiple alternate analytical approaches. History encourages us to expand the scope and variety of questions we ask – for example, not just what happened and why, but how it was related to other things happening in the same place and time, or in other places, or before, or after; how people understood it at the time; and what they did with that understanding. That expands our grasp of the spectrum of human perspectives, experiences, ideas, and traditions – in short of the human condition.

Second, studying and teaching History presents us with complex ethical challenges. Chapters 1 and 2 discussed what I see as the ethical assumptions of both historicist and more theoretically oriented ("social science" or "critical") History. The one asks us to treat the people of the past, the people we are studying, as fully human people, in a sense as interlocutors – we do not just write or speak *about* them; we also listen *to* them. The other asks us to acknowledge our own full humanity, not to deny our own present interests and concerns in the name of scholarly detachment. The same is true of our approach to teaching. One important aim of History teaching is to get students to take the past and its people seriously – to get them to expand their horizons by approaching the past with respect and care. But we need to engage our students' interest and concerns; we need to approach the past with them from where they are in the present. And we also must recognize our own interests, concerns, values, and histories, and their role in shaping our questions about and our perspective on the past. This is not just a matter of good historical method; it is a question of intellectual honesty and also of respect for our own humanity and historicity, and for that of our students.

In theory reconciling these different ethical imperatives should be difficult. As scholars and teachers, should we be loyal to or interested in the past or the present? In practice the effort to do justice to both simultaneously is exciting. It is good, clean, challenging, sometimes spooky intellectual fun. The point in each case is to recognize the fundamental and full humanity of the people we encounter, whether they are our students today, people in the past, or ourselves. When we do that, learning becomes an adventure. When we relinquish control over our encounter with others, we are free to encounter ideas that take us to new places, to learn new things, unexpected things. We are free not only to find unexpected answers to our questions, but to find unexpected questions. Both are exciting. And sometimes too we find that it is not really very exciting to have the power to pose the questions. Sometimes it is more exciting to find that we are not the one asking the questions. Rather, we are being asked to answer someone else's questions. That "someone else" can be our students. That is often interesting and rewarding, an opportunity to learn. But sometimes that other person is someone who is dead, but who is fully as much a human being as we are, and who is speaking to us, if we listen. That is spooky. That is fun. That is what being a member of the human species is like. And that is what History is about.

Bibliography

American Historical Association, "AHR Conversation: Explaining Historical Change; or, The Lost History of Causes," *American Historical Review* 120:4 (2015): 1369–1423.
American Historical Association, *History Anew: Innovations in the Teaching of History Today*, ed. Robert Blackey (Long Beach: California State University, Long Beach Press, 1993).
American Historical Association, "History Discipline Core" (2016). www.historians.org/teaching-and-learning/tuning-the-history-discipline/2016-history-discipline-core.
American Historical Association, "Statement on Excellent Classroom Teaching of History" (updated 2017). www.historians.org/jobs-and-professional-development/statements-standards-and-guidelines-of-the-discipline/statement-on-excellent-classroom-teaching-of-history.
American Historical Association, "Tuning the History Discipline in the United States." www.historians.org/teaching-and-learning/tuning-the-history-discipline.
Andrews, Stephen D., "Structuring the Past: Thinking about the History Curriculum," *Journal of American History* 95 (2009): 1094–1101.
Andrews, Thomas and Flannery Burke, "What Does It Mean to Think Historically?" *Perspectives* 45:1 (2007): 32–35.
Ankersmit, Frank, *History and Tropology: The Rise and Fall of a Metaphor* (Berkeley: University of California Press, 1994).
Ankersmit, Frank, "Manifesto for an Analytical Political History," in *Manifestos for History*, ed. Keith Jenkins, Sue Morgan, and Alun Munslow (New York: Routledge, 2007), pp. 179–196.
Ankersmit, Frank, "The Necessity of Historicism," *Journal of the Philosophy of History* 4 (2010): 226–240.
Armitage, David, "In Defense of Presentism," in *History and Human Flourishing*, ed. Darrin M. McMahon (Oxford: Oxford University Press, 2020), pp. 46–69.
Ashby, Rosalyn, Peter J. Lee, and Denis Shemilt, "Putting Principles into Practice: Teaching and Planning," in *How Students Learn: History in the Classroom*, ed. M. Suzanne Donovan and John D. Bransford (Washington, DC: National Academies Press, 2005), pp. 79–177.

Aydelotte, William O., "Notes on the Problem of Historical Generalization," in *Generalization in the Writing of History: A Report of the Committee on Historical Analysis of the Social Science Research Council*, ed. Louis Gottschalk (Chicago, IL: University of Chicago Press, 1963), pp. 145–177.

Baberowski, Jörg, *Der Sinn der Geschichte: Geschichtstheorien von Hegel bis Foucault* (Munich: Beck, 2005).

Bain, Robert B., "Into the Breach: Using Research and Theory to Shape History Instruction," *Journal of Education* 189 (2008/2009): 159–167.

Bain, Robert B., "'They Thought the World Was Flat?' Applying the Principles of How People Learn in Teaching High School History," in *How Students Learn: History in the Classroom*, ed. M. Suzanne Donovan and John D. Bransford (Washington, DC: National Academies Press, 2005), pp. 179–213.

Banner Jr., James M., *Being a Historian: An Introduction to the Professional World of History* (Cambridge: Cambridge University Press, 2012).

Banner Jr., James M., *The Ever-Changing Past: Why All History Is Revisionist History* (New Haven, CT: Yale University Press, 2021).

Barksdale, Scott T., "Good Readers Make Good Historians," *The History Teacher* 46 (2013): 231–252.

Barton, Keith C. and Linda S. Levstik, *Teaching History for the Common Good* (Mahwah, NJ: Lawrence Erlbaum, 2004).

Beard, Charles A., "Written History As an Act of Faith," *American Historical Review* 39 (1934), pp. 219–231.

Beiser, Frederick C., *The German Historicist Tradition* (Oxford: Oxford University Press, 2011).

Belanger, Elizabeth, "Bridging the Understanding Gap: An Approach to Teaching First-Year Students How to 'Do' History," *The History Teacher* 49 (2015): 35–62.

Bentley, Michael, "The Turn toward 'Science': Historians Delivering Untheorized Truth," in *The Sage Handbook of Historical Theory*, ed. Nancy Partner and Sarah Foot (Thousand Oaks, CA: Sage, 2013).

Berger, Stefan, "A Plea for Renewing a Left-of-Centre Engaged History Writing in 'Conversations: What Is History? Historiography Roundtable,'" *Rethinking History* 22 (2018): 500–524.

Berger, Stefan, ed., *The Engaged Historian: Perspectives on the Intersection of Politics, Activism and the Historical Profession* (New York: Berghahn, 2019).

Beringer, Richard E., *Historical Analysis: Contemporary Approaches to Clio's Craft* (New York: Wiley, 1978).

Berkhofer, Robert F., *Fashioning History: Current Practices and Principles* (New York: Palgrave MacMillan, 2008).

Bermúdez, Angela and Rosário Jaramillo, "Development of Historical Explanation in Children, Adolescents and Adults," *International Review of History Education* 3 (2001): 146–167.

Bevir, Mark, "Objectivity in History," *Theory and History* 33 (1994): 328–344.

Blackbourn, David, *Marpingen: Apparitions of the Virgin Mary in a Nineteenth-Century German Village* (New York: Knopf, 1994).

Blake, Christopher, "Can History Be Objective?" in *Theories of History*, ed. Patrick Gardiner (New York: Free Press, 1959), pp. 329–343.
Bloch, Marc, *The Historian's Craft* (New York: Vintage, 1953).
Bloxham, Donald, *History and Morality* (Oxford: Oxford University Press, 2020).
Booth, Alan, *Teaching History at University: Enhancing Learning and Understanding* (New York: Routledge, 2003).
Booth, Alan and Paul Hyland, "Introduction: Developing Scholarship in History Teaching," in *The Practice of University History Teaching*, ed. Alan Booth and Paul Hyland (Manchester: Manchester University Press, 2000), pp. 1–13.
Bourke, Joanna, "Foreword," in *Manifestos for History*, ed. Keith Jenkins, Sue Morgan, and Alun Munslow (New York: Routledge, 2007), pp. xi–xii.
Bradley Commission on History in Schools, "Building a History Curriculum: Guidelines for Teaching History in Schools," *The History Teacher* 23:1 (1989): 7–35.
Britt, M. Anne, Charles A. Perfetti, Julie A. van Dyke, and Gareth Gabrys, "The Sourcer's Apprentice: A Tool for Document-Supported History Instruction," in *Knowing, Teaching, and Learning History: National and International Perspectives*, ed. Peter N. Stearns, Peter Seixas, and Sam Wineburg (New York: New York University Press, 2000), pp. 437–470.
Brown, George, "Assessing the Quality of Education in History Departments," in *History and Higher Education: New Directions in Teaching and Learning*, ed. Alan Booth and Paul Hyland (Oxford: Blackwell, 1996), pp. 289–319.
Bullock, Alan, "The Historian's Purpose: History and Metahistory," in *The Philosophy of History in Our Time*, ed. Hans Meyerhoff (New York: Doubleday, 1959), pp. 292–299.
Butterfield, Herbert, "The Dangers of History," in Herbert Butterfield, *History and Human Relations* (New York: MacMillan, 1952), pp. 158–181.
Bynum, Caroline Walker, "Wonder," *American Historical Review* 102 (1997): 1–26.
Calder, Lendol, "Uncoverage: Toward a Signature Pedagogy for the History Survey," *Journal of American History* 92:4 (2006): 1358–1370.
Cannadine, David, *G. M. Trevelyan: A Life in History* (New York: HarperCollins, 1992).
Cannon, Lynn Weber, "Fostering Positive Race, Class, and Gender Dynamics in the Classroom," *Women's Studies Quarterly* 18 (1990): 126–134.
Cantor, Norman F., *Inventing the Middle Ages: The Lives, Works, and Ideas of the Great Medievalists of the Twentieth Century* (New York: Quill/William Morrow, 1991).
Cantor, Norman F. and Richard I. Schneider, *How to Study History* (Arlington Heights, IL: Harlan Davidson, 1967).
Carr, Edward Hallett, *What Is History?* (New York: MacMillan, 1961).
Chakrabarty, Dipesh, "History and the Politics of Recognition," in *Manifestos for History*, ed. Keith Jenkins, Sue Morgan, and Alun Munslow (New York: Routledge, 2007), pp. 77–87.
Chakrabarty, Dipesh, "History as Critique and Critiques of History," *Economic and Political Weekly* 26:37 (1991): 2162–2166.

Chakrabarty, Dipesh, "History and Historicality," review of Ranajit Guha, *History at the Limit of World History*, in *Postcolonial Studies* 7:1 (2004): 125–130.

Chakrabarty, Dipesh, *Provincializing Europe* (Princeton, NJ: Princeton University Press, 2009).

Chakrabarty, Dipesh, "Provincializing Europe: Postcoloniality and the Critique of History," *Cultural Studies* 6 (1992): 337–357.

Chapman, Arthur, "Causal Explanation," in *Debates in History Teaching*, 2nd edition, ed. Ian Davies (London: Routledge, 2017), pp. 130–143.

Chapman, Arthur and Terry Haydn, "Teaching History in Changing and Challenging Times," *History Education Research* 16 (2020): 1–3.

Chatterjee, Indrani, "Whose History? What Theory? A Postcolonial Response," *History of the Present* 10 (2020): 166–168.

Chesneaux, Jean, *Pasts and Futures, or What Is History For?* (London: Thames and Hudson, 1978 [1976]).

Christianson, Paul, "Patterns of Historical Interpretation," in *Objectivity, Method, and Point of View: Essays in the Philosophy of History*, ed. W. J. van der Dussen and Lionel Rubinoff (Leiden: Brill, 1991), 47–71.

Cobb, Richard, "Richard Cobb," in *Historians on History: An Anthology* ed. John Tosh (Harlow: Pearson, 2000), pp. 39–45.

Cohen, Stanley, *Folk Devils and Moral Panics* (London: MacGibbon & Keen, 1972).

Collingwood, R. J., *The Idea of History* (Mansfield Centre, CT: Martino, 2014 [1946]).

Commager, Henry Steele, *The Nature and the Study of History* (Columbus, OH: C. E. Merrill, 1965).

Corley, Christopher R., "From Mentoring to Collaborating: Fostering Undergraduate Research in History," *The History Teacher* 46 (2013): 397–414.

Cote, Jennifer L., "'None of My History Classes Were Like This': An Experiment in Mastery Pedagogy," *The History Teacher* 4 (2017): 597–627.

Cullen, Jim, *Essaying the Past: How to Read, Write, and Think about History* (Malden, MA: Wiley-Blackwell, 2012).

Daddow, Oliver J., "The Ideology of Apathy: Historians and Postmodernism," *Rethinking History* 8 (2004): 417–437.

Danto, Arthur C., "On Explanation in History," *Philosophy of Science* 23:1 (1956): 15–30.

Daston, Lorraine, "Die unerschütterliche Praxis," in *Auf der Suche nach der verlorenen Wahrheit: Zum Grundlagenstreit in der Geschichtswissenschaft*, ed. Rainer Marie Kiesow and Dieter Simon (Frankfurt: Campus, 2000), pp. 13–25.

Dening, Greg, "Enigma Variations on History in Three Keys: A Conversational Essay," *History and Theory* 39:2 (2000): 210–217.

Dening, Greg, "Performing Cross-Culturally," in *Manifestos for History*, ed. Keith Jenkins, Sue Morgan, and Alun Munslow (New York: Routledge, 2007), pp. 98–107.

Diaz, Arlene, Joan Middenfdorf, David Pace, and Leah Shopkow, "The History Learning Project: A Department 'Decodes' Its Students," *Journal of American History* 94 (2008): 1211–1224.
Dickinson, Alaric K. and Peter J. Lee, "'Educational Objectives for the Study of History' Reconsidered," in *History Teaching and Historical Understanding*, ed. Alaric K. Dickinson and Peter J. Lee (London: Heinemann, 1978), pp. 21–38.
Dickinson, Edward Ross, *Dancing in the Blood: Modern Dance and European Culture on the Eve of the First World War* (Cambridge: Cambridge University Press, 2017).
Dickinson, Edward Ross, "Dominion of the Spirit over the Flesh: Religion and Sexuality in the German Women's Movements before 1914," *Gender and History* 17 (2005): 1–32.
Dickinson, Edward Ross, "Liberalism with a Vengeance? Three Books on Social Policy in New Zealand," *Kotare* 2 (1999): pp. 48–56.
Dickinson, Edward Ross, "Policing Sex in Germany, 1882–1982: A Preliminary Statistical Analysis," *Journal of the History of Sexuality* 16 (2007): 204–250.
Dickinson, Edward Ross, "'Was There a Backlash against Weimar's Sexual Politics?' Some Further Reflections," Weimar Studies Network, May 12, 2016, https://weimarstudies.wordpress.com/2016/05/12/guest-post-edward-dickinson-on-weimars-sexual-politics-and-the-backlash-thesis/#more–1542.
Dickinson, Edward Ross, *The World in the Long Twentieth Century: An Interpretive History* (Berkeley: University of California Press, 2018).
Dietze, Carola, "Toward a History on Equal Terms: A Discussion of *Provincializing Europe*," *History and Theory* 47 (2008): 69–84.
Dirlik, Arif, *Postmodernity's History: The Past as Legacy and Project* (New York: Rowman & Littlefield, 2000).
Doan, Laura, *Disturbing Practices: History, Sexuality, and Women's Experience in Modern War* (Chicago, IL: University of Chicago Press, 2013).
Dobson, Miriam and Benjamin Ziemann, "Introduction," in *Reading Primary Sources: The Interpretation of Texts from Nineteenth- and Twentieth-Century History*, ed. Miriam Dobson and Benjamin Ziemann (New York: Routledge, 2009), pp. 1–18.
Douma, Michael J., *Creative Historical Thinking* (New York: Routledge, 2018).
Dozono, Tadashi, "The Passive Voice of White Supremacy: Tracing Epistemic and Discursive Violence in World History Curriculum," *Review of Education, Pedagogy, and Cultural Studies* 42 (2020): 1–26.
Dray, William, *Law and Explanation in History* (Oxford: Oxford University Press, 1957).
Dray, William, *Philosophy of History*, 2nd edition (Englewood Cliffs, NJ: Prentice Hall, 1993).
Duggan, Lisa, "The Theory Wars, or, Who's Afraid of Judith Butler?" *Journal of Women's History* 10 (1998): 9–19.
Dunn, Ross E., "Constructing World History in the Classroom," in *Knowing, Teaching, and Learning History: National and International Perspectives*, ed.

Peter N. Stearns, Peter Seixas, and Sam Wineburg (New York: New York University Press, 2000), pp. 121–140.

Elder, Linda, Meg Gorzycki, and Richard Paul, *The Student Guide to Historical Thinking: Going beyond Dates, Places and Names to the Core of History* (Lanham, MD: Rowman & Littlefield, 2019).

Eley, Geoff, *A Crooked Line: From Cultural History to the History of Society* (Ann Arbor: University of Michigan Press, 2005).

Elton, G. R., "G. R. Elton," in *The History Debate*, ed. Juliet Gardiner (London: Collins & Brown, 1990), pp. 6–12.

Elton, G. R., *The Practice of History* (New York: Thomas Crowell, 1967).

Elton, G. R., *Return to Essentials: Some Reflections on the Present State of Historical Study* (Cambridge: Cambridge University Press, 1991).

English, Richard, "History and the Study of Terrorism," in *The Cambridge History of Terrorism*, ed. Richard English (Cambridge: Cambridge University Press, 2021), pp. 3–27.

Erekson, Keith A., "From Archive to Awards Ceremony: An Approach for Engaging Students in Historical Research," *Arts & Humanities in Higher Education* 10 (2011): 388–400.

Ermarth, Elizabeth, "Sequel to History," in *The Post-Modern History Reader*, ed. Keith Jenkins (New York: Routledge, 1997), pp. 47–64.

Ermarth, Elizabeth Deeds, "Beyond History," *Rethinking History* 5 (2002): 195–215.

Estes, Todd, "Constructing the Syllabus: Devising a Framework for Helping Students Learn to Think Like Historians," *The History Teacher* 40:2 (2007): 183–202.

Etkind, Alexander, *Internal Colonization: Russia's Imperial Experience* (Cambridge: Polity Press, 2011).

Evans, Richard J., *In Defense of History* (New York: Norton, 1999).

Evans, Ronald W., "Educational Ideologies and the Teaching of History," in *Teaching and Learning in History*, ed. Gaea Leinhardt, Isabel L. Beck, and Catherine Stainton (Hillsdale, NJ: Lawrence Erlbaum, 1994), pp. 171–207.

Fairburn, Miles, *Social History: Problems, Strategies, and Methods* (New York: St. Martin's, 1999).

Farge, Arlette, *The Allure of the Archives*, trans. Thomas Scott-Railton (New Haven, CT: Yale University Press, 1989).

Faust, Drew, Hendrik Herzog, David A. Hollinger, et al., "Interchange: The Practice of History," *Journal of American History* 90 (2003): 576–611.

Festle, Mary Jo, "How They Change: Students Tell Us How History Transforms Them," *Perspectives in History* 53:9 (2015): 29–30.

Finney, Patrick, "Beyond the Postmodern Moment?" *Journal of Contemporary History* 40:1 (2005): 149–165.

Fischer, David Hackett, *Historians' Fallacies: Toward a Logic of Historical Thought* (New York: Harper & Row, 1970).

Foley, Malcolm, "History as Love," *Perspectives on History*, September 7, 2022, pp. 5–6.

Foucault, Michel, *The Archaeology of Knowledge* (New York: Pantheon, 1972).
Foucault, Michel, "Nietzsche, Genealogy, History," in *Michel Foucault: Language, Counter-Memory, Practice*, ed. Donald F. Bouchard (Ithaca, NY: Cornell University Press, 1977), pp. 139–164.
Foucault, Michel, "What Is Enlightenment?" in *Ethics: Subjectivity and Truth*, ed. Paul Rabinow, trans Robert Hurley and others (New York: New Press, 1998), pp. 303–320.
Frankel, Charles, "Explanation and Interpretation in History," in *Theories of History*, ed. Patrick Gardiner (New York: Free Press, 1959), pp. 408–427.
Fuentes, Marisa J., *Dispossessed Lives: Enslaved Women, Violence, and the Archive* (Philadelphia: University of Pennsylvania Press, 2016).
Fulbrook, Mary, *Historical Theory* (New York: Routledge, 1995).
Galgano, Michael J., "Liberal Learning and the History Major," *Perspectives* 28 (2007): 61–64.
Gadamer, Hans-Georg, *Methode und Wahrheit: Grundzüge einer philosophischen Hermeneutik* (Tubingen: Morh, 1965).
Gaddis, John Lewis, *The Landscape of History: How Historians Map the Past* (New York: Oxford University Press, 2002).
Galbraith, V. H., *An Introduction to the Study of History* (London: Watts, 1964).
Gannon, Kevin, "On Presentism and History; Or, We're Doing This Again, Are We?" https://thetattooedprof.com/2022/08/19/on-presentism-and-history-or-were-doing-this-again-are-we.
Geyl, Peter and Arnold Toynbee, "Can We Know the Pattern of the Past? A Debate," in *Theories of History*, ed. Patrick Gardiner (New York: Free Press, 1959), pp. 308–319.
Goarke, Leo, "Teaching History: The Future of the Past," in *The River of History: Trans-National and Trans-Disciplinary Perspectives on the Immanence of the Past*, ed. Peter Farrugia (Calgary: University of Calgary Press, 2005), pp. 59–75.
Goldstein, Leon J., "Evidence and Events in History," *Philosophy of Science* 29:2 (1962): 175–194.
Goldstein, Leon J., "A Note on Historical Interpretation," *Philosophy of Science* 42:3 (1975): 312–319.
Goswami, Manu, "Remembering the Future," *American Historical Review* 113 (2008): 417–424.
Gottschalk, Louis, "Categories of Historiographical Generalization," in *Generalization in the Writing of History: A Report of the Committee on Historical Analysis of the Social Science Research Council*, ed. Louis Gottschalk (Chicago, IL: University of Chicago Press, 1963), pp. 113–129.
Green, Dominic, "The Unmaking of American History by the Woke Mob," *Wall Street Journal*, August 26, 2022.
Greene, Stuart, "Students as Authors in the Study of History," in *Teaching and Learning in History*, ed. Gaea Leinhardt, Isabel L Beck, and Catherine Stainton (Hillsdale, NJ: Lawrence Erlbaum, 1994), pp. 209–255.
Grim, Valerie, David Pace, and Leah Shopkow, "Learning to Use Evidence in the Study of History," in *Decoding the Disciplines: Helping Students Learn*

Disciplinary Ways of Thinking (San Francisco, CA: Jossey-Bass, 2004), pp. 57–68.

Grinin, Leonid, David Baker, Esther Quadackers, and Andrey Korotayev, *Teaching and Researching Big History: Exploring a New Scholarly Field*, ed. Leonid Grinin, David Baker, Esther Quadackers, and Andrey Korotayev (Volgagrad: Uchitel, 2014).

Grossman, James, "History Isn't a 'Useless' Major," *Los Angeles Times*, May 30, 2016.

Grossman, James and Waldo E. Martin, "A Tribute to Leon Litwack," *Perspectives in History* 60 (2922): 7–9.

Guldi, Jo and David Armitage, *The History Manifesto* (Cambridge: Cambridge University Press, 2014).

Gutierrez, Christine, "Making Connections: The Interdisciplinary Community of Teaching and Learning History," in *Knowing, Teaching, and Learning History: National and International Perspectives*, ed. Peter N. Stearns, Peter Seixas, and Sam Wineburg (New York: New York University Press, 2000), pp. 353–374.

Gutman, Herbert, "Herbert Gutman," in *Visions of History*, ed. Henry Abelove, Betsy Blackmer, Peter Dimock, and Jonathan Scheer (Manchester: Manchester University Press, 1976), pp. 185–216.

Hacke, Jens and Matthias Pohlig, eds., *Theorie in der Geschichtswissenschaft: Einblicke in die Praxis des historischen Forschens* (Frankfurt: Campus, 2008).

Halldén, Ola, "On the Paradox of Understanding History in an Educational Setting," in *Teaching and Learning in History*, ed. Gaea Leinhardt, Isabel L. Beck, and Catherine Stainton (Hillsdale, NJ: Lawrence Erlbaum, 1994), pp. 27–46.

Hamerow, Theodore S., "What Is the Use of History?" in *Reflections on History and Historians*, ed. Theodore S. Hamerow (Madison: University of Wisconsin Press, 1987), pp. 205–243.

Handlin, Oscar, *Truth in History* (Cambridge, MA: Harvard University Press, 1979).

Hare, J. Laurence, Jack Wells, and Bruce E. Baker, *Essential Skills for Historians: A Practical Guide to Researching the Past* (London: Bloomsbury, 2020).

Harris, Steve, "Reading and Understanding History: An Introduction to Critical Thinking," unpublished ms, 2022.

Haskell, Thomas, "Objectivity Is Not Neutrality: Rhetoric vs. Practice in Peter Novick's *That Noble Dream*," *History and Theory* 29 (1990): 129–157.

Heineman, Elizabeth D., "The Economic Miracle in the Bedroom: Big Business and Sexual Consumption in Reconstruction West Germany," *Journal of Modern History* 78:4 (2006): 846–877.

Hempel, Carl G., "The Function of General Laws in History," *Journal of Philosophy* 39 (1942): 35–48.

Herf, Jeffrey, "Never Apologize for Telling the Truth," September 13, 2022, https://quillette.com/2022/09/13/never-apologize-for-trying-to-tell-the-truth.

Herman, Paul and Adriaan van Veldhuizen, "Introduction: Historicism as a Travelling Concept," in *Historicism: A Travelling Concept*, ed. Herman Paul and Adriaan van Veldhuizen (London: Bloomsbury Academic, 2021), pp. 1–12.

Himmelfarb, Gertrude, "Gertrude Himmelfarb," in *Historians on History: An Anthology*, ed. John Tosh (Harlow: Pearson, 2000), pp. 290–298.
Hitchcock, Tim, Robert B. Shoemaker, and John Tosh, "Skills and the Structure of the History Curriculum," in *The Practice of University History Teaching*, ed. Alan Booth and Paul Hyland (Manchester: Manchester University Press, 2000), pp. 47–59.
Hobsbawm, Eric, *On History* (New York: New Press, 1997).
Hofstadter, Richard, "History and the Social Sciences," in *Varieties of History*, ed. Fritz Stern (New York: Vintage, 1972 [1956]), pp. 359–370.
Holborn, Hajo, *History and the Humanities* (New York: Doubleday 1972).
Howell, Martha and Walter Prevenier, *From Reliable Sources: An Introduction to Historical Methods* (Ithaca, NY: Cornell University Press, 2001).
Hunt, Lynn, *History: Why It Matters* (Cambridge: Polity Press, 2018).
Hunt, Lynn, "Where Have All the Theories Gone?" *Perspectives on History* 40:3 (2002): 5–7.
Hunter, Emma, "Dialogues between Past and Present in Intellectual Histories of Mid-Twentieth-Century Africa," *Modern Intellectual History* 20 (2023): 630–638.
Husbands, Chris, *What Is History Teaching? Language, Ideas and Meaning in Learning about the Past* (Buckingham: Open University Press, 1996).
Iber, Patrick and Jennifer Ratner-Rosenhagen, "The Present Is a Foreign Country: Teaching the History of Now," *Modern Intellectual History* 20 (2023): 651–662.
Iggers, George G., "Historicism: The History and Meaning of the Term," *Journal of the History of Ideas* 56 (1995): 129–152.
Jameson, Fredric, "How Not to Historicize Theory," *Critical Inquiry* 34 (2008): 563–582.
Jantzen, Kyle, "Teaching the Practice of History with *The New York Times*," *The History Teacher* 49 (2016): 271–284.
Jenkins, Keith, "On Disobedient Histories," *Rethinking History* 7 (2003): 367–385.
Jenkins, Keith, *On "What Is History?"* (London: Routledge, 1995).
Jenkins, Keith, "A Postmodern Reply to Perez Zagorin," *History and Theory* 39 (2000): 181–200.
Jenkins, Keith, *Rethinking History* (New York: Routledge, 1991).
Jenkins, Keith, "Teaching History Theory: A Radical Introduction," in *History in Higher Education: New Directions in Teaching and Learning*, ed. Alan Booth and Paul Hyland (Oxford: Blackwell, 1996), pp. 75–95.
Jones, Jacqueline, "Presidential Address: Historians and Their Publics, Then and Now," *American Historical Review* 127 (2022): 1–30.
Jordanova, Ludmila, *History in Practice*, 2nd edition (London: Hodder, 2006).
Joyce, Patrick, "The End of Social History?" *Social History* 20:1 (1995): 73–91.
Joyce, Patrick, "The Gift of the Past: Towards a Critical History," in *Manifestos for History*, ed. Keith Jenkins, Sue Morgan, and Alun Munslow (New York: Routledge, 2007), pp. 88–97.
Joyce, Patrick, "History and Postmodernism," in *The Post-modern History Reader*, ed. Keith Jenkins (New York: Routledge, 1997), pp. 244–249.

Kalela, Jorma, *Making History: The Historian and Uses of the Past* (New York: Palgrave MacMillan, 2011).

Kansteiner, Wulf, "Mad History Disease Contained? Postmodern Excess Management Advice from the UK," *History and Theory* 39 (2000): 218–229.

Kelman, Ari and Jonathan Fetter-Vorm, *Battle Lines: A Graphic History of the Civil War* (New York: Hill & Wang, 2015).

Kendi, Ibrahim X., *How to Be an Antiracist* (New York: One World 2019).

King, Patricia M. and Karen Stronhm Kitchener, *Developing Reflective Judgment: Understanding and Promoting Intellectual Growth and Critical Thinking in Adolescents and Adults* (San Francisco, CA: Jossey-Bass, 1994).

Kleinberg, Ethan, "Just the Facts: The Fantasy of a Historical Science," *History of the Present* 6 (2016): 87–102.

Kleinberg, Ethan, Joan Wallach Scott, and Gary Wilder, "Theses on Theory and History," *History of the Present* 10 (2020): 157–165.

Kloppenberg, James T., "Objectivity in Historicism: A Century of American Historical Writing," *American Historical Review* 94 (1989): 1011–1030.

Knudsen, Heidi Eskelund, "History as a Designed Meaning-Making Process: Teacher Facilitation of Student–Subject Relationships," *Historical Education Research Journal* 17 (2020): 36–49.

Koch, Andrew K., "Many Thousands Failed: A Wakeup Call to History Educators," *Perspectives on History* 55 (2017): 18–19.

Kocka, Jürgen, *Facing Total War: German Society, 1914–1918* (Cambridge, MA: Harvard University Press, 1985 [original 1975]).

Kocka, Jürgen, "Geschichte – wozu?" in *Über das Studium der Geschichte*, ed. Wolfgang Hardtwig (Munich: Deutscher Taschenbuch Verlag, 1990), pp. 427–443.

Körber, Andreas, "German History Didactics: From Historical Consciousness to Historical Competencies – and Beyond?" in *Historicizing the Uses of the Past: Scandinavian Perspectives on History Culture, Historical Consciousness and Didactics of History Related to World War II*, ed. Hille Bjerg, Claudia Lenz, and Erik Thorstensen (Bielefeld: Transcript, 2011), pp. 145–164.

Kurfiss, Joanne Gainen, *Critical Thinking: Theory, Research, Practice, and Possibilities* (Washington, DC: Association for the Study of Higher Education, 1988).

Labaree, David, "Commentary on James Sweet's Essay about Historical Presentism," https://davidlabaree.com/2022/08/29/james-sweet-is-history-history-identity-politics-and-teleologies-of-the-present.

LaCapra, Dominick, "Resisting Apocalypse and Rethinking History," in *Manifestos for History*, ed. Keith Jenkins, Sue Morgan, and Alun Munslow (New York: Routledge, 2007).

LaCapra, Dominick, "Rethinking Intellectual History and Reading Texts," *History and Theory* 19:2 (1980): 245–276.

LaCapra, Dominick, *Understanding Others: Peoples, Animals, Pasts* (Ithaca, NY: Cornell University Press, 2018).

Lee, Peter, "History Education and Historical Literacy," in *Debates in History Education*, 2nd edition, ed. Ian Davies (London: Routledge, 2017), pp. 53–65.

Lee, Peter and Jonathan Howson, "'Two Out of Five Did Not Know That Henry VIII Had Six Wives': History Education, Historical Literacy, and Historical Consciousness," in *National History Standards: The Problem of the Canon and the Future of History Teaching*, ed. Linda Symcox and Arie Wilschut (Charlotte, NC: Information Age, 2009), pp. 211–263.

Leinhardt, Gaea, "History: A Time to Be Mindful," in *Teaching and Learning in History*, ed. Gaea Leinhardt, Isabel L Beck, and Catherine Stainton (Hillsdale, NJ: Lawrence Erlbaum, 1994), pp. 137–170.

Leinhardt, Gaea, "Lessons on Teaching and Learning in History from Paul's Pen," in *Knowing, Teaching, and Learning History: National and International Perspectives*, ed. Peter N. Stearns, Peter Seixas, and Sam Wineburg (New York: New York University Press, 2000), pp. 223–245.

Lévesque, Stéphan, *Thinking Historically: Educating Students for the Twenty-First Century* (Toronto: University of Toronto Press, 2008).

Lloyd, Christopher, "History and the Social Sciences," in *Writing History: Theory & Practice*, ed. Stefan Berger, Heiko Feldner, and Kevin Passmore (London: Arnold, 2003), pp. 83–103.

Loewen, James W., *Teaching What Really Happened: How to Avoid the Tyranny of Textbooks and Get Students Excited about Doing History*, 2nd edition (New York: Teachers College Press, 2018).

Lorenz, Chris, "Historical Knowledge and Historical Reality: A Plea for 'Internal Realism,'" *History and Theory* 33 (1994): 297–327.

Lowenthal, David, *The Past Is a Foreign Country* (Cambridge: Cambridge University Press, 1985).

Luhmann, Niklas, *Die Gesellschaft der Gesellschaft* (Frankfurt: Suhrkamp, 1997).

Luhmann, Niklas, *Introduction to Systems Theory*, ed. Dirk Baecker, trans. Peter Gilgen (New York: Polity, 2011).

Lutz, Raphael, "The Implications of Empiricism for History," in *The Sage Handbook of Historical Theory* (Thousand Oaks, CA: Sage, 2013), pp. 23–40.

MacMillan, Margaret, *Dangerous Games: The Uses and Abuses of History* (New York: Modern Library, 2008).

Mandell, Nikki and Bobbie Malone, *Thinking Like a Historian: Rethinking History Instruction* (n.p.: Wisconsin Historical Society Press, 2008).

Manly, Elizabeth S., Rien Fertel, Jenny Schwartzberg, and Robert Ticknor, "Teaching in the Archives," *The History Teacher* 53 (2019): 67–105.

Martell, Christopher C. and Kaylene M. Stevens, *Teaching History for Justice: Centering Activism in Students' Study of the Past* (New York: Teacher's College Press, 2021).

Martinez, Maria Elena, "Archives, Bodies, and Imagination: The Case of Juana Aguilar and Queer Approaches to History, Sexuality, and Politics," *Radical History Review* 120 (2014): 159–182.

Marty, Myron A., "Historians' Crafts: Common Interests in a Diverse Profession," *Journal of American History* 81 (1994): 1078–1087.

Marwick, Arthur, *The Nature of History*, 3rd edition (Chicago, IL: Lyseum, 1989).

Masuzawa, Tomoko, *The Invention of World Religions* (Chicago, IL: University of Chicago Press, 2005).
Maxwell, Mike, "More about General Principles of Historical Knowledge," http://futurefocusedhistory.blog/more-about-general-principles-of-historical-knowledge.
Maza, Sarah, *Thinking about History* (Chicago, IL: University of Chicago Press, 2017).
McCullagh, C. Behan, "The Truth of Historical Narratives," *History and Theory* 26:4 (1987): 30–46.
McNeill, William H., *Mythistory and Other Essays* (Chicago, IL: University of Chicago Press, 1986).
McNeill, William H., "Why Study History?" www.historians.org/about-aha-and-membership/aha-history-and-archives/historical-archives/why-study-history- (1985).
Megill, Allan, "'Grand Narrative' and the Discipline of History," in *A New Philosophy of History*, ed. Frank Ankersmit and Hans Kellner (Chicago, IL: University of Chicago Press, 1995), pp. 151–173.
Megill, Allan, "Recounting the Past: 'Description, Explanation, and Narrative in Historiography," *American Historical Review* 94:3 (1989): 627–653.
Middendorf, Joan, David Pace, Leah Shopkow, and Arlene Diaz, "Making Thinking Explicit: Decoding History Teaching," *National Teaching and Learning Forum* 16 (2007): 1–4.
Miller, Joseph C., *The Problem of Slavery as History* (New Haven, CT: Yale University Press, 2012).
Mink, Louis O., "The Autonomy of Historical Understanding," *History & Theory* 5 (1966): 24–47.
Monte-Santo, Chauncey, "Beyond Reading Comprehension and Summary: Learning to Read and Write in History by Focusing on Evidence, Perspective, and Interpretation," *Curriculum Inquiry* 41 (2011): 212–249.
Morgan, Edmund S., *American Slavery, American Freedom* (New York: Norton, 2003 [original 1975]).
Morin, Edgar, "From the Concept of System to the Paradigm of Complexity," *Journal of Social and Evolutionary Systems* 15 (1992): 371–385.
Moses, A. Dirk, "Hayden White, Traumatic Nationalism, and the Public Role of History," *History and Theory* 44 (2005): 311–332.
Motadel, David, "The Political Role of the Historian," *Contemporary European History* 32 (2023): 38–45.
Munslow, Alun, *Deconstructing History*, 2nd edition (New York: Routledge, 1997).
Munslow, Alun, "History, Skepticism and the Past," *Rethinking History* 21:4 (2017): 474–488.
Murphey, Murray G., *Our Knowledge of the Historical Past* (Indianapolis, IN: Bobbs-Merrill, 1973).
National Academy of Sciences (USA), *History as Social Science*, ed. David S. Landes and Charles Tilly (New York: Prentice-Hall, 1971).

National Center for History in the Schools (USA), "History Standards," available at the University of California at Los Angeles Public History Initiative, https://phi.history.ucla.edu/nchs/history-standards.

National Center for History in the Schools (USA), *Lessons from History: Essential Understandings and Historical Perspectives Students Should Acquire* (Los Angeles: University of California Press/National Center for History in the Schools, 1992).

National Council for History Education (UK), "Building a World History Curriculum: A Guide to Using Themes and Selecting Content" (1997), https://eric.ed.gov/?id=ED422238.

National Curriculum History Working Group (UK), "National Curriculum Working Group Final Report (England and Wales)," in *Teaching History*, ed. Hilary Bourdillon (London: Routledge, 1994), pp. 27–42.

Nokes, Jeffery D., "Recognizing and Addressing the Barriers to Adolescents' 'Reading Like Historians,'" *The History Teacher* 44 (2011): 379–399.

Norton, Claire, and Mark Donnelly, *Liberating Histories* (New York: Routledge, 2019).

Novick, Peter, *That Noble Dream: The "Objectivity Question" and the American Historical Profession* (New York: Cambridge University Press, 1988).

Oakeshott, Michael, *Experience and Its Modes* (Cambridge: Cambridge University Press, 1933, reprint 1966).

Oakeshott, Michael, *On History and Other Essays* (Carmel, IN: Liberty Fund, 1999 [1983]).

Oexle, Otto Gerhard, *Geschichtswissenschaft im Zeichen des Historismus: Studien zu Problemgeschichten der Moderne* (Gottingen: Vandenhoeck & Ruprecht, 1996).

Oexle, Otto Gerhard, "Im Archiv der Fiktionen," in *Auf der Suche nach der verlorenen Wahrheit: Zum Grundlagenstreit in der Geschichtswissenschaft*, ed. Rainer Marie Kiesow and Dieter Simon (Frankfurt: Campus, 2000), pp. 87–103.

Olwell, Russell, and Azibo Stevens, "'I Had to Double-Check My Thoughts': How the Reacting to the Past Methodology Impacts First-Year College Student Engagement, Retention, and Historical Thinking," *The History Teacher* 48 (2015): 561–572.

Pace, David, "The Amateur in the Operating Room: History and the Scholarship of Teaching and Learning," *American Historical Review* 109:4 (2004): 1171–1192.

Pace, David, "Beyond 'Sorting': Teaching Cognitive Skills in the History Survey," *The History Teacher* 26:2 (1993): 211–220.

Passmore, Kevin, "Poststructuralism and History," in *Writing History: Theory & Practice*, ed. Stefan Berger, Heiko Feldner, and Kevin Passmore (London: Arnold, 2003), pp. 119–126.

Perry, W. G., *Forms of Intellectual and Ethical Development in the College Years: A Scheme* (San Francisco, CA: Jossey-Bass, 1970).

Pihlainen, Kalle, "The Distinction of History: On Valuing the Insularity of the Historical Past," *Rethinking History* 20:3 (2016): 414–432.

Pihlainen, Kalle, "Narrative Objectivity versus Fiction," *Rethinking History* 2 (1998): 7–22.
Pihlainen, Kalle, *The Work of History: Constructivism and a Politics of the Past* (New York: Routledge, 2017).
Popper, Karl, *The Poverty of Historicism* (London: Ark, 1957).
Quality Assurance Agency for Higher Education, *Subject Benchmark Statement: History* (Gloucester: Quality Assurance Agency for Higher Education, 2022), www.qaa.ac.uk/docs/qaa/sbs/sbs-history-22.pdf?sfvrsn=beaedc81_2.
Reisman, Avishag, "Teaching the Historical Principle of Contextual Causation: A Study of Transfer in Historical Reading," in *Interpersonal Understanding in Historical Context*, ed. Matthias Martens, Ullrike Hartmann, Michael Sauer, and Marcus Hasselhorn (Rotterdam: Sense, 2009), pp. 43–60.
Renier, G. J., *History: Its Method and Purpose* (New York: Harper & Row, 1965).
Roberts, Clayton, *The Logic of Historical Explanation* (University Park: Pennsylvania State University Press, 1996).
Roberts, David G., *Nothing but History: Reconstruction and Extremity after Metaphysics* (Berkeley: University of California Press, 1995).
Rosa, Alberto and Ignacio Brescó, "What to Teach in History Education when the Social Pact Shakes?" in *Palgrave Handbook of Research in Historical Culture and Education*, ed. Mario Carretero, Stefan Berger, and Maria Grever (New York: Palgrave MacMillan, 2017), pp. 413–428.
Rubinoff, Lionel, "Historicity and Objectivity," in *Objectivity, Method, and Point of View: Essays in the Philosophy of History*, ed. W. J. van der Dussen and Lionel Rubinoff (Leiden: Brill, 1991), pp. 133–153.
Rüsen, Jörn, *History: Narration – Interpretation – Orientation* (New York: Berghahn, 2005).
Sa Cavalcante Schuback, Marcia, "Engaged History," in *The Ethos of History: Time and Responsibility*, ed. Stefan Helgesson and Jayne Svenungsson (New York: Berghahn, 2018), pp. 160–174.
Sage Foundation, *The Sage Handbook of Historical Theory*, ed. Nancy Partner and Sara Foot (Los Angeles: Sage, 2013).
Sakki, Inari, "Aims in Teaching History and Their Epistemic Correlates: A Study of History Teachers in Ten Countries," *Pedagogy, Culture, & Society* 27 (2019): 65–85.
Salevouris, Michael J. and Conal Furay, *The Methods and Skills of History: A Practical Guide* (Chichester: Wiley-Blackwell, 2015).
Sandwell, Ruth, "On Historians and Their Audiences: An Argument for Teaching (and not just Writing) History," in *Becoming a History Teacher: Sustaining Practices in Historical Thinking and Knowing*, ed. Ruth Sandwell and Amy von Heyking (Toronto: University of Toronto Press, 2014), pp. 61–90.
Sarup, Madan, *An Introductory Guide to Post-Structuralism and Postmodernism* (Athens: University of Georgia Press, 1989).
Satia, Priya, "The Presentist Trap," *Perspectives on History* 60 (2023): 6–7.
Satia, Priya, *Time's Monster: How History Makes History* (Cambridge, MA: Harvard University Press, 2020).

Schama, Simon, *Dead Certainties (Unwarranted Speculations)* (New York: Vintage, 1991).
Schools Council History Project (UK), *A New Look at History* (Edinburgh: Holmes MacDougal, 1976), www.schoolshistoryproject.co.uk/wp-content/uploads/2015/12/NewLookAtHistory.pdf.
Scott, James, *Seeing Like a State: How Certain Schemes to Improve the Human Condition Have Failed* (New Haven, CT: Yale University Press, 1998).
Scott, Joan, "Gender: A Useful Category of Analysis," *American Historical Review* 91 (1986): 1053–1075.
Scott, Joan, "History-Writing As Critique," in *Manifestos for History*, ed. Keith Jenkins, Sue Morgan, and Alun Munslow (New York: Routledge, 2007), pp. 19–38.
Sears, Alan, "Trends and Issues in History Education in International Contexts," in *Debates in History Teaching*, 2nd edition, ed. Ian Davies (London: Routledge, 2017), pp. 42–51.
Seixas, Peter, "The Community of Inquiry as a Basis for Knowledge and Learning: The Case of History," *American Educational Research Journal* 30 (1993): 305–324.
Seixas, Peter, "Schweigen! Die Kinder! Or, Does Postmodern History Have a Place in the Schools?" in *Knowing, Teaching, and Learning History: National and International Perspectives*, ed. Peter N. Stearns, Peter Seixas, and Sam Wineburg (New York: New York University Press, 2000), pp. 19–37.
Shephard, Todd, "Practices Make Pertinent: Prospecting and Histories of the Present," *Modern Intellectual History* 20 (2023): 639–650.
Simon, Zoltán Bolizsár, "Do Theorists of History Have a Theory of History? Reflections on a Non-discipline," *Historia da Historiografia* 12 (2009): 53–68.
Simon, Zoltán Bolizsár, "Historicism and Constructionism: Rival Ideas of Historical Change," *History of European Ideas* 45 (2019): 1171–1190.
Sipress, Joel M. and David J. Voelker, "From Learning History to Doing History: Beyond the Coverage Model," in *Exploring Signature Pedagogies: Approaches to Teaching Disciplinary Habits of Mind*, ed. Regan A. Gurung, Nancy L. Chick, and Aeron Haynie (Sterling, VA: Stylus, 2009), pp. 19–35.
Sleeter, Christine E. and Miguel Zavala, *Transformative Ethnic Studies in Schools: Curriculum, Pedagogy, and Research* (New York: Teachers College Press, 2020).
Smith, Mark A., "Teaching Jefferson," *The History Teacher* 42 (2009): 329–340.
Snyder, Timothy, *On Tyranny: Twenty Lessons from the Twentieth Century* (New York: Duggan, 2017).
Sofer, Reba N., *Discipline and Power: The University, History and the Making of an English Elite, 1870–1930* (Stanford, CA: Stanford University Press, 1994).
Southgate, Beverley, "'Humani nil alienum': The Quest for 'Human Nature,'" in *Manifestos for History*, ed. Keith Jenkins, Sue Morgan, and Alun Munslow (New York: Routledge, 2007), pp. 67–76.
Spiegel, Gabrielle M., "The Future of the Past: History, Memory and the Ethical Imperatives of Writing History," *Journal of the Philosophy of History* 8 (2014): 149–179.

Spiegel, Gabrielle M., "The Limits of Empiricism: The Utility of Theory in Historical Thought and Writing," *Medieval History Journal* 22 (2019): 1–22.

Spier, Fred, "Big History: The Emergence of an Interdisciplinary Science?" *World History Connected* 6 (2009), https://worldhistoryconnected.press.uillinois.edu/6.3/spier.html.

Spierenburg, Peter, *Men and Violence: Gender, Honor, and Rituals in Modern Europe and America* (Columbus: Ohio State University Press, 1998).

Spoehr, Kathryn T. and Luther W. Spoehr, "Learning to Think Historically," *Educational Psychologist* 29:2 (1994): 71–77.

Stearns, Peter N., "Getting Specific about Training in Historical Analysis: A Case Study in World History," in *Knowing, Teaching, and Learning History: National and International Perspectives*, ed. Peter N. Stearns, Peter Seixas, and Sam Wineburg (New York: New York University Press, 2000), pp. 419–436.

Stearns, Peter N., *Meaning over Memory: Recasting the Teaching of Culture and History* (Chapel Hill: University of North Carolina Press, 1993).

Stearns, Peter N., Peter Seixas, and Sam Weinburg, "Introduction," in *Knowing, Teaching, and Learning History: National and International Perspectives*, ed. Peter Stearns, Peter Seixas, and Sam Wineburg (New York: New York University Press, 2000), pp. 1–12.

Steinmetz, George, "Historicism and Positivism in Sociology: From Weimar Germany to the Contemporary United States," in *Historicism: A Travelling Concept*, ed. Herman Paul and Adriaan van Veldhuizen (London: Bloomsbury Academic, 2021), pp. 57–96.

Steinmetz-Jenkins, Daniel, "Introduction: Whose Present? Which History?" in *Modern Intellectual History* 20 (2023): 559–570.

Stern, Fritz, ed., *Varieties of History* (New York: Vintage, 1972 [1956]).

Stipling, Barbara, "Teaching Inquiry with Primary Sources," *Teaching with Primary Sources Quarterly* 2 (2009): 2–4.

Sugrue, Thomas J., "Responsibility to the Past, Engagement with the Present," *Labor History* 39 (1998): 60–69.

Sunderland, Willard, *The Baron's Cloak: A History of the Russian Empire in War and Revolution* (Ithaca, NY: Cornell University Press, 2014).

Sweet, James H., "Is History History? Identity Politics and Teleologies of the Present," *Perspectives on History*, August 17, 2022, www.historians.org/publications-and-directories/perspectives-on-history/september-2022/is-history-history-identity-politics-and-teleologies-of-the-present.

Sylvester, David, "Change and Continuity in History Teaching 1900–1993," in *Teaching History*, ed. Hillary Bourdillon (London: Routledge, 1994), pp. 9–26.

Symcox, Linda, "Internationalizing the U.S. History Curriculum: From Nationalism to Cosmopolitanism," in *National History Standards: The Problem of the Canon and the Future of Teaching History*, ed. Linda Symcox and Arie Wilschut (Charlotte, NC: Information Age, 2009), pp. 33–54.

Symcox, Linda and Arie Wilschut, "Introduction," in *National History Standards: The Problem of the Canon and the Future of Teaching History*, ed. Linda Symcox and Arie Wilschut (Charlotte, NC: Information Age, 2009), pp. 1–11.

Tanaka, Stefan, *History without Chronology* (n.p.; Lever, 2019).

Tanaka, Stefan, "Pasts in a Digital Age," in *Writing History in a Digital Age*, ed. Jack Doughtery and Kristen Navrotzki (Ann Arbor: University of Michigan Press, 2013), pp. 35–48.

Tanaka, Stefan, "Reconceiving Pasts in a Digital Age," in *Historein* 15:2 (2015): 21–29.

Thompson, E. P., *The Making of the English Working Class* (New York: Victor Gollancz, 1963).

Thompson, F. M. L., "F. M. L. Thompson," in *The History Debate*, ed. Juliet Gardiner (London: Collins, 1990), pp. 74–80.

Thompson, Willie, *What Happened to History?* (London: Pluto, 2000).

Toner, Carol, "Teaching Students to Be Historians: Suggestions for an Undergraduate Research Seminar," *The History Teacher* 27 (1993): 37–51.

Tosh, John, *The Pursuit of History*, 5th edition (Harlow: Longman, 2009).

Tosh, John, *The Pursuit of History*, 6th edition (New York: Routledge, 2015).

Tosh, John, *Why History Matters* (Basingstoke: Palgrave MacMillan, 2008).

Traub, Valerie, "The New Unhistoricism in Queer Studies," *PMLA* 128:1 (2013): 21–39.

Trevelyan, George Macaulay, *An Autobiography & Other Essays* (London: Longmans, Green & Co, 1949).

Trevelyan, George Macaulay, *Clio, A Muse and Other Essays* (Freeport, NY: Books for Libraries, 1913).

Trevelyan, George Macaulay, "History and the Reader," in *An Autobiography, and Other Essays* (London: Longman, Green, 1949), pp. 52–67.

Trevelyan, George Macaulay, "History and Literature," *Journal of the Historical Association* 9:34 (1924): 82–91.

Trouillot, Michel-Rolph, *Silencing the Past: Power and the Production of History* (Boston, MA: Beacon Press, 1995).

Upadhyay, Shashi Bhushan, *Historiography in the Modern World: Western and Indian Perspectives* (Oxford: Oxford University Press, 2016).

Van Bouwel Jeroen and Erik Weber, "A Pragmatist Defense of Non-relativistic Explanatory Pluralism in History and Social Science," *History and Theory* 47 (2008): 168–182.

Vansledright, Bruce A., *Assessing Historical Thinking and Understanding* (London: Taylor & Francis, 2013).

Veyne, Paul, *Writing History: Essay on Epistemology*, trans. Minna Moore-Rinvolucri (Middletown, CT: Wesleyan University Press, 1984).

Vianna, Hermano, *The Mystery of Samba: Popular Music & National Identity in Brazil*, ed. and trans. John Charles Chasteen (Chapel Hill: University of North Carolina Press, 1999).

Von Goethe, Johann Wolfgang, *Faust, Eine Tragödie* (original 1828), p. 9, www.digbib.org/Johann_Wolfgang_von_Goethe_1749/Faust_I_.pdf.

Von Ranke, Leopold, "A Fragment from the 1830s," in *The Varieties of History*, ed. Fritz Stern (Cleveland, OH: Meridian, 1956), pp. 58–60.
Von Ranke, Leopold, "A Fragment from the 1860s," in *The Varieties of History: From Voltaire to the Present*, ed. Fritz Stern (Cleveland, OH: Meridian, 1956), pp. 60–62.
Von Ranke, Leopold, "On the Character of Historical Science (A Manuscript of the 1830s)," in *The Theory and Practice of History*, ed. Georg C. Iggers and Konrad von Moltke, trans Wilma A. Iggers and Konrad von Moltke (Indianapolis, IN: Bobbs-Merrill, 1973), pp. 33–44.
Von Ranke, Leopold, "The Pitfalls of a Philosophy of History (Introduction to a Lecture on Universal History; A Manuscript of the 1840s)," in *The Theory and Practice of History*, ed. Georg G. Iggers and Konrad von Moltke, trans Wilma A. Iggers and Konrad von Moltke (Indianapolis, IN: Bobbs-Merrill, 1973), pp. 47–50.
Von Ranke, Leopold, "Preface to the First Edition of Histories of the Latin and Germanic Nations (October 1824)," in *The Theory and Practice of History*, ed. Georg G. Iggers and Konrad von Moltke, trans Wilma Iggers and Konrad von Moltke (Indianapolis: Bobbs-Merrill, 1973), pp. 55–58.
Von Ranke, Leopold, *The Secret of World History: Selected Writings on the Art and Science of History*, ed. Roger Wines (New York: Fordham University Press, 1981).
Walker, Clarence, *Mongrel Nation: The America Begotten by Thomas Jefferson and Sally Hemmings* (Charlottesville: University of Virginia Press, 2010).
Walsh, William H., "'Meaning' in History," in *Theories of History*, ed. Patrick Gardiner (New York: Free Press, 1959), pp. 296–307.
Walsh, William H., *Philosophy of History: An Introduction* (New York: Harper, 1958).
Walvoord, Barbara E. and John R. Breihan, "Arguing and Debating: Breihan's History Course," in B. E. Walvoord and L. P. McCarthy, *Thinking and Writing in College: A Naturalistic Study of Students in Four Disciplines* (Urbana, IL: National Council of Teachers of English, 1990), pp. 97–143.
Waring, Scott M., "Escaping Myopia: Teaching Students about Historical Causality," *The History Teacher* 43 (2010): 283–288.
Weber, Max, "Die 'Objektivität' sozialwissenschaftlicher und sozialpolitischer Erkenntnis," *Archiv für Sozialwissenschaft un Sozialpolitik* 19 (1904): 22–87.
Wertsch, James V., "Is It Possible to Teach Beliefs, as Well as Knowledge about History?" in *Knowing, Teaching, and Learning History: National and International Perspectives*, ed. Peter N. Stearns, Peter Seixas, and Sam Wineburg (New York: New York University Press, 2000), pp. 38–50.
White, Hayden, "Afterward," in *Manifestos for History*, eds. Keith Jenkins, Sue Morgan, and Alun Munslow (New York: Routledge, 2007), pp. 220–231.
White, Hayden, "Interpretation in History," in *Tropics of Discourse: Essays in Cultural Criticism* (Baltimore, MD: Johns Hopkins University Press, 1978), pp. 51–80.

White, Hayden, "The Public Relevance of Historical Studies: A Reply to Dirk Moses," *History and Theory* 44 (2005): 333–338.
Wilder, Gary, "From Optic to Topic: The Foreclosure Effect of Historiographical Turns," *American Historical Review* (2012): 723–745.
Williams, William Appleman, "Introduction," in *History as a Way of Learning* (New York: New Viewpoints, 1974), pp. 3–23.
Wilson, Norman J., *History in Crisis? Recent Directions in Historiography* (Upper Saddle River, NJ: Prentice Hall, 2005).
Windelband, Wilhelm, "Rectorial Address, Strasbourg, 1894," *History and Theory* 19:2 (1980): 169–185.
Wineburg, Sam, *Historical Thinking and Other Unnatural Acts: Charting the Future of Teaching the Past* (Philadelphia, PA: Temple University Press, 2001).
Wineburg, Sam, *Why Learn History (When Its Already on Your Phone)* (Chicago, IL: University of Chicago Press, 2018).
Wineburg, Sam, Mark Smith, and Joel Breakstone, "What Is Learned in College History Classes?" *Journal of American History* 104 (2018): 983–993.
Wood, Linda Sargent, "Hooked on Inquiry: History Labs in the Methods Course," *The History Teacher* 45 (2012): 549–567.
Woolf, Daniel, *A Concise History of History: Global Historiography from Antiquity to the Present* (Cambridge: Cambridge University Press, 2019).
Yilmaz, Kaya, "Historical Empathy and Its Implications for Classroom Practices in Schools," *The History Teacher* 40 (2007): 331–338.
Young, Robert J. C., *White Mythologies: Writing History and the West*, 2nd edition (London: Routledge, 2004).
Zagorin, Perez, "History, the Referent, and Narrative: Reflections on Postmodernism Now," *History and Theory* 38 (1999): 1–24.
Zagorin, Perez, "Rejoinder to a Postmodernist," *History and Theory* 39 (2000): 201–209.
Zimmerman, Jonathan, "In Search of 'College-Level Teaching,'" *Journal of the Gilded Age and Progressive Era* 14 (2015): 429–432.

Index

Akyeampong, Emmanuel, 128
American Historical Association, 6, 8, 24, 36, 38, 41, 90, 110, 160, 180, 185, 188, 213
argument
 in History education, 69–71
Arni, Caroline, 115

Baberowski, Jörg, 47
Bain, Robert, 4, 67
Banner, James M., 64, 83, 160, 167, 177
Barton, Keith, 32, 190, 196
Beard, Charles, 161, 167, 176
Berkhofer, Robert, 79
Bevir, Mark, 170–171
bias, 37, 185, 212, 243
 and critical thinking, 192, 195, 249
 and historicism, 49–50, 115, 138, 172–176
 and inquiry, 247
 and language, 163–166
 and reciprocity in pedagogy, 217
 and theory, 145
 assessing, 170
 in sources, 49–50, 52, 55, 95, 131–132, 143, 189, 237
 in the classroom, 221
 personal and political, 79, 162
 productivity of, 181
Blackbourn, David, 93
Blake, Christopher, 131, 166
Bloch, Marc, 149, 189, 204
Booth, Alan, 3, 8, 33, 62
Bourke, Joanna, 7, 13
Bynum, Caroline Walker, 110

Calder, Lendol, 7
Carr, Edward Hallett, 137, 160, 163, 176
cause, causation, causality in History, 109–124
 a challenge for students, 118
Chakrabarty, Dipesh, 39, 112–113, 116, 145, 168
Chesneaux, Jean, 41
Collingwood, Robin G., 86, 131

Commager, Henry Steele, 62, 134, 160, 194
critical thinking, 192, 195

deductive reasoning, 54, 56, 79, 190
democracy and History education, 40, 50, 65, 195–196, 197, 198–199, 201–202, 203, 226
Dening, Greg, 36, 104, 109
Doan, Laura, 7, 12, 49, 83
Droysen, Gustav, 130
Dunn, Ross E., 116

Elton, Geoffrey R., 38, 72, 89, 131, 182, 208
empiricism, 22, 79, 90–94, 109–111, 113, 116, 136–137, 143–145, 151, 152, 154–155, 158, 185
emplotment, 164, 175
engaged history, 40, 41, 43, 50, 53
Ermarth, Elizabeth, 165
Evans, Richard J., 117, 175
explanation in History, 8, 21, 31, 32, 33–34, 48, 56, 62, 64, 67, 79, 85, 89, 98, 104, 109–124, 191, 243
 alternative explanations, 125
 and inquiry, 125, 138
 and judgment, 195
 and perspective, 128
 and popular culture, 194–195
 and postmodern theory, 163–164
 multicausality, 117–118, 123
 narrative form, 100, 101, 102–103, 115–116

Fairburn, Miles, 35, 37, 48, 132, 152, 169
fiction, 14, 95, 103, 104–105, 108–109, 115, 168, 171
Finney, Patrick, 90
Foucault, Michel, 82, 165, 206
Fuentes, Marisa J., 126
Fulbrook, Mary, 6, 64

Gadamer, Hans-Georg, 18
Gaddis, John L., 33, 86, 101, 102, 117
Geyl, Peter, 80
Goethe, Johann Wolfgang von, 75

Goldstein, Leon J., 29, 101, 104
Grossman, James, 213

HARKing, 54, 98
Haskell, Thomas, 179
Havel, Vaclav, 210, 212
hermeneutics, 47, 93, 95, 111, 141, 148, 159, 175, 188, 222, 223, 225, 232
Himmelfarb, Gertrud, 175
historicism, 13, 20, 40, 46, 47–50, 51–56, 58, 60, 88, 90, 92, 93, 109, 111, 141, 142, 153, 181, 185
  and availability bias, 136
  and Big Data, 193
  and categorization, 148
  and explanation, 115, 119
  and lessons of history, 205–210
  and postmodernism, 155–166, 167, 171–176
  and presentism, 221
  and the environmental fallacy, 143
  compatibility with social/social science theory, 93–95, 114, 138, 144–145, 151, 154
  critique of social/social science theory, 82–88, 113
  critiques of, 79, 89, 143
  ethical position of, 47–50, 216, 217, 222, 249
  historicity of, 116–117, 161, 187
historicism, unconditional, 37, 39, 47–53, 54, 175
historicity, 45, 46, 49, 81, 87, 181, 204, 250
Hobsbawm, Eric, 14, 179, 205
holism, 33–37, 55, 59, 60, 61, 72, 85, 96, 112, 183, 186, 187, 189, 201, 248, 249
Howell, Martha, 33, 110–111, 161, 174

idiographic analysis, 57, 58, 59, 60, 75, 97, 99, 101, 164, 184
immersion, 35, 36, 45, 48, 79, 114, 136, 160, 175, 203, 222
inductive reasoning, 54–55, 56, 57, 58, 59, 60, 75, 79
inquiry, 17, 21, 77
  and argument, 71, 178
  and availability bias, 136
  and bias, 173
  and confirmation bias, 140
  and engaged History, 47
  and good questions, 72, 75
  and historicism, 142, 153
  and History education, 204, 212, 213, 216, 218, 221
  and interpretation, 181, 182
  and perspective, 177
  and theory, 31, 80, 82, 86, 94–95, 111, 154
  centrality to History, 2, 20, 29, 99, 112, 124, 182, 186, 188

History as a mode of, 1, 5, 7, 11, 31, 34, 58, 60, 66, 71, 92, 97, 155, 156, 170, 178, 183, 186, 201
  in History education, 222, 240–241, 243–248
  inductive, 54, 58
Internet, the
  and History education, 194, 228
interpretation in History, 4, 33, 54, 59, 60, 61–66, 67, 68–70, 82, 85, 92, 101–103, 104, 108, 130, 163, 164, 178, 179, 180, 184, 187, 188, 189
  and analysis, 190
  and bias, 157, 159, 161, 165, 173, 181, 229
  and historicity, 161
  and information, 191
  and language, 164
  and opinion, 181, 201
  and pedagogy, 200, 216, 218, 231, 237–243, 246, 247, 248
  assessing quality of, 168–171

Jenkins, Keith, 89, 166, 176, 195, 205
Jones, Jacqueline, 160, 180
Jordanova, Ludmila, 48, 80, 117, 172, 174
Joyce, Patrick, 49, 88, 167

Kendi, Ibrahim, 113
Kleinberg, Ethan, 84, 193
Kocka, Jürgen, 57, 93

LaCapra, Dominick, 70, 77, 90, 172, 213
Leinhardt, Gaea, 1–2
Lessons from History, 195, 198, 199, 201
Lowenthal, David, 160
Luhmann, Niklas, 95

MacMillan, Margaret, 205
Marwick, Arthur, 63, 155
Marxism, 14, 43, 57, 82, 87, 93, 94, 112, 119, 120, 145, 146, 157, 179
Masuzawa, Tomoko, 147, 173
Maza, Sarah, 58, 98, 117, 196
McCullagh, C. Behan, 131
McNeill, William H., 106, 184
Miller, Joseph C., 38, 62, 111, 211
Munslow, Alun, 131, 150, 162–166, 171

National Academy of Sciences, 32, 91
nominalism, 56, 114, 116, 184
nomothetic analysis, 55, 78, 98, 101

Oakeshott, Michael, 56, 183
objectivity, 14, 22, 37, 38, 41, 43, 81, 90, 91, 130, 131, 155–162, 165, 166, 167, 171, 176, 179–182, 195, 204, 228, 230

Painter, Nell Irvin, 159
postmodernism, 6, 21, 27, 89, 166
 and historicism, 114, 162–164, 166, 176
presentism, 6, 41, 205, 219, 221
Prevenier, Walter, 33, 110–111, 161, 174

Ranke, Leopold von, 5, 16, 24, 33, 37, 45, 91, 107, 111, 172, 176
reciprocity
 pedagogical, 17, 217
Renier, G. J., 63, 71

Sarup, Madan, 110
Satia, Priya, 39, 40, 81
Schama, Simon, 63, 108, 131
Scott, Joan, 173
Seixas, Peter, 114, 201, 222
Sipress, Joel M., 5, 69, 215
social science, 6, 54, 67, 90
 and Big Data, 193
 and deductive reasoning, 190
 and fragmentary sources, 153
 and historical inquiry, 154, 185, 186, 235
 and History in the 1970s, 91
 compatibility with historicism, 91, 99, 116
 corrective to availability bias, 138
 corrective to the environmental fallacy, 145
 critique of historicism, 143
 distinction from History, 71
 ethical position of, 81, 249
 historicist critique, 34
 historicist critique of, 84–86, 116
 historicity of, 87, 88
 History as, 5, 22, 26, 28, 51, 57, 60, 66, 82
 in History education, 233

social theory, 6, 60, 78, 81, 84–86, 88, 90, 112
 and categorization, 147
 and confirmation bias, 142
 and historicity, 177
 compatibility with historicism, 88
 corrective to availability bias, 136
 corrective to bias in sources, 153
 corrective to the environmental fallacy, 144
 historicist critique of, 86, 88, 117
 in History education, 188
 postcolonial critique of, 113, 114
spookiness, 75, 85, 125, 155, 191, 250
Sunderland, Willard, 125–126

Tanaka, Stefan, 34, 35
theory wars, 6, 89
Thompson, Edward P., 93
Thompson, F. M. L., 243
Tosh, John, 4, 28, 34, 46, 50, 53, 80, 85, 86, 89, 99, 109, 168, 174, 200
Toynbee, Arnold, 80, 126
Trevelyan, George Macauley, 38, 58, 83, 87, 104, 108, 111, 148, 163, 172, 179, 180, 188, 206
Trouillot, Michel-Rolph, 39, 49, 81, 87

Vansledright, Bruce A., 168
Veyne, Paul, 132
Voelker, David J., 5, 69, 215

White, Hayden, 13, 95, 164, 171
Wilder, Gary, 90
Windelband, Wilhelm, 28, 55, 98
Wineburg, Sam, 4, 10, 32, 35, 70, 184

Young, Robert C, 113

For EU product safety concerns, contact us at Calle de José Abascal, 56–1°, 28003 Madrid, Spain or eugpsr@cambridge.org.

www.ingramcontent.com/pod-product-compliance
Ingram Content Group UK Ltd.
Pitfield, Milton Keynes, MK11 3LW, UK
UKHW020422260326
469255UK00030B/399